'*The Globalisation of Urban Governance* is a must-read primer for any researcher interested in the role of cities in addressing global sustainable development goals. Through a diversity of case studies and theoretical perspectives, the editors offer a valuable guide to navigating the challenges and opportunities for the governance of safe and sustainable urban spaces. A virtuoso effort led by two of the world's leading scholars in this field of environmental governance.'

Prof. Benjamin J. Richardson, *University of Tasmania*

'How to govern our globe's cities well? That is, how to live up to the sustainable development ideals of SDG 11? This is one of the most pertinent questions of our time. *The Globalisation of Urban Governance* is an excellent volume that advances the emerging field of research on urban governance at the intersections of global governance, (international) law, political science and urban studies. Aust and du Plessis have put together a wonderful collection of clear and engaging chapters, which deal with various aspects of the globalisation of good governance of cities from a legal perspective. A highly innovative book relevant to both the scholarly and policy discourse on the meaning of SDG 11.'

Janne E. Nijman, *Academic Director of the T.M.C. Asser Instituut in The Hague and Professor of History and Theory of International Law, University of Amsterdam*

'Cities around the world have started to use whatever powers they have to achieve inclusiveness, safety, resilience and sustainability for their residents, not because they were empowered to do so by states, but simply because they experience the impact of poverty, discrimination, insecurity, pollution and climate change on a daily basis. This important new book, edited by world leading experts on the topic Aust and du Plessis, shows how cities thus have become essential global actors for the achievement of sustainable development, and what are the implications for urban governance.'

Jonathan Verschuuren, *Professor of International and European Environmental Law, Tilburg University*

The Globalisation of Urban Governance

The adoption of the Sustainable Development Goals (SDGs) by the UN General Assembly in 2015 represents the latest attempt by the international community to live up to the challenges of a planet that is out of control. Sustainable Development Goal 11 envisages inclusive, safe, resilient and sustainable cities around the world by the year 2030. This globally agreed vision is part of a trend in international policy toward good urban governance, and now awaits implementation. Fourteen original contributions collectively examine how this global vision has been developed on a conceptual level, how it plays out in various areas of (global) urban governance and how it is implemented in varying local contexts. The overarching hypothesis presented herein is that SDG 11 proves that local governance is recognised as an autonomous yet interrelated part of the global pursuit of sustainable development. The volume analyses three core questions: How have the normative ideals set forth in SDG 11 been developed? What are the meanings of the four sub-goals of SDG 11 and how do these relate to each other? What does SDG 11 imply for urban law and governance in the domestic context and how are local processes of urban governance internationalised?

The Globalisation of Urban Governance makes an important scholarly contribution by linking the narrative on globalisation of good urban governance in various social sciences with legal discourse. It considers global governance and connects the existing debate about cities and their place in global governance with some of the most pertinent questions that lawyers face today.

Helmut Philipp Aust is Professor of Law at the Freie Universität Berlin, Germany.

Anél du Plessis is Professor of Law and the SARChI Chair in Cities, Law and Environmental Sustainability (CLES) at the North-West University (NWU), South Africa.

Cities and Global Governance

The Routledge series *Cities and Global Governance* is composed of contributed volumes covering key areas of study at the intersection of urbanism and global governance. Each title explores dimensions of the relationship between the local and the global, between urban landscapes and global dynamics. Authors in the series make empirical and theoretical contributions that advance our understanding of the role of cities as sites and actors in global governance.

1. Cities, Networks, and Global Environmental Governance
Spaces of Innovation, Places of Leadership
Sofie Bouteligier

2. The Power of Cities in International Relations
Edited by Simon Curtis

3. Global Cities and Climate Change
The Translocal Relations of Environmental Governance
Taedong Lee

4. The Urban Climate Challenge
Rethinking the Role of Cities in the Global Climate Regime
Edited by Craig Johnson, Noah Toly, and Heike Schroeder

5. The Global City 2.0
From Strategic Site to Global Actor
Kristin Ljungkvist

6. Greening Post-Industrial Cities
Growth, Equity, and Environmental Governance
Corina McKendry

7. The Globalisation of Urban Governance
Legal Perspectives on Sustainable Development Goal 11
Edited by Helmut Philipp Aust and Anél du Plessis

The Globalisation of Urban Governance

Legal Perspectives on Sustainable Development Goal 11

Edited by
Helmut Philipp Aust and Anél du Plessis

Routledge
Taylor & Francis Group
New York London

First published 2019
by Routledge
52 Vanderbilt Avenue, New York, NY 10017

and by Routledge
2 Park Square, Milton Park, Abingdon, Oxon OX14 4RN

First issued in paperback 2020

Routledge is an imprint of the Taylor & Francis Group, an informa business

Library of Congress Cataloging-in-Publication Data
Names: Aust, Helmut Philipp, 1980- editor. | du Plessis, Anél, editor.
Title: The globalisation of urban governance : legal perspectives on Sustainable Development Goal 11 / edited by Helmut Philipp Aust and Anél du Plessis.
Other titles: Globalisation of Urban governance
Description: New York, NY : Routledge, 2019. | Series: Cities and global governance | Includes bibliographical references and index.
Identifiers: LCCN 2018029430| ISBN 9781138485495 (hardback) | ISBN 97811351049269 (master) | ISBN 9781351049252 (webpdf) | ISBN 9781351049245 (epub) | ISBN 9781351049238 (mobipocket/kindle)
Subjects: LCSH: City planning--Environmental aspects. | Urban ecology (Sociology) | Metropolitan government. | Sustainable Development Goals.
Classification: LCC HT166 .G5795 2019 | DDC 307.1/16--dc23
LC record available at https://lccn.loc.gov/2018029430

ISBN 13: 978-0-367-66382-7 (pbk)
ISBN 13: 978-1-138-48549-5 (hbk)

Typeset in Times New Roman
by Taylor & Francis Books

Contents

List of tables ix
List of contributors x
Preface xv

PART 1 1

1 Introduction: The Globalisation of Urban Governance – Legal Perspectives on Sustainable Development Goal 11 3
HELMUT PHILIPP AUST AND ANÉL DU PLESSIS

2 Including Cities in the 2030 Agenda – A Review of the Post-2015 Process 17
NOORA ARAJÄRVI

3 International Institutions and the City: Towards a Comparative Law of Glocal Governance 38
MICHAEL RIEGNER

4 City Limits: Sustainable Urban Governance in Planetary Infrastructural Regimes 65
BORIS VORMANN

PART 2 85

5 Funding and Good Financial Governance as Imperatives for Cities' Pursuit of SDG 11 87
OLIVER FUO

6 War and Peace in the City 108
CINDY WITTKE

7 Ensuring Access to Public Space as a Dimension of "Safe Cities": The Role of UN Entities in Shaping the Global Urban Governance Agenda 127
HANNAH BIRKENKÖTTER

8 The Challenges of Cultural Diversity for Safe and Sustainable Cities 151
FRANCOIS VENTER

PART 3 171

9 Global Goals and Urban Development: The Territorial Effects of Implementing the MDGs in Brazil 173
M. CECILIA OLIVEIRA

10 City Regions in Pursuit of SDG 11: Institutionalising Multilevel Cooperation in Gauteng, South Africa 186
JAAP DE VISSER

11 The Pursuit of SDG 11 Through the Lens of Integrated Development Planning 208
ANGELA VAN DER BERG

12 Governance in the Smart City: Sketches of a Research Programme in Legal Theory 227
PETER GAILHOFER

13 The Tensions Between Local Resilience-Building and Transnational Action: US-Mexican Cooperation in Crime Affected Communities in Northern Mexico, and What this Tells Us about Global Urban Governance 247
ALEJANDRO RODILES

14 Conclusion: Summary of Observations and Pointers for Future Research 267
ANÉL DU PLESSIS AND HELMUT PHILIPP AUST

Index 275

Tables

10.1 Population growth in the Gauteng Province 190
10.2 Overview of South African Constitutional Court judgments on "municipal planning" 194

Contributors

Noora Arajärvi currently works as a research officer on the The Accountability Deficits of Major Western Powers project at the School of Law at the University of Essex. Previously, she was a visiting scholar at the Max Planck Institute for Comparative Public Law and International Law in Heidelberg (2018) and a postdoctoral fellow with the Berlin Potsdam Research Group – The International Rule of Law – Rise or Decline? (2015–2017). She has also served at the Rule of Law Unit in the Executive Office of the Secretary-General of the UN (2013–2015). Arajärvi has published several articles on different areas of public international law and is the author of *The Changing Nature of Customary International Law: Methods of Interpreting the Concept of Custom in International Criminal Tribunals* (Routledge 2014). Her current research includes the conceptual aspects of the international rule of law, implementation of SDG 16, compliance and accountability in international law, and the continuing exploration of the essence of customary international law.

Helmut Philipp Aust is Professor of Law at the Freie Universität Berlin. Previously, he was a senior research fellow at Humboldt University of Berlin (2011–2016). He was also Visiting Professor at the University of Konstanz (2016) and Visiting Fellow at the Lauterpacht Centre of International Law, University of Cambridge (2008) and at the Institute of International Law and the Humanities at Melbourne Law School (2014–2015). His research interests lie in the fields of public international law and comparative constitutional law. He is the author of *Complicity and the Law of State Responsibility* (2011) and of *Das Recht der globalen Stadt* (2017). He has also co-edited the collection *The Interpretation of International Law by Domestic Courts* (with Georg Nolte, 2016). Since May 2017, he is Co-Chairman of a new study group, The Role of Cities in International Law, of the International Law Association.

Hannah Birkenkötter is a research assistant at Humboldt-Universität zu Berlin at the Chair for Public Law and Jurisprudence (Prof. Dr. Christoph Möllers, LLM) as part of a research group on overlapping spheres of authority and interface conflicts. She currently pursues a dissertation exploring rule of law discourses within the United Nations system, and was a visiting doctoral researcher at the New York University School of Law (2016–2017) and at Princeton University (2014). She has published several articles on formats of legal research, the role of judicial and quasi-judicial processes in international law, and on comparative constitutional law.

Jaap de Visser is Director of the Dullah Omar Institute at University of the Western Cape, a research and advocacy institution, specialising in governance and human rights in Africa. He is co-author of *Local Government Law of South Africa*. His research, teaching and consulting focuses on local government, multilevel government, good governance and federalism in Africa. He has published on local government in South Africa, Uganda, Zimbabwe, Ethiopia and Kenya and has advised UNICEF, UN-Habitat, UNDP, Forum of Federations, and the German Agency for Technical Cooperation (GIZ), as well as national, provincial and local governments in South Africa. He was the lead consultant in the drafting of the Western Cape Land Use Planning Act of 2014 and advised the UNDP on the 2015 review of Lesotho's Local Government Act. Prof. de Visser is a board member of the Commonwealth Local Government Forum, Secretary/Treasurer of the International Association of Centers for Federal Studies and serves on the editorial boards of the Hague Journal on the Rule of Law and the Commonwealth Journal on Local Governance.

Anél du Plessis is Professor of Law and the SARChI Chair in Cities, Law and Environmental Sustainability (CLES) at the North-West University (NWU), South Africa. She is author and editor of various publications, including *Environmental Law and Local Government in South Africa* (2015) and *Fulfilment of South Africa's Constitutional Environmental Right in the Local Government Sphere* (2009). Her research focuses on environmental, local government, and different aspects of constitutional law and governance. She is a member of the Executive Committee of the Environmental Law Association of South Africa, project coordinator for a long-standing local government capacity-building project of the NWU and the Konrad Adenauer Foundation and serves on the Teaching Committee of the IUCN Academy of Environmental Law. She is a rated researcher of South Africa's National Research Foundation and an alumnus of the scholarship programmes of the Deutscher Akademisher Austauschdienst (DAAD), the US Fulbright and the Alexander von Humboldt Foundation.

Oliver Fuo is an Associate Professor in the Faculty of Law, North-West University (NWU), South Africa. He obtained his LLB Degree in 2002 from the University of Buea. In 2009 and 2014, he obtained his LLM and LLD qualifications from the NWU. He was a postdoctoral fellow at the NWU in 2014 and a senior lecturer at the University of the Free State in 2015. Oliver Fuo has presented papers in national and international conferences and has published numerous articles in established national and international journals. He serves as a reviewer for several law journals and is Assistant Editor of the Potchefstroom Electronic Law Journal. His research addresses a range of issues that cut across constitutional law, local government law, socio-economic rights law and aspects of environmental law.

Peter Gailhofer is currently working as a lawyer and scientific researcher at Oeko-Institut Berlin, focussing on legal problems of sustainable development, urbanisation, digitalisation and on transnational implications of human rights. From 2016 to 2017 he was employed as an attorney for energy and climate protection law at Becker Büttner Held Berlin. Before completing his legal traineeship in 2015, he was a scientific researcher at the University of Zurich (chair for Philosophy and Theory of Law, Legal Sociology and Public International Law, 2008–2013). In 2014, he completed his dissertation *Rechtspluralismus und Rechtsgeltung* [Legal Pluralism and Legal Validity] which received the Prof. Walther Hug award and was published in 2016 with Nomos (funded by the German Research Foundation, DFG).

M. Cecilia Oliveira is project leader of Implementing the Paris Agreement at the Institute for Advanced Sustainability Studies in Potsdam, Germany. She holds a PhD in International Relations from the Catholic University of Sao Paulo and was a Fulbright Fellow at the Earth Institute, Columbia University, USA. Her thesis "Millennium Development Goals: Secure Life and Planetary Governmentality" focused on the effects of the MDGs in Brazil and new connections between security and development. Her main areas of study are development, critical approaches to sustainability, security, and climate change.

Michael Riegner is a postdoctoral researcher at Humboldt University of Berlin (Department of Public and Comparative Law & Law and Society Institute). He was a researcher at Max Planck Institute for Comparative Public Law and International Law in Heidelberg and at Justus-Liebig-University Gießen and consults regularly for development agencies and international institutions. He studied law at Passau University, Geneva University, and New York University School of Law. He has published inter alia in the Yale Journal of International Law and Transnational Legal Theory, and his book on global information governance in international institutional law appeared in 2017.

Alejandro Rodiles is Associate Professor of International Law and Global Governance at ITAM School of Law, in Mexico City. Previously, he was a research fellow at the Law Faculty of Humboldt University of Berlin. Rodiles has served as a diplomat at the Permanent Mission of

Mexico to the United Nations in New York. He is the author of *Coalitions of the Willing and International Law –The Interplay between Formality and Informality* (Cambridge University Press, 2018).

Angela van der Berg is a doctoral candidate at the Faculty of Law of the North-West University, South Africa, and Tilburg University, the Netherlands. Her doctoral research focuses on municipal planning law and policy for sustainable cities. Her research addresses a range of issues that cut across municipal and urban planning, sustainable development, sustainable cities, and matters of local government law and governance. Angela has presented papers at national and international conferences and has published articles in established national journals. She has also authored and co-authored book chapters. Angela is currently involved as co-project coordinator for an annual local government capacity-building project sponsored by the Konrad Adenauer Stiftung in South Africa.

Francois Venter is an extraordinary professor of the Faculty of Law of the North-West University in Potchefstroom, where he has taught constitutional law since 1974. He was dean of the faculty from 2001 to 2012. His research focus is on the comparison of constitutional law and theory and he has published three monographs in the field, the latest being *Constitutionalism and Religion* (Edward Elgar, 2015).

Boris Vormann is Professor of Politics and head of the politics section at Bard College Berlin. He has held visiting research and teaching positions at the CUNY Graduate Center, Freie Universität Berlin, Harvard University, and New York University. His most recent books are *Global Port Cities in North America: Urbanisation Processes and Global Production Networks from Routledge* (2015), *A handbook on U.S. politics and policy* (Springer VS, 2016), and a monograph on the crisis of democracy, co-authored with Christian Lammert (Aufbau Verlag, 2017). His long-term research project examines the role of states in building the urban infrastructures of expanding global trade networks.

Cindy Wittke is leader of the research group Frozen and Unfrozen Conflicts at the Leibniz Institute for East and Southeast European Studies in Regensburg. From 2014–2017 she held the position of a senior researcher with the Department of Politics and Public Administration of the University of Konstanz. Additionally, she is an external programme associate of the Political Settlement Research Programme, University of Edinburgh. Her research is situated at the intersection of international law and politics. Wittke earned a Magistra Artium (MA) in East European Studies and a PhD in Law from the Freie Universität Berlin. Her previous affiliations include interdisciplinary research centres like Governance in Areas of Limited Statehood at the Freie Universität Berlin (2006–2010), the Lauterpacht Centre for International

Law in Cambridge (2009, 2010), and the Centres for Law, Society & Culture, and for Constitutional Democracy at Indiana University's Maurer School of Law (2013–2014). Her first monograph *Law in the Twilight – International Courts and Tribunals, the Security Council and the Internationalisation of Peace Agreements between State and Non-State Parties* was recently published by Cambridge University Press (2018).

Preface

This volume is the result of a three-year long German-South African research project which started out under the title of Safe and Sustainable Cities in 2016. It was funded by the Alexander von Humboldt Foundation under their Research Group Linkage programme line. When we applied for the funding for this project in early 2015, the adoption of a separate goal on cities as part of the Sustainable Development Goals had not yet been decided on. The adoption of the SDGs in 2016 encouraged us to broaden the focus of the book project to look more generally into what we perceived to be an intensifying globalisation of questions of urban governance. More and more, we find, there are international normative expectations of what it means for a city or locality to be well-governed. This scholarly work is about these processes and their implications. Its contributions look at both the international dimensions bringing about these normative expectations and the local contexts in which these expectations are playing out. We trust that the book will inform scholarly research in law as well as in other disciplines.

We have several people to thank at this point in time. First of all we should like to acknowledge the wonderful support that we enjoyed at our respective home institutions in Potchefstroom and Berlin. At the North-West University (NWU) in Potchefstroom, we wish to thank Saritha Marais and Elsabé Roux for all their administrative assistance. In Berlin, our gratitude needs to be shared between two institutions, as the project started while one of us was still affiliated with Humboldt University of Berlin (HU) before later moving on to Freie Universität Berlin (FU). At HU, we wish to thank Juliane Brauer for supporting us in the day-to-day running of the programme. At FU, Bozena Sikora has been a constant source of help. Alexander Silke and Natalie Reglinski have also been steady supporters of this collective endeavour.

At both NWU and FU, we are grateful to a number of colleagues who have helped us with the editing process. Our warmest thanks go out to Erna Cassarà, Felix Schott, Johannes Siegel, Melandri Steenkamp, Andrew Molaiwa and Alan Brimer for helping us with putting together the manuscript. At Routledge we should like to thank Natalja Mortensen and Maria

Landschoot for seeing this publication through, as well as the anonymous reviewers for their feedback on the concept and structure of the volume as well as the chapters under review.

Of course, this volume would not exist without the contributions of our authors. It has been a genuine pleasure to work with all of them and we were delighted to see the chapters evolving from one draft to the next, and also how speedily and swiftly responses came in to reviewer feedback, queries and comments. Part of the process of working towards the publication of this volume were two intensive workshops in Potchefstroom and Berlin, where we had the chance to discuss matters of content and scope not only with one another but also with other expert colleagues whose critical input and scholarly guidance contributed considerably to the quality of this book. Our thanks are due to Ariane Berger, Sué Gonzalez Hauck, Markus Heintzen, Jaco Karsten, Kristine Kern, Myrone Stoffels, Juliana Streva, Bruck Teshome and Johanna Wolff for engaging with us in these workshops and for having served as rigorous peer reviewers of the content, scope and level of analysis in individual chapters.

Finally, we should like to thank some institutions. At the Alexander von Humboldt Foundation we are grateful to Alexandra Justus and Markus Lambertz for their assistance and reliable guidance. At FU Berlin, the May 2017 workshop enjoyed additional support from the Department of Law, the FU Centre for International Cooperation and the Ernst-Reuter-Gesellschaft e.V.

Helmut Aust and Anél du Plessis,
Berlin and Potchefstroom, 30 October 2018

Part 1

1 Introduction

The Globalisation of Urban Governance – Legal Perspectives on Sustainable Development Goal 11

Helmut Philipp Aust and Anél du Plessis

Sustainable Development Goal 11 and the Changing Dynamics of Urban Governance

The adoption of the Sustainable Development Goals (SDGs) by the UN General Assembly in 2015 represents the latest attempt by the international community to live up to the challenges of a planet on which population growth is out of control (French and Kotzé 2018). The steadily growing world population has to live and prosper within the limitations of the resources that our planet can generate. Climate change is a particularly pressing issue which is set to change the way people live dramatically in the next couple of generations. There is also the constant trend of urbanisation. More and more people live in cities and other urban areas such as towns and suburbs marked by the density of human structures such as houses, commercial buildings, road and railway infrastructure and the construction necessary for basic service delivery. This has led many to proclaim that we are living in an "urban age", while others are sceptical of the underlying statistics and normative projects (Brenner and Schmidt 2014). Be that as it may, it is not disputed that the current rate of urbanisation poses challenges with respect to environmental protection, the living conditions and the safety of city dwellers in informal settlements, the co-habitation of diverse communities in multilingual and multicultural spaces, the resilience of the earth system, and a host of other issues. At the same time, cities are increasingly being viewed as important stakeholders in the provision and maintenance of global public goods (Bulkeley and Betsill 2005, p. 44; Sassen 2013, p. 243; du Plessis 2017, pp. 242–244). Cities are now important partners in the concerted management and the promotion of the sustainable use of the global natural commons. Cities have formed cross-border associations that pride themselves on doing more than their respective nation states (their national governments) to mitigate and adapt to climate change (Aust 2015). Cities and urban areas are simultaneously part of the problems characteristic of the "urban age" and of the solutions to such problems.

This dual character of cities finds expression in SDG 11. The urban goal aspires to "make cities and human settlements inclusive, safe, resilient and sustainable" (UN General Assembly 2015). The goal is disambiguated in a number of sub-targets which address *inter alia* issues such as safe and affordable housing, slum upgrading, access to transport systems, participatory urban planning, the protection of world cultural and natural heritage, responding to natural disasters, reducing the adverse environmental impact of cities, and providing access to safe, inclusive and accessible green public spaces. Indicators specific to these targets are expected to be the yardsticks with which to assess whether and to what extent UN member states are on track to fulfil their pledges.

SDG 11 is noteworthy in several respects. First, it is the only actor-specific goal among the SDGs, which otherwise focus on concrete questions such as the reduction of poverty (Goal 1), the achievement of gender equality (Goal 5) or the combatting of climate change (Goal 13). Goal 11 stands out insofar as it addresses a particular level of governance. Secondly, it states an internationally agreed vision for good urban governance. Thirdly, SDG 11 bridges global and local levels of governance. While the SDGs were adopted by UN member states and are also directed at states for their implementation, SDG 11 emphasises that many local issues have a cascading effect as they escalate beyond mere local concern (Aust and du Plessis 2018).

These features of SDG 11 are analysed in this book. The contributions to this volume focus on aspects of the globalisation of good urban governance from a legal perspective. The book also includes contributions from other disciplines, notably political science, which makes it possible to analyse the legal nature of urban governance while being sensitive to the political context(s) in which the globalisation of urban governance takes place.

Urban governance was traditionally a remit of the state, and was confined mainly to domestic law, policy and regulations. International law used to be disinterested in the internal workings of the state (Aust 2017). Almost all international law commitments were aimed at securing certain end-results. The ways and means by which a state managed to arrive at such results were considered to be immaterial. This applied *a fortiori* also to the internal organisation of states, including the institutions of local government.

These certainties are no longer beyond question. The adoption of SDG 11 typically calls for a nuanced and differentiated assessment of why and how questions of urban governance are becoming global. Why is it that cities have entered the global governance arena in a fashion that seems to bypass sovereignty at times, and how is our conception of the boundaries of city governance changing? At the outset, it should be made clear that we do not understand the globalisation of urban governance to mean that every urban governance issue has become of direct global concern. Neither is the local, as a governed and governing space, disappearing. Nor is the importance of the state as a central organising category of our contemporary global world diminishing. And not every aspect of the globalisation of urban governance has legal relevance or implications.

At the same time, however, we can see how global forces have local impact and how international institutions such as the United Nations (UN) are taking a keen interest in how local governance is organised. This is happening by way of programme-based initiatives and other operations within different UN structures, for example. Other international organisations such as the World Bank and the International Organisation for Standardisation (ISO) also increasingly help to shape urban governance (International Organisation for Standardisation 2014). Transnational coalitions and other informal associations between cities and other actors contribute to the internationalisation of local matters. And cities and their local authorities find themselves at the receiving end of this trend. More and more often, they are required to take international normative expectations into account when they plan and make decisions. Their cooperation with institutions such as the UN or the World Bank and their participation in global climate change networks such as the C40 – Climate Leadership Group or ICLEI show, however, that they are not just "at the receiving end" – cities and local governments are also actively participating in the globalisation of local matters. Several of these developments have legally relevant implications which command of scholars to rethink established legal relationships (Blank 2006; Nijman 2011).

This is an essential point for the premise and shared understanding of the contributions to this volume. The overarching hypothesis is that SDG 11 demonstrates how local governance is recognised as an autonomous yet interrelated part of the global pursuit of sustainable development. This is a consequence of what is and what ought to be happening in and among the cities of the world. Still, none of the contributors to this volume aims to oversell the current importance of cities and their institutions. City structures inevitably operate in global, regional and national contexts which determine the leeway and scope for manoeuvre in their governance operations. No city nor its government function as an island. When we thus speak of the globalisation of urban governance, the real world picture comprises a fragmented matrix of institutional arrangements, political regimes and sources of governing power that transcend real and virtual administrative boundaries. This is owed not least to the enormous differences between the cities and local governments of the world (also see Le Galès 2002, p. 183; Curtis 2016, pp. 30–35). The distinctions stem from the size, resources, spatial formation, social make-up and institutional organisation of cities as well as from their constitutional status and authority within different states, some of them being situated in what is colloquially called the 'Global South' as opposed to the so-called 'Global North' (more explanation on these categories Roy 2014, p. 15). Some cities and their local authorities are situated in strong multilevel federal government systems and democratic structures, while others are part of unitary states with far less governance autonomy. These conceptual metaphors and comparisons may be misleading in their binary simplicity, yet they are useful to show at a very basic level how different the conditions are in which cities operate.

This book brings together a group of scholars from diverse geographical and disciplinary backgrounds. Most of the contributions are rooted in law and take an interest in the legal dimensions of urban governance. However, the volume does not adopt a unitary legal perspective. Instead, the analyses testify to the diversity within legal scholarship insofar as some contributions approach the urbanisation of local governance from an international law perspective, whereas others zoom in on the state level and the relevance of domestic administrative and local government law and practice. There is a robust streak of comparative analysis and understanding in most of the contributions, which adds texture and context to the issues under discussion. In addition, this book was conceived in the context of a joint German-South African research project on questions of urban governance. This explains a certain geographical emphasis among the contributors. However, a number of different voices from other jurisdictions also feature in this volume, which enhances our insights and findings on the globalisation of urban governance. The contributions set in political science create an important contextual backdrop for the legal analyses. In this sense, the volume also pays tribute to the strong interdisciplinary heritage of urban studies and wishes to make a contribution to that stream of scholarship.

Key Concepts and Methodological Issues

This volume embraces diversity in scholarly approach and research methodology. At the same time, the contributions are anchored in certain common assumptions. Unless indicated otherwise in the respective contributions themselves, the chapters in this book follow a shared terminology set forth in this introduction.

First of all, the "globalisation of urban governance" referred to in the title of the book is not meant to convey the idea that all contemporary questions of urban governance have become globalised. We understand urban governance to inclusively refer to the institutional design, operations (including planning and management), institutions, as well as the rules and principles binding on and generated by local governments. The reference to governance underscores that "traditional", hierarchical forms of the exercise of state power (via formal government in the public sector context) are now supplemented by other governance actors and instrumentation (Holley 2010, pp. 128–131; Kotzé 2012). Public actors, for example, also work in conjunction with the private sector, be it in the form of "public-private partnerships" (PPPs) or other mechanisms. It is acknowledged that the "power" of non-governmental actors such as the media, NGOs, investors and donors, the education sector and industry is real and influential in shaping urban governance. The same goes for the different types of interaction between various legal subjects. In terms of governance instrumentation, command and control type governance is today supplemented by instrumentation such as incentives and disincentives, agreement-based instruments, as well as civil society-based instruments such as measures for community participation in decision-making processes. The term urban governance is thus broad enough to encapsulate a variety of techniques, instrumentation and approaches through which cities and other urban areas are today governed, administered and organised, and by means of which they themselves govern in increasingly diversified communities (Pierre and Peters 2012, pp. 82–83).

When we talk about cities and urban areas more generally, we are focusing on delineated local jurisdictions and the role of municipal governments. While cities are spaces with various dimensions and features, it is their immediate authorities (municipalities; local governments) as very specific public actors in which we are particularly interested. In this context, it is difficult to conceive of a specific definition of a city or "urban area", as every legal and government system of the world differs in that regard. Many countries know some kind of constitutional protection of "self-government" or "self-administration" for local authorities. This is the case, for instance, with respect to Germany and South Africa (on Germany see Aust 2017, pp. 75–120; on South Africa, du Plessis 2012, pp. 367–372). In other jurisdictions, such as the United States and Australia, this is not the case, and the autonomy of the local level of government merely flows from the statutory enactments of the individual states (for a comparison Grant and Drew 2017, pp. 177–209). Still, most cities face common challenges and similar limitations that come with growing urbanisation, an unprecedented flow of people and goods, climate change, and their limited natural, financial and other resources. For this reason we consider it useful to discuss the globalisation of urban governance in comparative fashion, being constantly mindful of the risk attached to blindly transplanting findings from one case (one legal jurisdiction) to another (Legrand 1997).

It should be stressed, however, that this project adopts a comparative mind-set without necessarily being a comparative law project in the traditional sense. Accordingly, authors were not supplied with a uniform set of questions or benchmarks with which to unearth and evaluate similarities and differences between different jurisdictions, for example. Instead, almost all of the contributions to this volume embrace a form of contextualising comparative analysis with a focus on relative similarities and comparable phenomena. The comparative mind-set is used to determine and explain, for instance, how various legal systems respond to the occurrence of cultural diversity in today's globalised urban areas, whether good financial governance is imperative at the local level, how the era of digital governance plays out locally, and how the World Bank's direct entry into agreements with local governments is being accommodated in different jurisdictions.

The globalisation of urban governance presupposes some kind of standard for (local) governance practice and the quality of life of those inhabiting the urban space. One such yardstick is provided by SDG 11. Its aspirations to make cities inclusive, safe, resilient and sustainable is representative of the current debates about good urban governance. SDG 11 serves as a globally recognised reference point against which the individual contributions to this book assess how urban governance is globalising and what the concomitant implications and effects are. In this context, one is reminded that SDG 11 is not legally binding in and of itself – at least insofar as the UN member states and their cities and local governments are concerned. The SDGs were adopted by the UN General Assembly (GA). Generally, the GA lacks law-making powers (Klabbers 2017, p. 94). Instead, its resolutions have the characteristics of recommendations and cannot bind the UN member states directly. This applies *a fortiori* to the subnational divisions of states.

This statement should be qualified in two ways. First, the binding nature of GA resolutions may be a different matter when it comes to the internal workings of the UN system. Here too it would be far-fetched to attribute to the resolutions their being binding across the whole UN system. Too much depends on the context in which resolutions were adopted and on how they relate to the mission and competences of individual UN organs, agencies and sub-groupings. Yet what frequently happens is that GA resolutions effectively become yardsticks for the implementation of further UN programmes. In this way, what initially started out as a non-binding document becomes crucial for how different parts of the UN understand their missions.

Secondly, the non-binding nature of the SDGs should also not trivialise their importance in practical terms. It has often been observed that at times non-binding, informal documents may have as large a 'compliance pull' as binding legal documents (Finnemore and Toope 2001). Based on the expectation that this may also be the case with SDG 11, this volume makes an innovative contribution both to the literature on different aspects of global governance and to legal scholarship specifically. In existing legal scholarship much attention focuses on how international (or EU) legal norms are implemented domestically (see, for instance, the contributions in Aust and Nolte 2016). This is an important question which continues to pose new challenges. Yet, how non-binding documents are taken into account by domestic governance actors is more difficult for lawyers to assess. After all, they usually share a penchant for clear distinctions between law and non-law, between what is binding and mere voluntary, political or moral commitments. To this extent, the contributions to this volume deliberately avoid speaking of "soft law" in characterising SDG 11 and its effects. In our view, the use of the term "soft law" in the present context may create an artificial separation between "hard law" and the rest (also see Klabbers 1996).

At the same time, the attempt by state parties to realise SDG 11 may require novel legal interventions and the establishment of new, or the strengthening of existing types of legal relationships within and across state borders. Together, the chapters in this volume explore how the different legal frameworks applicable to urban governance are being transformed (directly and/or indirectly) by informal practices, transnational lobbying and non-binding international commitments such as the SDGs. To this end, questions are being asked about the limitations created by existing domestic law and governance systems where the SDG commitments and international peer pressure are expected to penetrate in the short to medium term. This volume thereby makes a contribution to the global governance literature, which is often more interested in informal processes, international relations and political workings than in concrete questions of the architecture of governance and the functioning of existing and future domestic and international law.

The scholarly and policy discourse on the subsidiary goals of inclusivity, sustainability, resilience and safety in SDG 11 is in the process of being developed. For this reason we do not adopt any fixed meanings for any of these goals. Their meaning, level of relevance and parameters are largely dependent on national and local contexts and should be considered in the context of all of the other SDGs. We thereby acknowledge the fluidity of SDG 11 – that a state of urban safety and security in Mexico and South Africa will be different in its conception and experience from what it would be in countries such as Germany, the United States or Australia. Urban inclusivity can, for example, be understood from the micro-level perspective of neighbourhood diversity as well as from the perspective of bridging the access barriers between a country's rural and urban areas by way of transportation infrastructure, affordable housing and basic services. These examples show that the meaning of SDG 11 still needs to be written.

Main Research Questions

Based on the shared assumptions sketched above, the chapters in this volume together and separately address a number of key questions. In the collective, the contributions offer a clearer picture of a) how urban governance is becoming global and what role SDG 11 plays in this regard; and b) how international, national and local law and governance systems are reacting or may have to react and/or adjust in future.

First, how have the normative ideals set out in SDG 11 been developed? Which genealogies are at play in stating that cities are expected to become inclusive, safe, resilient and sustainable? How do these categories relate to broader trends in (global) governance and (international) law? What may be some of the unintended legal consequences of SDG 11?

Second, what are the respective meanings of the four sub-goals of SDG 11 – inclusiveness, safety, resilience, sustainability – and how do these relate to one another? Is there tension between these sub-goals, and if so, why? How can any tension be resolved and accommodated? Do local initiatives to implement some of the sub-goals contribute to a lack of attention to others? If so, how? Which ideological and political preferences are, or may potentially be, bolstered by initiatives focusing on some of the goals?

Third, what does SDG 11 imply for urban law and governance in the domestic context and how are local processes of urban governance internationalised? How does international influence manifest itself in different domestic contexts and what are the legal and institutional limitations and barriers, if any? Is there evidence of direct contact between local governments (individually or by way of networks) and other international institutions? Is there a weaker and more indirect form of engagement by local governments with global norms, goals and expectations? Which local governance instrumentation, projects or legal constructs exist that already contribute or may in future contribute to the pursuit of SDG 11 in the context of developing and developed countries?

A host of issues could not be addressed in this volume, a fact which highlights the need for continued research on the globalisation of urban governance. Some of these issues include the development of international indicators for sustainable cities, the meaning of the so-called right to the city in the context of SDG 11, the rural-urban interface, the prominent role of politics in how city governments plan and arrive at decisions, and the impact of other international forces such as economic and geo-political drivers, international immigration patterns and international conflict on the present trend of urbanisation. Other questions remain to be asked about the meaning of community participation at the city level and responsive democratic government in an era of populism, as well as about the role of the courts and judicial activism in interpreting and applying the underlying international and transnational forces behind the design of progressive or regressive new domestic laws and policies.

The Structure of the Volume

The book has three parts. The first part looks at the genesis and development of SDG 11 in context and analyses what it means for the globalisation of urban governance. The second part looks at specific contexts of the globalisation of urban governance whereas the third part focuses on the local dimensions of this phenomenon.

Following this introduction, the first part of this volume continues with Chapter Two, in which Noora Arajärvi discusses how cities came to be included in the 2030 Agenda. The Rio+20 outcome document recognised the need for systematic urban development to strengthen sustainability, and outlined the sub-themes, which formed the basis for negotiating SDG 11 on cities and human settlements. Arajärvi reviews the role of cities in the post-2015 negotiations, with a focus on the Open Working Group on SDGs. She sets out the background of the notion of sustainable cities in the UN framework, and looks at the process of drafting the targets and indicators for SDG 11. She concludes that while some concerns have surfaced on the mounting role of local governance, there appears to be a broadly shared understanding among UN members on the importance of cities in achieving the SDGs.

The international dimension of urban governance is further fleshed out in Chapter Three by Michael Riegner. This chapter analyses legal relationships between international institutions and cities, especially in the fields of sustainable development and urban security. As global cities have emerged as para-diplomatic actors and international institutions have discovered local governments as partners, another dimension has been added to multilevel global governance: the “glocal” city. A key element of “glocal governance” is the formation of direct legal relationships between international institutions and local governments. Hence, this chapter looks into the public law that frames, limits and legitimates relations between local governments and international institutions. In particular, it analyses how international institutional law regulates such institutions’ relationships with cities and how domestic local government law addresses and evolves in response to relations between cities and international institutions.

The first part of the volume concludes with Chapter Four, in which Boris Vormann critiques dominant discourses on sustainable urban governance on two grounds. First, their limited focus on cities as territorially bounded and separate entities presents a truncated understanding of urbanisation processes that distort what sustainability means in problematic ways. Second, because the flows that are crucial in shaping urbanisation processes are not articulated just at the local level, the definition of urban governance needs to be extended to patterns of state intervention on many levels. The concept of *infrastructural regimes* serves in this chapter as a heuristic device to understand how the state, in different constellations and degrees of centralisation, shapes socio-spatial arrangements to create, stabilise and guarantee the market flows that over-determine urban development. The author discerns three infrastructural regimes for the case of the United States to unpack the historically specific, shifting patterns of state intervention. He concludes with the thought that debates on urban sustainability, regardless of whether they address the global south or the global north, need to be upscaled to map onto these urban realities and to provide a meaningful conceptual language. On a more normative level, given their stakes and leverage in spatial restructuring processes, local governments have the potential to overcome the divisive logics of urban entrepreneurialism and the vicious circle of zero-sum competition for flows of capital, commodities and tourists.

In the second part of this book, the focus falls on specific dimensions of the globalisation of urban governance. In Chapter Five, Oliver Fuo reminds the reader that cities across the globe need adequate funding and good financial management in order to be able to realise the targets set in SDG 11. Informed by this caveat, the chapter discusses how some international and African regional instruments seek to promote good financial governance. This is followed by a reflection on sources of funding that can generally be utilised by cities in developing countries for the envisaged transition to sustainability. The chapter uses South Africa's legal framework as an example to demonstrate some of the complexities faced by cities in developing countries in attempting to generate and effectively manage the fiscal resources needed to transition to a sustainable future. The South African example shows that although a genuine attempt has been made in law to protect the fiscal autonomy of cities and to accommodate the core principles of good financial governance canvassed by international and African regional instruments, serious challenges are experienced in the implementation of relevant laws, which may affect the pursuit of SDG 11 in a very direct way.

In Chapter Six, Cindy Wittke discusses how twenty-first century cities are objects, subjects, laboratories, and agents of emerging formal and informal modes of global, local and transnational governance. She argues that cities have started using the language of inter-state relations and international law and mimicking states' practised forms of institutionalised and legalised interaction. From a global comparative perspective, twenty-first century cities are also vulnerable and prone to various forms of intra-city violent conflicts. This chapter provides an explorative overview of the fast-changing variety of urban conflict constellations, which asks for continuous interdisciplinary, theoretical, and comparative investigations of the forms and patterns of violent intra-city conflicts. Such investigations are necessary to unpack and understand what is at stake in urban warfare and when building peace in cities. In the course of these explorations the chapter also debates from a twenty-first century city-perspective the spatial adaptions and re-conceptionalisations that originally state-centred concepts like warfare and peace are undergoing.

Chapter Seven then turns to another dimension of urban safety. Hannah Birkenkötter discusses the understanding of safe cities in the 2030 Agenda and the New Urban Agenda as access to public space free of physical violence, to be implemented by a variety of actors through multi-stakeholder partnerships. Placing the substantive content of SDG 11.7 in the wider context of the UN's human settlements agenda, the author argues that the focus on the planning and design of public space is the result of slow normative change that has partly been shaped by the operational activities of UN entities and their direct interaction with city governments.

An examination of operational activities on safer cities by the UN Human Settlements Programme (UN-Habitat) and the UN Entity on Gender Equality (UN Women) shows that operational activities have an impact on norm evolvement within the UN system. Operational activities might be supervised, but are not primarily guided, by state-composed governing structures. This does not imply that UN entities have replaced states as the main drivers of normative change, but their role is not limited to implementing international standards. Rather, they are important actors in normative interpretation and development. The result is an interplay between interpretation and standard-setting, between executive agencies and their principals, with implications for international institutional law.

Chapter Eight concludes the second part of the book. Francois Venter explains that given the fact that local governments are usually entrusted with the primary responsibility for culturally and religiously sensitive matters, the promotion of social development and a safe environment are complex demands faced by cities. The potential for development-inhibiting tension and conflict caused by improperly governed multi-cultural cohabitation is clearly present. Around the world, many issues concerning culture-related conflict, both between members of society and between the institutions of government and citizens, have challenged governments, and the cases that reached the courts were often concerned with the complexities of urban cohabitation. This chapter explores typical instances of tensions arising from cultural differences in urban societies for the purposes of drawing attention to the nature of the problems that the authorities are required to resolve. The manner in which especially courts in jurisdictions professing liberal democracy tend to seek solutions by invoking cultural and religious neutrality is investigated against the background of the notion of constitutionalism. The core question being addressed is whether a principled solution can be found for the mitigation of tensions arising from the increasing cultural diversity in the cities of a globalising world, in order to promote cultural inclusiveness and urban safety.

In Part Three of the book, local contexts of the globalisation of urban governance are addressed. In Chapter Nine, Cecilia Oliveira traces the development of the SDGs from its predecessors, the Millennium Development Goals (MDGs), with a particular focus on municipal policies to ensure safety in Rio de Janeiro. The author explains that the inclusion of a self-standing goal on cities in the SDGs is often portrayed as progress from the position established by the MDGs. However, the absence of reference to cities in the MDGs does not mean that local governments were irrelevant for their implementation. On the contrary, this chapter shows that municipalities and cities already played a key role in implementing the MDGs within UN member states. It demonstrates this point through a case study of the efforts to implement the MDGs in Brazil, at the local level generally and in the city of Rio de Janeiro more specifically.

It is argued that by studying the local implementation of the MDGs, we can draw some conclusions about the role of cities under the SDGs. In particular, the author takes a critical view on the combination of social and security policies especially targeted at low-income neighbourhoods, in particular the favelas.

In Chapter Ten of the book, Jaap de Visser turns to a crucial issue for the successful implementation of the SDGs, the organisation of metropolitan areas. The author focuses on the Gauteng City Region (GCR), a conglomeration of cities and towns around the City of Johannesburg, a major contributor to the economy of South Africa and the African continent. The population of the GCR is growing fast and its economy is vibrant. However, spatial and institutional fragmentation among the various levels of government in the GCR is hampering development. It is against this background that this chapter discusses the constitutional and legal options for closer multilevel collaboration with a specific focus on the provincial and municipal organs of state in the Gauteng Province in South Africa. It locates the debate in the international normative framework on decentralisation. The author discusses legal options, ranging from the most intrusive (such as merging institutions) to the least intrusive (intergovernmental collaboration). The chapter concludes that legal frameworks may place a high premium on the protection of municipal autonomy but also offer a range of mechanisms to facilitate collaboration across jurisdictional boundaries.

Following on from that perspective, Chapter Eleven by Angela van der Berg departs from the understanding that integrated development planning is central to promoting sustainable development in the urban context. In South Africa specifically, it has been more than 15 years since the introduction of integrated development planning into municipal planning practice. The UN 2030 Agenda for sustainable development frames the context within which global sustainability must be pursued. SDG 11 requires specific action from cities across the globe to ensure sustainability in the urban context. This chapter questions how the notion of integrated development planning can serve as a vehicle for the pursuit of SDG 11 in the South African context. Emphasis is placed on the Integrated Development Plan (IDP) of the City of Johannesburg Metropolitan Municipality.

In Chapter Twelve Peter Gailhofer turns to one of the most pressing issues of contemporary urban governance and one which has a crucial role to play in the realisation of the SDGs. In his contribution he outlines a legal theoretical approach to the "smart city". The concept of the "smart city" conflates two transformative "mega-trends" of the twenty-first century – digitisation and urbanisation – both of which are often deliberated in the social sciences and, at least recently, in jurisprudence. Focusing on the implications of smart cities for law and governance means reformulating many of the legal theoretical problems commonly associated with transnationalisation – like legal polycentricity or fragmentation – yet from a new, different perspective, which reproduces notions of "glocalism" in a rather radical way. With his legal theoretical reconstruction of the concept of the smart city the author diagnoses new challenges for the law, which are fundamental and practical at once. The chapter also clarifies the conceptual role and the practical importance of overarching legal values, principles or objectives like those in SDG 11 which may be of use in the challenging task of reconstructing their substance. The contribution concludes with a general and preliminary proposal for a deepened exploration of the normative consequences of the digitisation of urban spaces.

In Chapter Thirteen, Alejandro Rodiles turns to the specific context of the so-called Mérida Initiative, a US–Mexican partnership aiming at strengthening law-enforcement cooperation in the fight against the violent illegal narcotics trade. Although less known for this feature, the Initiative also comprises an action plan which, without referring to it, accords with SDG 11: it seeks to make Mexican cities and communities (other human settlements) affected by organised crime safer by enhancing their inclusiveness and sustainability through resilience-building strategies. This chapter analyses the relationship between local resilience-building and transnational cooperation in the framework of the Mérida Initiative, and inquires into what this analysis suggests about global urban governance more broadly.

The book concludes with Chapter Fourteen, in which the editors to this volume draw together the various strands of discussion of the individual chapters. They summarise key findings of the volume and propose future routes for inquiry.

Bibliography

Literature

Aust, Helmut Philipp. 2015. Shining cities on the hill" *The Global City, Climate Change and International Law. European Journal of International Law*, 26, 255–278.

Aust, Helmut Philipp. 2017. *Das Recht der globalen Stadt – Grenzüberschreitende Dimensionen kommunaler Selbstverwaltung*. Tübingen: Mohr Siebeck.

Aust, Helmut Philipp and Nolte, Georg. 2016. *The Interpretation of International Law by Domestic Courts – Uniformity, Diversity, Convergence.* Oxford: Oxford University Press.

Aust, Helmut Philipp and du Plessis, Anél. 2018. Good Urban Governance as a Global Aspiration: On the Potential and Limits of Sustainable Development Goal 11. In: Duncan French and Louis Kotzé (eds). *Sustainable Development Goals – Law, Theory and Implementation*. Cheltenham, UK: Edward Elgar. pp. 201–221.

Blank, Yishai. (2006). The city and the world. *Columbia Journal of Transnational Law*, 44. 868–931.

Brenner, Neil and Schmid, Christian. 2014. The "urban age" in question. *International Journal of Urban and Regional Research,* 38. 731–755.

Bulkeley, Harriet and Betsill, Michèle. 2005. Rethinking Sustainable Cities: Multilevel Governance and the "Urban" Politics of Climate Change. *Environmental Politics*, 14. 42–63.

Curtis, Simon. 2016. *Global Cities and Global Order*. Oxford: Oxford University Press.

Du Plessis, Anél. 2012. Climate Governance in South African Municipalities: Opportunities and Obstacles for Local Government. In: Benjamin R. Richardson (ed). *Local Climate Change Law*. Cheltenham, UK: Edward Elgar. pp. 353–388.

Du Plessis, Anél. 2017. The Readiness of South African Law and Policy for the Pursuit of Sustainable Development Goal 11. *Law, Democracy and Development* 21, 239–262.

Finnemore, Martha and Stephen Toope. 2001. Alternatives to "legalization": Richer views of law and politics. *International Organization*, 55, 743–758.

French, Duncan and Kotzé, Louis (eds). 2018. *Sustainable Development Goals – Law, Theory and Implementation*. Cheltenham. UK. Edward Elgar.

Grant, Bligh and Drew, Joseph. 2017. *Local Government in Australia – History, Theory and Public Policy*. Singapore: Springer.

Holley, Cameron. 2010. Facilitating monitoring, subverting self-interets and limiting discretion: Learning from "new" forms of accountability in practice. *Columbia Journal of Environmental Law*, 25, 127–211.

Klabbers, Jan. 1996. The reduncancy of soft law. *Nordic Journal of International Law*, 65, 167–182.

Klabbers, Jan. 2017. *International Law*, 2nd edn. Cambridge: Cambridge University Press.

Kotzé, Louis. 2012. *Global Environmental Governance*. Cheltenham, UK: Edward Elgar.

Le Galès, Patrick. 2002. *European Cities – Social Conflicts and Governance*. Oxford: Oxford University Press.

Legrand, Pierre. 1997. The Impossibility of "Legal Transplants". *Maastricht Journal of European and Comparative Law*, 4, 111–124.

Nijman, Janne. 2011. The Future of the City and the International Law of the Future. In: Sam Muller, Stavros Zouridis, Morly Frishman and Laura Kistemaker. (eds). *The Law of the Future and the Future of Law*. The Hague, NL: Torkel Opsahl. pp. 213–239.

Pierre, Jon and B. Guy Peters. 2012. Urban Governance. In: Peter John, Karen Mossberger and Susan E. Clarke (eds). *The Oxford Handbook of Urban Politics*. Oxford: Oxford University Press. pp. 71–86.

Roy, Ananya. 2014. Worlding the South – Towards a Post-Colonial Theory of Urban Governance. In: Susan Parnell and Sophie Oldfield (eds). *The Routledge Handbook on Cities of the Global South*. New York: Routledge. pp. 9–20.

Sassen, Saskia. 2013. A Focus on Cities Takes us Beyond Existing Governance Frameworks. In: Joseph Stiglitz and Mary Kaldor (eds). *The Quest for Security: Protection without Protectionism and the Challenge of Global Governance*. New York: Columbia University Press. pp. 238–259.

Documents

International Organization for Standardization "ISO 37120:2014: Sustainable Development of Communities – Indicators for City Services and Quality of Life". (2014). Available at www.iso.org/standard/62436.html.

United Nations General Assembly. (2015). Sustainable Development Goals. UN Doc. A/RES/70/1.

2 Including Cities in the 2030 Agenda – A Review of the Post-2015 Process

Noora Arajärvi

"Cities Are Where the Battle for Sustainable Development Will be Won or Lost."

(The Report of the High-Level Panel of Eminent Persons 2013:17)

Introduction and Background

At the 70th session of the General Assembly on 25 September 2015, the UN Member States adopted the new development agenda "Transforming our World: the 2030 Agenda for Sustainable Development". It adopted 17 sustainable development goals (SDGs) and 169 targets, covering three dimensions of sustainable development: social, economic, and environmental. SDG 11 is titled "Make Cities and Human Settlements Inclusive, Safe, Resilient and Sustainable", and it includes seven substantive targets and three targets that detail the means of implementation.

The 2030 Agenda was set up to have sustainable development at its core and poverty eradication as its highest priority, with the catch phrase "Leave no one behind". The Rio+20 outcome document "The Future We Want" required that the "SDGs should be action-oriented, concise and easy to communicate, limited in number, aspirational, global in nature and universally applicable to all countries while taking into account different national realities, capacities and levels of development and respecting national policies and priorities" (The Future We Want 2012, para 247). It provided the mandate for negotiating a new sustainable development agenda, setting up the Open Working Group on Sustainable Development Goals (OWG) and the subsequent intergovernmental process "with a view to developing global sustainable development goals to be agreed by the General Assembly" (para 248).

"The Future We Want" recognised systematic urban development as an important factor in strengthening sustainability and outlined its subthemes, which formed the basis for negotiating SDG 11. Further, it emphasised the need for holistic approaches in delivering and implementing sustainability strategies in cities and human settlements (para 134). While it is beyond doubt that cities and local governance structures are relevant in achieving sustainable development for environmental, social, political, economic, and cultural dimensions (eg Barral 2012; Parnell 2016), it was by no means certain that there would be sufficient support of states for a stand-alone goal for urban sustainable development (De Boer 2015). To date, it has not been a typical goal for development, and it merges issues of safe and affordable housing, basic urban services, affordable transport, participatory planning, disaster risk planning, environmental protection, public spaces, and good governance.

Within the SDGs framework, cities are also relevant in achieving additional goals and targets beyond SDG 11, such as sustainable economic regeneration and decent work, the eradication of inequalities, education and culture, food security and nutrition, waste management, water and sanitation, energy and transport, climate and risk resilience, sustainable consumption and production, and democracy and accountability (Sustainable Development Solutions Network Thematic Group on Sustainable Cities 2013; Bizikova and Searcy 2017). In this chapter, however, the focus is on the specific issue of the inclusion of cities in the 2030 Agenda, and in particular, their capacities, decision-making powers and competences, as recognised and discussed by states in the OWG. While these issues bear links to inclusiveness and representation, this chapter does not engage with the question of participatory decision-making in general, or the inclusion of affected communities, the public and individuals in development strategies, but limits the review and analysis to the treatment of cities as subjects and potential norm-makers and norm-entrepreneurs.

Sustainable Cities in the Post-2015 Process

From MDGs to SDGs

The Millennium Development Goals (MDGs) did not address the role of cities as subjects in the development discourse but instead concentrated on slums (Oliveira 2019, Chapter 9 in this volume). The implementation of MDG 7(d) has shown the many benefits of having a target focusing on slums, while its limitations have highlighted the need for a more systemic approach to addressing the scale and pace of urbanisation. The omission of a more holistic goal on urbanisation has been widely viewed as one of the major pitfalls of the MDGs, and states have expressed a desire to mend this in the new development agenda (Miyazawa and Zusman 2015). Such lacunae in the MDGs brought on increased demands to shift the focus to structural issues that may hinder development. Importantly, this has led to an understanding among many member states that cities and human settlements function across different areas of sustainable development. At the same time, given the key role of cities in the promotion of sustainable development, support for a stand-alone goal has become more vocal (Barnet and Parnell 2016).

As set out in "The Future We Want", the government-led process and negotiations were headed by the OWG, consisting of 77 member states in 30 groups. The OWG convened its first meeting in March 2013 and was chaired by the Permanent Representatives of Kenya and Hungary. In August 2014, after having held 13 formal sessions and countless informal consultations and "informal-informal" meetings, the OWG delivered a final set of 17 proposed SDGs, including 169 targets. In December 2014 the Secretary-General submitted the synthesis report "The Road to Dignity by 2030: Ending Poverty, Transforming All Lives and Protecting the Planet" (2014), presenting a summary of the inputs to the post-2015 process. This was followed by intergovernmental negotiations co-facilitated by the Permanent Representatives of Kenya and Ireland. The negotiations ran from November 2014 to July 2015, culminating at the United Nations Sustainable Development Summit in September 2015, which adopted the 2030 Agenda with the SDGs, as proposed by the OWG.

Preparatory Work of the United Nations Technical Support Team

The work of the OWG was supported by the United Nations Technical Support Team (TST), which first drafted issues briefs to inform the OWG of the relevant areas for consideration and later provided technical input on goals and targets, including language from existing instruments and tools for measuring each proposed target. UN-Habitat and the United Nations Environment Programme (UNEP) led the drafting of the "Issues Brief on Sustainable Cities and Human Settlements" (Issues Brief 2014), with 12 other UN entities contributing to it.[1] In addition, many other entities highlighted the role of sustainable cities and human settlements for the post-2015 agenda, including:

- Group of Friends of Sustainable Cities
- Sustainable Development Solutions Network
- Global Task Force of Local and Regional Governments
- Communitas Coalition for Sustainable Cities and Regions
- World Urban Campaign
- Institute for Advanced Sustainability Studies
- C40 Cities Climate Leadership Group.

The TST Issues Brief emphasised the relevance of cities and urban areas to the new development agenda, consolidated different approaches, and provided some basic data to support the inclusion of an urban SDG (Issues Brief 2014). It underlined the links between urban development and human rights, inequalities, crime, economics, and other social and environmental implications. It also noted that "with the benefit of decentralization, city governments are playing an increased role in ensuring wellbeing for their citizens" (Issues Brief 2014, p. 3). In addition, it drew links to matters discussed in other issues briefs. Moreover, the Issues Brief recognised the need for transformative policies on many levels of governance, namely, national, regional and local, "with the city-region as geographical key to implementing solutions beyond administrative boundaries", and noted the importance of a "regional and global networks of cities" (Issues Brief 2014, p. 3). Stopping short of saying that cities have or should have legal competences in the area of development strategies, the Issues Brief did acknowledge that enhancing capacities, strengthening legal authority and improving fiscal bases are essential and that "countries should [...] support [cities] by adopting proactive national urban policies and enhancing the capacities of urban actors to address the challenges of city-regions" (Issues Brief 2014, p. 4).

First, the Issues Brief proposed three potential strategies for bringing sustainable cities into the SDGs. The first aimed at securing cities as a stand-alone goal. This approach was supported by UN-Habitat,[2] the Global Task Force of Local and Regional Governments for Post-2015 and Habitat III,[3] the Sustainable Development Solutions Network,[4] and the Mayors Adaptation Forum "Bonn Declaration of Mayors"[5] (Issues Brief 2014, pp. 4-5). Second, the mainstreaming of urban issues across the development agenda or the inclusion of cities as a cross-cutting area across multiple goals was endorsed by the High-level Panel in its Report to the Secretary-General[6] and the United Nations Global Compact[7] (Issues Brief 2014, p. 5). Third, it was noted that targets addressing cities and sustainable urban development may be reflected under other Goals (Issues Brief 2014, pp. 5-6). Based on these approaches, the Issues Brief recommended identifying core targets which were not addressed in other SDG proposals at that point in time,[8] and to construct a proposal of a stand-alone SDG on cities based on these (Issues Brief 2014, p. 6). Alternatively, it was noted that "The Future We Want"[9] lists some subthemes to be further explored as potential targets (Issues Brief 2014, p. 6).

Open Working Group on Sustainable Development Goals

The OWG held its first session in March 2013, reflecting on the initial input of the Secretary-General (Initial Input of the Secretary-General 2012) and discussing general aspects of the SDGs. From its second to the eighth session, the OWG considered different subject-matters in general, conducting its work through keynote addresses, introductions of issue briefs by the TST, panel discussions and an interactive debate. The areas under consideration included poverty eradication; food security, agriculture, water and sanitation; employment, health and population dynamics; economic, trade and energy areas; means of implementation, global partnerships, human rights and global governance; cities, consumption and production, and climate change; and biodiversity, equality, conflict prevention, peacebuilding, the rule of law and governance (Progress Report of the OWG 2014).[10]

The seventh session of the OWG saw the first substantive discussion on cities, in which states began to articulate their positions. At this point the discussion centred on the question of whether to include a stand-alone goal or to mainstream urban issues, and on the specific topics to be covered in the targets.

The troika of Cyprus, Singapore, and the United Arab Emirates (UAE) highlighted the importance of governance in addressing the topic of cities in the new development agenda.[11] On behalf of the least developed countries, Bangladesh called for strengthening the urban-rural linkage,[12] a topic that gained much traction in later discussions. Brazil and Nicaragua pointed to the need for a holistic approach to urban development and human settlements, and stated that this should be incorporated into the post-2015 agenda either in the form of a specific objective or as a set of targets and indicators.[13] Furthermore, they argued that local authorities cannot formulate and implement urban development and planning policies on their own, nor should these objectives overburden them.[14] It was evident that this statement arose from concerns that the increased competencies of local actors might minimize the importance of national and regional authorities. Such concern, however, was not strongly vocalised at later stages of the negotiations.

On behalf of the troika including the USA and Canada, Israel called for a multi-stakeholder and multi-sectoral participation in building sustainable cities and support for good governance, and endorsed "networks of cities, such as C40, connecting the world's megacities in an effort to reduce greenhouse gas emissions".[15] Nonetheless, at this point of the negotiations the troika was not convinced that a stand-alone goal on cities would be the best way forward, and instead, suggested that emphasis should be directed at targets relevant to urban dwellers across the agenda.

Germany, Switzerland, and France consistently called for the involvement and recognition of "the critical role of local authorities".[16] More precisely, they endorsed "strong local and regional authorities and the engagement of civil society [and] democratic local governance".[17] This was one of the more articulate statements in recognising that local and regional authorities should take more ownership of the development and implementation of public policies, including financial capabilities.

Romania and Poland likewise highlighted the need for national, regional and local solutions beyond administrative boundaries, including accountable local authorities.[18] Similarly, the EU stated that "the political role of local authorities, legally competent and primary managers of urban development, has to be strengthened" through adopting an "integrated approach to urban planning and governance".[19] Australia, the Netherlands, and the

UK suggested developing "new flexible forms of governance, which can cope with evolving circumstances and empower citizens", and proposed that city governance should be integrated with other levels of government.[20] Japan called for local governments to be included in the quest towards sustainable cities as they possess experience and knowledge in this area, and hence should be given the ownership of the targets.[21]

The eighth session of the OWG did not provoke much discussion on cities, and most states did not engage with the question of whether or not the issue of sustainable cities should form a stand-alone goal. Generally, states accepted that at the very least the cross-cutting nature of cities should be recognised, and called for an integrated approach addressing linkages with other sustainable development issues (Progress Report of the OWG 2014, para 154). The "Progress Report of the Open Working Group" and the "Focus Areas Document" released before the ninth session (19 Focus Areas 2014) introduced 19 focus areas, with focus area 13 addressing sustainable cities and human settlements. It sets a long list of topics for consideration and draws interlinkages to other focus areas but remains silent on the actual role of cities and their competences vis-à-vis governance structures and administrative arrangements. The Progress Report does, however, recognise the lack of consensus among the membership on whether the topic of cities should form a stand-alone goal or should rather be incorporated in other focus areas (Progress Report of the OWG 2014, para 152).

During the ninth session, cities as actors in sustainable development did not feature in the discussions of the OWG, with the exception that France, Switzerland, and Germany explicitly recognised that the inclusion of cities in the new agenda should incorporate participatory and inclusive processes, including within local and regional levels.[22]

Prior to the tenth session of the OWG the co-chairs proposed that the focus areas would be considered in clusters. Cluster 5 brought together sustainable cities and human settlements, sustainable consumption and production, and climate. In March 2014 a new Focus Areas document was released, which detailed 11 items (interchangeably called targets in the OWG) under Focus Area 13 on sustainable cities and human settlements (Focus Area Document, March 2014). The items focused for the most part on substantive issues, with the exception of item f on enhancing capacities for urban planning, and item k on appropriate means of implementation.

On 1 April 2014 a compilation of existing targets and indicators was circulated to the Member States of the OWG (Compendium of Existing Goals and Targets 2014). The spreadsheet listed 48 existing targets on sustainable cities and human settlements, which had been identified in consultation with the TST (Compendium of Existing Goals and Targets 2014, rows 222-269). The formulation of this compilation document drew from many instruments: for example, "The Future We Want", "Local Agenda 21", "Urban Environmental Accords", "UN-Habitat Governing

Council Resolution 23/17", "Universal Declaration on Human Rights", and the MDGs, and was drafted in most part by UN-Habitat and UNEP. The purpose of the compilation was to illustrate that for many items measuring tools and national strategies were already in place, and to serve as an assurance that the new agenda was neither taking any subject matter beyond its mandate nor creating new obligations on states.

Importantly, some input by the TST focused on the role and competence of cities in relation to several areas of sustainable development: "to recognize the important role of municipal governments in setting a vision for sustainable cities [...]" ("(The) Future We Want" 2012, para 136), "promot[e] decentralization and the role of local authorities and enabling institutional frameworks for partnerships with service providers and civil society, sustainable financing, pro-poor policies and environmental sustainability in the delivery of basic services for all"; "improve[e] the competencies and capacities of local and regional authorities in the field of land and property valuation and taxation"; "invite international agencies to facilitate the improvement of access by cities, and by local and regional authorities, to climate change mitigation and adaptation financing [...]" (UN-Habitat Governing Council Resolution 23/17, and noting "the commitment of mayors and subnational leaders to scale up climate action, urge engagement with the global level on climate change, and enhance access to finance" (Nantes Declaration of Mayors and Subnational Leaders on Climate Change 2013).

At the tenth session of the OWG, Saudi Arabia, the troika of China, Indonesia and Kazakhstan, as well as Belarus, agreed that the urban focus area should be a stand-alone goal, and generally supported the items included under Focus Area 13.[23] Similarly, the Caribbean Community (CARICOM) voiced clear support for a stand-alone goal on cities, and noted that the success of such a goal depends heavily on local government for implementation.[24] Also, France, Germany and Switzerland expressed their continuing support for a stand-alone goal, recognising the need to build the capacities of local and regional authorities for planning and implementing urban policies, and calling for participatory processes.[25] Bulgaria and Croatia noted that "local authorities, civil community and private sector have a large responsibility in it all, but also a significant existential interest and business perspectives as well",[26] and Norway, Ireland and Denmark pointed to the importance of inclusive, effective and accountable local governance.[27] The troika of Italy, Spain and Turkey made a suggestion to define item f on enhancing the capacities for urban planning by indicating specific principles attached to it, such as integrated urban development plans based on participatory and inclusive processes.[28]

Cyprus, Singapore and UAE proposed the inclusion of "safe" in the title of the focus area.[29]

Somewhat conversely, Canada, Israel, and the USA called attention to the downside of a stand-alone goal on cities, "particularly if it creates an artificial distinction between urban and rural environments, livelihoods, and issues", and asked for this concern to be taken into account in the next draft document of the SDGs.[30] On the same lines, India noted that it was not fully wedded to the idea of a separate urban goal,[31] and Sweden proposed the integration of cities into the other goal areas.[32]

While most states at the tenth OWG session did not anchor their comments on the Focus Areas document or the Existing Targets document, some began to direct their comments to specific items. China, Indonesia and Kazakhstan, for instance, gave specific proposals for items, including "enhancing the carrying capacity of cities [and] improving functions of cities", and proposed alternative language for some of the other items.[33] Likewise, Pakistan provided a concrete proposal for the item on increasing the number of cities adopting and implementing policies and plans.[34]

For the eleventh OWG session the focus areas were renumbered and the Working Document for the Eleventh Session of the Open Working Group on SDGs was circulated, containing Focus Area 10 on sustainable cities and human settlements, titled "Build inclusive, safe and sustainable cities and human settlements" (Document for the Eleventh Session of the Open Working Group, May 2014 p. 5 *et seq*). The number of items was reduced to eight, with item c on enhancing capacities for integrated urban planning and management, and e on increasing the number of cities adopting and implementing policies and plans towards resilience and adaptation to climate change and natural disasters. The appropriate means of implementation within each focus area were not specified at this point but Focus Area 15 listed potential implementation items directed at the national and international levels.

At the eleventh session, Barbados, on behalf of CARICOM, raised concerns over the vagueness and the absence of benchmarking of items, in particular calling for reasoning on how item h (protect and safeguard the world's cultural and natural heritage) related to achieving sustainable cities, and noting that item c was a means of implementation rather than a substantive item or target.[35] The Group of 77 and China, recognising the crucial importance of transformative policies, multiple levels of governance, and the role of local actors in addressing cities in the SDGs, called "for new modalities of interaction between nations at the international level, as well as between central and local governments at the national level, in order to fulfil their respective roles as governmental stakeholders in global efforts on sustainability. Other non-state actors also play important complementary roles."[36] Brazil and Nicaragua supported the inclusion of an item on participatory decision-making at the local level.[37]

Cyprus, Singapore, and the UAE stated their strong support for a stand-alone goal,[38] as did the troika of Indonesia, China, and Kazakhstan,[39] but the latter joined India[40] and Argentina[41] in voicing concern about the emphasis on "cities" at the expense of rural areas and other human settlements. These states were of the view that it is notionally and pragmatically better to discuss sustainable cities in conjunction with sustainable agriculture, as issues of urbanisation and ruralisation are to an extent two sides of the same coin. This line of critique ran in most part parallel to highlighting the need for special assistance for developing countries in enhancing their capacities, as advocated by Indonesia, China and Kazakhstan,[42] Iran,[43] India,[44] and Benin on behalf of the least developed countries.[45]

France, Germany, and Switzerland reiterated their support for good governance through enhancing decision-making at the local level, and proposed an amended item "c to build the capacities of local and regional authorities, through participatory processes, for planning and implementing urban policies. Only local authorities are likely to strengthen national policies."[46] In addition, they acknowledged "the need, as expressed by many developing cities, for local economic development" but noted that this target could also be included in the goal on economic growth. Although not endorsing a stand-alone goal, Croatia and Bulgaria recognised the "large responsibility" of local authorities as well as their "significant existential interest".[47]

On behalf of the Southern African Countries, Zimbabwe called for the elimination of terms such as "universal" and "adequate", for they might have varied interpretations.[48] This directly contradicted the proposal by the troika of Italy, Spain, and Turkey to add the term "adequate" for item f, to read "By 2030 enhance social cohesion and personal security and ensure universal access to inclusive, adequate and safe public spaces."[49] Italy, Spain, and Turkey also proposed adding a target to address vulnerable groups in cities, in particular migrants, noting that "cities must adapt to migration flows through the provision of necessary shelters and basic services."[50] Some states insisted on the deletion of item d on reducing the ecological footprints of cities, maintaining that the concept of an "ecological footprint" has no definition and has not been accepted at the international level.[51]

As in the previous OWG sessions, Norway, Denmark, and Ireland stated their hesitation to press for a stand-alone goal while referencing the importance of good, inclusive, effective and accountable local governance in achieving the SDGs.[52] Furthermore, Croatia and Bulgaria,[53] and Australia, the Netherlands, and the United Kingdom,[54] without expressly opposing the stand-alone goal, noted that the targets address cross-cutting areas to be reflected across multiple goals. Finally, the troika of the USA, Canada, and Israel stated that they welcomed any form of inclusion of cities in the SDGs, be it as a stand-alone goal or incorporated across the agenda.[55]

The twelth session of the OWG was held in June 2014, prior to which the co-chairs circulated the draft chapters and the zero-draft of goals and targets, bringing the total number of goals to 17 with 212 targets. No references to the capacities of cities and local communities were explicitly included in the zero-draft under SDG 11 or means of implementation. At the close of the twelth session of the OWG the co-chairs distributed a revised zero-draft, which aimed "to more closely reflect areas of agreement and expressed priorities [and] to simplify and harmonize the phrasing of some of the goals" (Letter of OWG Co-chairs 2014). At this point the wording in the draft was changed from "focus areas" to "proposed goals" and the term "items" was changed to "targets".

The title of the focus area ("Build inclusive, safe and sustainable cities and human settlements") attracted some criticism for including the word "build", as this could be read to exclude those urban areas that are not yet built. The co-chairs then proposed a revised title, "Make cities and human settlements inclusive, safe and sustainable". This was supported by UN-Habitat and the formulation was retained for the final version of the SDGs, with the addition of "resilient". There was concern among some UN entities that the proposed SDG 11 had deviated from the delicate balance between the three branches of sustainability – the environmental, the social and the economic – to the disadvantage of the environmental dimension, and called for its reinforcement, with little opposition.

At the thirteenth and final session of the OWG, the states made no references to the SDG 11 or cities in general, although a number of other targets were mentioned at this point, in particular those of a more controversial nature under SDG 5 (Achieve gender equality and empower women and girls – references to gender and reproductive rights), SDG 14 (Conserve and sustainably use the oceans, seas and marine resources for sustainable development – reference to the United Nations Convention on the Law of the Sea) and SDG 16 (Promote peaceful and inclusive societies for sustainable development, provide access to justice for all and build effective, accountable and inclusive institutions at all levels – national rule of law elements). This indicates that states were generally content with the language and objectives of SDG 11 and did not perceive it to be problematic in substance or in its implementation strategies.

The uncontested passage of SDG 11 is not only a result of its broadly accepted subject-matter or a strong global commitment to making cities and human settlements inclusive, safe and sustainable. It stems also from the vague and non-committal – or some may say flexible and general – language of the targets, which was easier for states to agree upon than precise and (semi-) binding formulations. For instance, 11.a calls for "Support [for] positive economic, social and environmental links between urban, peri-urban and rural areas by strengthening national and regional development planning", but the practical measures of providing such support can be set by each state. Of course, the indicators patch up the framework to an extent in defining the focus of the measurement and review. In the case of 11.a, the outcome is measured by the "Proportion of population living in cities that implement urban and regional development plans integrating population projections and resource needs, by size of city" (indicator 11.a.1.). The exact methodology, meaning and purpose of 11.a, alongside other targets, can be better assessed once national implementation measures are adopted and, possibly, at the point of the first comprehensive review in 2020 (UNGA resolution on the Work of the Statistical Commission 2017, para 1; also Barnet and Parnell 2016).

SDG 11 is certainly not alone in its nebulous language. Most targets in the 2030 Agenda have been formulated in such an open-ended manner, which may reduce the impetus of the SDGs in practice, as even feeble efforts could be deemed sufficient to "strengthen", "enhance", "reduce" or "support". For the member states to reach an intergovernmentally agreed outcome, however, this approach was the only acceptable one, and towards the end of the negotiations it was obvious that there was little prospect of reaching any agreement on detailed and unambiguous language for the targets.

The Secretary-General's Synthesis Report and Intergovernmental Negotiations

The Secretary-General's synthesis report, "The Road to Dignity", compiled the full range of inputs related to the post-2015 process, outlining the many work streams and consultations that had fed into the 2030 Agenda, and delivered a cautiously optimistic and encouraging outlook with transcendental references to a "universal call to action", "shared ambitions", and being "together in a universal compact" (Road to Dignity 2014). The main purpose of the report was to support the intergovernmental negotiations which followed the conclusion of the work of the OWG.

The synthesis report drew from two decades of development experience (paras 26–35) and the discussion of the post-2015 sustainable development agenda (paras 36–47), and then proposed "six essential elements for delivering on the sustainable development goals": dignity, people, prosperity, planet, partnership, and justice (paras 66–81). It also addressed the broader aspects of implementing and delivering the 2030 Agenda. In conclusion, the synthesis report recognised and commended the OWG's proposal for the goals and targets.

The synthesis report includes multiple references to local mechanisms, local governments and authorities, and implementation partnerships between global, regional, national and local levels. It notes that the SDGs reinforce the commitment to the unaccomplished MDGs and break new ground with goals on inequalities, economic growth, decent jobs, cities and human settlements (para 45). In order to achieve the SDGs, the Report calls for consideration of the investments at the subnational level, which are to be led by local authorities (para 94). Moreover, it highlights that sustainable development strategies will have to be reviewed and implemented at the local level, with the full engagement of local authorities. In relation to this, it explicitly acknowledges "the role of mayors in leading the way for sustainable development" (para 128).

The intergovernmental negotiations took place from November 2014 to July 2015 and echoed largely the concerns of states as expressed at the final session of the OWG. The negotiations amounted to a test of whether the wider UN membership could find consensus on the goals and targets proposed by the OWG. Much of the discussion focused on the global partnership and the relationship between the Addis Ababa Action Agenda on Financing for Development (2015) and the Post-2015 Development Agenda. Only a few targets were amended, mostly due to the reluctance of G77 and China to reopen the OWG document (Dodds et al. 2016). During the intergovernmental negotiations many states noted that all levels of cooperation – international, regional and local – should be encouraged, but omitted any specific mention of the capacities or competencies of cities, nor did they draw attention to SDG 11 otherwise, with the exception of a few technical remarks.

Indicators for Measuring the SDGs

Simultaneously with the final phase of the post-2015 process, the UN Statistical Commission set up an Inter-Agency Expert Group on SDG Indicators (IAEG-SDG) composed of 28 representatives of national statistical offices and, as observers, representatives of regional commissions and regional and international agencies. It was tasked to develop an indicator framework for the SDGs to support the implementation and review processes. IAEG-SDG delivered a proposal of 230 indicators to the Statistical Commission in March 2016 (Report of the Inter-Agency and Expert Group on Sustainable Goal Indicators 2016). On 6 July 2017, the General Assembly adopted the global indicator framework for the sustainable development goal and targets of the 2030 Agenda for Sustainable Development (UNGA Resolution on the Work of the Statistical Commission 2017). It noted that this framework is intended to be voluntary and country-led, and it is to be refined annually and reviewed comprehensively every five years. In addition, the global indicators are to be complemented by indicators at the regional and national levels, which will be developed by member states.

While the development and selection of indicators by the IAEG-SDG was intended as a technical exercise, it was not void of political pressure, which is reflected in the selection of the indicators and the negligible attention given to the consideration of some of the indicators supporting the targets under SDG 11. The process of the formulation of indicators was a contested issue – there was a strong feeling at the UN and among some member states that the politicization of the process reflected negatively on the outcomes, refuted more technical aspects, and led to the omission of some of the more methodologically sound indicators (Hák et al. 2016; Beisheim et al. 2015). In addition, there were internal battles between UN agencies, with each pushing its own agenda and its own indicators.

The 2030 Agenda emphasises the need for multilevel governance in implementing, reviewing and measuring the SDGs (eg Fenton and Gustafsson 2017), which can be read to include cities as actors in advancing sustainable development. The Report of the IAEG-SDG, however, proposes only a few indicators that touch upon the competences of cities or local administrations as such (Report of the Inter-Agency and Expert Group on Sustainable Development Goal Indicators 2016). These are 11.3.2 "Proportion of cities with a direct participation structure of civil society in urban planning and management that operate regularly and democratically" and 11.b.1 "Proportion of local governments that adopt and implement local disaster risk reduction strategies in line with the Sendai Framework for Disaster Risk Reduction 2015–2030". Evidently, these indicators reveal nothing of the quality of the activities as such, for they measure "proportion", a numeric value relative to the comparison group. In addition to these, under SDG 17 indicator 17.16.1 measures the number of countries reporting progress in multi-stakeholder development effectiveness monitoring frameworks that support the achievement of the sustainable development goals. This could potentially include cities, but again it is a strictly quantitative indicator which says little of the type and level of the frameworks.

It has been argued that not only were there challenges in selecting the indicators, but additional issues arose from the limited availability of standardised, open and comparable data, the lack of support for monitoring the data collection at the local/city level, and the complexity of the actors involved in the different types of cities globally (Klopp and Petretta 2017). The 2016 Sustainable Development Report recognises some particular issues in measuring urban data, such as the need to update urbanisation patterns for better means to address current and emerging urban challenges. It also proposes to look at the unique challenges and structures of refugee camps, for which applications of urban social policy may provide potential solutions (Sustainable Development Goals Report 2016, p. 86).

Universality and Implementation

The SDGs are based on the principle of universality, conversely to the MDGs, which addressed issues largely pertaining to developing countries (Oliveira 2019, in this volume). The quest for substantive universality proved to be problematic during the OWG and intergovernmental negotiations, and it still remains undetermined how it materialises within the SDGs. While endorsing the universal nature of the 2030 Agenda in general, many targets – in particular regarding the implementation of the SDGs – recognise and call for international cooperation and capacity-building support especially for developing countries. Furthermore, a number of targets require more effort from developing countries, whereas the most developed nations may already be performing up to and above the standard. Such targets include, for instance, 16.9 on the provision of legal identity and birth certificates; 3.2 on reducing infant mortality below a specified threshold; and 4.1 on ensuring free, equitable and quality primary and secondary education. Indeed, some confusion on the measuring of the SDGs arises from the uneasy relationship between a universal agenda and a highly pluralised world. Some targets are global[56] whereas many are strictly domestic,[57] and others are intentionally left open-ended[58] or explicitly integrate all levels.[59]

States have so far been relatively slow in implementing the SDGs into their national plans and strategies (Sustainable Development Goals Report 2017, p. 2; Winkler and Williams 2017, p. 1027). The Preamble of the 2030 Agenda declares that "All countries and all stakeholders, acting in collaborative partnership, will implement this plan." The effective implementation of the SDGs presumes that all actors acknowledge the need for simultaneous application of both formal and informal rules and mechanisms in promoting and enabling development policies as well in providing transformative force for the realisation of the SDGs (Soyeju 2015, p. 372). In addition to the global and national indicators and implementation strategies, for the SDGs to be effective and universal, transparent and inclusive follow-up, review and accountability mechanisms must be in place, as acknowledged and explored in subsequent UN reports also (eg Report of the Secretary General on Critical Milestones 2016, paras 64-66, 74, 105, 109-110).

In 2016 the "New Urban Agenda" (NUA), focusing in large part on the local implementation of urban development policies, was adopted at the United Nations Conference on Housing and Sustainable Urban Development (Habitat III) intergovernmental meeting in Quito, Ecuador. The NUA was spearheaded by UN-Habitat and negotiated through regional representatives, policy experts, stakeholders and the Habitat III bureau, consisting of ten member states selected for their geographic spread. While there is a clear connection between SDG 11 and the NUA, the latter addresses a wider range of urban issues, "presents a paradigm shift" and recognises the role of cities more explicitly, noting the relevance of national, sub-national, and local institutional and regulatory frameworks (New Urban Agenda 2016 foreword, para 83). NUA states that one of its aims is to "contribute[to the implementation and localization" of 2030 Agenda "in an integrated manner, and to the achievement of the Sustainable Development Goals and targets, including Goal 11" (New Urban Agenda 2016, para 9). In short, NUA facilitates the implementation of SDG 11 through its focus on urban policies, governance frameworks and legislation, spatial planning and local finance frameworks, and places heightened emphasis on the implementation at the local level and the need to develop the capacity of local authorities and other local actors. The follow-up and review process of the NUA is complementary to the SDGs and in order to avoid the duplication of efforts, the NUA results will be fed into the SDG review process.

Conclusion

The importance of cities as actors in global governance is increasingly recognised, as this volume serves to illustrate. Within the development discourse, the prevalence of broadening the impetus set in the MDGs became obvious in the years leading up to and during the post-2015 process. This chapter has described the process of negotiating and formulating SDG 11, with an emphasis on the statements delivered during the post-2015 process, in particular in the OWG.

Perhaps it would be too idealistic to call the issues of cities cross-cutting features of the 2030 Agenda, but the inclusion of SDG 11, "Make cities and human settlements inclusive, safe, resilient and sustainable", was not met with contestation by the member states. Nonetheless, it is noteworthy that there was no real consensus on the final document as a whole among the membership of the OWG, as noted by the representative of Tanzania in the final meeting of the OWG: "Truly, we cannot claim to have achieved a meaningful consensus under these circumstances!" Member states generally were not comfortable with the outcome of the negotiations, but at the same time there was evident negotiation fatigue and no strong political will to re-open the document for discussion.

Unlike the situation with some other SDGs, SDG 11 was at no point the cause for a heated debate. Rather, it was generally accepted that cities must be represented in the agenda, and while some states were hesitant to question the value of having a stand-alone urban goal, they were eventually persuaded by the majority in the OWG. There were no evident alliances of geographic or political groupings vouching strongly for or against the inclusion of the stand-alone goal. Developing countries especially, however, directed attention to the importance of the urban-rural relationship for sustainable development and called for special assistance for developing countries in enhancing their capacities.

Given the political climate during the OWG negotiations, it is safe to say that any attempt that may have been viewed as reducing the competence of the state and affecting the national ownership over development policy – be it for the benefit of the international or local actors – would have been met with intense resistance. In that sense, SDG 11 is a success in setting universally accepted standards while being multidimensional and packing many issues into one goal. In order to convert the aspirations of SDG 11 into reality, the indicator framework must be strengthened, responsibility of which lies with the states and, to an extent, with cities and other local actors.

Notes

1 Economic Commission for Latin America and the Caribbean, Economic and Social Commission for Asia and the Pacific, International Fund for Agricultural Development, International Labour Organization, United Nations Development Programme, United Nations Population Fund, United Nations Children's Fund, The United Nations Office for Disaster Risk Reduction, United Nations Entity for Gender Equality and the Empowerment of Women, World Health Organization, World Meteorological Organization and the World Bank.

2 Proposed Goal: "promote cities that are environmentally sustainable, socially inclusive, economically productive and resilient". See http://mirror.unhabitat.org/downloads/docs/11918_1_594773.pdf. (Accessed: 31 May 2018).

3 No specific goal proposed but eight "objectives". See http://www.uclg.org/sites/default/files/ENG_Press_Release_UCLG_Global_TFnew%20%281%29.pdf. (Accessed: 7 May 2018).

4 Proposed Goal: "[e]mpower inclusive, productive and resilient cities", addressing their social, economic and environmental dimensions. See http://unsdsn.org/wp-content/uploads/2013/06/140505-An-Action-Agenda-for-Sustainable-Development.pdf. (Accessed: 31 May 2018).

5 No specific wording was proposed, but rather a general for adoption of a universal Goal for cities. See http://resilient-cities.iclei.org/fileadmin/sites/resilient-cities/files/Resilient_Cities_2013/MAF_2013_Bonn_Declaration_of_Mayors.pdf. (Accessed: 7 May 2018).

6 It recommends "a local, geographic approach to the post-2015 agenda", "disaggregating data by place and giving local authorities a bigger role in setting priorities." See https://www.un.org/sg/sites/www.un.org.sg/files/files/HLP_P2015_Report.pdf. (Accessed: 31 May 2018).

7 Noting that urbanisation is a key to addressing resource scarcity and access to infrastructure and services. See http://www.unglobalcompact.org/docs/news_events/9.1_news_archives/2013_06_18/UNGC_Post2015_Report.pdf. (Accessed: 7 May 2018).

8 Eg urban sprawl, public space, slum reduction, shelter, safety, mobility, resilience and air pollution reduction.

9 These include: affordable housing, infrastructure and slum upgrading; cultural heritage and urban revitalization; participatory decision-making; urban safety and health; sustainable transport and energy and green space; water and sanitation; resilience; urban planning and design; and partnerships for sustainable urban development. *The Future We Want*, paras 134–137.

10 For summaries of OWG sessions and statements of States, see https://sustainabledevelopment.un.org/owg.html. (Accessed: 7 May 2018).

11 https://sustainabledevelopment.un.org/content/documents/5393singapore.pdf. (Accessed: 7 May 2018).

12 https://sustainabledevelopment.un.org/content/documents/5418Bangladesh.pdf. (Accessed: 7 May 2018).

13 https://sustainabledevelopment.un.org/content/documents/5423brasil.pdf. (Accessed: 7 May 2018).

14 *Ibid.*

15 https://sustainabledevelopment.un.org/content/documents/7572us13.pdf. (Accessed: 7 May 2018).

16 https://sustainabledevelopment.un.org/content/documents/6550france1.pdf. (Accessed: 7 May 2018).

17 *Ibid.*

18 https://sustainabledevelopment.un.org/content/documents/5838romania2.pdf. (Accessed: 7 May 2018).
19 https://sustainabledevelopment.un.org/content/documents/5553eu1.pdf. (Accessed: 7 May 2018).
20 https://sustainabledevelopment.un.org/content/documents/5488australia.pdf. (Accessed: 7 May 2018).
21 https://sustainabledevelopment.un.org/content/documents/5453japan.pdf. (Accessed: 7 May 2018).
22 https://sustainabledevelopment.un.org/content/documents/7257SDG%20OWG%209_Statement%20Trio%20FRA%20CHE%20GER_final.pdf. (Accessed: 7 May 2018).
23 https://sustainabledevelopment.un.org/content/documents/7942saudiarabia3.pdf. (Accessed: 7 May 2018); https://sustainabledevelopment.un.org/content/documents/7762china5.pdf. (Accessed: 7 May 2018); https://sustainabledevelopment.un.org/content/documents/7857belarus2.pdf. (Accessed: 7 May 2018).
24 https://sustainabledevelopment.un.org/content/documents/8177caricom5.pdf. (Accessed: 7 May 2018).
25 https://sustainabledevelopment.un.org/content/documents/8087france14.pdf. (Accessed: 7 May 2018).
26 https://sustainabledevelopment.un.org/content/documents/8357bulgaria5.pdf. (Accessed: 7 May 2018).
27 https://sustainabledevelopment.un.org/content/documents/7782denmark1.pdf. (Accessed: 7 May 2018).
28 https://sustainabledevelopment.un.org/content/documents/7792italy5.pdf. (Accessed: 7 May 2018).
29 https://sustainabledevelopment.un.org/content/documents/7802cyprus5.pdf. (Accessed: 7 May 2018).
30 https://sustainabledevelopment.un.org/content/documents/8477us21.pdf. (Accessed: 7 May 2018).
31 https://sustainabledevelopment.un.org/content/documents/8498india5.pdf. (Accessed: 7 May 2018).
32 https://sustainabledevelopment.un.org/content/documents/8247sweden.pdf. (Accessed: 7 May 2018).
33 https://sustainabledevelopment.un.org/content/documents/7762china5.pdf. (Accessed: 7 May 2018).
34 https://sustainabledevelopment.un.org/content/documents/8202pakistan.pdf. (Accessed: 7 May 2018).
35 https://sustainabledevelopment.un.org/content/documents/10217caricom6.pdf. (Accessed: 7 May 2018).
36 https://sustainabledevelopment.un.org/content/documents/10182g775.pdf. (Accessed: 7 May 2018).
37 https://sustainabledevelopment.un.org/content/documents/9694brazil6.pdf. (Accessed: 7 May 2018).
38 https://sustainabledevelopment.un.org/content/documents/9226uae.pdf. (Accessed: 7 May 2018).
39 https://sustainabledevelopment.un.org/content/documents/9222indonesia3.pdf. (Accessed: 7 May 2018).
40 https://sustainabledevelopment.un.org/content/documents/9202india3.pdf. (Accessed: 7 May 2018).
41 https://sustainabledevelopment.un.org/content/documents/8774argentina2.pdf, p. 12. (Accessed: 7 May 2018).
42 https://sustainabledevelopment.un.org/content/documents/9222indonesia3.pdf. (Accessed: 7 May 2018).

43 https://sustainabledevelopment.un.org/content/documents/9662iran6.pdf. (Accessed: 7 May 2018).
44 https://sustainabledevelopment.un.org/content/documents/9202india3.pdf. (Accessed: 7 May 2018).
45 https://sustainabledevelopment.un.org/content/documents/9634ldc6.pdf. (Accessed: 7 May 2018).
46 https://sustainabledevelopment.un.org/content/documents/9598france4.pdf. (Accessed: 7 May 2018).
47 https://sustainabledevelopment.un.org/content/documents/9390bulgaria3.pdf. (Accessed: 7 May 2018).
48 https://sustainabledevelopment.un.org/content/documents/9318zimbabwe3.pdf. (Accessed: 7 May 2018).
49 https://sustainabledevelopment.un.org/content/documents/9294spain5.pdf. (Accessed: 7 May 2018).
50 *Ibid.*
51 For example, Argentina; Indonesia, China and Kazakhstan; Brazil and Nicaragua; India; and Iran. All *supra note.*
52 https://sustainabledevelopment.un.org/content/documents/9474denmark2.pdf. (Accessed: 7 May 2018).
53 *Supra note.*
54 https://sustainabledevelopment.un.org/content/documents/9350australia5.pdf. (Accessed: 7 May 2018).
55 https://sustainabledevelopment.un.org/content/documents/9190canada3.pdf. (Accessed: 7 May 2018).
56 For example, 3.1 By 2030, reduce the global maternal mortality ratio; 3.6 By 2020, halve the number of global deaths and injuries from road traffic accidents; 7.3 By 2030, double the global rate of improvement in energy efficiency; 11.4 Strengthen efforts to protect and safeguard the world's cultural and natural heritage; 15.c Enhance global support for efforts to combat poaching and trafficking of protected species.
57 1.3 Implement nationally appropriate social protection systems and measures for all, and by 2030 achieve substantial coverage of the poor and the vulnerable; 2.3 By 2030, double the agricultural productivity and incomes of small-scale food producers; 8.1 Sustain per capita economic growth in accordance with national circumstances.
58 1.1 By 2030, eradicate extreme poverty for all people everywhere; 5.1 End all forms of discrimination against all women and girls everywhere; 16.10 Ensure public access to information and protect fundamental freedoms, in accordance with national legislation and international agreements.
59 1.b Create sound policy frameworks at the national, regional and international levels, based on pro-poor and gender-sensitive development strategies, to support accelerated investment in poverty eradication actions; 2.5 By 2020, maintain the genetic diversity [...] including through soundly managed and diversified seed and plant banks at the national, regional and international levels [...].

Bibliography

Literature

Barnett, Clive and Parnell, Susan. 2016. Ideas, implementation and indicators: epistemologies of the post-2015 urban agenda. *Environment and Urbanization*, 28(1), 87–98.

Barral, Virginie. 2012. Sustainable development in international law: Nature and operation of an evolutive Legal norm. *European Journal of International Law*, 23(2), 377–400.

Beisheim, Marianne and Løkken, Hedda and aus dem Moore, Nils and Pintér, László and Rickels, Wilfried. 2015. Measuring Sustainable Development: How Can Science Contribute to Realizing the SDGs? Background Paper (2 April 2015) with Results from the Conference (20 May 2015) Deutsche Forschungsgemeinschaft and the United Nations University. 2015. Available at www.dfg.de/download/pdf/dfg_im_profil/geschaeftsstelle/dfg_praesenz_ausland/nordamerika/2015/150421_dfg_unu_konferenz/backgroundpaper.pdf (Accessed: 7 May 2018).

Bizikova, Livia and Searcy, Cory. 2017. Cities and the SDGs: An Interdependent Partnership. 19 September 2017, Guest article on *SDG Knowledge Hub, International Institute for Sustainable Development.*Available at: http://sdg.iisd.org/commentary/guest-articles/cities-and-the-sdgs-an-interdependent-partnership/. (Accessed: 7 May 2018).

Chasek, Pamela S. and Wagner, Lynn M. and Leone, Faye and Lebada, Ana-Maria and Risse, Nathalie. 2016. Getting to 2030: Negotiating a sustainable development agenda. *Review of European Community and International Environmental Law*, 25(1), 5–14.

De Boer, John. 2015. The sustainable development fight will be won or lost in our cities. 24 September 2015. *World Economic Forum's Agenda* [online]. Available at: www.weforum.org/agenda/2015/09/the-fight-for-sustainable-development-will-be-won-or-lost-in-our-cities/. (Accessed: 7 May 2018).

Dodds, Felix, Ambassador Donoghue, David and Leiva Roesch, Jimena. 2016. *Negotiating the Sustainable Development Goals: A Transformational Agenda for an Insecure World.* London: Routledge.

Fenton, Paul and Gustafsson, Sara. 2017. Moving from high-level words to local action — governance for urban sustainability in municipalities. *Current Opinion in Environmental Sustainability*, 26–27, 129–133.

Hák, Tomáš and Janoušková, Svatava and Moldan, Bedřich. 2016. Sustainable Development Goals: A need for relevant indicators. *Ecological Indicators*, 60, 565–573.

Klopp, Jacqueline M. and Petretta, Danielle L. 2017. The urban sustainable development goal: Indicators, complexity and the politics of measuring cities. *Cities*, 63, 92–97.

Miyazawa, Ikuho and Zusman, Eric. 2015. A Quantitative Analysis of the Effect of Governance on the Millennium Development Goals (MDGs): Implications for the Post-2015 Development Agenda. Institute for Global Environmental Strategies Discussion Paper No. 2014–02. January 2015. Available at https://pub.iges.or.jp/system/files/publication_documents/pub/discussionpaper/4410/MDGs_and_Governance_IGES_Discussion_Paper_2014-02_FINAL_rev.pdf (Accessed: 7 May 2018).

Oliviera, M. Cecilia. 2019 Global Goals and Urban Development: The Territorial Effects of Implementing the MdGs in Brazil. In H.P Aust and A.A. du Plessis (eds). *The Globalisation of Urban Governance - Legal Perspectives on Sustainable Development Goal 11*. London: Routledge. pp. 173–185.

Parnell, Susan. 2016. Defining a global urban development agenda. *World Development*, 78, 529–540.

Soyeju, Olufemi. 2015. Making a case for a development-driven approach to law as a linchpin for the post-2015 development agenda. *Potchefstroom Electronic Law Journal*, 18(2), 363–396.

Sustainable Development Solutions Network Thematic Group on Sustainable Cities. Why the World Needs an Urban Sustainable Development Goal. 18 September 2013. Available at https://sustainabledevelopment.un.org/content/documents/2569130918-SDSN-Why-the-World-Needs-an-Urban-SDG.pdf. (Accessed: 7 May 2018).

Winkler, Inga T. and Williams, Carmel. 2017. The sustainable development goals and human rights: A critical early review. *The International Journal of Human Rights*, 21(8), 1023–1028.

Documents

2005 World Summit Outcome, 24 October 2005, A/RES/60/1.

Addis Ababa Action Agenda of the Third International Conference on Financing for Development. 27 July 2015. A/RES/69/313.

Charter of the United Nations, 24 October 1945. 1 UNTS XVI.

Compendium of Existing Goals and Targets under the 19 Focus Areas being considered by the Open Working Group. 1 April 2014. Available at:https://sustainabledevelopment.un.org/content/documents/3507Existing%20targets_1_April_version.xlsx. (Accessed: 21 July 2018).

Document for the Eleventh Session of the Open Working Group on SDGs. 5–9 May 2014. Available at: https://sustainabledevelopment.un.org/content/documents/3686WorkingDoc_0205_additionalsupporters.pdf. (Accessed: 7 May 2018).

19 "Focus Areas". 21 February 2014. Available at: https://sustainabledevelopment.un.org/content/documents/3276focusareas.pdf. (Accessed: 7 May 2018).

Focus Area Document. 19 March 2014. Available at: https://sustainabledevelopment.un.org/content/documents/3402Focus%20areas_20140319.pdf. (Accessed: 7 May 2018).

The Future We Want. 27 July 2012. A/RES/66/288.

Habitat Governing Council Resolution 23/17. Report of the Governing Council of the United Nations Human Settlements Programme (2011), A/66/8, 37–42.

Initial Input of the Secretary-General to the Open Working Group on Sustainable Development Goals. 17 December 2012. A/67/634.

Introduction and Proposed Goals and Targets on Sustainable Development for the Post-2015 Development Agenda. 2 June 2014. Available at: https://sustainabledevelopment.un.org/content/documents/4528zerodraft12OWG.pdf. (Accessed: 7 May 2018).

Issues Brief on Sustainable Cities and Human Settlements. October 2014. Available at: https://sustainabledevelopment.un.org/content/documents/2306TST%20Issues%20Brief%20Cities_FINAL.pdf. (Accessed: 21 July 2018).

Letter of Open Working Group Co-chairs. 30 June 2014. Available at: https://sustainabledevelopment.un.org/content/documents/4324lettercochairs30june14.pdf. (Accessed: 7 May 2018).

Millennium Declaration, 8 September 2000. A/RES/55/2.

Nantes Declaration of Mayors and Subnational Leaders on Climate Change. 28 September 2013. Available at: http://archive.iclei.org/fileadmin/user_upload/documents/Global/initiatives/2013_Nantes_Summit/WorldMayorsSummit2013_Nantes_EN_Declaration_only.pdf. (Accessed: 7 May 2018).

New Urban Agenda. 20 October 2016. A/RES/71/256.

Progress Report of the Open Working Group, 14 February 2014. Available at: https://sustainabledevelopment.un.org/content/documents/3238summaryallowg.pdf. (Accessed: 7 May 2018).

Report of the High-Level Panel of Eminent Persons on the Post-2015 Development Agenda, "A New Global Partnership: Eradicate Poverty and Transform Economies through Sustainable Development". 30 May 2013. New York: United Nations Publications.

Report of the Inter-Agency and Expert Group on Sustainable Development Goal Indicators. 19 February 2016. E/CN.3/2016/2/Rev.1.

Report of the Secretary General on Critical Milestones Towards Coherent, Efficient and Inclusive Follow-up and Review at Global Level. 15 January 2016. A/70/684.

Rio Declaration on Environment and Development. 14 June 1992. A/CONF.151/26.

(The) Road to Dignity by 2030: Ending Poverty, Transforming All Lives and Protecting the Planet. 4 December 2014. A/69/700.

Secretary-General's Remarks to the General Assembly on the Synthesis Report on the Post-2015 Agenda, New York. 4 December 2014. Available at: www.un.org/sg/statements/index.asp?nid=8250. (Accessed: 7 May 2018).

Transforming Our World: The 2030 Agenda for Sustainable Development. Adopted 25 September 2015. A/RES/70/1.

United Nations Department of Economic and Social Affairs. The Sustainable Development Goals Report 2016. 13 July 2016. New York: United Nations Publications. Available at: https://unstats.un.org/sdgs/report/2016/. (Accessed: 21 July 2018).

United NationsDepartment of Economic and Social Affairs. The Sustainable Development Goals Report 2017. 17 May 2017. New York: United Nations Publications. Available at https://unstats.un.org/sdgs/report/2017/. (Accessed: 21 July 2018).

United Nations General Assembly Resolution, Work of the Statistical Commission Pertaining to the 2030 Agenda for Sustainable Development. 6 July 2017. A/RES/71/313.

UN-Habitat Governing Council Resolution 23/17 on sustainable urban development through expanding equitable access to land, housing, basic services and infrastructure in the Report of the Governing Council of the United Nations Human Settlements Programme (2011). 15 April 2011. A/66/8, 37-42. Available at: https://unhabitat.org/wp-content/uploads/2017/04/Twenty-third-session-11-15-April-2011-Supplement-No.-8-A668-GC23.2011.pdf. (Accessed: 21 July 2018).

3 International Institutions and the City

Towards a Comparative Law of Glocal Governance

Michael Riegner

Introduction: International Institutions and the "Glocal City"

In 2010, the city of Rio de Janeiro in Brazil became the first municipality worldwide to receive a World Bank development policy loan amounting to more than one billion USD in direct budget support. The loan agreement, signed by the mayor of Rio and the World Bank country director, obliged the Bank to pay out the loan into a municipal account. In return, the city committed to a reform programme including pension cuts, simplified business registration procedures, and public-private infrastructure investments, as well as the upgrading of health and educational services in low-income neighbourhoods (World Bank 2010). The loan was notable because it established direct legal relations between an international institution and a local government with unprecedented financial volume and political impact. In doing so, it took the engagement of international institutions with local government to a new level – but it was by no means the first such engagement: The Bank has been funding urban development projects since the 1970s, which initially focused on national governments and specific investment projects. The United Nations (UN) has been formulating standards for local government since the 1970s as well. Since then, over 10,000 cities in 150 countries have received more than 60 billion USD in international aid. Significant changes in local governance have resulted from advice and policy diffusion through international institutions (Cohen 2001, pp. 39, 41 *et seq*). A new high point of international engagement was reached with the Sustainable Development Goals (SDGs) adopted by the UN in 2015. They devote an entire global goal, SDG 11, to making cities "inclusive, safe, resilient and sustainable" (UN General Assembly Res. 70/1, 2015).

Despite their increasing significance, relations between international institutions and cities are still an unusual topic for legal research. While international lawyers have accepted international organisations as legal subjects and significant actors, cities are still treated primarily as subnational entities mediated by their nation states. Likewise, local government lawyers have traditionally paid little attention to cities' international relations. More recently, however, this dualist framework has been challenged by legal scholars who argue that an "international local government law" or a "law of the global city" is emerging (Aust 2017; Frug and Barron 2006; Blank 2006; SFDI 2002). These new approaches respond to developments which sociologists, geographers and international relations scholars have been observing for some time. "Global cities" have emerged as self-confident centres of transnational economic networks and as paradiplomatic actors in relations with foreign governments and in city alliances (Tavares 2016; Sassen 1991). Conversely, international institutions have discovered local governments as allies in the fulfillment of their global mandates. Aid institutions promote decentralisation as a development strategy, and the UN forges global city networks to combat climate change (Eslava 2015; Aust 2015). These two dynamics, one bottom-up and one top-down, have added another dimension to multilevel global governance: the "glocal" city.

The term "glocalisation" is used by anthropologists to describe social processes in which the (socially constructed) categories of the global and the local interpenetrate each other and generate hybrid cultural and legal spaces (Robertson 1995; Swyngedouw 1997; Randeria 2003; Eberhard 2009). This chapter proposes a more specific, legal understanding. A key element of "glocal governance" is direct legal relationships between international institutions and local governments. From an anthropological perspective, these relations are key in the social constructions of scale that underlie the unstable dichotomy of "global" and "local". From a legal perspective, these direct relations are unusual, for when local governments go global and international institutions go local they increasingly bypass the national. They leapfrog, so to speak, the central government. This may create opportunities for more effective cooperation but also raises concerns regarding legitimacy, distributive justice and political conflict (Fainstein 2001; Korff 1987). The 2010 Rio loan illustrates these concerns. At that time the federal government of Brazil was dominated by the leftist workers' party with a lower-income constituency, while the Rio mayor was from the conservative party PMDB, which pursued a business-friendly agenda and later orchestrated the impeachment of the workers' party president Dilma Rousseff. Translating political conflicts and legitimacy concerns into questions of legality is a classical function of public law. Hence, this chapter looks into the public law that frames, limits and legitimates relations between local governments and international institutions. How does international institutional law regulate relationships with cities? And how does domestic local government law address, and evolve in response to, relations between cities and international institutions?

With these questions, the chapter focuses on aspects that have not yet been addressed systematically in extant literature. Existing research on "international local government law" tends to concentrate on two dimensions: either on the influence of international law on cities as objects of regulation, or on para-diplomatic relations of local governments in city networks or with foreign governments. (For an overview see Aust 2017, pp. 6–10; Frug and Barron 2006, pp. 23–52, each with further references.) While international institutions are often instrumental for these two dimensions, this chapter places the focus on their legal relations with cities as analytically distinct phenomena.

The analysis proceeds in two steps. The first section discusses the role of the city in international institutional law, asking what founding treaties, secondary law and human rights norms say about relationships between cities and international institutions. The focus will be on those institutions which have been involved with local governments early and substantially, especially the World Bank and UN agencies like Habitat.

The next section looks at the comparative law of glocal cities. What does domestic law say about local government relations with international institutions? And how does it evolve in response to international influences? This chapter can only begin to address these comparative questions by discussing some methodological challenges and by illustrating them with examples from selected jurisdictions and themes. The geographic focus will be on cities in the Global South which have the most intensive ties to the World Bank and the UN, especially Rio de Janeiro and Johannesburg. The thematic focus will be on the legal treatment of informal settlements, which poses a key challenge for creating safe and sustainable cities and raises key questions of glocal governance: What is, legally speaking, a city, and who is a part of it? Whose rights are protected by a "right to the city" or the right to housing, and whose are not?

The International Institutional Law of Glocal Cities

This section analyses the role of the city in international institutional law, addressing relevant institutions and legal sources, systematising the legal relationships international institutions establish with cities, and concluding with remarks on the substance of international norms on urban development.

Institutional Evolution and Legal Sources

Under the paradigm of sovereignty that pervades the international legal order, international institutions deal only with nation states and central governments – not with cities. Nevertheless, worldwide urbanisation and the increasing role of cities have been reflected in the institutional architecture of international cooperation since the 1970s. This institutional evolution is driven by the competing paradigm of functionalism, i.e. the search for technical solutions by international expert agencies (cf Klabbers 2014). Development agencies were among the first to engage with local governments in a functionalist vein. In 1972 the World Bank published an

"Urbanisation Sector Working Paper", marking the starting point of systematic development assistance for urban development (Cohen 2001). The UN followed suit in 1976 with the "Habitat I" conference and the resulting Vancouver Declaration, a format repeated periodically every twenty years, in 1996 with Habitat II and the Istanbul Declaration, in 2016 with Habitat III and the "New Urban Agenda". The conferences were institutionalised in 2002 when the General Assembly established the UN Human Settlements Program (UN-Habitat) as a subsidiary organ under Art. 22 UN Charter (see in detail Birkenkötter 2019, in this volume). UN-Habitat collaborates closely with other UN agencies that deliver aid and advice to local governments, especially the UN Development Programme (UNDP) and UNESCO. Until today, development institutions entertain the most intensive and most legally formalised relations with cities.

Relevant legal sources can be found on three levels: the primary law of international institutions and applicable general international law, especially human rights; the secondary law of the institutions; and the bilateral agreements they conclude with cities. The primary level is chiefly formed by the institutions' founding treaties or acts. The World Bank's Articles of Agreement, the UN Charter and the General Assembly resolutions establishing UN-Habitat lay down the mandates and competences of the institutions, the principles and instruments of their cooperation with recipients of aid and advice, as well as representation of local concerns in their organs and decision-making procedures. Many of these provisions are relevant for cooperation with cities. For instance, the institutional mandates to promote development were initially interpreted as aiming at aggregate development at the level of the nation state, measured by gross *national* product. Cooperation with local governments became the order of the day only when this interpretation changed in the 1970s towards a more functionalist understanding. Urbanisation accelerated, development was seen in a disaggregated manner, and municipalities became the locus of decentralised development efforts (Eslava 2015, pp. 139 *et seq*). Similarly, primary law has evolved with respect to institutional decision-making. Representation in political organs remains reserved to national governments until today, but UN-Habitat now provides for the participation of local authorities in its deliberations, and the international bureaucracies of the World Bank und UNDP use their relative autonomy to negotiate aid projects directly with city officials (UN General Assembly Res. 56/206, 2002: para 3; UN-Habitat Governing Council Rules of Procedure, as amended 2017, rules 64–65).

Yet the paradigm of sovereignty remains alive and kicking, namely in the Bank's non-political mandate and the UN's impartiality requirement. These requirements embody the general principle of non-intervention and function as legal limits on their cooperation with cities. International agencies must not get involved in partisan politics between city representatives and central governments. The Bank declined requests to fund the construction of entirely new capital cities in Nigeria and Brazil because they were considered "political" projects (Cohen 2001). Mandate limitations also complicate the application of another body of international law to the urban development operations of international institutions: namely, human rights law (Boulden 2005; Killinger 2003). Today, however, there is growing consensus that international institutions are bound by basic human rights norms, be it by virtue of their founding charters, customary international law, or general principles in the sense of Art. 38(1) lit. c ICJ-Statute (Dann 2013, pp. 263 *et seq*; Darrow and Arbour 2009). Consequently, human rights law is also applicable to urban development projects and thus governs the legal relationship of both international and municipal authorities with local citizens and affected residents. While there is no explicit "right to the city" in international law, a range of human rights is relevant to urban development (Oomen et al. 2015; UNESCO 2006; Brown and Kristiansen 2009). Especially relevant is the right to adequate housing (Herrle et al. 2015; Cohen 2014, p. 271; Hohmann 2013; UN-Habitat/OHCHR 2014).

While primary law and human rights provide quasi-constitutional foundations, the concrete rules that govern day-to-day operations are found mainly in secondary law. Over time UN and Bank organs have laid down a voluminous body of general rules applicable to cooperation with cities, ranging from norms on the choice of municipalities as contractual partners to safeguards for project-affected urban residents. These rules are contained in resolutions of the UN General Assembly, in decisions by governing bodies of UN-Habitat and other UN agencies, or in "Operational Policies" and "Bank Procedures" ("OP/BPs") at the World Bank. This body of norms might be termed "Glocal Administrative Law", or more modestly, a "law of urban development cooperation" (see generally Kingsbury et al. 2005; Dann 2013). Besides administrative rules, the General Assembly has formulated global goals in resolutions on the Millennium Development Goals (Res. 55/2 of 2000; "MDGs") and on the Sustainable Development Goals (Res. 70/1 of 2015; "SDGs"). The MDGs did not lay down a separate goal on cities, but MDG 7 on environmental sustainability contained a sub-target in MDG 7.11 to achieve "significant improvement in the lives of at least 100 million slum dwellers" in developing countries (UN General Asembly Res. 2/55, 2000; UN Secretary-General 2001). The SDGs now devote an entire goal, SDG 11, to making cities "inclusive, safe, resilient and sustainable". This goal is applicable to all member states, including industrialised countries like Germany (see in detail Arajärvi 2019, in this volume). These goals are significant because they influence urban governance at the international, national and local level through governance by information (Kanie 2017; Rittich 2010).

The legal effects of secondary norms differ according to the type of instrument and the addressees concerned. Stipulations on urban governance in UN General Assembly resolutions or in the World Bank's OP/BPs are not as such binding on member states. They can, however, be internally binding within the international institution where they explicitly or implicitly impose obligations on its own organs and administrative staff. These obligations are enforced through a hierarchy, including a system of regular reporting and supervision by the UN Secretary-General within the UN system. In addition, the World Bank established the quasi-judicial Inspection Panel, which hears non-compliance complaints brought by project-affected people against the Bank management (Dann 2013, pp. 452 *et seq;* Bradlow and Fourie 2013). Internally binding norms can become legally relevant for member states, cities and individuals in several ways. They exercise international public authority by means of information, they function as a conditionality and incentive for those who want to access the funds of international donors, they contain certain procedural and substantive entitlements for affected populations, and they are incorporated into the bilateral funding agreements with recipients.

The bilateral legal agreements concluded between international institutions and the recipients about specific urban development projects constitute the third and most concrete level of sources. Such funding agreements are generally considered to be treaties under international law (Head 1996). Although they are concluded anew for each project or programme, they are heavily pre-structured by primary and secondary institutional law, both in terms of their substance and of the procedures for their conclusion and execution. Even though these agreements are formally bilateral contractual treaties, they have features of multilateral, normative treaties: The many bilateral agreements form a network of standardised treaties comparable to standard contracts with general conditions in domestic contract law. This network effectively externalises and multilateralises the internal institutional law which governs the bilateral agreements. This makes it possible to speak of an international institutional law of glocal cities, formed by primary and secondary law and by the bilateral agreements which externalise the internal rules of international institutions.

Legal Relationships Between International Institutions and Cities

International institutions establish legal relationships with cities through several modalities of action. A first modality is the conclusion of a bilateral legal agreement with the city on the transfer of financial assistance (loans or grants) or on the transfer of knowledge (technical assistance or advisory services). Such agreements on financial or technical assistance are also concluded with networks of cities. Besides these contractual modes, international institutions also establish relationships with cities through unilateral governance by information, such as by publishing rankings of cities. While bilateral assistance agreements occur mostly between development institutions and cities in the Global South, networked cooperation and governance by information are also used by institutions like UNESCO and are spread across the globe, as shown below.

Under the classical paradigm of sovereignty, legal agreements on financial or technical assistance were concluded between international institutions and nation states, both of which are recognised as subjects of international law. Yet as early as 1946, the World Bank's Articles of Agreement allowed for loans to be extended not only to member states but also to "any political sub-division thereof" (IBRD Art. III Sec. 4). These political subdivisions can be cities, metropolitan agglomerations, publicly owned corporations, or federal states or provinces with legal responsibilities for urban development (Cohen 2001, pp. 46, 48). The type of support has extended over time: While cities initially received financing for concrete infrastructure projects, the Bank now also extends direct budget support in exchange for institutional and legal reform programmes, as exemplified by the Rio development policy loan. The elaboration of such reform programmes is often accompanied by technical assistance and expert advice (on these instruments, Dann 2013, pp. 361 *et seq,* 416 *et seq*; Riegner 2017, pp. 327 *et seq*).

The establishment of direct legal relations with cities follows a functionalist logic. The Bank wants to deal directly with and have legal legal claims against the entity implementing the project. This rationale is made explicit in the Bank's secondary law: the Operational Policy (OP) 7.00 on "Choice of borrower" stipulates a preference for loans to be made directly to the entity responsible for project implementation, so that the Bank has the legal means to monitor and ensure that loan proceeds are used for the intended purpose (OP 7.00 para 2; IBRD Art. III Sec. 5(b)). The functionalist logic has also been extended to "sovereigntist" legal agreements concluded between the Bank and the central government: If such agreements concern urban development, they often designate municipalities as implementing agencies and oblige the central government to channel the funds to them. In that case, the Bank concludes an additional project agreement with the municipality, which contains the obligations on project implementation otherwise included in the loan agreement (IBRD OP 7.0. para 12). Similar arrangements are made when the International Finance Corporation, the Bank's private sector arm, lends to corporate entities that are publicly owned or involved in public-private partnerships.

This practice raises salient legal questions: Are loan agreements and project agreements with cities treaties under international law? If so, have cities become subjects of international law? And what if national constitutions reserve the competence to conclude international treaties to national governments, as they often do? The Vienna Conventions on the Law of Treaties do not mention sub-state entities. Aid agreements concluded with national governments are generally considered to be international treaties. They are treated as such by the Bank, by the UN and by their member states, and their object and purpose is served better if they are subject to the uniform treaty regime of international law rather than to the diverse contract laws of 150 national legal orders (Head 1996, pp. 216 *et seq*; Broches 1959). These arguments also apply, *mutatis mutandis*, to agreements with cities. A possible counter-argument is that cities are not subjects of international law and thus cannot acquire international rights and obligations. Yet this reasoning is somewhat circular, given that the agreements are concluded precisely to confer international rights and obligations on cities (Aust 2017, pp. 142–148). The concern with treaty competences under national law is also alleviated: Bank officials are legally required to perform a due diligence assessment on the recipient entity's legal status, its relations to the central government, and its capacity to repay the loan and implement the project (World Bank Legal Vice-Presidency Law Digest (LEGVP) 2014). In sum, the better view seems to be that agreements with cities are international treaties, unless the parties stipulate otherwise. To the extent that cities thus acquire international legal rights and obligations, they are (partial) subjects of international law (Aust 2017, pp. 147–148).

This conclusion raises another pressing legal question: What is the role of the national government, especially when it is not a party to the agreement concluded directly between the Bank and a city? This question becomes especially salient when national and city government disagree on the substance of the agreement, or when they represent politically opposed camps, as was the case with the loan to Rio de Janeiro. The Bank's Articles of Agreement include national governments at two levels: Firstly, each loan or grant agreement is ultimately voted upon by the Board of Directors, in which the central government is represented. Secondly, when the recipient is a subnational entity, the Articles require the national government or the central bank to guarantee the repayment of the loan and the interest (IBRD Art. III Sec. 4 (i)(iii), Art. V Sec. 4 and 7). These provisions ensure, in principle, that the Bank does not render assistance to a city against the will of a national government. Still, the possibility of granting direct assistance to cities creates powerful incentives for all players and can affect the bargaining power and political economy at competing levels of government. In this light, the Rio loan agreement's provisions on upgrading low-income neighbourhoods may well have been part of a bargain with the federal government and a concession to the workers' party constituency.

Legal questions also arise when international institutions use another instrument in their global governance toolkit, that of network building. City networks often emerge as bottom-up initiatives by local governments, but the UN and the World Bank have also turned to transnational networks to implement their mandates and have midwifed some of them at the outset. These networks serve as knowledge sharing platforms and policy diffusion mechanisms, disseminating best practices and setting global agendas (Acuto and Rayner 2016; Aust 2015). In 1999 the Bank and UN-Habitat co-founded the "Cities Alliance", funded by the Bank's global programme line (Cohen 2014, p. 266; World Bank IEG 2007). The Alliance succeeded in focusing the global agenda on one policy issue, namely informal settlement upgrading, encapsulated in the Alliance slogan "Cities without Slums" (World Bank and UN-Habitat 1999). This goal later informed the formulation and interpretation of MDG 7.11 on slums.

Again, a first legal question that arises here is the role of central government involvement. Unlike with bilateral treaties, there is no requirement in international institutional law for central governments to consent to such networking arrangements, raising the potential of bypassing national governments. Besides, there are issues with transparency. Unlike bilateral assistance agreements, such network arrangements are not routinely published. For instance, in 2011 the World Bank concluded a cooperation agreement with the C40 coalition of cities to combat climate change. This agreement has not been made public and was released only in April 2017 upon an access to information request filed by the author of this chapter under the Bank's Access to Information Policy (AI Request No. AI4914, submitted 1 April 2017). The request revealed an intensive collaboration on city climate action plans, standardised reporting frameworks, financial and technical assistance, knowledge sharing and coordinated public communications (World Bank 2011, para 7 (a)). The agreement, signed by World Bank president Robert Zoellick and the chair of the C40, then-New York mayor Michael Bloomberg, is entitled "Memorandum of Understanding" and explicitly states that it "does not constitute a legally binding commitment by either Participant to undertake any obligation or responsibility." Nevertheless, participants seem to have acted upon their commitments, driven by the determined leadership of the C40 secretaries: first, Michael Bloomberg of New York, followed in 2013 by the mayor of Rio de Janeiro, Eduardo Paes, who had arranged the Rio loan with the Bank in 2010.

Finally, international institutions establish legal relationships with cities through instruments of governance by information. They collect, process and disseminate data and information about cities and urban development in the form of reports, rankings or statistical indicators. Numbers travel particularly well across borders and between local and global levels of governance (Davis et al. 2012). Such information can affect urban development policies and local governments through economic or reputational incentives resulting from global competition among cities. The World Bank's "Doing Business" indicators, for instance, rank the business-friendliness of jurisdictions by measuring the regulatory environment in the major business city. Given the global competition for foreign direct investment, the ranking has induced hundreds of legal reforms around the world, some of them limited to the cities where the data is collected (Besley 2015). Similarly, UNESCO's listing of urban spaces as World Heritage Sites creates incentives for cities competing for tourists to conform to UNESCO's standards, as the German city of Dresden discovered when it saw its listing cancelled over a controversial bridge construction (Zacharias 2010). Finally, the MDGs and SDGs not only create reputational incentives by measuring progress through indicators but also exercise discursive power by defining parameters and key notions of urban development debates: MDG 7.11 (and now SDG 11.1) placed the problematic notion of "slums" high on the international agenda and narrowed down global urban development debates to focus on "slum reduction" (Cohen 2014; see the section below).

The examples confirm that governance by information can amount to an exercise of international public authority. Despite its informality, it thus requires a legitimating legal framework (Bogdandy and Goldmann 2008). This necessitates a careful analysis of what I have termed the "international institutional law of information", i.e. the rules and principles applicable to the collection, processing and distribution of information by international institutions (Riegner 2017; Riegner 2015). This analysis shows that informational action relevant to cities is often not based on bilateral legal agreements and thus occurs without the concrete consent of affected national or local governments. Yet even unilateral informational action is regulated to some extent by primary and secondary law. In that sense, informational relationships are legal relationships too. A key question is whether an international institution has the legal mandate to establish a particular kind of informational relationship. While the founding treaties of the UN and the Bank contain a general competence to publish studies and reports (Art. 13(1)(b), 62(1) UN Charter; IBRD Art. V Sec. 13), a more specific mandate from political organs may be required to empower international bureaucracies to informational action that amounts to an exercise of international public authority (Bogdandy and Goldmann 2008). This requirement is not always met in practice: The indicators for MDG 7.11 and for Doing Business were not based on a decision by political organs in which member states were represented. In contrast, the indicators for SDG 11 were developed in a process laid down by General Assembly Resolution 70/1 and were approved by the political organs of the UN. This may have politicised the process at the expense of statistical quality, but has arguably improved its legitimacy from a legal point of view (see in detail Riegner 2016).

The Substance of International Norms: The Example of Informal Settlements

The substance of international norms on urban development has expanded over time and has come to address a broad range of issues ordinarily governed by local government law. Thus far, the existing literature has mainly identified "guiding images", "concepts" or "programmes" which diffuse certain normative understandings of urban safety, sustainability, economic competitiveness and good local governance (Aust 2017, pp. 273

et seq; Lindemann 2014, pp. 17 *et seq*; Frug and Barron 2006, pp. 30 *et seq*). Others provide ethnographies of the everyday workings of international norms in specific cities at the grassroots – or rather: at the street – level (Eslava 2015). These approaches leave a gap at the intermediary level which this chapter proposes to address by focusing on the norms of international institutional law that govern urban development projects in one exemplary thematic area.

One theme that emerges prominently from the substance of international norms on urban development is the legal treatment of informal settlements. Informality designates areas beyond the framework of state law, which are typically unplanned, underserviced, unauthorised and/or characterised by insecure land tenure. International institutions' preoccupation with informality reflects their engagement with cities in the Global South, where a significant share of current urban settlements and of projected urban growth is unplanned (Ledeneva 2018, pp. 7–37; Arfvidsson et al. 2016; UN-Habitat 2015). Informality is also a useful lens for legal analysis because it captures key questions of urban governance: What is a city as a matter of international law? Which spaces belong to it? How should it be governed, and where should social and environmental services be rendered? Who belongs to the city, and who should be treated as rights-holders or illegal occupants?

Unlike many domestic legal orders, international law does not provide a uniform definition of what a city is. International institutions work with the political and administrative units which national law constitutes and defines as cities. Yet where the administrative city is outgrown by economic and demographic expansion, institutions like the World Bank pursue a more functional notion of the city. This functional approach does not follow jurisdictional and historical boundaries but treats agglomerations as economic and social entities that follow necessities of production, mobility, trade, environment and integration into world markets (World Bank 2015; Cohen 2001, p. 48). It also highlights the existence of informal settlements and economies in urban and peri-urban areas beyond the reach of official city institutions. Long before MDG 7.11 and SDG 11.1 put the global spotlight on "slums", urban development projects pursued a strategy of the legal formalisation of property rights, housing and service provision in informal neighborhoods (Eslava 2015, pp. 162 *et seq*; Cohen 2014; Mitchell 2005). This strategy found support in human rights law, especially in the right to adequate housing in Art. 11(1) ICESCR. In its General Comment No. 4 of 1991 the UN Committee on Economic and Cultural (ESC) Rights interprets the "adequacy" of housing to include legal security of tenure in informal settlements. State parties are required to "take immediate measures at conferring legal security of tenure upon those persons and households lacking such protection" (CESCR 1991, para 8a). Taken together, these legal approaches arguably convey another guiding image of what a city is, or should be, as a matter of international law: the image of a "legally formalised" city.

This image also influences views on how the formal city should be governed and serviced. International institutions emphasise urban planning as an element of legalisation and as a contrast to the disorderly "slum". International requirements for planning aim at creating the preconditions for orderly urbanisation, access to housing and public services, infrastructure development and environmental management. World Bank and UN secondary law condition access to international aid on specific forms of planning by the recipients. OPs/BPs and GA resolutions require multi-year country-level planning of assistance, including to urban development, and they subject the preparation of concrete urban development projects to an elaborate administrative procedure requiring planning, environmental impact assessments, and public participation (Riegner 2017, pp. 305 *et seq;* Dann 2013, pp. 303 *et seq,* 353 *et seq).* At the level of individual projects, the World Bank used budget support loans to promote housing policy reforms that "enable markets" and "unlock the value of land" until the 2000s. In contrast, UN institutions tended to emphasise the public good aspects of land and housing (Buckley and Kalarickal 2006; Lindemann 2014, p. 37 *et seq*; UN Human Rights Council 2011b). The UN Committee on Economic Social and Cultural Rights advocates a rights-based approach that does not require the state to provide large-scale housing but to construct and implement a policy framework which makes privately provided housing "affordable" and "accessible", prioritising the housing needs of disadvantaged and vulnerable groups (Saul et al. 2014, p. 931; CESCR 1991, paras 8, 11–14).

While formalisation and planning often correlate with improved service delivery and environmental management, they can have unintended consequences. The guiding image of the formal city walks a fine line between "legally formal", "informal" and "illegal". Under certain circumstances it may reinforce the stigma of illegality and lawlessness associated with informal settlements and residents that prevail in many local contexts (Eslava 2015, p. 190 *et seq*; Fernandes and Varley 1998). This can sustain policies and practices that discriminate on the basis of race, social origin, property, birth or other grounds prohibited by Art. 2(2) ICESCR and compromise the equal enjoyment of other rights, such as housing, water or health (CESCR 1991, para 8c, f; UN Human Rights Council 2011a, para 13).

Such unintended consequences are well documented in the implementation of MDG 7.11. The target to "improve the lives of 100 million slums dwellers" was interpreted in line with the Cities Alliance's objective of "Cities without Slums", and UN-Habitat's biannual "World Cities Report" promoted this framing by referring to MDG 7.11 as the "slum reduction target". "Improving the lives of slum dwellers" thus became synonymous with "escaping" or "moving out of" the slum. As a result, evictions and slum demolitions became a frequent policy to produce the statistics showing progress towards the MDG 7.11 indicator. Whether slum dwellers were forcibly evicted or resettled in new, often informal settlements in the periphery was irrelevant for the purposes of MDG 7.11 (Cohen 2014; Huchzermeyer 2013).

These unintended consequences raise the question of how international institutions protect the rights of city residents affected by urban development projects, especially in informal neighborhoods. At the level of secondary law, institutions have developed environmental and social safeguards. The Bank's safeguards have evolved since the 1990s and were consolidated in 2016 in a new "Environmental and Social Framework". The UNDP enacted "Environmental and Social Standards" in 2014. These norms require consultation with affected residents and impact assessments, which were initially focused on environmental impacts but have evolved to cover social effects as well. The social safeguards have been interpreted as concretisations of human rights norms applicable to development projects, and the most recent versions now include an explicit commitment to respect for human rights and, in the case of UNDP, to human rights due diligence (Dann and Riegner (forthcoming); Riegner 2017, p. 317; Naudé Fourie 2009, pp. 260 *et seq*).

For urban development projects, standards on land acquisition, involuntary resettlement and use restrictions are particularly relevant. These standards grant affected residents a right to a hearing and require compensation for eligible residents in case of involuntary resettlement (World Bank 2016; UNDP 2014). The eligibility of informal occupants has been a consistent point of disagreement between international institutions, governments, and local residents. While the right to housing also protects informal occupants against forced evictions (CESCR 1991: para 8a; CESCR 1997), national law and local authorities often treat informal dwellers as illegal occupants unworthy of protection. International institutional law is situated in between these positions. On the one hand, the Bank and UNDP tend to give more legal protection to informal occupants than national law, and they increasingly work together with local NGOs and social movements (cf World Bank 2016, para 10; Herrle et al. 2015; Cohen 2014, p. 271).

On the other hand, the Bank's safeguards fall short of human rights obligations, for instance by allowing resettlement into inadequate housing if affected residents already lived in inadequate conditions prior to resettlement (UN Human Rights Council 2013, para 35). Moreover, recurring cases before the World Bank's Inspection Panel demonstrate systemic compliance problems in urban resettlement and land titling projects (World Bank Inspection Panel 2010; World Bank Inspection Panel 2005). In sum, the role of international institutions seems ambivalent and fraught with inherent tensions. How these tensions play out in practice cannot be analysed in the abstract at the international level but depends on the complex interplay of global, national and local norms and contextual determinants in specific cases. It is this interplay that the following section now turns to.

The Comparative Law of Glocal Cities

This section looks at the responses of domestic local government law to the globalisation of the city, and more specifically to legal relations between cities and international institutions. It first discusses the comparative approach it adopts, and then highlights responses in two areas of local government law, namely city relations with international institutions and substantive impacts on the legal treatment of informal settlements.

Comparing "Open Cityhood" in Domestic Local Government Law

While international norms on cities gain importance, most local government law is still found at the domestic level in national constitutions, national legislation, sub-national law at the level of federal states, and in legal acts and bylaws of local governments. This law, however, is also responding to the global forces shaping urban governance and is opening cities for international influences. They are thus evolving towards "open cityhood", the local correlate of open statehood in federal systems (cf Fassbender 2007). Open cityhood raises a series of legal questions: How does local government law regulate a city's international relations in general, and its cooperation with international institutions in particular? How do these rules function as mechanisms for the reception and localisation of international norms? How does the interplay of global, national and local norms change urban governance? Studying these questions poses methodological problems that this chapter proposes to address through a comparative law approach. This approach requires, firstly, enriching the literature on global cities with methodological insights from comparative law; and secondly, enlarging the geographical horizon of comparative local government law to include the Global South. By thus comparing the internationalisation of local government law across jurisdictions, we can understand urban change in its global context and as a global phenomenon.

While the first wave of legal literature on global cities tended to focus primarily on single jurisdictions (eg Aust 2017), the next step is to compare developments across domestic legal orders. Sociology and urban studies already adopt such comparative approaches to the globalisation of the city (Deville et al. 2016; Robinson 2016). Within this field, the literature on global cities assumes at least implicitly a measure of economic and socio-cultural convergence that justifies the "global" label in the first place (cf Rodriguez and Shoked 2016, p. 124). But are global cities also defined by converging legal structures? Does their local government law regulate international relations in a comparable way? Does the localisation of international norms on urban governance lead to convergence in local government law? A systematic study of these questions can draw on long-standing debates in comparative law among functionalists, contextualists and critical comparatists, which generally counsel against *a priori* assumptions of similarity or difference (Frankenberg 2016; Hirschl 2014; Michaels 2006). If anything, they suggest making questions of convergence the explicit object of empirically informed research and paying particular attention to diverging contextual determinants. This also goes for studying the localisation of international norms, as renewed approaches to comparative international law remind us. Despite its inherent claim to universality, international law is interpreted differently across regions, jurisdictions and cities, and it has different effects in national legal orders and local settings (see generally Roberts 2017; Mattei and Mamyluck 2011). We thus cannot assume that international norms on local government have the same meaning and effects everywhere, but need to compare their localisation across different urban contexts.

Comparing open cityhood also requires crossing the North-South divide in comparative local government law. Existing comparative studies of local government law are mostly focused on the US-American and European context (cf Panara and Varney 2011; Kuhlmann 2009; Kushner 2003). Within this geographical horizon they have defined some useful dimensions for comparison, which are outlined in the section below, and have addressed some aspects of open cityhood (Rodriguez and Shoked 2016; Nicola and Forster 2016). Taking a global perspective, however, requires expanding this analysis in two directions. Firstly, open cityhood represents another comparative dimension along which we may observe convergence and orient typologies of more or less internationally open cities, as exemplified in the sub-section below. Secondly, comparison must broaden its horizon to include the Global South if the comparative sample is to be representative enough to allow for real generalisations (cf Hirschl 2014; Saunders 2009). A global comparison across the North-South divide requires new legal typologies capturing the variations between settler cities, colonial capitals and socialist urbanism, to name but a few (Therborn 2017; Parnell and Oldfield 2014; Edensor and Jayne 2011; Montgomery 2004). These typologies must consider socio-legal variations such as the degree of and approaches to informality in local government law. This type of socio-legal comparison can draw especially on anthropological work and multi-sited ethnographic studies of urban informality and of the localisation of global norms in this context (Eslava 2015; generally Merry and Goodale 2007). Besides providing empirical grounding, anthropology counsels against reifying the analytical categories of "global" and "local" and calls for seeing them as socio-legal constructions of scale that shift with time and place.

The following subsections will illustrate this comparative approach with examples drawn mostly from cities in the Global South, where most of the worldwide urban growth is occurring and where the effects of international and development cooperation can be expected to be particularly pronounced. Examples will focus especially on the cities of Rio de Janeiro and Johannesburg, two "global cities" which have been particularly exposed to international cooperation and yet remain understudied in this particular respect.

Relations Between Cities and International Institutions in Local Government Law

A prerequisite for cities to establish relationships with international institutions is that national law allows them to do so. A comparative inquiry thus needs to first identify the relevant provisions in constitutional law, federal legislation, and possibly other layers of national law. These provisions rarely address the issue explicitly and thus have to be interpreted. Constitutions typically assign the competence to conduct foreign affairs and to conclude treaties to the central government. This is the case, for instance, in Brazil (Art. 49, 84), Germany (Art. 32, 59 (2)), and South Africa (Sec. 84(2), 231(1)). But are these provisions exclusive, or do they leave room for other actors, including cities, to engage in para-diplomatic relations? Some jurisdictions distinguish between core aspects of foreign affairs exclusively reserved to the central government, and other forms of international relations that remain open to other actors. This view is taken in German law, where formal legal relations with subjects of international law are reserved for the federal government (and federal states in some circumstances), but non-legal forms of international engagement remain open to cities (Aust 2017, pp. 70–74). A more permissive practice prevails in Brazil, where cities engage in a host of para-diplomatic activities, including the conclusion of agreements with international institutions like the World Bank (Dias 2010; Tavares 2016).

If the national level has no diplomatic monopoly, the next question is which provisions empower cities to cooperate internationally, as opposed to intermediate levels of federal states or provinces – or in other words, how do we distinguish open cityhood from open statehood in federal systems? Most constitutions surveyed here contain provisions on local government (e.g. Art. 29 *et seq* in Brazil; Art. 28(2) in Germany; Sections 40, 41, 151–157, 163 in South Africa). These constitutional provisions are usually spelled out in detail at the level of legislation. In some cases legislation addresses international relations explicitly, for instance the Mexican Federal Law on Treaties and the constitutional charter of Mexico City, whose Art. 20 addresses the "Global City" (Miguel-Stearns 2014). In most other cases there are no explicit provisions. Instead, norms typically use the language of "local matters" or some variant to define the competences of local governments. Traditionally, this did not include international relations, but the wording does not preclude a progressive interpretation where cities turn global and local matters become global.

At this point, the anthropological insight that "global" and "local" are constructions of scale that often co-constitute each other gains legal relevance. This relevance is illustrated by legal disputes about so-called "human rights cities" (Baumgärtel and Oomen 2014; Krajewski 2014) or about UNESCO's involvement with world heritage sites in cities (Reyes 2015, p. 33). A particularly illustrative example is a dispute between the Italian city of Florence and the global food corporation McDonalds. In November 2016 the corporation sued the local government because the city had refused a permit for a McDonalds restaurant in the historical old town of Florence. The refusal was based on local bylaws requiring restaurants in the old town to sell traditional food typical of the region. What seems like a straightforward conflict between the global and the local becomes a "glocal" process on closer inspection. For one, McDonalds had offered to adapt its globally standardised menu to local culinary norms. More importantly, the municipal bylaws on local food were not age-old but had just been enacted in January 2016 in response to a UNESCO recommendation which aimed at preserving the status of the city as world cultural heritage site (UNESCO 2017, p. 25). The global and the local thus co-constitute each other in a process that is best described by the concept of glocalisation, which can explain simultaneous tendencies of convergence and divergence and avoids politically charged dichotomies of global vs local.

In the light of these developments it should not come as a surprise that the "local" competences of cities are increasingly interpreted to encompass relationships with international institutions. This is common practice in Brazil, where the Federal Foreign Ministry has set up a support unit to facilitate and coordinate the para-diplomatic activities of cities and federal states (Dias 2010). In South Africa international practice is more limited, but the city of Johannesburg brands itself as "A World Class African City" on the international stage (Sihlongonyane 2016). Many factors need to be considered to account for differences in interpretive practice, including the general understandings of the nature and purpose of local governments. Are they understood simply as decentralised state units which derive their legitimacy mainly from effective administration? Then their para-diplomatic powers will depend on their relative effectiveness to centralised diplomacy, and they need to derive their democratic legitimacy from the national level and legislation. This may look different if cities are considered as communities of self-governing citizens with their own democratic legitimacy. In Germany, for instance, cities have been associated with a certain tradition of political freedom (Aust 2017, pp. 79 *et seq*). In Latin America decentralisation and local self-government have contributed to nation-wide democratisation in formerly autocratic regimes (Blank 2006, pp. 894 *et seq*; Campbell 2003).

A last set of questions arises if cities are indeed empowered to cooperate with international institutions: What forms, conditions and limits are stipulated in national law, if any? Constitutional law may impose a general condition, and possibly limitation, through norms on loyal cooperation among federal, regional and state governments: cities must not act in a way that is disloyal to or contradicts national foreign policy or the international obligations of the state (cf Sec. 40(2) Constitution of South Africa; on Germany, see Aust 2017, pp. 122–130). More specific conditions and limitations result from legislation on local government, especially provisions on municipal finance and debt. For instance, in many jurisdictions local governments cannot autonomously take out loans, whether from commercial lenders or multilateral development banks, but require permission from provincial or national governments, as is the case in South Africa. While primarily intended to prevent over-indebtedness, this additional check may also go some way in addressing the unsustainability of temporary international project funding.

In sum, the national legal framework is evolving in response to the international cooperation of cities, but much of this evolution remains at the level of interpretation in administrative practice. Courts rarely adjudicate city competences on international cooperation, partly because international institutions mostly play a supporting role less amenable to legal conflict, partly because there are other, political avenues for resolving disputes when they occur. However, this picture changes if we now turn to evolutions in the substance of local government law that concerns the rights of residents.

Impact on the Substance of Local Government Law: Glocalising Informality

When considering the impact of international cooperation on the substance of local government law, it is important to understand that the focus of such cooperation has shifted since the 1990s from investments in physical infrastructure at the neighbourhood-level to issues of city-wide governance and institutional reform (Lindert 2016; Cohen 2014, pp. 265 *et seq*). As a result, cooperation with international institutions impacts on all comparative dimensions of local government law (cf Kuhlmann 2009): functional responsibilities (namely legal competences and autonomy), territorial profile (size, metropolitan governance), political organisation (especially organs and local democracy), and administrative profile (bureaucratic organisation, service delivery, public-private partnerships).

Decentralisation projects extend the functional responsibilities of local governments by enhancing their legal competences and autonomy (Eslava 2015, pp. 178 *et seq*; Cohen 2001, pp. 44 *et seq*). Cooperation also encourages changes in the territorial profile, especially when it comes to metropolitan governance reforms. Political organisation becomes more participatory in response to consultation requirements in Bank Safeguards and to projects promoting participatory budgeting and the inclusion of civil society organisations in decision-making procedures (World Bank 2008; Shah 2007; Sousa Santos 1998). The administrative profile of local governments has evolved in projects on the privatisation of public services and public-private infrastructure investments (World Bank IEG 2014; Lindemann 2014, pp. 1–3, 37–44; World Bank 2013, p. 37; Cohen 2001, p. 51 *et seq*). All dimensions come together in the legal debates and norms on informal settlements, which impact upon all aspects of safe, sustainable and inclusive cities. The comparative law of informal settlements is thus a promising area for further research, whose possible direction I should like to exemplify with snapshots of Johannesburg and Rio de Janeiro.

South Africa and the metropolitan Region of Gauteng around Johannesburg exemplify the impact of international networks like the City Alliance and of global goals (on Johannesburg, see also De Visser 2019, Van der Berg 2019, both in this volume). The South African constitution establishes an "hourglass model" of federalism with a strong central and local level on the one hand and weak provincial governments on the other. Inspired by international human rights law, the Constitution also guarantees the right to housing in Sec. 26(2), which the Constitutional Court fleshed out in its 2000 landmark case *Grootboom* (Saul et al. 2014, pp. 957–959). The socio-economic context of urban development remains shaped by the legacy of apartheid, including racially segregated settlements and often sub-standard and insecure housing in townships inhabited by black and brown South Africans. In this context the central government seized on the MDGs in the early 2000s and communicated an MDG "obligation" to achieve "slum-free" cities by 2014. In 2005 the Gauteng provincial department responsible for housing vowed to achieve that goal in time for the FIFA World Cup in 2010, and the city of Johannesburg even promised to "eradicate informal settlements" by 2008. Soon provinces adopted legislation on slum elimination that expanded local governments' powers to evict informal inhabitants, that further criminalised land invasion, and that mandated security measures in the prevention of new informal settlement formation. Many of these mechanisms had been used during apartheid and had been repealed during the early days of democratisation in the 1990s (Huchzermeyer 2013).

In the ensuing litigation a provincial authority initially convinced the High Court that the "Slums Act" had nothing to do with forced evictions but was a measure to address the UN Millennium Development Goals and constitutional goals (cf Huchzermeyer 2013). In 2009 the Constitutional Court eventually struck down the Act's core provision on eviction powers on the grounds that they violated the constitutional right to housing, in turn inspired by the international human right to housing (Constitutional Court of South Africa 2009). This snapshot illustrates that glocal governance may well consist of countervailing processes in which global norms re-awaken dormant local legal traditions for the worse, while local norms and courts bring to life the global remedies that put them back to sleep, at least for now.

Rio de Janeiro evidences the impact of large-scale World Bank investments in city infrastructure and informal neighborhoods, or "favelas". Informality is a defining feature of the context for local government law and urban development in Brazil. 50 percent of the population of the major urban areas live in informal urban communities with inadequate housing, water supply and sanitary conditions (CESCR 2009, para 33). The 1988 Constitution introduced an ambitious chapter on urban development, which was fleshed out in 2001 by the enactment of the federal "City Statute". This law recognised a "right to the city" and gave municipalities powers for urban planning and to restrict the private property rights to that effect (Klink 2013; Fernandes 2007; generally, Lefebvre 1968). Since then, the city of Rio has embarked on an ambitious urban improvement programme. In that context the Bank granted the one billion USD loan mentioned earlier and supported a range of infrastructure projects such as the modernisation and privatisation of Rio's old port, as well as policing, social and land formalisation programmes in the favelas, which are reputed to be controlled by drug traders and criminal gangs. In particular, the Bank supported the "Police Pacification Units" programme (UPP), which combined the quasi-military occupation of neighborhoods with the extension of social services to the pacified territories (see Oliveira 2019, in this volume; Dias and Eslava 2013; World Bank 2012).

Unlike in South Africa, these internationally supported programmes did not envisage large-scale evictions, and the World Bank safeguards tended to alleviate the consequences of resettlement where it did occur. The safeguards were unable, however, to manage other problems: the abuse of force by police remains a persistent problem denounced by NGOs and UN human rights institutions (Amnesty International 2015; UN Human Rights Council 2017, paras 17–19; generally on urban violence, see Wittke 2019, in this volume). Besides, even where the state did not force out local residents, market forces often did. Especially in centrally located favelas, upgrading and property formalisation have led to rising costs of living and real estate prices. Many residents have thus suffered economic displacement towards the periphery, as a result of market forces unleashed by Rio's exposure to the global economy. The Rio example thus illustrates an important limitation of the law of glocal governance as it stands: If it is understood only as a law of relations among public actors, its positive implications may well be undercut by globalised private forces. Glocal governance has neither mobilised the "social function" ascribed to private property by the Brazilian Constitution nor localised norms on the affordability and locational adequacy of housing derived from Art. 11(1) ICESCR (cf CESCR 1991, para 8c, f); UN Human Rights Council 2011a, para 13.

Conclusion: Judging Glocal Governance Law

After all, cooperation between international institutions and cities emerges as an ambivalent endeavour. International cooperation mobilises resources for local investment, enables mutual learning and the exchange of experience across countries, and it incentivises local actors to consider problems and externalities that transcend city boundaries. International institutions can be and often have been advocates of more equitable city development. At the same time, such cooperation faces criticisms of a lack of effectiveness, legitimacy, and distributive justice. Cities may not be the right level for effective cooperation on issues with mobile causes and spill-over effects (also see the chapter in this volume by Vormann 2019). Local climate change coalitions may simply displace emissions to the next city, or not even include cities with emission-heavy industry. Upgrading informal neighbourhoods within the bounds of a city leads to the physical or economic displacement of poor populations to the periphery beyond the municipal boundaries. In these situations, the risks of bypassing higher levels of government become particularly apparent.

The modalities of international cooperation may also cause problems. Project-based funding may be unsustainable and donor-driven and thus complicate planning based on local needs. The diffusion of global models may threaten diversity and reduce the value of the city as a laboratory for innovation and experimentation. Finally, there are concerns with respect to the substance of international cooperation. Privatisation, resettlement and orientation towards global markets and global concerns do not always benefit local populations equitably. The public law applicable to international cooperation alleviates some of these concerns and offers mechanisms to harness some of its potential. In this respect, international institutional law seems to have progressed further than local government law within some states, but neither seems able to address the negative externalities of private global forces that states have unleashed in the first place. In the end, this leads to an ultimately unsurprising question: Is it time to bring the state back into the law of glocal governance?

Bibliography

Literature

Acuto, Michele and Rayner, Steve. 2016. City networks. Breaking gridlocks or forging (new) lock-ins? *International Affairs*, 92(5), pp. 1147–1166.

Amnesty International. 2015. *Homicides by Military Police in the City of Rio de Janeiro*. Rio de Janeiro: Amnesty International.

Arajärvi, Noora. 2019. Including Cities in the 2030 Agenda – A Review of the Post-2015 Process "Cities Are Where the Battle for Sustainable Development Will Be Won or Lost. In Aust, Helmut Philipp and du Plessis, Anél (eds). *The Globalisation of Urban Governance: Legal Perspectives on Sustainable Development Goal 11*. London: Routledge. pp. 17–37.

Arfvidsson, Helen and Simon, David and Oloko, Michael and Moodley, Nishendra. 2016. Engaging with and measuring informality in the proposed Urban Sustainable Development Goal. *African Geographical Review*, 36(1), 100–114.

Aust, Helmut Philipp. 2015. Shining Cities on the Hill? The Global City, Climate Change, and International Law. *European Journal of International Law*, 26(1), pp. 255–278.

Aust, Helmut Philipp. 2017. *Das Recht der globalen Stadt*. Tübingen: Mohr Siebeck.

Baumgärtel, Moritz and Oomen, Barbara. 2014. Human Rights Cities. In: Mark Gibney and Anja Mihr (eds). *The Sage Handbook of Human Rights*. Thousand Oaks, CA: SAGE. pp. 709–729.

Besley, Timothy. 2015. Law, Regulation, and the Business Climate: The Nature and Influence of the World Bank Doing Business Project. *Journal of Economic Perspectives* 29(3), 99–120.

Birkenkötter, Hannah. 2019. Ensuring Access to Public Space as a Dimension of "Safe Cities": The Role of UN Entities in Shaping the Global Urban Governance Agenda. In Aust, Helmut Philipp and du Plessis, Anél (eds). *The Globalisation of Urban Governance: Legal Perspectives on Sustainable Development Goal 11*. London: Routledge. pp. 127–150.

Blank, Yishai. 2006. The City and the World. *Columbia Journal of Transnational Law*, 44, 868–931.

Boulden, Jane. 2005. Mandates Matter: An Exploration of Impartiality in United Nations Operations. *Global Governance*, 11(2), 147–160.

Bradlow, Daniel D. and Naudé-Fourie, Andria. 2013. The Operational Policies of the World Bank and the International Finance Corporation. *International Organizations Law Review* 10(1), 3–80.

Broches, Aron. 1959. International Legal Aspects of the Operation of the World Bank. *Recueil des Cours*. 98, 297–409.

Brown, Alison and Kristiansen, Annali. 2009. *Urban Policies and the Right to the City*. Paris: UNESCO, UN-Habitat.

Buckley, Robert and Kalarickal, Jerry (eds). 2006. *Thirty Years of World Bank Shelter Lending. What Have We Learned?*. Washington DC: World Bank.

Campbell, Tim. 2003. *The Quiet Revolution. Decentralization and the Rise of Political Participation in Latin American Cities*. Pittsburgh, PA: University of Pittsburgh Press.

Cohen, Michael. 2001. Urban Assistance and the Material World: Learning by Doing at the World Bank. *Environment and Urbanization*, 13(1), 37–60.

Cohen, Michael. 2014. The City is Missing in the Millennium Development Goals. *Journal of Human Development and Capabilities*, 15(2–3), 261–274.

Dann, Philipp. 2013. *The Law of Development Cooperation. A Comparative Analysis of the World Bank, the EU and Germany*. Cambridge: Cambridge University Press.

Dann, Philipp and Riegner, Michael. In press. The World Bank's Environmental and Social Framework and the Evolution of Global Order. *Leiden Journal of International Law*.

Darrow, Mac and Arbour, Louise. 2009. The Pillar of Glass: Human Rights in the Development Operations of the United Nations. *American Journal of International Law*, 103, 446–501.

Davis, Kevin and Kingsbury, Benedict and Merry, Sally Engle. 2012. Indicators as a Technology of Global Governance. *Law and Society Review*, 46(1), 71–104.

De Sousa Santos, Boaventura. 1998. Participatory Budgeting in Porto Alegre: Toward a Redistributive Democracy. *Politics Society*, 26, 461–510.

Deville, Joe and Guggenheim, Michael and Hrdlicková, Zuzana (eds). 2016. *Practising Comparison. Logics, Relations, Collaborations.* Manchester, UK: Mattering Press.

De Visser, Jaap. 2019. City Regions in Pursuit of SDG 11: Institionalising Multi-level Cooperation in Gauteng, South Africa. In Helmut Philipp Aust and Anél du Plessis (eds). *The Globalisation of Urban Governance: Legal Perspectives on Sustainable Development Goal 11*. London: Routledge. pp. 186–207.

Dias, Maria Clara and Eslava, Luis. 2013. Horizons of Inclusion: Life Between Laws and Developments in Rio de Janeiro. *Inter-American Law Review*, 44(2), 177–218.

Dias, Reinaldo. 2010. *Um tema emergente nas Relações Internacionais: A para-diplomacia das cidades e municípios. Âmbito Jurídico*, 79 [online]. Available at: www.ambito-juridico.com.br/site/index.php?n_link=revista_artigos_leitura&artigo_id=8156 (Accessed: 8 March 2018).

Eberhard, Christoph. 2009. Law and Anthropology in a 'Glocal' World: The Challenge of Dialogue. In: Freeman, Michael and Napier, David (eds). *Law and anthropology: Current Legal Issues*,Volume 12. Oxford: Oxford University Press. pp. 67–88.

Edensor, Tim and Jayne, Mark. 2011. *Urban Theory Beyond the West*. London: Routledge.

Eslava, Luis. 2015. *Local Space, Global Life. The Everyday Operation of International Law and Development*. Cambridge: Cambridge University Press.

Fainstein, Susan S. 2001. Inequality in Global City-Regions. *Planning Review*, pp. 37(144), 20–25.

Fassbender, Bardo. 2007. *Der offene Bundesstaat. Studien zur auswärtigen Gewalt und zur Völkerrechtssubjektivität bundesstaatlicher Teilstaaten in Europa.* Tübingen: Mohr Siebeck.

Fernandes, Edésio. 2007. Implementing the Urban Reform Agenda in Brazil. *Environment and Urbanization*, 19(1), 177–189.

Fernandes, Edésio and Varley, Ann (eds). 1998. *Illegal Cities. Law and Urban Change in Developing Countries.* London: Zed Books.

Frankenberg, Günter. 2016. *Comparative Law as Critique.* Cheltenham, UK: Elgar.

Frug, Gerald and Barron, David. 2006. International Local Government Law. *Urban Lawyer* 38(1), pp. 1–62.

Head, John W. 1996. Evolution of the Governing Law for Loan Agreements of the World Bank and Other Multilateral Development Banks. *American Journal of International Law* 90(2), 214–234.

Herrle, Peter and Ley, Astrid and Fokdal, Josefine. 2015. *From Local Action to Global Networks. Housing the Urban Poor.* London: Routledge.

Hirschl, Ran. 2014. *Comparative Matters. The Renaissance of Comparative Constitutional Law.* Oxford: Oxford University Press.

Hohmann, Jessie. 2013. *The Right to Housing. Law, Concepts, Possibilities.* Oxford: Hart.

Huchzermeyer, Marie. 2013. "Slum' Upgrading or 'Slum" Eradication? The Mixed Message of the MDGs. In: Langford, Malcolm and Sumner, Andy and Ely Yamin, Alicia (eds). *Millennium Development Goals and Human Rights. Past, Present, and Future.* New York: Cambridge University Press. pp. 295–315.

Kanie, Norichika (ed). 2017. *Governing Through Goals: The Sustainable Development Goals and a New Governance Strategy in the 21st Century.* Boston: MIT Press.

Killinger, Stefanie. 2003. *The World Bank's Non-political Mandate.* Köln: Heymann.

Kingsbury, Benedict and Krisch, Nico and Stewart, Richard B. 2005. The Emergence of Global Administrative Law. *Law and Contemporary Problems*, 68(3–4), pp. 15–61.

Klabbers, Jan. 2014. The Emergence of Functionalism in International Institutional Law: Colonial Inspirations. *European Journal of International Law*, 25(3), 645–675.

Klink, Jeroen. 2013. Development Regimes, Scales and State Spatial Restructuring. Change and Continuity in the Production of Urban Space in Metropolitan Rio de Janeiro, Brazil. *International Journal of Urban and Regional Research*, 37 (4), pp. 1168–1187.

Korff, Ruediger. 1987. The World City Hypothesis: A Critique. *Development and Change* 18(3), 483–493.

Krajewski, Markus. 2014. Kommunaler Menschenrechtsschutz. *Die Öffentliche Verwaltung*, 17, pp. 721–729.

Kuhlmann, Sabine. 2009. *Politik- und Verwaltungsreform in Kontinentaleuropa. Subnationaler Institutionenwandel im deutsch-französischen Vergleich.* Baden-Baden, Germany: Nomos.

Kushner, James A. 2003. *Comparative Urban Planning Law. An Introduction to Urban Land Development Law in the United States Through the Lens of Comparing the Experience of Other Nations.* Durham, NC: Carolina Academic Press.

Lefebvre, Henri. 1968. *Le droit à la ville.* Paris: Éd. Anthropos (Société et urbanisme).

Ledeneva, Alena (ed). 2018. *The Global Encyclopaedia of Informality.* London: UCL Press.

Lindemann, Helena. 2014. *Kommunale Governance. Die Stadt als Konzept im Völkerrecht.* Tübingen: Mohr Siebeck.

Lindert, Paul van. 2016. Rethinking Urban Development in Latin America: A Review of Changing Paradigms and Policies. *Habitat International*, 54, 253–264.

Mattei, Ugo and Mamyluck, Boris. 2011. Comparative International Law. *Brooklyn Journal of International Law*, 36(2), pp. 386–452.

Merry, Sally Engle and Goodale, Mark. 2007. *The Practice of Human Rights. Tracking Law Between the Global and the Local.* Cambridge:Cambridge University Press.

Michaels, Ralf. 2006. The Functional Method of Comparative Law. In: Zimmermann, Reinhard and Reimann, Mathias (eds). *The Oxford Handbook of Comparative Law.* Oxford: Oxford University Press. pp. 340–382.

Miguel-Stearns, Teresa. 2014. Mexico. In: Gaebler, Ralph and Shea, Alison (eds). *Sources of State Practice in International Law.* 2nd edn. Leiden: Brill. pp. 370–388.

Mitchell, Timothy. 2005. The Work of Economics: How a Discipline Makes Its World. *European Journal of Sociology* 46(2), pp. 297–320.

Montgomery, Mark R. 2004. *Cities Transformed. Demographic Change and Its Implications in the Developing World.* London: Earthscan.

Naudé-Fourie, Andria. 2009. *The World Bank Inspection Panel and Quasi-judicial Oversight.* Utrecht, NL: Eleven International Publishing.

Nicola, Fernanda and Foster, Sheila. 2016. Comparative Urban Governance for Lawyers. *Fordham Urban Law Journal*, 42(1), pp. 1–24.

Oliveira, M. Cecilia. 2019. Global Goals and Urban Development: The Territorial Effects of Implementing the MDGs in Brazil. In Aust, Helmut Philipp and du Plessis,

Anél (eds). *The Globalisation of Urban Governance: Legal Perspectives on Sustainable Development Goal 11*. London: Routledge. pp. 173–185.

Oomen, Barbara and Davis, Martha and Grigolo, Michele (eds). 2016. *Global Urban Justice. The Rise of Human Rights Cities.* Cambridge: Cambridge University Press.

Panara, Carlo and Varney, Mike. 2011. *Local Government in Europe.* London: Routledge.

Parnell, Sue and Oldfield, Sophie (ed). 2014. *The Routledge Handbook on Cities of the Global South.* London: Routledge.

Randeria, Shalini. 2003. Glocalization of Law. Environmental Justice, World Bank, NGOs and the Cunning State in India. *Current Sociology* 51(3–4), pp. 305–328.

Reyes, Victoria. 2015. Investigating Global Culture: Its Creation, Structure, and Meanings. In: Vujnovic, Marina and Mele, Vincenzo (eds). *Globalizing Cultures.* Leiden: Brill. pp. 21–38.

Riegner, Michael. 2015. The International Institutional Law of Information. *International Organizations Law Review* 12(1), pp. 50–80.

Riegner, Michael. 2016. Implementing the "Data Revolution" for the Post-2015 Sustainable Development Goals - Toward a Global Administrative Law of Information. In: Boisson de Chazournes, Laurance and Davis, Kevin E. and Fariello, Frank (eds). *The World Bank Legal Review: Financing and Implementing the Post-2015 Development Agenda.* Washington, DC: World Bank. pp. 17–39.

Riegner, Michael. 2017. *Informationsverwaltungsrecht internationaler Institutionen. Dargestellt am Entwicklungsverwaltungsrecht der Weltbank und Vereinten Nationen.* Tübingen, Germany: Mohr Siebeck.

Rittich, Kerry. 2010. Governing by Measuring. The Millenium Development Goals in Global Governance. In: Ruiz Fabri, Hélène and Wolfrum, Rüdiger and Gogolin, Jana (eds). *Select proceedings of the European Society of International Law.* Vol. 2. Oxford: Hart. pp. 463–487.

Roberts, Anthea. 2017. *Is International Law International?* Oxford: Oxford University Press.

Robertson, Roland. 1995. Glocalization: Time-Space and Homogeneity-Heterogeneity. In: Featherstone, Mike and Lash, Scott and Robertson, Roland (eds). *Global Modernities.* London: SAGE. pp. 25–44.

Robinson, Jennifer. 2016. Comparison. In: Jayne, Mark und Ward, Kevin (eds). *Urban Theory. New Critical Perspectives.* London: Routledge. pp. 84–98.

Rodriguez, Daniel and Shoked, Nadav. 2016. Comparative Local Government Law in Motion. How Different Local Government Law Regimes Affect Global Cities' Bike Share Plans. *Fordham Urban Law Journal* 42(1), pp.123–191.

Sassen, Saskia. 1991. *The Global City.* Princeton, NJ: Princeton University Press.

Saul, Ben and Kinley, David and Mowbray, Jacqueline. 2014. *The International Covenant on Economic, Social and Cultural Rights. Commentary, Cases and Materials.* Oxford: Oxford University Press.

Saunders, Cheryl. 2009. Towards a Global Constitutional Gene Pool. *National Taiwan University Law Review,* 4(1), pp.1–38.

SFDI - Société française pour le droit international (ed). 2002. *Les collectivités territoriales non-étatiques dans le systeme juridique international.* Paris: Pedone.

Shah, Anwar (ed). 2007. *Participatory Budgeting.* Washington, D.C: World Bank.

Sihlongonyane, Mfaniseni. 2016. The Global, the Local and the Hybrid in the Making of Johannesburg as a World Class African City. *Third World Quarterly* 37(9), pp. 1607–1627.

Swyngedouw, Erik. 1997. Neither Global Nor Local: 'Glocalization' and the Politics of Scale. In: Cox, Kevin R. (ed): *Spaces of Globalization. Reasserting the Power of the Local*. New York: Guilford Press. pp. 137–166.

Tavares, Rodrigo. 2016. *Paradiplomacy. Cities and States as Global Players*. New York: Oxford University Press.

Therborn, Göran. 2017. *Cities of Power. The Urban, the National, the Popular, the Global*. London: Verso.

Van der Berg, Angela. 2019. The Pursuit of SDG 11 Through the Lens of Integrated Development Planning. In Aust, Helmut Philipp and du Plessis, Anél (eds). *The Globalisation of Urban Governance: Legal Perspectives on Sustainable Development Goal 11*. London: Routledge. pp. 208–226.

von Bogdandy, Armin and Goldmann, Matthias. 2008. The Exercise of International Public Authority Through National Policy Assessment. The OECD's PISA Policy as a Paradigm for a New International Standard Instrument. *International Organizations Law Review*, 5, 241–298.

Vormann, Boris. 2019. City Limits: Sustainable Urban Governance in Planetary Infrastructural Regimes. In Aust, Helmut Philipp and du Plessis, Anél (eds). *The Globalisation of Urban Governance: Legal Perspectives on Sustainable Development Goal 11*. London: Routledge. pp. 65–83.

Zacharias, Diana. 2010. Advancing International Institutional Law. The UNESCO Regime for the Protection of World Heritage as Prototype of an Autonomy-Gaining International Institution. In: von Bogdandy, Armin and Dann, Philip and Wolfrum, Rüdiger, Bernstorff, Jochen and Goldmann, Matthias (eds). *The Exercise of Public Authority by International Institutions*. Berlin: Springer. pp. 201–335.

Case Law

South Africa

Constitutional Court of South Africa (Moseneke, J.). 2009. Judgment (majority). Abahlali BaseMjondolo and Sibusiso Zikode v Premier of the Province of KwaZulu-Natal and Other, judgement of 14.10. 2009, Case CCT12/09, [2009] ZACC 31.

Documents

CESCR – Committee on Economic, Social and Cultural Rights. 1991. General Comment No. 4: The right to adequate housing. UN Doc. E/1992/23.

CESCR – Committee on Economic, Social and Cultural Rights. 1997. General Comment No. 7 Forced evictions. UN Doc. E/1998/22.

CESCR – Committee on Economic, Social and Cultural Rights. 2009. Concluding Observations - Brazil. UN Doc. E/C.12/BRA/CO/2.

UN-Habitat. 2015. *Informal Settlements. Habitat III Issue Paper*. Nairobi.

UN-Habitat; OHCHR. 2014. The right to adequate housing. New York, Geneva.

UN Human Rights Council. 2011a. Report of the Special Rapporteur on adequate housing as a component of the right to an adequate standard of living, and on the right to non-discrimination in this context, Raquel Rolnik. Preliminary note on the mission to the World Bank Group. A/HRC/16/42/Add.4.

UN Human Rights Council. 2011b. Report of the Special Rapporteur on the promotion and protection of the right to freedom of opinion and expression, Frank La Rue. A/HRC/17/27.

UN Human Rights Council. 2013. Report of the Special Rapporteur on adequate housing as a component of the right to an adequate standard of living, and on the right to non-discrimination in this context, Raquel Rolnik. Mission to the World Bank. A/HRC/22/46/Add3.

UN Human Rights Council. 2017. Universal Periodic Review - Compilation on Brazil - Report of the Office of the United Nations High Commissioner for Human Rights. A/HRC/WG.6/27/BRA/2, 24.10.2017.

UNDP. 2014. Environmental and Social Standard 5 - Displacement and Resettlement.

UNESCO (ed). 2006. *Urban Policies and the Right to the City.* Paris: UNESCO.

UNESCO. 2017. Report: Advisory mission to the World Heritage site of The Historic Centre of Florence, Italy.

UN Secretary-General. 2001. Road map towards the implementation of the United Nations Millennium Declaration. A/56/326.

World Bank. 2008. Brazil: Toward a More Inclusive and Effective Participatory Budget in Porto Alegre (Report No. 40144-BR).

World Bank. 2010. Loan Agreement (Rio de Janeiro Municipality Fiscal Consolidation for Efficiency and Growth Development Policy Loan / Projeto de Política de Desenvolvimento do Município do Rio de Janeiro) between Municipality of the city of Rio de Janeiro and International Bank for Recontruction and Development, Dated August 20, 2010, Loan Number 7942-BR.

World Bank. 2011. Memorandum of Understanding between IBRD, IDA, IFC and the C40 Cities Climate Leadership Group Ref. Collaboration on Emissions, 1 June 2011.

World Bank. 2012. *Bringing the State Back to the Favelas of Rio de Janeiro.* Washington DC.

World Bank. 2013. *Planning, Connecting and Financing Cities.* Washington DC.

World Bank. 2015. *Metropolitan Governance in Brazil.* Washington DC.

World Bank. 2016. Proposed Environmental and Social Standard 5: Land Acquisition, Restrictions on Land Use and Involuntary Resettlement [online]. Available at: http://documents.worldbank.org/curated/en/383011492423734099/pdf/114278-WP-REVISED-PUBLIC-Environmental-and-Social-Framework-Dec18-2017.pdf (Accessed: 8 March 2018).

World Bank IEG – Independent Evaluation Group. 2007. *The Cities Alliance.* Washington DC.

World Bank IEG – Independent Evaluation Group. 2014. *World Bank Group Support to Public-Private Partnerships.* Washington DC.

World Bank Inspection Panel. 2005. India - Mumbai Urban Transport Project Investigation Report 34725, 21.12.2005.

World Bank Inspection Panel. 2010. Cambodia: Land Management and Administration Project, Investigation Report 58016, 23.11.2010.

World Bank Legal Vice Presidency (LEGVP). 2014. Choice of an IBRD Borrower or an IDA Recipient. Law and Policy Digest. Washington DC.

World Bank and UN-Habitat. 1999. *Cities Alliance for Cities without Slums.* Washington DC.

4 City Limits

Sustainable Urban Governance in Planetary Infrastructural Regimes

Boris Vormann

The Prospect of Sustainable Development[1]

From Manhattan to Tokyo, from London to Hamburg, steel and glass structures dotting the edges of disused urban waterfronts, urban agricultural projects, and electric transportation options made possible by the sharing economy all give the impression of global progress, the beginnings of which are subtly making themselves known in other parts of the world as well. The hard labour and grime of the industrial age has all but disappeared in many cities in the Global North. Throughout the 1950s and 1960s, Bochum, Detroit, and Manchester were urban powerhouses of the Fordist industrial system. After the 1970s, they gradually became symbols of a failed industrial era, barren memorial landscapes. Meanwhile, they have become showcases of post-industrial rejuvenation and revitalisation. In the course of economic reconstruction in European and North American cities alike, the industrial age came to be seen as an undesired *intermezzo*, an outlier sandwiched between a sustainable pre-industrial and post-industrial time.[2]

As such, many now see sustainable and smart cities as a panacea for the challenges of globalisation. Proponents of this view suggest that the success of the post-industrial city can be replicated globally, thereby fostering social progress even in the most remote corners of the world. In the tradition of liberalism, cities are assigned a special role in this "civilizing" process. According to Edward Glaeser, a prominent supporter of this thesis, cities are incubators of scientific and cultural innovation. Through the innovative spirit prevailing in urban agglomerations, the necessary technologies and social mechanisms will arise and lead the way to an environment-friendly and democratic future. If globalisation is to become more sustainable, more democratic and more inclusive, then it will happen in urban space through the triumph of the city (Glaeser 2011).

City rankings, which have become an omnipresent tool in urban debates, supposedly reveal truths about the sustainability, smartness, and other potential advantages of any particular city. These rankings suggest that cities have an endless potential to become ever more sustainable, and that through some manner of a trickle-down effect one city after another can climb to the summit of the sustainability pyramid "greening" the planet to a new splendour. The cultural practice of city rankings represents the principal problem of this urban globalisation debate. Such rankings completely ignore the many, highly-uneven relationships of interdependency among cities. Cities are not self-sufficient. When one city becomes more sustainable, unsustainable practices (the extraction of resources, production, distribution, etc.) are often simply shifted out of view to other places. The utopian visions of the urban age that dominate contemporary discourses on social development do not tell the full story. By liberating the city from larger social contexts, such narratives reproduce the myth of globalisation as an aspatial and apolitical process.

The idea of the post-industrial city as a place of progress that will gradually spread to all the corners of the world represents a false necessity. Highly visible representational urban spaces conceal the processes that made these seemingly sustainable and smart versions of urbanisation possible in the first place. By no means did the industrial era suddenly come to an end after the 1970s. The rise of London, Frankfurt, and New York to financial metropolises was not an indication of a sudden and full departure from production, as it so often seems. Rather, this post-industrial urban era is a spatial fiction. The global cities and smart cities are more or less sustainable islands in the middle of a globally reconstructed economy, one that is much less sustainable than the High Lines and the Elbphilharmonies of the transatlantic world would have us believe.

In turn, the hopes placed in cities of the Global South as pioneers of social development ring just as hollow. To be sure, it would be cynical not to appreciate that international institutions such as the United Nations (UN) have begun to include urban questions on their agenda. There is no doubt that the Sustainable Development Goals' (SDGs)' focus on inclusiveness and safety, on resilience and sustainability in cities is generally desirable. Who would oppose these aims? Unfortunately, they are not just ambiguous and underdefined – even though they are that – more importantly, these agendas misrepresent the problem. These cities of the Global South, just like their counterparts in the North Atlantic world, are imagined as individual units, severed from the complex networks of flows and political interrelations of which they are an integral part and on which they depend.

This fetish of the urban era also leads to an impoverished understanding of patterns of state intervention. Without such an understanding, actually attaining more sustainable development in any of these contexts is less than likely. In fact, such a truncated vision of cities could even distract from the actual problems that would need to be addressed. Global metropolitan regions are part of global networks of production. This means that post-industrial cities are not the harbingers of a better, more sustainable, urban future. These cities are standing on stilts. They are dependent on things that do not happen within their borders. That is why an analytical understanding of spatial processes is so crucial. If we shift our view away from the representative spaces of globalisation and toward its infrastructures, the role of politics and the state that otherwise seem only to occupy a passive position at the edges of market forces, become more essential.

State Politics of Circulation: Governing Infrastructural Regimes

From a methodological standpoint then, the infrastructures of metropolitan areas and global city-regions can serve as an analytical prism enabling a better understanding of the politics of globalisation and the interplay among different levels of government. These physical coordination systems form the backbone of global trade and inter-city exchange networks. They offer a heuristic device that can help us systematically chart state action, and to conceptualise the meaning of space for the politics of globalisation.[3] If one moves state infrastructural regimes to the fore of the analysis, as this chapter sets out to do, it becomes necessary to confront questions of social justice. Who governs? Whom does urbanisation benefit and whom does it harm? Just how democratic are such processes of integration? And finally: how sustainable are these processes really?

From such a perspective, the parameters of sustainability can be revisited. Crucially, the wider socio-scientific field needs to rethink the relationship between globalisation and urbanisation in order to develop a more meaningful concept of sustainability; that is, one that takes into consideration urbanisation processes beyond the city limits. In this chapter I demonstrate how such a re-conceptualisation can occur. How does the state, on different levels of government, influence the development of global cities and urban regions, and thereby of sustainability itself? I use the US context as a case in point to delineate patterns of state intervention, because it is both the most important and the most unlikely context for such an analysis. It is *important*, because the US is still the hegemonic power in global economic and political relations. Its influence on the organisation of trade networks has cascading effects elsewhere. Its example provides us with a typology of functions states have to fulfill in order to make networks of exchange possible. At the same time, the US is an *unlikely* example because it is generally regarded as an exceptional nation where the state is particularly reticent and politically negligible in market affairs.[4] As we will see, even in this supposedly unique context the state is pivotal in creating globalisation processes. Obviously, what holds true there, in the most liberal of all market economies, should equally apply in more state-centric systems around the globe.

As the following analysis shows, state action encompasses a series of functions that seem to be more universally necessary for market economies to be able to engage in trade relations. These state politics of circulation encompass elements of market creation, stabilisation, and guarantee. Within this ideal type, for the transatlantic context, we can historically differentiate between imperial, Keynesian-Fordist, and planetary infrastructural regimes, in which the state fulfils these duties in different yet essential ways. All in all, we can observe an historic shift to indirect forms of intervention, which, in many cases, renders the state invisible, while its role as creator, stabiliser, and guarantor of the market continues. State action in the geographical South seems to mirror and complement this northern trajectory, even if not in fully symmetrical terms. On a planetary scale, these multilevel state actors interrelate in networks of uneven economic development that in turn shape different functional requirements on the part of these individual political systems.

From these empirical observations, theoretical implications for urban and globalisation research on sustainability can be deduced, which in turn also have practical consequences for the functioning of state politics and democracy in the context of global dependencies. Since urbanisation is a process performed through global networks, current methodological approaches such as global city rankings and individual city analyses need to be scrutinised and reworked on a theoretical level. This holds true for the SDGs as well. What does it mean to render cities more resilient, inclusive, and safe, when one takes processes beyond the city's edges into account? And who are the political subjects responsible for and capable of creating more sustainable urbanisation processes? Since sustainable cities are not coequal with sustainable urbanisation, sustainable urban governance needs coordination at higher echelons than that of local governments. If municipal actors do not wish to be pitted against one another, in the battle for resources and capital – a competition which is ultimately unsustainable – then networks of urban actors need to find common ground and should connect more closely on an institutional level.

Contours of the Invisible State

Globalisation, understood as the increasing mobility of various actors and factors, is neither exclusively the result nor the sole cause of urbanisation. Both processes are, however, deeply interrelated. The increased mobility of people, capital, and goods necessitates a suitable spatial infrastructure – airports, highways, server farms, etc. (Graham 2001; Harvey 2001) – that for various reasons often materialises in and between the metropolitan nodes of globalisation. Without that corresponding spatially-fixed infrastructure, global flows would be unthinkable. And inversely, for reasons that are still to be clarified, cities seem to be increasingly dependent on global networks. The global city and the inter-urban networks in which it operates are thus the counterparts of global circulation, as research on urbanisation has emphasised for a long time (Friedman 1986; Sassen 1991; Taylor 2004).

That urbanisation consists of a set of processes that clearly extend beyond the city proper is a claim with considerable theoretical and empirical implications, aptly discussed in the literature on "planetary urbanisation" (Brenner 2013; Brenner and Schmid 2015), the "global-urban imagination" (Madden 2012) and "methodological city-ism" (Angelo and Wachsmuth 2014).[5] What is important for the purpose of this chapter is that from this perspective urban sustainability means more than what the term usually denotes. As Hillary Angelo, David Wachsmuth and Daniel Aldana Cohen contend, the "social, economic and ecological issues behind sustainability problems are regional or global in scale," while "urban policy usually addresses single ecological issues in individual neighbourhoods." As such, they argue, "sustainability research and policymaking should shift focus from city centres to urban regions and global networks of production, consumption and distribution" (Angelo et al. 2016, p. 391). This in turn means that sustainable urban governance needs to be understood as something that involves other levels of government.

If urbanisation extends to the planetary scale, however, how are the global flows that intersect in the world's leading city-regions actually articulated? How could they take a more sustainable form? Sustainable urbanisation necessitates sustainable globalisation. This seems to leave us with an oxymoron, because globalisation is often viewed as a set of external processes that undercuts and disintegrates state action. How can such processes be governed? Or even sustainably governed? In response, this chapter claims that multilevel state intervention is essential for globalisation and urbanisation processes to happen. This argument is also the basis for a reassessment of urban sustainability.

A Typology of State Functions

Which are the precise state functions that render free markets possible in the first place? First, global markets are never wholly free from state intervention. The assumption that they could be is a misconception. The idea of a "free market" is fundamentally an over-simplification. At the very least, the state is required to protect property rights and to ensure contract compliance, as well as to ensure law and order, and a stable currency. On this point proto-liberal state theorists such as Thomas Hobbes and John Locke were unanimous: without institutional stability and security there can be no property and no accumulation, and with that, no globalisation. However, beyond these very basic functions the state undertakes other tasks without which globalisation would be impossible. Even Adam Smith, the classic theorist of liberal political economy, oft quoted for his idea of a self-regulating market, wrote an entire book in his *Inquiry into the Nature and Causes of the Wealth of Nations* on the role of the state in the creation of markets. In it (Book V) he also anticipates the contemporary debate on market failure by stressing the necessity of state intervention in matters of national defence, the construction of infrastructure, and education.

Beyond these basic state capacities, governments do much more for globalisation processes to be possible. The state first determines the parameters for *market creation*, which include legal and technological norms for trading in expanding market networks.[6] This encompasses among other things the financing of telecommunication and transportation infrastructure projects in order to lower transaction costs. Beyond the basic material functions, trade is also facilitated through supranational agreements that set standards for bilateral exchange to which international investment treaties and the infamous courts of arbitration also belong. Moreover, states create markets by ensuring that certain health and labour standards are in place, by educating and housing the work force, and by improving the business environment (eg through accelerated permitting, advantageous public-private partnerships, etc.). Finally, market creation also implies the exploration (and exploitation) of foreign markets – through investments, exports, and other forms of exchange – as well as the stabilisation of demand at home through redistribution, cheap credit, or other forms of intervention.

In addition to guaranteeing the fundamental framework, another major purpose of the state is as a *stabiliser* of global trade relations. When we think of the global trade of goods, this includes first and foremost the maintenance and development of geographically strategic, critical infrastructure. The repair of such infrastructures over long periods of time is often neglected; however, it is of major significance to the budgets of different levels of government. Research and development in telecommunications and transportation technology are equally investments that allow for long-term competitive advantage but that are often ignored as crucial state work. Moreover, the state fulfills its stabilising function in that it mitigates globalisation's negative system effects, ensures the macroeconomic calibration of its national currency, and encourages diplomacy and other forms of durable interstate relationships.[7]

Third, the state has a *guarantor function* in the case of a (possible) disruption. Preserving circulation is one of the most important aspects of state policy. This includes interventions in crisis situations such as financial bailouts as well as less invasive, preventative measures to ensure uninterrupted trade. Friction in circulation networks is tied to high economic costs, since the global division of labour in "just-in-time" networks is dependent upon the unimpeded flow of goods (Rodrigue 2013). These circuits must be protected from disruptive factors, as much against terrorists and pirates as smugglers and thieves. As such, risk management in the supply chain has become a field of study and a lucrative business strategy (Sheffi 2005). For states, maintaining security is therefore a very high priority. This dimension of state intervention has gained greater meaning following the terrorist attacks on September 11, 2001, and in the name of system optimisation has in the meantime expanded to include other potential disruptions of circulation such as labour strikes, demonstrations, and the blockade of critical infrastructure (Cowen 2014; Vormann 2015).

If the state engages in these central functions of global trade and production, what role is then played by the municipal level? That depends on the geographical and historical context. Since the nineteenth century North Atlantic states have performed these three types of state intervention in various forms and with very different emphases. Over the course of time the intrastate division of labour has shifted between different levels of government. Focusing on the historical development of these state intervention patterns gives us a better understanding of the changing roles of urban and regional nodes in the global economy and in global politics. In relation to the back-story of these permutations, it becomes clear that urban space has not disintegrated, but rather has gained geopolitical importance. While states might, at first glance, appear to have lost significance on the national level, they remain nonetheless of crucial consequence for globalisation.

To attain a richer and politically viable understanding of sustainable development, debates on urban governance will have to factor these multi-scalar dynamics into any plausible proposal for policy reform. Yet, while state functions are relatively clear in theory, in practice, they are shape-shifting and come in different forms. A look at history can help develop a conceptual vocabulary to come to terms with these changing governance arrangements over time and allow pivotal strategic insights at a historical moment that might turn out to constitute a fundamental shift in state politics of circulation and globalisation patterns.

Periodising Intervention Patterns

So far, I have argued that global flows require an appropriate apparatus consisting of both technological infrastructures and political institutions, an apparatus which historically only states have been able to provide. Nonetheless, the constellations change from context to context. The various scales of geopolitical engagement (local, subnational/regional, national, and supranational) interact with varying degrees of importance, and in fluid relation to one another. The spatial regimes of infrastructure are thus based on a continuously shifting interplay among state institutions. Neil Brenner refers to a so-called "scalar fix" to describe such an organisation of different levels of government and geopolitical action horizons (Brenner 2004). This concept presupposes a *longue-durée* periodisation – an idea that is often deployed in critical geography and political economy, and was refined by the work of the Regulation School – that is also helpful in the illustration of infrastructural regimes explored here.

The American case, which will be analysed below, is particularly well-suited to illustrate these infrastructural regimes. As the liberal market economy *par excellence,* where state intervention appears fundamentally less important than elsewhere, the American example is where one would least suspect the state playing a significant role in globalisation. If systemic patterns of intervention can be isolated there, then they should be evident in the European context, where states have always engaged in more direct monitoring and controlling of the market, as well as in other political contexts that have over time been integrated into the global circuits of trade and exchange.

The transition from a Keynesian moment in North Atlantic nation states, in which a Fordist compromise made national accumulation possible, to a post-Fordist "relativisation of scales" stands above all else in the foreground of any such historical periodisation (Jessop 2000). This relativisation has been characterised by the new influence of subnational, especially city-regional, actors, as well as of supranational institutions and coalitions of interest, to which we will return later. For now, the decisive point is that congruence exists among specific, historically-distinct politics of space and the corresponding restructuring of a given infrastructural regime.[8] Within these spatio-political arrangements, different levels of government have different tasks.

Seen from a historical perspective, the Keynesian shift has been one from a redistributive, spatially-equalising set of policies with strong co-operation among the different scales of government and political spaces to a new arrangement in which municipal, regional, and national levels compete against one another. During this process a similar privatisation of public goods and deregulation of trade relations and markets took hold on both sides of the Atlantic, albeit with divergent emphases and despite inherent institutional path dependencies and political-cultural differences.

Because of the important role of regulationist influences on the debates surrounding state theory, Fordism and its failures are often of central interest in these theoretical debates. To understand the infrastructures of global trade networks and the role of city-regional players in globalisation, however, one must also consider the period before the Great Depression. This is when the US and other North Atlantic states built the capital-intensive groundworks of globalisation. In sum, we can therefore isolate three concrete North Atlantic infrastructural regimes: (1) The imperial regime (from roughly the 1870s to the Great Depression); (2) the Fordist regime (from the 1930s New Deal Era to the 1970s); and (3) the planetary regime (since the mid-1970s). I will use the remainder of this chapter to explore these regimes from the perspective of changing intra-governmental relations in order to conclude on what this multilevel dimension implies for sustainable urban governance.

The Imperial Infrastructural Regime

The imperial regime, spanning the latter third of the nineteenth and the first two decades of the twentieth century, was crucial for the rise of modern globalisation and urbanisation, as states erected the fundamental infrastructure of transport mobility and communication networks during this period. Government interventions were very direct, and as such, more immediate in market creation and market stabilisation: the construction of canals, the laying of transatlantic telegraphic cables, the expansion of the rail network at a transcontinental level, the creation of new regulatory agreements on interstate trade at the sub-national level, to name a few examples. The US government also engaged in market-protective interventions by providing military support for westward expansion and continental integration, as well as by interceding after the repeated financial crises of the late nineteenth century. Only with the consolidation of these physical and institutional infrastructures did a modern central state begin to emerge in the US (Skowronek 1982).

Within the context of the so-called *dual federalism* model, municipalities in the US were subsumed as individual corporate entities within their states. Political action at the local level was nonetheless assigned an important role, as a hub for the organisation and consolidation of the continental land grab.[9] As early as the late eighteenth and early nineteenth centuries New York City and its mercantile elites had become an indispensable node for the conquest of the continent, competing with other East Coast cities such as Philadelphia, Baltimore and Boston for the resources of the Appalachian hinterland (Abu-Lughod 1999). In the course of industrialisation, these cities developed into the powerhouses and industrial hubs of the US economy. The US Civil War (1861–1865) and Reconstruction stimulated the economy and led to a boom for cities in the Midwest. As the link between East Coast financiers and the Western expansion, Chicago became the heartbeat of the new American industrial economy.

Government coordination efforts, especially at the national level, were equally crucial for the development and expansion of modern transportation and communications networks, since what was generally true for market players also applied to the cities on the US frontier: the competition between city elites (sometimes referred to as *boosterism*) would have made the efficiency of nineteenth century national trade networks impossible. The self-interest vested in small towns on the frontier would have clashed too spectacularly to allow for a coherent national economy to emerge. Here, it cannot be emphasised enough that this early historical moment of globalisation, profoundly marked by land grabs and the subsequent subdivision and exploitation of space, was indeed such a spatial process that any analytical distinction from the political process would be nonsensical. Only through the construction of a continental national economy was the central state in its modern form created in the first place.

To put it more succinctly, globalisation did not make states disappear, but sparked their emergence, even in the exceptional, deeply market-oriented US. Also decisive for this development were the extraterritorial nodes of global trade which the imperial state erected locally. The clearest example is certainly the construction of the Panama Canal, which efficiently connected West Coast trade with transatlantic shipping. But the annexation of geo-strategically important islands in the Pacific was also critical for the rise of the US economy, since coal-powered ships required refuelling stations in order to cover long distances.[10] Opening the Chinese market, a key component of US foreign trade policy at the turn of the nineteenth century, thus meant the expansion of American geopolitical networks. As such, the promotion of globalisation was essential in establishing the US as a world power from the outset and *vice versa*.

The Fordist Infrastructural Regime

The Great Depression marked the end of the imperial regime in the US. Dual federalism had been an arrangement that required coordination between the federal state and the individual states of the union. *Cooperative federalism*, in turn, was to become the context in which towns and cities truly became political actors. With the increase in the number of global transactions, which was fundamental to the transition to the Fordist-Keynesian regime, the municipal level developed into a geopolitical pivot. Growing urban problems led to the restructuring of relations among the various levels of government after the New Deal in the 1930s, the most important result of which was the establishment of direct relations between the federal and local governments. In the wake of the Great Depression, and in the face of high unemployment and other social problems triggered by the crisis, none of which individual state governments had managed to get under control, this immediate connection allowed for the circumvention of the cumbersome intermediary of the (subnational) states in the implementation of counter-cyclical political measures. Direct relations between federal and municipal levels were made possible above all by a reciprocal dependence. Just as cities needed financial support from the federal government, so too did the federal government need municipal administrations to efficiently implement the emergency programmes of the New Deal. The individual states on their part agreed to the restructuring of the existing federalist model, since they profited from greater rights to oversee local governments in the implementation of federal education, health, and welfare programmes.

In the US, just as in Europe, the state was expected to redistribute the fruits of the economic boom after the New Deal, to encourage mobility, and to create full employment (Blyth and Matthijs 2017). Local actors have played a central role in the cooperative federalism of the US in several respects: in the provision of public goods in the context of the redistributive welfare and interventionist policies, in the implementation of large-scale infrastructure projects such as the highway system, and in the modernisation and expansion of logistics hubs. Overall, the federal government's compensatory national spatial policy, implemented through cross-financing and the special promotion of individual cities and regions, reflected the redistributive ideal of social citizenship and state duty-of-care – even if it never lived up to its promises for all.

In this regime the building blocks for a planetary restructuring of production were first put into place. These conditions of possibility were brought about not only by the Bretton Woods institutions, which fashioned a global trade architecture, but also through infrastructure construction, such as the Cam Ranh Bay's logistic hub (built during the Vietnam War), and domestically through the establishment of new container ports in the growing global cities of New York City and Los Angeles. Investments in research and development, as well as a militaristically and economically competitive infrastructure, were essential in maintaining a coordinated economy that combined mass consumption and mass production (Mazzucato 2015). Nonetheless, this emerging infrastructure also provided the starting point for the emergence of the global manufacturing networks that undermined the Fordist compromise between capital, labour and the state.

The Planetary Infrastructure Regime

After the crises of the 1970s and under the auspices of devolution, the federal government began to delegate greater responsibilities to local governments, often without commensurate federal funding. This generated a litany of unfunded mandates. Within the so-called *new federalism* of the Reagan era, federal intervention was increasingly pushed into the background. Local governments became entrepreneurial actors themselves, who through various measures attempted to lure global flows into their cities through tax incentives, infrastructure, and market-friendly conditions, all in the hope of increasing tax revenues and attaining privileged access to global circulation (Harvey 1989; Keil and Mahon 2009). A new balance was found between the shifting geopolitical scales, in which municipal and city-regional institutions as well as private actors gained greater influence, but in which nation states continued to play a decisive, albeit changed role.

Despite the dominant view, represented in countless policy reports and planning debates, that states are simply passive subordinates and dependents, there is sufficient opportunity for political action, even for competitive states and cities. In many ways the American tradition of urban boosterism was continued under conditions of fiscal austerity, fashioning an urban policy that abandoned its welfare mandate to seek the salvation of the city in economic growth. The main task of the "entrepreneurial city" (Harvey 1989), which had to increasingly focus on appealing to new global investors, large enterprises, and tourism flows, became the creation of a business-friendly environment through tax incentives, for example, and an attractive and secure living environment for the new elites of the service economy. On the municipal level, functions and responsibilities were often transferred to quasi-public, frequently appointed, non-elected officials. Supporters of this shift often highlight the benefits of public authorities or public-private partnerships (PPPs) as if the state were only a junior partner. In fact, bonds and other government-guaranteed financial instruments more often than not were precisely the reason that such investments were made profitable in the first place.[11] Mitigating risk, and in a crisis shouldering it entirely, has become a major task of state intervention, thereby erasing the state from public perception but by no means absolving it from responsibility.

Market-friendly government policies, risk strategies, and tax incentives for investors at the municipal level are not the only reasons why it would be wrong to write off the state as a political actor. It is true that state interventions may no longer be instantly decipherable, not least because of the overemphasis in public discourse on the importance of self-regulating markets and technological innovation that obscures the role of the political. And undoubtedly, the immediately interventionist state of the Fordist-Keynesian post-war era no longer exists. Since the crises of the 1970s, however, a state that follows the dictates of austerity policy and inflation stability – functions that safeguard and guarantee the world economy above all else – has taken its place, creating highly flexible labour markets and demand through cheap credit to keep global trade circuits flowing.

Despite the funeral speeches of the 1990s, the nation-state also remains the decisive actor in global bodies. The Bretton Woods institutions – the IMF, the World Bank, and the WTO (successor to the GATT) – may have played important roles in expanding markets globally, but their work is still carried out in close coordination with nation states. In global institutions such as UN-Habitat or the G20 summits they are the *only* key players. With a view to ensuring globalisation processes, supranational coordination since the 1980s has expanded to include, in particular, the negotiation of free trade agreements and the fixing of the legal operations of international transactions. Given resurgent neo-mercantilist tendencies, this type of state work has become more and more visible and increasingly an apple of discord in public debates.

An equally important area of active state work is that of securing global transport and communication networks, through both the maintenance and development of infrastructure (harbours, satellites, fibre-optic cables, etc.), and by means of the military defence of trade and exchange routes (Ritter et al. 2007; Bogatu 2008). In addition to the facilitation and guarantee of global economic networks, non-regulation is another central part of nation-state action. Included here are the lack of state sanctions on nitrogen oxides and heavy crude oil, which keeps transport costs artificially low in the shipping industry and is essential for global trade, but causes colossal environmental damage paid by others elsewhere. Similarly, environmentally and socially destructive resource extraction and production in the Global

South must be counted as further state-enabled externalisation processes (Vormann 2015).

Massive cost shifting unlocks opportunities for economic arbitrage, which in turn makes economic globalisation profitable for businesses in the first place. Such cost shifting is tolerated and sometimes even encouraged by nation states. In short, in considering the urban age and its conjoined hopes for sustainable globalisation, the flows and networks that overdetermine the urban are by no means as arbitrary and external as they may seem. Space remains crucial in globalisation. It is a question of transaction costs, effective communication, and cheap transportation over long distances – functions provided by the state, not by the market. Beyond that, we must consider the market-creating subsidisation of global trading through tax breaks, investments in research and development, and labour market-friendly social and educational policy to arrive at a fuller understanding of patterns of state interventions.[12]

Variations of the Invisible State

The orientation towards global markets and trade that has taken place since the 1970s has resulted in a sort of tunnel effect in the global cities of Europe and North America (Graham 2001). In the course of restructuring, cities on both sides of the Atlantic realigned their institutions and infrastructures in order to more easily tap into strategic global flows. Through this reorientation, the politics of metropolitan regions gained space and government intervention gained importance. We have not seen the dissolution of the nation state, but instead the constitution of a new kind of state which within its various levels of government ensures the basic functions of globalisation. To this end actors have been reimagined as new entrepreneurial entities that are brought into interurban and interregional competition. Unlike the imperial or Fordist states' directly funded initiatives, today the state has withdrawn its support to a much less visible role, usually by way of state guarantees, subventions, and risk assumption. As such, it no longer operates with the mechanisms of accountability and legitimacy it had in earlier eras.

We have developed our understanding of state functions in the North Atlantic context. There are of course variations between countries in this regard, much as there are differences in the degree of state intervention in national contexts elsewhere. A state's involvement depends on the embeddedness of a given economy in global circulation processes, on institutional path dependencies, on resource endowments and cultural legacies, and on power relationships within and between states. For instance, China has pursued these state politics of circulation with much more vigour, through heavy investments in large-scale infrastructure, the facilitation of Special Economic Zones (SEZs) and subsidies of export-led industries (Douglass 2001; Turok 2014) than, say, its landlocked northern neighbour Mongolia. In many ways, Chinese policies of "steering" (Chen

2014) growth to the coastal cities on its eastern seaboard since the late 1970s has constituted a much accelerated version of what European nation states and the US accomplished over the course of two centuries under very different historical and technological circumstances: the establishment of viable infrastructural regimes. Meanwhile, the externalities of this project for rural *and* urban populations have been enormous.

For its part, the case of urbanisation on the African continent allows us an insightful glimpse into the indispensable dependence of the private sector on state work. Echoing numerous sanguine reports on urbanisation in Africa from the World Bank and other private sector institutions (see Pieterse and Parnell 2014, p. 14), the McKinsey Global Institute praises the young and cheap labour force, the untouched resources, and its rapidly expanding consumer markets (McKinsey Global Institute 2016). But it does something that might come as a surprise to students of transatlantic state-market relations: it tells state actors not to *step back* – not to let the free market rule – but to *step up* and procure what is necessary for economic globalisation to function.

As such, McKinsey's list encompasses private sector recommendations unheard of in the North, suggesting to African governments that they should "strengthen public-sector capabilities, [...] increase housing for 190 million new urbanites by 2025, [...] ensure healthy urbanisation, [...] create tomorrow's new talent, [...] increase tax collection [and] accelerate infrastructure development" (McKinsey Global Instute 2016, p. 104). In short, McKinsey and other consulting firms, are suggesting to African governments that they should become more active facilitators and guarantors of the market. They should create the conditions for markets and globalisation to become possible.

At this point, this should come as less of a surprise. The ideal-typical functions of creating, stabilising and guaranteeing market exchange might vary in degree, but ultimately need to be met in one way or another. In order for states to materially engage in global trade, a minimum of physical and institutional infrastructures needs to be in place. States might fulfill these tasks in ways that are sometimes more, sometimes less visible. They might strike particular intra-governmental balances and enter into more complex, semi-private set-ups, but they cannot get around meeting these basic requirements. This insight leaves us with two final questions. First, how can sustainability debates be upscaled to map onto the realities of planetary infrastructural regimes? And second, how can active state actors use their political agency on various scales to attain more environmentally sustainable development patterns?

Globalising urban sustainability

While in recent years many scholars and policy-makers have begun to speak of the rise of the urban century and sustainable, smart cities have entered this debate as a global *Leitbild* for a more democratic and environmentally sustainable globalisation, this discourse reduces political action to a matter of mere detail. Such optimistic thinking about the city as the saviour of globalisation grants a meaningful role to technological change and private initiatives, whereas state action is downgraded to procedural "governance" strategies, or is dismissed entirely. Similarly, cities appear as entities completely detached from one another, wherein sustainability and democracy can be achieved wholly independent from outside factors. This narrative of the uncoupled city is a counterpart to the discourse of globalisation as an aspatial process. It distorts our understanding of urban sustainability to a degree where the concept seems almost devoid of meaning.

As we have seen, states engage in historically specific manifestations of market creation, stabilisation, and guarantee in order to facilitate processes of globalisation. Through a division of labour across various levels of government they enable the formation of infrastructural regimes. For actors at the local level, the linchpin of globalisation, this cooperation means that their futures also depend on political actors outside of local government. An examination of the infrastructures of globalisation reveals not only the various dimensions of cost displacement but also the fact that the state has in no way become obsolete. Quite the opposite: state spatial politics are fundamentally important for the processes of globalisation, even if they have become more complex and less visible.

This has a series of implications. On a theoretical level, urbanisation can no longer be analysed on a case-by-case basis. Instead, it must be newly conceptualised as a series of interurban and transnational interconnected processes. This, in turn, also means that sustainable cities and smart cities, which have been imbued with all of the hope of the "urban age", cannot be viewed independently from context. A sustainable city can be understood as such only when the network on which it depends also fulfils the necessary criteria. A focus on the structuring of spaces of globalisation and the participation of state actors also reveals their relative responsibilities. From this perspective, processes that could otherwise seem technical and technocratic no longer appear to be directed by outside forces or to have no alternatives. Following this logic, municipalities can regain direct political influence through a politics of space. They should engage in new inter-governmental alliances to prevent spatial arbitrage.

What exactly does this imply? Production processes are and remain spatial. The possibility of offshoring rests on economic locational factors, but also on the character and type of work itself. Not all tasks can be easily shifted to other places. Flows that we associate with globalisation are often bound to their locations: tourists and business people; markets controlled by traders in Frankfurt, Chicago, or London, dependent on local infrastructure. Even the transfer of ideas (the most intangible of all possible flows) has a particular infrastructure. When global urban regions simply compete with one another over these flows, then the governing principle remains *divide et impera*: divide and conquer! Attracting the most tourists, goods, and capital becomes a zero-sum game between subnational actors. This dependence on flows, however, also has emancipatory potential. The liberal democracies of the nineteenth century grew and evolved at the nodes of such networks (Mitchell 2011). It is not without reason that protest movements in the recent past have blockaded critical infrastructure like the Oakland harbour during Occupy Wall Street or the spaces of logistics in Hamburg during the G20 protests. Space is still political, and social movements are awakening us to this fact.

What is more: Infrastructure is expensive. It creates path dependencies for societal and economic development; and, as we have seen, without it, globalisation is impossible. This means that cities also have a certain, heretofore-unused bargaining power that can be leveraged in inter-governmental negotiations, especially in federal contexts. This is particularly the case when more cities and urban regions organise themselves in clusters of solidarity. This method of domestic organisation seems increasingly to be a viable tool, as the most recent tendencies of renationalisation and renunciation of globalisation change the role of subnational entities. This phenomenon is especially visible in the US, where cities are currently declaring themselves sanctuary cities, places of protection for immigrants threatened by federal deportation, and where cities are forming subnational alliances aimed at fighting and protecting themselves against climate change.

These emerging political entities are as yet still institutionally weak. Whether we are standing at the beginning of a new infrastructural regime, in which the scale of politics and spatial-political horizons of trade are pushed even further, and whether such subnational structures solidify or not, is a question to which we currently have no answer. And yet: Over the course of the last century the importance of metropolitan regions and their policies has steadily increased. The scope of influence of such subnational, city-regional actors seems to be consolidating in the twenty-first century. We cannot dismiss the possibility that such metropolitan regions could become even more important in the foreseeable future, especially considering the extent of existing interdependencies and the thrusts of urbanisation. Fundamental questions of politics and societal behaviour in such an emergent context will also have to be considered anew. The idea of the end of geography has never been an accurate description of a possible state of affairs, but always an ultimately unattainable normative aspiration. As citizens grapple with the future of democracy, rediscovering the spaces and politics of globalisation will be essential to rejuvenate its utopian promises.

Notes

1 The author would like to thank Emily Bereskin for her extraordinary support in crafting this manuscript. He is also grateful to the participants of the course *Statecraft in the New Global Order* at Bard College Berlin for their questions

throughout the 2017 Fall term and their comments on an earlier version of this manuscript.

2 I develop this argument more fully elsewhere (Vormann 2015). For an analysis of different urban contexts in both the Global North and Global South see Vormann and DeDauw (2018).

3 This article takes its methodological cues from a recent turn towards infrastructures in the social sciences. For more meta-theoretical treatments of this matter see Calhoun et al., 2013; Angelo and Hentschel, 2015;, Burchardt and Hoehne, 2015; Klinenberg, 2018; and Van Heur, 2018. Moreover, some authors have begun to critically engage with logistics and trans-border infrastructure in particular, eg Shapira, 2013; Cowen, 2014; Wachsmuth, 2017; and Danyluk, 2017.

4 This distinction is generally made in the literature on the *Varieties of Capitalism* (VoC). See Hall and Soskice 2001. The myth of American exceptionalism has accompanied the nineteenth century state-building process of the US and finds a voice throughout the twentieth century in the work of influential authors such as Louis Hartz and Seymour Martin Lipset. For a comparative analysis of the nation-building process and critiques of exceptionalist research paradigms see Vormann, 2012, 2014, 2018.

5 Also see the edited collection by Neil Brenner, 2014 which assembles some of the most important essays in the field.

6 The legal implications of how global cities act in the international realm are discussed by Helmut Aust, 2017.

7 On the negative externalities of global trade see Vormann, 2015 and the edited volume by Monios and Wilmsmeier, 2018.

8 The idea of the "scalar fix" is derived from David Harvey's concept of the "spatial fix" (Harvey 2001, for an overview). Moreover, see Keil and Mahon, 2009; Wachsmuth, 2017; Keil, 2018; for analyses of geopolitical restructuring at the city-regional scale.

9 For the classical analysis of the US central state's consolidation see Skowronek 1982.

10 See McCormick, 1990.

11 On public authorities in the US context see Sbragia, 1996.

12 For details see Vormann, 2015. Levy et al. 2015 offer a helpful overview of the literature on state persistence.

Bibliography

Literature

Abu-Lughod, Janet L. 1999. *New York, Chicago, Los Angeles: America's Global Cities.* Minneapolis, MN: Minnesota University Press.

Angelo, Hillary, Cohen, Daniel A. and Wachsmuth, David. 2016. Expand the frontiers of urban sustainability: Social equity and global impacts are missing from measures of cities' environments friendliness. *Nature*, 536 (7618), 391–393.

Angelo, Hillary and Hentschel Christine. 2015. Interactions with infrastructure as windows into social worlds. A method for critical urban studies. *CITY*, 19(2–3), 306–312.

Angelo, Hillary and Wachsmuth, David. 2014. Urbanizing urban political ecology: A critique of methodological cityism. *International Journal of Urban and Regional Research* 39(1), 16–27.

Aust, Helmut Philipp. 2017. *Das Recht der globalen Stadt - Grenzüberschreitende Dimensionen kommunaler Selbstverwaltung*. Tübingen: Mohr Siebeck.

Blyth, Mark and Matthijs, Matthias. 2017. Black swans, lame ducks, and the mystery of IPE's missing macroeconomy. *Review of International Political Economy*, 24(2), 203–231.

Bogatu, Christian. 2008. *Smartcontainer als Antwort auf logistische und sicherheitsrelevante Herausforderungen in der Lieferkette*. Berlin: Universitätsverlag der TU Berlin.

Brenner, Neil. 2004. *New State Spaces. Urban Governance and the Rescaling of Statehood*. Oxford: Oxford University Press.

Brenner, Neil. 2013. Theses on urbanization. *Public Culture*, 25(1), 85–114.

Brenner, Neil (ed.). 2014. *Implosions/Explosions. Towards a Study of Planetary Urbanisation*. Berlin: Jovis.

Brenner, Neil and Schmid, Christian. 2015. Towards a new epistemology of the urban? *CITY*, 19(2–3), 151–182.

Burchardt, Marian and Höhne, Stefan. 2015. The infrastructures of diversity: Materiality and culture in urban space – an introduction. *New Diversities*, 17(2), 1–13.

Calhoun, Craig and Sennett, Richard and Shapira, Harel. 2013. Infrastructures of the urban. *Public Culture*, 25(2).

Chen, Xiangming. 2014. Steering, Speeding, Scaling: China's Model of Urban Growth and its Implications for Cities in the Global South. In: Parnell, Susan and Oldfield, Sophie (eds). *The Routledge Handbook on Cities of the Global South*. New York: Routledge. pp. 155–172.

Cowen, Deborah. 2014. *The Deadly Life of Logistics: Mapping Violence in Global Trade*. Minneapolis. MN: University of Minnesota Press.

Danyluk, Martin. 2017. Capital's logistical fix: Accumulation, globalisation, and the survival of capitalism. *Environment and Planning D: Society and Space*. Available at: http://journals.sagepub.com/loi/epd?expanded=2017.

Douglass, Michael. 2001. Intercity Competition and the Question of Economic Resilience: Globalization and Crisis in Asia. In: Scott, Allen J. (ed). *Global City-Regions. Trends, Theory, Policy*. Oxford: Oxford University Press. pp. 236–262.

Friedmann, John. 1986. The world city hypothesis. *Development and Change*, 17 (1), 69–83.

Glaeser, Edward. 2011. *Triumph of the City. How our Greatest Invention Makes us Richer, Smarter, Greener, Healthier, and Happier*. New York: Penguin.

Graham, Stephen. 2001. Flow City: Networked Mobilities and the Contemporary Metropolis. *disP—The Planning Review*, 1(144), 4–11.

Hall, Peter A. and Soskice, David (eds). 2001. *Varieties of Capitalism. The Institutional Foundations of Comparative Advantage*. Oxford: Oxford University Press.

Harvey, David. 1989. From managerialism to entrepreneurialism: The transformation in urban governance in late capitalism. *Geografiska Annaler. Series B, Human Geography*, 71(1), 3–17.

Harvey, David. 2001. Globalization and the "spatial Fix". *Geographische Revue*, 2, 23–30.

Jessop, Bob. 2010. Redesigning the State, Reorienting State Power, and Rethinking the State. In: Leicht, Kevin T. and Jenkins, J. Craig (eds). *Handbook of Politics. State and Society in Global Perspective*. New York: Springer. pp. 41–61.

Keil, Roger. 2018. *Suburban Planet. Making the World Urban from the Outside In*. Cambridge: Polity Press.

Keil, Roger and Mahon, Rianne. 2009. *Leviathan Undone? Towards a Political Economy of Scale*. Vancouver: University of British Columbia.

Klinenberg, Eric. 2018. *Palaces for the People: How Social Infrastructure Can Help Fight Inequality, Polarization, and the Decline of Civic Life*. New York: Crown.

Levy, Jonah D. and Leibfried, Stephan and Nullmeier, Frank. 2015. Changing Perspectives on the State. In: Leibfried, Stephan and Huber, Evelyne and Lange, Matthew, Levy, Jonah D. and Stephens, John D. (eds). *The Oxford Handbook of Transformations of the State*. Oxford: Oxford University Press.

Madden, David. 2012. City becoming world: Nancy, Lefebvre and the global-urban imagination. *Environment and Planning D: Society and Space*, 30(5), 772–787.

Mazzucato, Mariana. 2015. *The Entrepreneurial State: Debunking Public vs. Private Sector Myths*. New York: Anthem Press.

McCormick, Thomas J. 1990. *China Market. America's Quest for Informal Empire 1893–1901*. Chicago: Elephant.

McKinsey Global Institute. 2016. *Lions on the Move II: Realizing the Potential of Africa's Economies*. New York: McKinsey & Company, Sept 2016.

Monios, Jason and Wilmsmeier, Gordon (eds). 2018. *Maritime Mobilities*. New York: Routledge.

Mitchell, Timothy. 2011. *Carbon Democracy. Political Power in the Age of Oil*. London: Verso.

Pieterse, Edgar and Parnell, Susan. 2014. Africa's Urban Revolution in Context. In: Pieterse, Edgar and Parnell, Susan (eds). *Africa's Urban Revolution*. London: Zed Books. pp. 1–17.

Ritter, Luke and Barrett, Michael J. and Wilson, Rosalyn. 2007. *Securing Global Transportation Networks: A Total Security Management Approach*. New York: McGraw-Hill.

Rodrigue, Jean-Paul. 2013. Supply Chain Management, Logistics Changes and the Concept of Friction. In: Hall, Peter V. and Hesse, Markus (eds). *Cities, Regions and Flows*. New York: Routledge.

Sassen, Saskia. 1991. *The Global City. New York, London, Tokio*. Princeton: Princeton University Press.

Sbragia, Alberta M. 1996. *Debt Wish. Entrepreneurial Cities, U.S. Federalism, and Economic Development*. Pittsburgh, PA: University of Pittsburgh Press.

Shapira, Harel. 2013. The border: infrastructure of the global. *Public Culture*, 25 (2), 249–260.

Sheffi, Yossi. 2005. *The Resilient Enterprise. Overcoming Vulnerability for Competitive Advantage*. Cambridge, MA: The MIT Press.

Skowronek, Stephen. 1982. *Building a New American State. The Expansion of National Administrative Capacities 1877–1920*. Cambridge: Cambridge University Press.

Taylor, Peter J. 2004. *World City Network: A Global Urban Analysis*. New York: Routledge.

Turok, Ivan. 2014. The Urbanization-Development Nexus in the BRICS. In: Parnell, Susan and Oldfield, Sophie (eds). *The Routledge Handbook on Cities of the Global South*. New York: Routledge. pp. 122–138.

Van Heur, Bas. 2018. Creative Cities and the Infrastructural Fragmentation of Socio-economic Space. In: Van Damme, Ilja and De Munck, Bert and Miles,

Andrew (eds). *Cities and Creativity from the Renaissance to the Present*. New York: Routledge.

Vormann, Boris. 2012. *Zwischen Alter und Neuer Welt. Nationenbildung im transatlantischen Raum*. Heidelberg: Synchron.

Vormann, Boris. 2014. Who needs American Studies? Globalization, nationalism, and the future of area studies. *American Studies/Amerikastudien*, 59(3), 387–406.

Vormann, Boris. 2015. *Global Port Cities in North America: urbanization and Global Production Networks*. New York: Routledge.

Vormann, Boris. 2015. Toward an infrastructural critique of urban change. Obsolescence and changing perceptions of New York City's waterfront. *CITY*, 19(2–3), 332–340.

Vormann, Boris. 2018. Greater than the Sum of its Parts. The Unrealized Potentials of Interdisciplinary Area Studies. In: Kelleter, Frank and Starre, Alexander (eds). *Projecting American Studies: Essays on Theory, Method, and Practice*. Heidelberg: Winter.

Vormann, Boris and DeDauw Patrick. 2018. Off Shore: The Sustainable City and its Logistical Costs. In: Monios, Jason and Wilmsmeier, Gordon (eds). *Maritime Mobilities*. New York: Routledge.

Wachsmuth, David. 2017. Infrastructure alliances: Supply-chain expansion and multi-city growth coalitions. *Economic Geography*, 93(1), 643–653.

Part 2

5 Funding and Good Financial Governance as Imperatives for Cities' Pursuit of SDG 11

Oliver Fuo

Introduction

Over the past three decades, decentralisation has become accepted across the globe as a tool to facilitate sustainable development (Chigwata and De Visser 2017; Fuo 2015, pp. 168–169). It is also accepted that protecting the autonomy of local governments, including their fiscal powers, in decentralised systems of government is a key requirement for cities' pursuit of sustainability (African Charter Articles 5(2), 7(1), 9(1) and 16(5); European Charter Articles 2–11; UN-Habitat 2009, paras 17–18, 20, 28, 48; Fessha and Kirkby 2008, pp. 255–264). In line with this thinking, it is therefore not surprising that Goal 11 of the UN Sustainable Development Goals (SDGs) is exclusively dedicated to the role of cities in the pursuit of urban sustainability. Although there is no universally accepted metrics of what constitutes a "sustainable" city, SDG 11 contains specific targets on a wide range of issues that should be realised by cities across the globe by 2030 (SDG 11 paras 11.1–11.7, 11.a-11.c). These targets could generally be considered as pointers to urban sustainability.

According to Local Governments for Sustainability (ICLEI), cities and local authorities across the world would have to invest trillions of US dollars (ICLEI 2015, p. 3) in building resilient infrastructure and the provision of services if they were to realise SDG 11 (Schmidt-Traub and Sachs 2015, p. 115). Securing the required infrastructure investment represents a major challenge even for cities that enjoy a degree of fiscal autonomy (World Bank 2015, p. 52). This challenge is omnipresent in developing countries, which have traditionally struggled to raise funding for development projects (ICLEI 2015, p. 3 para. 41; SDGs Goal 11 para. 11.c; SDG 17 paras 17.1–17.5). Worse still, not all cities that can generate the requisite finances can effectively utilise such resources to transition to sustainability. In addition to adequate funding, good financial governance is mandatory if cities are to transition to sustainability (Federal Ministry for Economic Cooperation and Development 2014, pp. 3–4; UN 2015, para 66). Good financial governance in this context is defined as transparent, legitimate and development-oriented local government action in the area of public finance on both the revenue generation and expenditure sides (Federal Ministry for Economic Cooperation and Development 2014, p. 8). It describes how the decision-making and functional activities performed by city officials can be directed towards ensuring the optimal use of limited resources to achieve the desired city objectives in an effective and efficient manner (Visser and Erasmus 2002, p. 8). Good financial governance falls within the broad field of public financial management. Experts in this area agree that appropriate systems for budgeting, accounting, strategic planning, auditing and reporting, public procurement and financial risk management are some of the core instruments that should be used by governments to promote the good management of public finances (Visser and Erasmus 2002, p. 8; Fourie 2014, pp. 272–274).

The quest for an effective management approach that can enable the transition to sustainability is not new. Following empirical and theoretical insights, interdisciplinary research in the area of transition studies led to the development of the transition management approach as a framework that could be used to support this transition (also in cities) (Roorda et al. 2014; Loorback 2010; Rotmans et al. 2001). Transition management recognises that both the liberal free market approach and the top-down management approach are outdated as mechanisms that by themselves could be used by governments to generate sustainable solutions at the societal level. It calls for a new system of management that strikes a balance between state, market and society (Loorback 2010, p. 162). The approach recognises that despite the best efforts of many cities, citizens, NGOs and companies to adopt and implement initiatives to contribute towards a sustainable future, they are confronted with complex sustainability problems that are deeply embedded in society (Roorda et al. 2014, p. 9). Therefore, addressing such complex challenges requires fundamental societal changes which can be achieved only by influencing, supporting and accelerating transition towards sustainability (Roorda et al. 2014, p. 9). The transition management approach offers six implementation principles to be utilised by city officials to influence the direction and pace of the dynamics of societal change towards sustainability (Roorda et al. 2014, p. 9–10). The proposed principles do not specifically speak to financial management but they do find relevance for present purposes. For example, the requirement that city officials should engage multiple stakeholders beyond simply providing inputs could enhance inclusiveness, accountability and transparency (eg in the context of city budgeting). The transition management principles are supposed to complement other governance activities rather than replace them (Roorda et al. 2014, p. 11; Rotmans et al. 2001, p. 24).

Against the above background, this chapter seeks to address a set of interrelated objectives. Firstly, it begins by discussing some international and African regional responses directed towards promoting good financial governance. Secondly, the chapter reflects on sources of funding that can generally be utilised for the envisaged transition to sustainable cities in the developing country context. Using South Africa's legal framework as an example, this chapter exposes the broader complexities cities face in securing the financial sustainability required for the pursuit of SDG 11.

International and African Regional Responses to Promoting Good Financial Governance

Corruption, mismanagement and the waste of public resources remain major impediments towards sustainable development in many developing countries. A recent report estimates that, over the past five decades, Africa has lost in excess of 1 trillion US dollars in illicit financial flows (IFF) and that this sum is equivalent to all official development assistance (ODA) received by the continent during the same timeframe. (For the adopted definition of illicit financial flows (IFFs), see AU and ECA Conference of Ministers of Finance, Planning and Economic Development 2015, p. 9.) The Report notes that up to one third of Africa's wealth is being held abroad and that this wealth and its associated income are beyond the reach of Africa's tax authorities (AU and ECA Conference of Ministers of Finance, Planning and Economic Development 2015, p. 56). According to the Report, a major source of IFF is money stolen by government officials through corrupt practices. As a result of this practice, African countries are deprived of some of the resources that could be used to build resilient infrastructure and expand social services (AU and ECA Conference of Ministers of Finance, Planning and Economic Development 2015, p. 56). Beyond Africa, systemic corruption and the looting of public funds is widely reported in many developing countries in other regions of the world (Gendreau and McLendon 2017, p. 6; Transparency International 2017, pp. 8–27).

In order to address the perennial problem of the mismanagement of public resources, the discussion of development policy among the UN system, donor countries/agencies and global financial institutions has increasingly stressed that good financial governance is a prerequisite for achieving long-term development goals in developing countries (Deutsche Gesellschaft für Technische Zusammenarbeit 2006, pp. 6–7). There are numerous commitments at the global and regional levels to give effect to this recognition, such as the Monterrey Consensus on Financing for Development (2003) (paras 3–4, 11, 13 and 14), the UN Convention Against Corruption (2003) (UNCAC)[1], the African Union Convention on Preventing and Combating Corruption (2003) (AUCPCC),[2] the Paris Declaration on Aid Effectiveness (2005) (paras 1, 3–4, 25 and 30), the Accra Agenda for Action (2008) (paras 24(a)-(d)), the Doha Declaration on Financing for Development (2008) (paras 2, 9, 16 and 20–21), and the Addis Ababa Action Agenda (2015) (paras 5 and 20).

The Addis Ababa Action Agenda specifically recognises that, in order to realise the targets set by the SDGs, institutions at the sub-national level have to be effective, efficient, accountable and transparent in the mobilisation and use of resources (Addis Ababa Action Agenda paras 5–11). Despite this recognition there is no specific goal expressly dedicated to good financial governance in the SDGs. Even though the importance thereof is acknowledged in a piecemeal fashion (UN 2015, para 66), SDG 11 is completely mute on this issue. Goal 16 of the SDGs, considered the governance goal, requires countries to implement certain core actions that resonate with the commitment to promote good financial governance (SDG 16 paras 16.3, 16.6, 16.7 and 16.10). The proceeding paragraphs specifically discuss attempts made in the UNCAC and the AUCPCC to promote good financial governance. Although these instruments also focus on criminalisation and international cooperation as mechanisms to combat corruption, these matters are not extensively addressed in this chapter.

One of the objectives of the UNCAC is to promote integrity, accountability and the proper management of public affairs and public property. Chapter 2 of the UNCAC, which outlines measures that can be implemented by state parties to prevent corruption, directly speaks to the core activities that can be used to promote good financial governance. Article 9 of the UNCAC urges each state party, in accordance with the fundamental principles of its legal system, to take the necessary steps to establish appropriate systems of procurement based on transparency, competition and objective criteria in decision-making (UNCAC Art. 9(1)). In addition, state parties are urged to set out the procedures for the adoption of national budgets; to ensure timely reporting on revenue and expenditure; to implement an appropriate system of accounting, auditing standards and related oversight; to implement effective and efficient systems of risk management and internal control; and where appropriate to implement corrective action in the case of failure to comply with established rules (UNCAC Art. 9(2)(a)-(e)). Furthermore, state parties are encouraged to implement civil and administrative measures that will preserve the integrity of accounting books, records, financial statements and all other documents related to public expenditure and revenue as well as to prevent the falsification of such documents (UNCAC Art. 9(3)).

Although the UNCAC has been acclaimed as a blueprint for policy reform on a global level, the language in Chapter 2 is non-mandatory (Webb 2005, pp. 206, 218). In addition, while the UNCAC is quite detailed on what is needed to ensure that established procurement systems are appropriate (UNCAC Art. 9(10(a))-(e)), it is almost silent on what is required in terms of budgeting, accounting, auditing and risk management. Overall, emphasis is placed on the need to ensure that the measures adopted promote the participation of society, the principles of the rule of law, integrity, transparency and accountability in the management of public finances. The non-mandatory wording of Chapter 2 of the UNCAC and the lack of precise guidance on what constitutes appropriate systems of budgeting, accounting, auditing and risk management mean that state parties enjoy significant discretion to decide if and how far they are prepared to incorporate relevant provisions of the Convention into domestic law (Webb 2005, p. 221).

In terms of the African Union Convention on Preventing and Combating Corruption (AUCPCC), one of its objectives is to "establish conditions to foster transparency and accountability in the management of public affairs" (AUCPCC Art. 2(5)). Article 5(4) of the Convention is expressly committed to fostering some of the key activities identified above as critical to cities' pursuit of good financial governance. In terms of this provision, state parties undertake to adopt and implement legislative and other measures that "create, maintain and strengthen internal accounting, auditing and follow-up systems, in particular, in the public income, custom and tax receipts, expenditures and procedures for hiring, procurement and management of public goods and services." Apart from this commitment, there is no concrete detail or qualifiers on the type of accounting, auditing or procurement systems that should be established by state parties. Generally, although the AUCPCC requires state parties to abide by the principles of good governance, the rule of law, transparency and accountability in the management of public funds (AUCPCC Art. 3), the Convention "suffers from excessive use of draw-back clauses", which are inclined to limit the effectiveness of its provisions (Olaniyan 2004, p. 85). As Olaniyan argues, many of the provisions of the Convention are subject to domestic legal systems and the provisions of national legislation, which makes it possible for state parties to use their discretion in restricting treaty obligations to eradicate corruption within their territories (Olaniyan 2004, pp. 85–86).

A reading of the UNCAC and the AUCPCC indicates that significant discretion is given to state parties to adopt and implement legislative and administrative measures, in accordance with the principles of their domestic legal systems, which promote the participation of society in government's fiscal activities, ensures access to information, transparency and accountability in the mobilisation and use of public resources. In the area of procurement, emphasis is also placed on the need to promote fair competition and access to redress mechanisms. Apart from these overarching principles, which could also be used to guide how cities mobilise and manage their finances, these instruments do not, however, attempt to regulate all relevant financial processes and procedures. This said, the existence of appropriate financial management systems alone cannot guarantee cities' transition to sustainability. Adequate revenue generation is equally indispensable.

Sources of Funding for Cities' Pursuit of SDG 11

The inability of developing countries to generate the funding required to realise internationally agreed development goals has always been a challenge. In an attempt to address this, the UN has spearheaded several initiatives. The most recent initiative is the Addis Ababa Action Agenda (2015) (paras 20–102), which is considered an integral part of the 2030 Agenda. A reading of SDG 17 and the Addis Ababa Action Agenda shows several sources of funding that could be explored by cities to ensure their transition to sustainability (SDG 17 paras 17.1–17.5; Addis Ababa Action Agenda para 20; Dethier 2013, p. 7; Paulais 2012, p. 13).

In terms of SDG 17 and the Addis Ababa Action Agenda, emphasis is placed on own revenue as the main source of funding for cities (Development Finance International (DFI) and Oxfam 2015, p. 37; SDG 17 para 17.1; Addis Ababa Action Agenda para 20). This is not surprising given the fact that the fiscal autonomy of cities is recognised as indispensable in their pursuit of sustainability (Fesha and Kirkby 2008, p. 261). Own revenue in this context could be interpreted as referring to money generated by cities through the collection of local taxes, property rates and charges for services they provide, patents, and other income-producing activities (Paulais 2012, p. 14). The preference for this source of funding is informed by the view that internally generated revenue is potentially more stable and predictable, and can more easily be aligned with locally defined priorities (DFI and Oxfam 2015, p. 37; Dethier 2013, p. 7). Reliance on own revenue in these countries is constrained by the limited taxation powers of many local authorities and the absence of the economic infrastructure needed to generate tax (KfW Development Bank 2016). In addition, a lack of urban planning capability, limited implementation and enforcement capacity, uncertainty about future regulatory policies such as tariff structures, corruption and socio-political instability inhibit the revenue-generating ability of many cities (World Bank 2015, pp. 45, 47). Attempts to increase own revenue through land value capture mechanisms such as the sale of land owned and controlled by cities carries the risk of corruption and the abuse of power (Schmidt-Traub and Sachs 2015, pp. 115–116; Dethier 2013, p. 9; Paulais 2012, pp. 17–18).

The limited quantities of internal revenue generated by cities in developing countries means that they may have to rely on intergovernmental fiscal transfers from higher levels of government (Dethier 2013, p. 7; World Bank 2015, p. 52). This is an inevitable outcome, given the fact that own revenues from subnational governments in these countries constitute less than 3 percent of the gross domestic product (GDP) (Dethier 2013, pp. 7–8). Increased intergovernmental allocations can be better achieved in countries with institutionalised fiscal decentralisation systems through intensified lobbying by city governments (SDG 17 para 17.1; Dethier 2013, p. 9). This may prove to be a herculean task for local authorities, given that intergovernmental transfers to cities have dwindled following the recent global economic crisis (Dethier 2013, pp. 1, 6). Dependence on unreliable and insufficient transfers make it difficult for cities to manage their budgets.

A third source of potential funding is grant funding from external partners which, for example, includes Official Development Assistance (SDG 17 para 17.2; Addis Ababa Action Agenda paras 22 and 51; Paulais 2012, p. 14). SDG 17 generally urges developed countries to fully implement their ODA commitments, including the specific commitment of some developed countries to achieving the target of 0.7 percent of gross national income for ODA to developing countries and 0.15 to 0.20 percent to least developed countries (SDG 17 para 17.2). Although grant funding from ODA is free money, it is always linked to specific goals, which may not necessarily correspond with the highest priorities of the cities, and grant funding rarely pays for future maintenance, repair and operation costs (Dethier 2013, p. 9). In addition, donor commitments in relation to grant funding are not always met (Asia-Europe Foundation (ASEF) 2015, p. 166). Although the failure to meet the frequently pledged donor targets is now linked to the effects of the recent global financial crisis, this pattern has been consistent over the past four decades (AU and ECA Conference of Ministers of Finance, Planning and Economic Development 2015, p. 53; ASEF 2015, p. 166). Given these weaknesses, cities should not heavily rely on ODA.

A fourth source of funding is borrowing. This occurs when a city takes a loan from a commercial bank or other specialised institution, and when it issues bonds (Paulais 2012, p. 14). Borrowing might be the most efficient financing mechanism for municipal infrastructure development and assets that have a long life (Dethier 2013, p. 10; Paulais 2012, p. 14). This mechanism provides city managers an opportunity to capture returns from infrastructure investments while deferring repayments (Dethier 2013, p. 10). It is suggested that borrowing should be used only to finance capital investments, in order to minimise the risks of running into an endless cycle of loan rollovers (Paulais 2012, p. 14). Generally, big cities are often in a better position to use debt markets to finance assets with a long lifespan because they have stronger economic bases and the willingness to pay for unmet services may be higher in urban areas (Dethier 2013, p. 10). However, even with big cities there are problems associated with debt as a financing mechanism. Firstly, the cost of borrowing is often high and in least developing countries, direct municipal debt financing on capital markets takes place on a very limited scale. In African countries, access to direct municipal debt financing is generally limited, for diverse reasons (Paulais 2012, pp. 15, 43; World Bank 2015, pp. 45–56). Bond markets are new in many developing countries, largely because the institutional environment does not support them. There is a general lack of legal and regulatory frameworks that can inspire investor confidence (Paulais 2012, p. 43; World Bank 2015, pp. 45–56).

In the light of the above, it has been argued that a credit rating system for sub-sovereign borrowers is indispensable to developing a capital market for local governments (Paulais 2012, p. 43; World Bank 2015, p. 45). Obtaining good sub-sovereign rating enables cities to access finance on better terms and helps them improve on the management of their finances (Paulais 2012, p. 44; World Bank 2015, pp. 54–55). However, even where a credit rating system for cities exists, access to finance by local authorities is strongly influenced by the governance performance of central governments (Paulais 2012, pp. 38, 43). In addition to the complexities related to credit ratings, central governments usually limit the borrowing powers of cities, for example by imposing a fiscal rule that places ceilings on borrowing, imposing a deficit target, and imposing rules related to debt repayment capacity (Ahmad, Albino-War and Singh 2005, pp. 14–15). This approach is generally acceptable in order to avoid uncontrolled city spendings being shifted to higher levels of government or becoming intergenerational debt (Ahmad, Albino-War and Singh 2005, p. 4).

Public-private partnerships (PPP) have also been identified as a finance mechanism that could be utilised by cities to build infrastructure. The involvement of private corporations in the delivery of public goods and services is mostly perceived as privatisation, and this strategy has proven to be highly contentious in many countries for a variety of reasons (McDonald and Ruiters 2005; Bakker 2007, pp. 430, 432). The problematic nature of this strategy is well documented in the area of the provision of water services (Kirkpatrick et al. 2006, pp. 143, 158–159; Kotzé and Fuo 2016, pp. 207–309). Research shows that PPPs have generally added relatively little value to city financing in developing countries in the past two decades (Paulais 2012, p. 16; World Bank 2015, p. 53). The record of full cost recovery is weak and many cities are reluctant to commit to the types of tariff levels that could attract private investors in infrastructure development (Dethier 2013, p. 11; Paulais 2012, pp. 16–17). Despite these challenges, the concept of PPP should not be jettisoned, but should be explored by cities in innovative ways that promote the involvement of local businesses. By using local businesses as private partners, local authorities may enhance the success of PPP and tap into the long-term relationships that exist between community residents, local officials, and their private sector partners (Paulais 2012, p. 17).

Commitments to addressing climate change provide cities with innovative funding options on mitigation and adaptation projects (Dethier 2013, p. 13; Paulais 2012, pp. 24–28). The Kyoto Protocol and Paris Agreement created the Clean Development Mechanism (CDM), which has resulted in the establishment of several funds to finance adaptation and mitigation measures, often with different areas of focus. Examples of such funds include: the Green Climate Fund; the Climate Investment Fund (CIF) consisting of the Clean Technology Fund (CTF) and the Strategic Climate Fund (SCF); the Global Environmental Facility; the Adaptation Fund;

and ICLEI's EcoBudget Programme, to name but a few. However, the main problem with these funds is that they are extremely fragmented. In addition, almost half of the approved CDM financing is directed towards reducing the emission of hydrofluorocarbons from the chemical industry (Paulais 2012, pp. 25–26). The CDM mechanism is complicated to use and requires knowledge which is generally beyond the reach of most city officials in developing countries. Furthermore, the use of the CDM mechanism requires complex project assessments, the costs of which may outweigh the resources obtained (Paulais 2012, pp. 26–27).

The various challenges faced by local governments to fund projects for the realisation of SDG 11 can be evidenced by the South African example. As the discussion below shows, although South Africa's legal framework guarantees a certain degree of fiscal autonomy to cities and obliges them to secure sound and sustainable management of their finances, they face challenges similar to those described above.

The Case of South Africa

Background

The Constitution of the Republic of South Africa, 1996 (the Constitution) fundamentally transformed the institution of local government in the country (Fedsure Life Assurance v Greater Johannesburg Transitional Metropolitan Council 1998 (12) BCLR 1458 (CC); City of Cape Town v Robertson 2005 (2) SA 323 (CC)). Chapter 7 of the Constitution is dedicated to various aspects of local government, including the status, objects, powers, functions and duties of municipalities and how local government representatives are elected (Constitution Sections 151–164). The local sphere of government is constituted by about 257 municipalities of different categories (Du Plessis and Nel 2015, p. 25). Although interrelated and interdependent with national and provincial government, municipalities are recognised as a distinct sphere of government (Constitution Sec. 40(1)) with a certain degree of legislative, executive and fiscal autonomy (Constitution Sections 151(2), 157, 158; City of Cape Town v Robertson 2005, para 60). All spheres of government are obliged to work together within the framework of the constitutional principle of co-operative government (Constitution Sections 40(2) and 41). The three spheres of government are obliged to avoid instituting legal proceedings against one another and to assist and support one another in the pursuit of sustainable development (Constitution Sec. 41(1); Du Plessis and Du Plessis 2012, p. 436). Municipalities have an expanded developmental mandate which puts them at the forefront of promoting local sustainability, including socio-economic development (Constitution Sections 152–153; Joseph v City of Johannesburg 2010 (3) BCLR 212 (CC) paras 27, 34–40; Fuo 2015, pp. 171–172).

They are typically responsible for the provision of a wide range of services such as municipal health services; municipal public transport; water and sanitation services; the control of air and noise pollution; municipal roads; refuse removal, refuse dumps and solid waste disposal. (For a full list of services, see Sec. 156 and Schedules 4B and 5 B of the Constitution.) Schedules 4 and 5 of the Constitution provide guidance on the allocation of powers and competences among the three spheres of government and are framed in very broad terms which often require judicial interpretation for clarity (Fuo 2017). Some of the functional areas of municipalities outlined in Schedules 4B and 5B mirror the substance of SDG 11.

Good Financial Governance in South African Local Government Law

Apart from the above reforms, the Constitution recognises the need for good financial governance at the local level (Constitution Sec. 153). In exercising their fiscal powers and functions, municipalities must be guided by the values and principles governing public administration in section 195 of the Constitution. This section prescribes that municipal administration must be informed by a high standard of professional ethics; the efficient, economic and effective use of resources; the provision of public services in an unbiased, impartial, fair and equitable manner; public participation; accountability and responsiveness; transparency and the granting of access to timely, accessible and accurate information; and good human resources management (Constitution Sec. 195(1)(a)-(i)). Where a municipality does not thoroughly manage its finances, national or provincial government could exercise its supervisory powers by taking over the administration of the affairs of that municipality (Constitution Sections 100 and 139).

In terms of legislation, the Prevention and Combating of Corrupt Activities Act 12 of 2004 (PCCAA) directly gives effect to South Africa's obligations emanating from the anti-corruption instruments discussed above. However, the PCCAA deals only with the criminal prosecution of persons involved in corruption and does not contain any civil measures to address the mismanagement of public resources. The PCCAA is therefore irrelevant for our current purposes.

In general, the Local Government: Municipal Finance Management Act 56 of 2003 (MFMA) seeks to secure the sustainable management of the financial affairs of municipalities. The MFMA seeks to achieve this objective by establishing treasury norms and standards that cut across a diverse range of municipal fiscal activities (MFMA Sec. 2). Overall, the MFMA emphasises the importance of ensuring transparency, accountability and appropriate lines of responsibility in the fiscal and financial affairs of municipalities and municipal entities. The MFMA is the most relevant legislation directed towards promoting good financial governance in South African municipalities. The sixteen chapters of this Act and the numerous regulations that accompany it cannot be exhaustively discussed in any book chapter. For the sake of convenience, this sub-section specifically focuses on budgeting and procurement to illustrate the extent to which the South African local government law framework further reflects the overarching principles captured in the UNCAC and the AUCPCC, as well as the complexities faced in their implementation.

Legal Framework for Municipal Budgeting

The Constitution bestows on municipal councils the power to approve budgets (Constitution Sec. 160(2)(b)). In line with the principles highlighted in the UNCAC and the AUCPCC, municipalities are constitutionally mandated to ensure that their budgets and budgetary processes promote transparency, accountability and effective financial management (Constitution Sec. 215(1)). Although the Constitution obliges national legislation to prescribe the form of municipal budgets, it generally requires that budgets in the local sphere of government must show the sources of revenue and the way in which proposed expenditure will comply with national legislation (Constitution Sections 215(2)(a) and (c)). In addition, municipal budgets must contain estimates of revenue and expenditure, differentiating between capital and current expenditure; proposals for financing any anticipated deficit for the period to which they apply; and an indication of their intentions regarding borrowing and other forms of public liability that will increase public debt during the ensuing year (Constitution Sec. 215(3)(a)-(c)).

The MFMA gives legislative effect to the constitutional budgeting powers of cities. The Act covers only annual budgets and adjustment budgets (MFMA Sections 16 and 28 respectively). An annual budget must be approved by a municipal council shortly before the start of each financial year and is supposed to inform municipal expenditure for the entire year (MFMA Sec. 16(1)). On the other hand, an adjustment budget is any amendment of an annual budget that occurs within the year (MFMA Sections 28(1)-(7) for details). The MFMA prescribes that municipalities may incur expenditure only in terms of an approved budget and within the limits of the amounts appropriated for the different votes in an approved budget (MFMA Sections 15(a) and (b)). This has the potential of preventing unjustified deviations from appropriations allocated to specific sustainability projects. Failure to comply with this requirement generally results in unauthorised, irregular or fruitless and wasteful expenditure which may attract personal liability and criminal prosecution (MFMA Sec. 32). This notwithstanding, unauthorised municipal expenditure in the 2015–2016 financial year stood at 12.77 billion ZAR in total, while fruitless and wasteful expenditure in the same period stood at 901 million ZAR (Auditor General South Africa (AGSA) 2017, p. 12). Such trends deplete financial resources that could be used by cities to transition towards sustainability.

Municipal budgeting is generally supposed to take place within the framework for integrated development planning prescribed by Chapter 5 of the Local Government: Municipal Systems Act 32 of 2000 (Systems Act). Each municipal council must, at the start of its five-year elected term, adopt a single, inclusive and strategic plan (known as the Integrated Development Plan or IDP) for the municipality. The wide scope of the IDP, the legal requirements for public participation and alignment to other sector-specific plans suggests that it is a strategic instrument which could be used by all municipalities to facilitate the transition to an inclusive and sustainable future (Fuo 2013; Du Plessis 2017, pp. 251–252).

The budget preparation and approval processes as well as the content and format of the annual budget are outlined in the MFMA (Sections 21–28). Section 23 of the MFMA specifically obliges municipalities to consult local communities when annual budgets are tabled in council. Mechanisms, processes and procedures established in terms of the Systems Act should be used to facilitate public consultation during the design and implementation of municipal budgets (Systems Act Sections 17–21). Despite these guarantees, most communities lack the skills needed to effectively engage in the intricacies of municipal budgeting and the local mechanisms established for public participation are largely dysfunctional (Fuo 2015, p. 174; AGSA 2015, p. 117). The public participation obligation is watered-down by the jurisprudence of courts, which clearly indicates that city officials are not obliged to accept community preferences (Fuo 2015, pp. 179–188). In brief, this jurisprudence merely requires city officials to create an environment conducive to the expression of communities' views, and for such views to be considered. This position is different from the type of consensus-building approach advocated in transition management studies. The desire for inclusivity is defeated when communities, business and city officials cannot forge a shared vision of sustainability.

The municipal council is required to consider the approval of the budget at least 30 days before the start of the budget year (MFMA Sec. 24(1)). There are serious consequences where a municipality fails to approve an annual budget and relevant revenue-raising measures to give effect to the annual budget by the first day of the budget year (MFMA Sections 25 and 26). This failure requires the executive of the relevant province to intervene in the municipality by taking appropriate steps to ensure that the budget is approved. The failure to approve the budget could also lead to the dissolution of the municipal council and the appointment of an administrator to run the affairs of the municipality until a newly elected council is established (Constitution Sec. 139; MFMA Sec. 26(1)). There have been several provincial interventions in municipalities on this basis (SA Local Government Briefing No. 9/2017, p. 8). Intervention may have significant implications for a municipality's authority to govern. In some instances, city officials have unsuccessfully approached courts to block provincial interventions (Ngaka Modiri Molema District Municipality v Chairperson,

North West Provincial Executive Committee and Others 2015 (1) BCLR 72 (CC)).

Non-compliance with the statutory requirements of the budgeting process is dealt with by section 27 of MFMA. Although the Act makes provision for the process which municipalities should follow when they anticipate the possibility of non-compliance with the generally prescribed process (MFMA Sec. 27(1)-(3)), section 27(4) categorically provides that "[N]on-compliance by a municipality with a provision of this Chapter relating to the budget process or a provision in any legislation relating to the approval of a budget-related policy, does not affect the validity of an annual or adjustment budget." Due to the existence of this provision, there has been unsuccessful litigation to set aside the budgets of two municipalities because they were adopted without properly following the prescribed processes for public consultation. In these cases, the courts held that the constituent elements of an annual or adjustment budget such as tariffs and property rates remain valid even though they were imposed without sufficient public consultation (South African Property Owners Association v The Council of the City of Johannesburg [2012] ZASCA 157 (8 November 2012) paras 33–40, 68–80; Borbet South Africa (Pty) Ltd v Nelson Mandela Bay Municipality 2014 (5) SA 256 (ECP) paras 35–109).

Legal Framework for Municipal Procurement

The Constitution also prescribes principles which should guide public procurement. When a municipality contracts for goods or services, it must do so in accordance with a system which is fair, equitable, transparent, competitive and cost-effective (Constitution Sec. 217(1)). The Preferential Procurement Policy Framework Act 5 of 2000 (PPPFA) gave effect to section 217(3) of the Constitution which obliged national government to adopt legislation that prescribes a framework within which preferential procurement policies should be designed by municipalities. However, the MFMA sets out the overarching statutory regulatory framework for procurement by municipalities and municipal entities (Sections 110–119). The MFMA mandates each municipality and municipal entity to have a supply chain management policy (SCMP) to regulate its procurement practices (Sec. 111).

In order to minimise corruption and promote good fiscal management, the MFMA discourages municipalities from accepting unsolicited bids and urges that for such a bid to be accepted, it must be in accordance with a city's SCMP (MFMA Sec. 113). Furthermore, where a municipality decides to approve a tender other than the one recommended by its tender committee, the Auditor General, the Provincial Treasury, and the National Treasury must be notified of such deviations (MFMA Sec. 114). This seeks to ensure that due process is followed and that the tender process is not abused by self-seeking politicians. Political office bearers such as mayors are barred from impeding the ability of accounting officers to implement SCMPs (MFMA Sec. 115(2)). In order to improve the integrity and objectivity of tender processes, elected councillors are barred from becoming members of municipal bid or tender committees (MFMA Sec. 117). Municipal councillors are not allowed to participate in any committee that evaluates bids or approves tenders, quotations or contracts, and they may not attend any such meeting as an observer (MFMA Sec. 117). To improve compliance, all officials involved in the implementation of a municipality's SCMP must meet the prescribed competency levels (MFMA Sec. 119(1)).

Despite the above measures, the Auditor General has identified common procurement findings that continue to test the integrity of the system. These include the frequent award of tenders to suppliers who submit fraudulent declarations, the failure of municipal employees to disclose interests in suppliers, the payment of suppliers by municipalities in spite of poor delivery, the payment of fictitious suppliers by municipalities, the failure to invite competitive bidding, a general lack of adequate internal controls, and corruption (AGSA 2017, pp. 47–48, 57–58). In addition, more than half of the total number of municipalities audited displayed a lack of readiness to comply with key supply chain management reforms such as the use of the central supplier database and the eTender portal, which became compulsory for all organs of state from 1 July 2016 (AGSA 2017, pp. 48–49).

The design of the law concerning financial management in South African cities is such that it should help to secure and protect the financial resources necessary for the transition to sustainability. The failure of South African municipalities to generally adhere to the core principles of good financial governance is real, and may be replicated in the story of local government in many other countries. This poses significant risk to the prospect of achieving any successful transition to sustainability of the kind envisioned in SDG 11.

Fiscal Powers and Sources of Funding for SA Municipalities

A reading of the Constitution points to three main sources of funding for municipalities. Firstly, as part of their fiscal autonomy, municipalities have the power to self-generate revenue by imposing rates on property and surcharges on fees for services provided for or on behalf of the municipality (Constitution Sec. 229(1)(a)). These fiscal powers are described as original municipal powers because they can be taken away only through an amendment of the Constitution (Rates Action Group v City of Cape Town 2007 (1) All SA 233 (SCA) paras 1–20; Fuo 2017, p. 333). However, they can be regulated by national legislation and through ministerial norms and standards. The Constitution does not entitle national government to usurp the fiscal power of municipalities (Minister of Local

Government, Environmental Affairs and Development Planning, Western Cape v The Habitat Council and Others; Minister of Local Government, Environmental Affairs and Development Planning, Western Cape v City of Cape Town and Others 2014 (5) BCLR 591 (CC) para 22). In a recent judgment, Justice Jafta declared section 8 of the Water Services Act 108 of 1997 (WSA) unconstitutional because it impermissibly empowered a national Minister to vary or set aside surcharges imposed on water services by Merafong City on the ground that it completely overlooked the original constitutional fiscal powers of municipalities (Merafong City Local Municipality v AngloGold Ashanti Ltd [2016] ZACC 35 (24 October 2016) paras 157–158). The constitutional fiscal powers of municipalities are given legislative effect through several statutes (Systems Act Sections 4(1)(c), 74; Municipal Fiscal Powers and Functions Act 12 of 2007 (MFPFA); and Local Government: Municipal Property Rates Act 6 of 2004).

Also aligned to the fiscal autonomy of municipalities are the powers to generate revenue by borrowing money from banks and other financial institutions, subject to national legislation (Constitution Sections 160(2)(d), 230A). A municipal council may raise loans for capital or current expenditure but loans for current expenditure may be raised only when necessary for bridging purposes during a fiscal year (Constitution Sec. 230A(1)(a)-(b)). A recent report shows that local government's consolidated outstanding long-term debt increased to 63.5 billion ZAR in the third quarter of the 2016/2017 municipal financial year, from 62.9 billion ZAR in the previous quarter. While 29 percent of this consolidated debt is in the form of bonds, the remaining 71 percent is in the form of long-term loans (SA Local Government Briefing No. 10/2017, p. 2). The country's municipal borrowing market is dominated by its metropolitan municipalities (SA Local Government Briefing No. 10/2017, p. 2).

As discussed above, national credit ratings influence the credit rating of cities and therefore their cost of borrowing. In the wake of the recent downgrades of South Africa's sovereign credit rating by global rating agencies, largely as a result of weaknesses in national leadership, Moody's announced the downgrading of the credit rating of ten South African municipalities (Gillham 2017; Moody's Investor Service 2017). Most of the municipalities maintained sound national credit rating standings but were downgraded to a Negative Outlook, thereby making the cost of future borrowing more expensive (Moody's Investor Service 2017). The downgrade of the credit rating of South African municipalities demonstrates the close operational and financial linkages that exist between national and local governments and raises questions about the fairness of such credit evaluations (Gillham 2017). The high cost of borrowing will negatively affect the ability of municipalities to raise the loans needed to build and maintain the infrastructure needed for climate resilience, for example.

Furthermore, a major source of revenue for municipalities is national equitable allocations (Constitution Sec. 214(1)). Each year the Minister of

Finance tables a Division of Revenue (DORA) Bill in Parliament, which is subsequently adopted as an Act, to provide for the equitable division of revenue raised nationally to all three spheres of government. The majority of rural municipalities without an adequate tax base depend almost entirely on the transfer of funds by national government for the delivery of basic services. Municipalities receive conditional grants from other spheres of government for specific projects such as the municipal infrastructure grant. However, some cash-strapped municipalities often use these grants to fund operating expenditure rather than to build much-needed infrastructure (AGSA 2017, pp. 12–13).

Apart from the sources of funding expressly provided for in the Constitution, South African municipalities can also generate revenue by requesting donations from the public, including from international partners (MFMA Sec. 12); the selling and leasing of assets; engaging in public-private partnerships (Systems Act Sections 76, 79, 80); imposing and collecting fines for violations of by-laws; and through investments (Steytler and De Visser 2014, pp. 12–36). In terms of PPP arrangements, there is the view that their use has increasingly led to the commercialisation of basic services, which has increased the hardship experienced by people living in poverty (Dugard 2010b). The privatisation of municipal services does not always lead to improved performance or value for money, and provides fertile ground for corruption at the local level in South Africa (Kotzé and Fuo 2016, pp. 308–309).

Despite their fiscal autonomy, most municipalities in the country cannot generate the revenue needed to deliver on their mandate. This has been attributed *inter- alia* to the non-existence of an adequate tax base, especially in largely rural areas, and the prevalence of a culture of non-payment for municipal services. Attempts by municipalities to ensure "100 percent cost recovery on operating and maintenance costs, even if capital investments are subsidized" has in some instances led to the disconnection of services in poor households (Dugard 2010a, p. 177) and community resistance. This was the cause of litigation in the famous *Mazibuko* case (Mazibuko and Others v City of Johannesburg and Others 2010 (3) BCLR 239 (CC)). Although the Constitutional Court declared the installation of pre-paid metres as lawful in the *Mazibuko* case, there is still resistance in some areas to cost-recovery programmes. Consumers currently owe municipalities a total of 128.4 billion ZAR (SA Local Government Briefing No. 10/2017, pp. 7–8). Unless the requisite finances are made available to them, preaching about good financial governance may sound hollow in the ears of municipal officials.

Conclusion

This chapter has used the case of South Africa to demonstrate some of the complexities faced by cities in developing countries in attempting to generate and effectively manage the fiscal resources needed to transition to a sustainable future. While attempts have been made at the international and African regional levels to improve the management of public finances through the adoption of the UNCAC and the AUCPCC, these instruments have weaknesses. Although they contain overarching principles that can guide the fiscal activities and decision-making processes of cities, it is entirely up to national governments to adopt and implement the detailed regulatory frameworks needed to ensure good financial governance at the domestic level. The weak wording of the duties of state parties in these instruments shows that they can decide what to include or exclude in domestic legislation. Therefore, the success of cities in promoting good financial governance is largely dependent on the existence of an enabling national regulatory framework. Generally, this challenge is further compounded by the fact that, in the midst of dwindling intergovernmental fiscal transfers, it is the dominant responsibility of cities to raise the financial resources required to transition to a sustainable future. While some cities may not enjoy the type of fiscal autonomy required to self-generate the much-needed revenue, even those with the requisite fiscal powers often struggle.

An analysis of the South African legal framework reveals a genuine attempt to protect the fiscal autonomy of cities and to generally accommodate the core principles of good financial governance canvassed by the UNCAC and the AUCPCC in the fiscal processes and activities of local government. However, the implementation of the law reveals serious challenges common to many developing countries and may affect the pursuit of SDG 11 in a very direct way.

Notes

1 This Convention was adopted on 31 October 2003 and entered into force on 14 December 2005. South Africa signed the Convention on 9 December 2003 and ratified it on 22 November 2004.

2 This Convention was adopted on 11 July 2003 and it entered into force on 5 August 2006. South Africa signed the Convention on 16 March 2004.

Bibliography

Literature

Auditor General South Africa (AGSA). 2015. Consolidated general report on the audit outcomes of local government 2013–2014. Pretoria: AGSA.

Auditor General South Africa (AGSA). 2017. Consolidated general report on the local government audit outcomes – MFMA 2015–16. Pretoria: AGSA.

Ahmad, Ehtisham, Albino-War, Maria and Singh, Raju. 2005. *Subnational Public Financial Management: Institutions and Macroeconomic Considerations.* Washington DC: IMF.

Asia-Europe Foundation (ASEF). 2015. Outlook report 2014/2015. Facts and perspectives. Volume II: Perspectives on sustainable development. Singapore: Asia-Europe Foundation.

AU (African Union) and ECA (Economic Commission for Africa) Conference of Ministers of Finance, Planning and Economic Development. 2015. Illicit financial flows: Report of the High Level Panel on Illicit Financial Flows from Africa. Available at: www.uneca.org/sites/default/files/PublicationFiles/iff_main_report_26feb_en.pdf (Accessed: 13 February 2018).

Bakker, Karen. 2007. The "commons" versus the "commodity": alter-globalisation, anti-privatisation and the human right to water in the global south. *Antipode*, 39(3), pp. 430–455.

Chigwata, Tinashe and De Visser, Jaap. 2017. Local government in the 2013 Constitution of Zimbabwe: defining the boundaries of local autonomy. *Hague Journal on the Rule of Law*, October 2017 [online]. Available at: www.readcube.com/articles/10.1007/s40803-017-0063-0 (Accessed: 12 February 2018).

Dethier, Jen-Jacques. 2013. *Coping with Urban Fiscal Stress Around the World.* Washington DC: World Bank.

Development Finance International (DFI) and Oxfam. 2015. Financing the Sustainable Development Goals: lessons from government spending on the MDGs. Available at: www.governmentspendingwatch.org/images/pdfs/GSW_2015_Report/Financing-Sustainable-Development-Goals-Report-2015.pdf (Accessed: 13 February 2018).

Deutsche Gesellschaft für Technische Zusammenarbeit (GTZ). 2006. *Good Financial Governance – Good Governance in Public Finance.* Eschborn: GTZ.

Dugard, John. 2010a. Can human rights transcend the commercialization of water in South Africa? Soweto's legal fight for an equitable water policy. *Review of Radical Political Economics*, 42(2), 175–194.

Dugard, John. 2010b. Civic action and legal mobilisation: the Phiri water meters case. In: Handmaker, Jeff and Berkhout, Remko (eds). *Mobilising Social Justice in South Africa: Perspectives from Researchers and Practitioners.* Pretoria: PULP. pp. 71–99.

Du Plessis, Anél A. 2017. The readiness of South African law and policy for the pursuit of Sustainable Development Goal 11. *Law, Democracy and Development*, 21, 239–262.

Du Plessis, Anél A. and Nel, J.G. 2015. An introduction. In: Du Plessis, Anél A. (ed). *Environmental Law and Local Government in South Africa.* Cape Town: Juta. pp. 3–37.

Du Plessis, Willemien and Du Plessis, Anél A. 2012. Striking the sustainability balance in South Africa. In: Faure, Michael and Du Plessis, Willemien (eds). *The Balancing of Interests in Environmental Law in Africa*. Pretoria: PULP. pp. 413–458.

Federal Ministry for Economic Cooperation and Development. 2014. *Good financial Governance in German Development Cooperation.* Bonn: BMZ.

Fessha, Yonatan and Kirkby, Coel. 2008. A critical survey of sub-national autonomy in African states. *Publius: The Journal of Federalism*, 38(2), 248–271.

Fourie, David. 2014. Improving budgeting and financial management. In: Thornhill, Christopher et al. (eds). *Public Administration and Management in South Africa: A Developmental Perspective.* Oxford: Oxford University Press. pp. 270–294.

Fuo, Oliver. 2013. A critical investigation of the relevance and potential of IDPs as a local governance instrument for pursuing social justice in South Africa. *Potchefstroom Electronic Law Journal*, 16(5), 221–269.

Fuo, Oliver. 2015. Public participation in decentralised governments in Africa: making ambitious constitutional guarantees more responsive. *African Human Rights Law Journal* 15, 167–191.

Fuo, Oliver. 2017. Intrusion into the autonomy of South African local government: advancing the minority judgment in the Merafong City case. *De Jure*, 50(2), pp. 324–345.

Gendreau, Brian and McLendon, Timothy E. 2017. *Latin American Business Environment Report*. Gainesville, FL: University of Florida.

Gillham, Shaun. 2017. Downgrade hits Bay borrowing. Available at: www.heraldlive.co.za/news/2017/06/17/downgrade-hits-bay-borrowing/?platform=hootsuite (Accessed: 19 June 2017).

KfW Development Bank. 2016. Current topics. Available at: www.kfw-entwicklungsbank.de/PDF/Entwicklungsfinanzierung/Themen-NEU/Governance-Good-Financial-Governance-EN-2014.pdf (Accessed: 27 April 2017).

Kirkpatrick, Colin, Parker, David and Zhang, Yin-Fang 2006. An empirical analysis of state and private-sector provision of water services in Africa. *World Bank Economic Review*, 20(1),143–163.

Kotzé, Louis J. and Fuo, Oliver. 2016. Bridging the public-private regulatory divide: South African mines and the right of access to water. *Journal of Energy and Natural Resources Law*, 34(3), 285–312.

Local Governments for Sustainability (ICLEI). 2015. Implementing the SDGs in cities - ICLEI briefing sheet, Urban Issues, No. 05. Available at: www.iclei.org/fileadmin/PUBLICATIONS/Briefing_Sheets/SDGs/05_-_ICLEI-Bonn_Briefing_Sheet_-_Implementing_SDGs_2015_web.pdf (Accessed: 5 May 2017).

Loorback, Derk. 2010. Transition management for sustainable development: a perspective, complexity-based governance framework. *Governance: An International Journal of Policy, Administration, and Institutions*, 23(1), 161–183.

McDonald, David and Ruiters, Greg (eds). 2005. *The Age of Commodity: Water Privatisation in Southern Africa*. London: Earthscan.

Moody's Investor Service. 2017. Rating action: Moody's downgrades 13 South African sub-sovereigns and changes the outlook to negative. Available at: www.ekurhuleni.gov.za/3029-moodys-final-press-release-for-sa-sub-sovereign-issuers-12-june-2017/file (Accessed: 19 June 2017).

Olaniyan, Kolawole. 2004. The African Union Convention on Preventing and Combatting Corruption: a critical appraisal. *African Human Rights Law Journal*, 4(1), 74–92.

Paulais, Thierry. 2012. *Financing Africa's Cities: The Imperative for Local Investment*. Washington DC: World Bank.

Roorda, Chris et al. 2014. *Transition Management in the Urban Context: Guidance Manual*. Rotterdam, NL: DRIFT, Erasmus University.

Rotmans, Jan, Kemp, Rene and Van Asselt, Marjolein. 2001. More evolution than revolution: transition management in public policy. *Foresight*, 3(1), 15–31.

SA Local Government Briefing No. 9/2017: 28 July 2017.

SA Local Government Briefing No. 10/2017: 31 August 2017.

Schmidt-Traub, Guido and Sachs, Jeffrey David. 2015. Financing sustainable development: implementing the SDGs through effective investment strategies and partnerships. Available at: http://unsdsn.org/wp-content/uploads/2015/04/150408-SDSN-Financing-Sustainable-Development-Paper.pdf (Accessed: 13 February 2018).

Steytler, Nico and De Visser, Jaap. 2014. *Local Government Law of South Africa*. Durban: LexisNexis.

Transparency International. 2017. People and corruption: Asia Pacific. Available at: http://files.transparency.org/content/download/2118/13484/file/2017_GCB_AsiaPacific_EN.pdf (Accessed: 13 February 2018).

UN (United Nations). 2015. *Transforming Our World: The2030 Agenda for Sustainable Development*. New York: United Nations.

UN-Habitat. 2009. *International Guidelines on Decentralisation and Access to Basic Services for All*. Nairobi: United Nations Human Settlements Programme.

Visser, C.B. and Erasmus, P.W. 2002. *The Management of Public Finance*. Oxford: Oxford University Press.

Webb, Philippa. 2005. The United Nations Convention Against Corruption: global achievement or missed opportunity? *Journal of International Economic Law*, 8 (1), pp. 191–229.

World Bank. 2015. *Investing in Urban Resilience: Protecting and Promoting Development in a Changing World*. Washington DC: World Bank.

Case law

Borbet South Africa (Pty) Ltd v Nelson Mandela Bay Municipality 2014(5) SA 256 (ECP)

City of Cape Town v Robertson 2005(2) SA 323 (CC)

Fedsure Life Assurance v Greater Johannesburg Transitional Metropolitan Council 1998(12) BCLR 1458 (CC)

Joseph v City of Johannesburg 2010(3) BCLR 212 (CC)

Mazibuko and Others v City of Johannesburg and Others 2010(3) BCLR 239 (CC)

Merafong City Local Municipality v AngloGold Ashanti Ltd [2016] ZACC 35 (24 October 2016)

Minister of Local Government, Environmental Affairs and Development Planning, Western Cape v The Habitat Council and Others; Minister of Local Government, Environmental Affairs and Development Planning, Western Cape v City of Cape Town and Others 2014(5) BCLR 591 (CC)

Ngaka Modiri Molema District Municipality v Chairperson, North West Provincial Executive Committee and Others 2015(1) BCLR 72 (CC)

Rates Action Group v City of Cape Town 2007(1) All SA 233 (SCA)

South African Property Owners Association v The Council of the City of Johannesburg [2012] ZASCA 157 (8 November 2012)

Legislation

Constitution of the Republic of South Africa, 1996

Local Government: Municipal Finance Management Act 56 of 2003

Local Government: Municipal Property Rates Act 6 of 2004

Local Government: Municipal Systems Act 32 of 2000

Municipal Fiscal Powers and Functions Act 12 of 2007

Preferential Procurement Policy Framework Act 5 of 2000
Prevention and Combating of Corrupt Activities Act 12 of 2004
Water Services Act 108 of 1997

Documents

Accra Agenda for Action (2008)
Addis Ababa Action Agenda (2015)
African Union African Charter on the Values and Principles of Decentralisation, Local Governance and Local Development (2014)
African Union Convention on Preventing and Combating Corruption (2003)
Doha Declaration on Financing for Development: Outcome Document of the Follow-up International Conference on Financing for Development to Review the Implementation of the Monterrey Consensus (2008)
European Charter on Local Self-Government (1985)
Monterrey Consensus on Financing for Development (2003)
Paris Declaration on Aid Effectiveness (2005)
UN Convention Against Corruption (2003)

6 War and Peace in the City

Cindy Wittke

Introduction

Academic articles and policy papers addressing contemporary cities and global urbanisation frequently start with the sound statement that we face a new urban age with more than 50 percent of the world's population living in cities and city regions. This announcement of another "spatial turn" puts twenty-first century cities (again) at the centre of interest.[1] Cities and city regions are imagined to operate not only within but also parallel to and beyond the territories of states on the local, regional as well as global levels. They become objects, loci, subjects and agents of global regulation and transnational co-operation (see eg Aust 2013; Daase 2014; Nijman 2009; Nijman 2011). The numeric appraisal of the scale of on-going global urbanisation processes is neither disputed in the academic literature nor by practitioners. Disputes in both spheres start with diverging visions and expectations of what the twenty-first century urban age will bring. One line divides "utopian" from "dystopian" visions regarding the global urban age and the challenges that it bears for global legal and political regulation. According to some security analysts, unregulated urban migration flows, exploding city growth and ecological challenges could lead to "violent political breakdown" and new forms of "anarchy" in cities, especially in the developing world (Evans 2016, p. 40). Evans points out "Pessimists foresee a coming era of 'feral cities' or of huge 'population bombs', in which armed conflict will occur mainly in sprawling megalopolises from Karachi and Dhaka in Asia to Kinshasa and Lagos in Africa" (Evans 2016, p. 40).[2] According to Sampaio, the current security literature makes a "grim reading" when it comes to military responses in urban spaces and their dimensions (Sampaio 2016, p. 74; see also Graham 2010). In contrast to such "dystopian" security-focused analysis, "utopians" view the transition from a rural to an urban world as an opportunity for global economic growth and transnational social mobility, and thus for fighting poverty and political instability. From this perspective, global urbanisation processes could even contribute to the "three traditional pillars of sustainable development: economic growth, social stability and environmental protection" (Evans 2016, p. 41). A 2014 research report of the United Nations (UN) supports this vision:

> Cities are important drivers of development and poverty reduction in both urban and rural areas, as they concentrate much of the national economic activity, government, commerce and transportation, and provide crucial links with rural areas, between cities, and across international borders. Urban living is often associated with higher levels of literacy and education, better health, greater access to social services, and enhanced opportunities for cultural and political participation.
>
> (United Nations 2014, p. 3)

This short sketch of visions about the impacts of global urbanisation illustrates the polyphony of voices according to which twenty-first century cities seem to be simultaneously spaces of opportunity and resilience but also of inequality and violence (Evans 2016, p. 41). From a research perspective Evans points out that "In the emerging science of cities, it seems as if hypothesis and heterogeneity will prevail over paradigm and homogeneity" (Evans 2016, p. 42). This chapter will pay tribute to this complexity and heterogeneity. It will also aim to avoid nourishing either utopian or dystopian visions of twenty-first century cities. However, it will take a starting point from another alarming numeric appraisal, namely that an estimate of 50 million people across the globe are currently affected by short term and/or protracted intra-city violent conflicts (Bernard 2016, p. 9, with further references). Peter Maurer, President of the International Committee of the Red Cross (ICRC), gave the following account of wars in cities in 2016:

> When wars are fought in cities, the vital infrastructure that makes communities function is damaged or destroyed. There is often no safe water to drink, electricity to power homes and businesses, or health services to vaccinate or cure disease. Health and humanitarian workers are deliberately attacked, and people are forced to leave looking for safety.
>
> (Maurer 2016, p. 640).[3]

Thus, twenty-first century cities, also those that are not situated in fragile or conflict-affected countries, are vulnerable to and by violent intra-city conflict (Sampaio 2016, p. 71). It is pressing to investigate politico-legal challenges that arise when looking at violent intra-city conflicts, modi for their regulation as well as processes of building sustainable peace in cities from a global comparative perspective. Therefore, this chapter aims to provide a broader exploration of the politico-legal dimensions of regulating (urban) violent conflicts that challenge peace, security and good governance in cities temporarily or even permanently. It goes beyond looking at the effect of international conflicts between states or of intra-state conflict situations between the state and/or different non-state parties on cities. Instead, the chapter aims to give account to the variety of intra-city violent conflicts reaching from so-called "gang-wars", to threats of terrorist attacks, to cities as places of regime change and revolutions as well as of separatism and secessionism. How does this analytical endeavour relate to this volume's framework focus on the UN's Sustainable Development Goals (SDGs) and specifically SDG 11? SDG 11[6] calls for making cities inclusive, safe, resilient and sustainable; it incorporates the vision of cities as emerging spaces for new modes of good urban governance and sustainable urban development. This chapter presumes that cities need to be more resilient to security challenges and urban violent conflicts for being able to build up and sustain inclusive institutions and services so that cities, their citizens and eventually the global urban community can thrive. Based on these introductory observations, the chapter's explorations start from the assumption that variations of contemporary urban conflict constellations take place within cities, but in their effect would go beyond cities' as well as states' borders. The chapter will discuss concepts of cities, urban conflicts and peace in the global urban age. It will also turn its focus to challenges for international humanitarian responses to violent conflicts and international engagement in building peace in cities. Such investigations come with the necessity of discussing the application, adaptation and re-conceptualisation of local and international concepts for shaping the transitions from violent conflict to sustainable peace (see also Maurer 2016, p. 639 *et seq*).

Twenty-first Century Cities – General Considerations

Violent armed conflicts are increasingly associated with city names. For example, Rio de Janeiro and Johannesburg stand for unregulated population growth, rising inequality, criminal violence, and conflict with and between gangs. Karachi and Dhaka are associated with unprecedented urban demographic growth, struggles for the right to the city, conflicts about housing, clean water and the availability of and access to services. These examples are illustrative of the challenges for good urban governance in twenty-first century cities. Other cities enter this picture because they are situated in zones of inter-state but mostly intra-state conflicts. Cities become battlegrounds in so-called asymmetric conflicts between the state and armed groups or between armed groups. Yet, cities also become zones of violent conflict without necessarily being situated in a state that faces inter- or intra-state violent conflict. These other variations of intra-city violent conflicts can reach for instance from conflicts between territorial gangs to terrorist attacks and activities in cities. Thus, cities also become battlefields in which political struggles and conflict are continued with violent means. Sampaio comes to the conclusion that "Most intense battles in recent years have taken place in cities, with state and non-state parties to the violent armed conflict fighting each other on the territories of cities and amongst (large) civilian city populations" (Sampaio 2016, p. 73). The fight for Aleppo could be considered as another variation of intra-city violent conflicts as well as the battles of Mosul or Raqqa, which both became nodal points of a cluster of cities and city regions conquered and "ruled" by the so-called Islamic State. Characteristic for these conflicts is that cities became the core of conflicts and their battleground. Consequently, cities are not only one territorial conquest necessary for continuing the conquest of a country. These recent forms of urban warfare add even more complexity to the picture of twenty-first century violent intra-city conflicts.

Moreover, recent conflict constellations in Ukraine, reaching from the so-called EuroMaidan or Revolution of Dignity in Kyiv to the conflicts in Donbas that started in Donetsk and Luhansk, complement the set of presented examples. The Revolution of Dignity had its centre in Kyiv on the Maidan Nezalezhnosti (Independence Square). The civil uprising conquered the public space of the city. After the use of force by the police and special forces, the civil demonstrations escalated to a militarised conflict in January/February 2014.[5] The movement spilled over to other urban centres in the country, especially the western parts of Ukraine. The resistance and resilience of "Anti-Maidan" demonstrations in turn can be connected to the start of separatist movements in Donetsk and Luhansk, highly urbanised and industrialised regions in East Ukraine. Furthermore, with the attempt to create spill over effects and conquer other cities like Kharkiv and Odessa at the Black Sea cities were again in focus for pushing forward this momentum of separatism. These examples also make clear that not only so-called mega-cities should be in the focus of this chapter (Evans 2016, p. 46).[6] Of course, this sketch does not give full account of the individual causes, courses, and consequences of each violent city conflict. Yet, together these examples lead to an important question: How can we approach this highly complex collage of violent conflict constellations and threats to peace and security in and of cities?

However, before we can discuss forms, patterns and variations of violent city conflicts, their legal and political regulation, and which concepts are fit to deal with the settlements of these conflicts, we need to define the politico-legal spaces or places that are in the centre of interest: cities. What makes a "city" from a politico-legal perspective?

A "bureaucratic conception" of cities envisions cities as objects and territories of municipal law, and hence as "integral parts" of the state, as "administrative convenience", or local branches of the central government (Blank 2006). A "democratic conception" of the city, in contrast, perceives local governments to be independent and autonomous semi-sovereign entities distinct from and independent of the state, ideally depending on and reflecting the will of the local population (Blank 2006). The analytical challenge of these conceptions is underlined by the fact that state constitutions and domestic laws usually treat "localities" as parts of the central state-apparatus, while they empower locally elected officials to run local governments granting them autonomy and freedom from central intervention at the same time (Nijman 2011, p. 214; Blank 2006, pp. 887–888; Frug and Barron 2006, pp. 1–22). Moreover, "Local issues are no longer local, but are becoming crucially embedded in global dynamics. [...] big cities situated in different continents and at diverse levels of economic development face similar challenges. In addition, the rapid movement of people, ideas, money and information across borders have caused the collapse of state boundaries in certain aspects and promoted transnational interdependence and interconnection." (Macaluso and Briscoe 2015, p. 13). Furthermore, "locality" is a term used to address cities as well as other municipal entities to capture a potentially emerging legal understanding of this concept in international law (see Blank 2006, pp. 870–871, 883, 887). For Blank for instance neither the democratic nor the bureaucratic legal conceptualisation of "locality" is satisfying (Blank 2006, p. 887). He stresses that "Although localities existed throughout human history as spatial, political, social and economic phenomena, there is no coherent doctrine that explains their changing legal status in international law." (Blank 2006, pp. 890–891 (including also a historical perspective)).

Other authors identify a legal and political dimension of an emerging "global public city" that acts on the domestic, regional and global level, within, out of, but also independently from the state, ideally based on the immediate will of an urban population (Nijman 2009, p. 17; Nijman 2011, pp. 216–218), some are even talking of an emerging "international local government law" (Frug and Barron 2006, pp. 1–22). And more recently, Helmut Aust asked for the legal relevance of co-operations between cities as well as between cities and international organisations (Aust 2013, pp. 674–675; see also Blank 2006, pp. 868, 891–892). He admits that international law is at first glance rather "blind" when it comes to local levels of (public) power (Aust 2013, p. 677; see also Blank 2006, pp. 868, 891–892; Frug 1999, pp. 2, 12–29). Aust argues for a broad and open understanding of international law when it comes to a law of the global public city perspective without, however, neglecting the difference between law and non-law, i.e. legally relevant and non-relevant forms of city-conduct and co-operations (Aust 2013, p. 674).[7] He implicitly also points us to another question that will inform the discussions in the next sections: How much law or legal regulation does the twenty-first century city need to be governed? From a general perspective, city governments have started to internalise global norms directly, on their own initiative, especially in the field of environmental law and climate change, to give effect to international law on the local, and eventually also on the transnational and transregional level even if the central government of state is not legally bound by it, or unwilling or unable to enforce it (Nijman 2009, p. 17;

Nijman 2011, pp. 221–223; Schroeder and Bulkeley 2009, pp. 314–319). Furthermore, international organisations and initiatives have started to directly address the city. The UN-Habitat[8]-led Global Campaign on Urban Governance, for instance, identified a set of universal principles that characterise "good urban governance" — such as sustainability, subsidiarity, equity, efficiency, transparency and accountability, civic engagement and citizenship, as well as security — that are intended to pave the way for an "inclusive city" (The Global Campaign on Urban Governance 2002, pp. 3, 12; Nijman 2011, pp. 219–221, 226; Pieterse 2008, pp. 14, 62–83). "The concept of an 'inclusive city' can potentially be applied in the Global North as well as in the Global South. Yet, the notion of inclusivity could have different dimensions in the North and South, in particular it may resonate with different groups who are either 'significant' or marginalised'" (The Global Campaign on Urban Governance 2002, p. 9). With "good urban governance" UN-Habitat added a strong normative dimension to the discourses about the governance of twenty-first century cities (The Global Campaign on Urban Governance 2002, p. 8).

Hence, we can conclude that twenty-first century cities' actions and interactions on the local and global levels are increasingly being understood as vehicles for the transfer and diffusion of normative standards for good urban governance, creating an informal and formal "trias" of state–city/locality–world, the components of which cannot be approached and analysed separately from each other (Aust 2013, pp. 681–682; Blank 2006, pp. 881–883). In sum, twenty-first century cities are more than sub-units of the state.

Against this background our focus turns back again to intra-city violent conflicts: What characterises violent intra-city conflicts and what is "urban warfare" in twenty-first century cities? What are the politico-legal and humanitarian challenges to regulate these intra-city violent conflicts and possible responses to make peace in cities? The following two sections are dedicated to the importance of understanding the analytical challenges when applying originally state-centred concepts of armed conflict and peace to violent intra-city conflicts.

More than Gangs – Violent Conflicts in Twenty-first Century Cities

Global urbanisation and asymmetric violent conflicts seem to go hand in hand, and more and more violent conflicts are taking place in urban spaces or become intra-city violent conflicts (Sampaio 2016, p. 73). As pointed out earlier, conceptual thinking about the politico-legal dimensions of intra-city violent conflicts in scholarship and practice is just at its beginnings. This section will focus on how legal scholarship as well as non-lawyer experts of international humanitarian law and humanitarian aid and development have addressed intra-city violent conflict constellations in recent years. Debates about intra-city violent conflicts have seen noteworthy turns, which become especially visible at the example of two special issues of the *International Review of the Red Cross.*

The 2010 special issue on "urban conflicts" focussed especially on conflicts with and between gangs, organised crime and informal governance structures that were established by these actors in parts of cities to secure their interest (Sampaio 2016, pp. 71 *et seq*). Rio de Janeiro or Johannesburg were leading examples to underline the urgency of investigating violent conflict in cities, new modes of peacebuilding, and political settlements for cities (Sampaio 2016, pp. 71 *et seq*). The urban conflicts at the centre of interest were those about the right to the (inclusive) city related to demographic growth and changes. Poor neighbourhoods, the growth of slums, and concentrated deprivations were seen to go hand in hand with the emergence of urban violence and riots, which were frequently related to urban territorial gang activities (Sampaio 2016, pp. 71 *et seq*).[9] At the same time informal modes of governance were discussed, which emerge in such contested and "fragile" urban spaces, creating informal norms and cultures of governance for the population. Cities, or parts of cities become non-places for effective governance by formal public authorities, like city governments. According to the editorial, one of the best-known manifestations of urban violence was "gang violence" connected with the debate about the applicability of rules of international humanitarian law regarding non-international armed conflicts to gangs as "organised armed groups" (Bernard 2010, pp. 309–311). Beyond "gang wars", climate change and natural disasters were seen as key-challenges to peace in the city. Three years after this special issue, Macaluso and Briscoe complemented the picture by pointing out that in what they called "fragile city contexts" public city institutions also became perpetrators of violence, while the population would rely on gangs and other irregular groups that provided stability and guaranteed security through informal practices and modes of governance (Macaluso and Briscoe 2015, p. 5). A city is "fragile" "… because its public spaces are the target of attack, and because its ungoverned, unpatrolled and impenetrable built-up areas are perceived to harbour the threats themselves" (Jütersonke and Krause 2013, p. 5). Subsequently, especially policy-oriented publications put a strong focus on large-scale urban violence in a form of what is addressed as "unconventional conflicts", i.e. not intra-state civil wars (Graham 2010, p. 27; Organisation of American States (OAS) 2015). Milliken on the other hand preferred to address such conflict constellations as "urban peace challenges" claiming that: "The link between chronic violence and poverty underlines the critical need for practical innovation to respond to violence and fragility in urban settings. While much of UN peacebuilding practice is limited by the prerogatives of state sovereignty with respect to city-level efforts, there is clearly an interest and capability in the larger peacebuilding community to respond to the urban challenge" (Milliken 2013, Documents and Reports). The substantial and procedural challenges of "urban peace challenges", according to Milliken, lie in addressing and dealing with the resilience of shadow governance and hybrid institutions that exist within and parallel to cities' official institutions (Milliken 2013). Consequently, these settings will also demand going beyond conventional forms of strong-arm approaches in clearing city conflicts by seeking instead for mediated and inclusively negotiated new political settlements.

Moreover, international and international humanitarian organisations face difficulties in understanding the situation on city level in a country and effectively responding to these situations as well as translating this conduct into conceptual approaches for addressing "unconventional conflicts" in twenty-first century cities. Altogether, the outlined developments were found to create new factual and conceptual relations between global-state-city-levels (trias – state-city/locality-world) as well as between state-city-citizens.

At the same time other authors stressed that "… there is evidence that violence in urban areas is itself highly heterogeneous, multi-causal, and spatially uneven …." (Jütersonke and Krause 2013, p. 3). They underlined the core-difference between a "civil war" narrative that makes the conquest of cities and especially the capital key for claiming a victory in intra-state violent conflicts and intra-city violent conflicts, in which cities, and their populations are not stakes to be won in inter- or intra-state conflicts but themselves places and sources of violent struggle, insecurity and fragility. Once mobilised, the populations of cities can bring down governments and change regimes as we have seen for instance at the example of Ukraine (Jütersonke and Krause 2013, p. 5; Geneva Peacebuilding Platform 2015, p. 7).

Cities also increasingly become foci of terrorist attacks and since the rise of the so-called Islamic State also of terrorist conquest. Moreover, cities can be starting points for regime changes, revolutions and secessionist movements. Thus, what becomes clear is that violent conflicts in cities are much more diverse than clashes between gangs. Increasing variations and complexities of intra-city violent conflicts raised questions of what characterises intra-city violent conflicts and to which of them are international humanitarian law and international law are applicable. Or putting it differently, what constitutes a humanitarian situation in a city and which actions and response of external actors, i.e. states and international organisations, does such a situation justify? These still mostly open questions are guided by the desire to govern and regulate large scale intra-state violence, to reduce the suffering of the predominantly civilian population and to support cities in making and keeping the peace to be able to reach the visions of cities outlined in SDG 11.

In 2016 the *Review of the Red Cross* published another special issue, this time on "war in cities", putting a stronger focus on asymmetric conflicts that could also be considered as intra-city violent conflicts or "urban warfare". Taking this security perspective at cities in conflict and "fragile cities" on the brink of conflict takes into consideration but goes beyond discussing cities in states at war; these debates turn to protracted conflicts in cities and "cities at war". In these urban conflict constellations it is the "urban fabric itself that becomes the battleground" (Bernard 2016, p. 2). Turning cities into battlegrounds was a common instrument of twentieth century "total war" but took a different direction with the rise of asymmetric conflicts.[10] In the 2016 *International Review of the Red Cross*, armed conflict in cities is discussed as the organised practice of armed violence of a sufficient intensity with a political purpose, involving state as well as non-state actors. Collective violence is considered as a broader category, including protracted but less intensive conflicts involving non-state actors such as militias, insurgents, and gangs with territorial ambitions and political affiliations, i.e. more than organised crime activities (Sampaio 2016, pp. 75 *et seq*). Furthermore, across the contributions to the 2016 special issue of the *Review of the Red Cross* authors point out that despite still on-going global urbanisation processes and strong interdisciplinary research on cities and urbanisation, we can safely claim that there is a lack of exchange and engagement between research on political and legal dimensions of violent conflicts (in cities) and urban studies. Thus, research on the role of cities in armed conflicts and armed conflict in cities is still at its very beginnings (Evans 2016, p. 38). This finding might be related to the fact that twenty-first century cities – as described and defined *supra* – are highly diverse. This might create obstacles for comparative research on intra-city violent conflicts entering into and connecting to the broader interdisciplinary field of urban studies.[11] Cities as places of violent conflict and "urban warfare" are also increasingly seen related to the debated term of "hybrid warfare" (Evans 2016, p. 38, Sampaio 2016, pp. 72, 78). The armed conflict in Donbas and the creation of the two separatist entities of the People's Republic of Donetsk and the People's Republic of Luhansk could serve as illustration for such a debate. Leaving the debates about the forms and degrees of Russian involvement in these separatist conflicts aside, the examples of Donetsk and Luhansk share earlier discussed characteristics of violent conflicts in cities and city regions (Neuman and Hull 2009). The violent separatist conflict took place and is still taking place highly populated areas. These areas, once a core urbanised and industrial hub of Ukraine, have been experiencing shelling, civilian fatalities and homes destroyed (Maurer 2016, p. 644 with further references to conflict events in Ukraine; see also Shveda and Park 2016; Diuk 2014; Davies 2016; Wilson 2016).

In sum, the discussed examples underline that violent conflicts in cities, like urbanisation, have international, global as well as transnational dimensions and effects (Maurer 2016, p. 645; Sampaio 2016, p. 84). They illustrate the need to approach violent conflicts in twenty-first century cities from different perspectives to gain a better idea of them. What is at stake when focussing on "urban warfare"? "Urban warfare" is not just a variation of the engagement of traditional armies in fights about cities with other armies or armed groups but it is first and foremost about violent conflicts or some say "war" within and of cities which still are outside the scope of traditional analysis and debates regarding the application of rules of international humanitarian law and subsequent humanitarian aid and development. In a recent report, the ICRC addressed possible humanitarian responses to violence in urban areas and especially the lack of essential public services during protracted armed conflicts but also broader social and security effects (Maurer 2016, p. 640 with further references). This leads us to the challenges for international humanitarian responses to violent conflicts in cities. Earle for instance points out:

> Humanitarian actors struggle to deal with the complexity of towns and cities and to take full advantage of the capabilities and resources present in urban areas. [...] The exclusion of development perspectives in immediate humanitarian response can impede long-term recovery. While humanitarian actors cannot solve structural urban problems, they can operate in ways that better support city systems and establish new frameworks within which future urban development can flourish, while limiting disruption to urban development trajectories.
>
> (Earle 2016, p. 221)

And Bernard adds in the same special issue:

> Whether the city is a theatre of war or a place of refuge, the lines between emergency intervention and development become blurred. In addition, many modern conflicts are protracted, and efforts to help residents must take into account the time factor. As we see over and over again in the news, residents and people involved in providing urban services who remain inside cities often show incredible tenacity, endurance and ability to withstand hardship, which humanitarians refer to as "resilience".
>
> (Bernard 2016, p. 10)

Both quotes underline how closely related urban violent conflicts, their regulation, and international humanitarian aid responses and development are to the implementation of SDG 11. The growing extent and complexity of intra-city violent conflicts have led to a search for new policy ideas amongst different expert communities (Sampaio 2016, p. 74). For instance, during the World Humanitarian Summit of 2016 the Global Alliance for Urban Crises was established. The Alliance for Urban Crisis is a platform of experts and expertise on cities, reaching from "humanitarian responders" to actors with urban expertise, among them networks of local authorities, professional associations of planners, architects and engineers. This way, the Alliance aims to connect urban expertise and humanitarian aid as well as development expertise. The Alliance *inter alia* agreed on a set of urban recommendations.[12] The Alliance's practice is guided by a series of principles, developed by the urban expert group and formalised in the Urban Crises Charter.[13] The Alliance has 65 institutional members working to "strengthen their institutional set up, capacity and programming in order to contribute more effectively towards the goal of improved prevention; preparedness and response to urban humanitarian crises".[14] The Alliance itself characterises its work as follows:

> The Global Alliance for Urban Crises is a global, multi-disciplinary and collaborative community of practice. It is a 'network of networks' working to prevent, prepare for and effectively respond to humanitarian crises in urban settings. [….] The Alliance promotes a vision of inclusive, safe, resilient, and sustainable cities and towns in which urban communities, their leaders and members have the power, capacities and resources to address the risks and reality of humanitarian crises, to mitigate crisis impacts on the most vulnerable, including the displaced, and to enable affected people to determine, with dignity, the course of their lives and their futures.[15]

The Alliance makes explicit reference to SDG 11 by using its language.[16] It also seems as if the Alliance as a network of networks builds on the idea of connecting urbanists with humanitarians in order to facilitate collaborations between them to meet short-term humanitarian and longer-term development needs in conflicted cities (Earle 2016, pp. 221–222). This vision leads us to the next section that will focus on discussing which concepts to use and adapt for approaching the transformation from humanitarian response to politico-legal settlement of intra-city violent conflicts.

Peacebuilding and Political Settlements for Twenty-first Century Cities?

Like armed conflict or war, humanitarian response as well as peace making are usually thought as response to inter- or intra-state humanitarian crisis and peace processes i.e. in the dimension of peace in and between states (Macaluso and Briscoe 2015, p. 4; Sampaio 2016, pp. 77 *et seq*). Again, cities in conflict zones of international and non-international armed conflicts (asymmetric conflicts) are familiar territory for international humanitarian aid organisations and peacebuilding initiatives. Yet, building and keeping peace specifically in cities affected by the variety of intra-city conflicts introduced in this chapter raises new conceptual challenges for scholars and practitioners alike, Sampaio even refers to it as responding to "urban lawlessness" (see also Sampaio 2016, pp. 73 *et seq*). It also demands discussing adapting and re-conceptualising concepts of humanitarian aid and development, of peacebuilding and peacekeeping as well as of alternative modes of governance in conflict-prone urban settings. Turning the focus back to humanitarian responses and humanitarian aid, Earle for instance stresses that "area" and "settlement" focused approaches can render humanitarian interventions more legible to local actors and institutions to ensure their cooperation. Such approaches would take a specific geographical area (a municipality or neighbourhood, for example) as the primary reference for planning and delivering humanitarian aid. In the end this apparently could lead to the effect that humanitarian aid would provide a range of different types of support to the whole population of an affected urban area (Earle 2016, p. 223).

Following this suggestion could be one answer to expressed concerns of policy-oriented authors. Milliken (2013) for instance expressed concern that international humanitarian aid and peacebuilding organisations' entry into urban violence regulation and reduction could also risk generating sovereignty and reputation-based resistance from states' governments. States could be alarmed that peacebuilders' involvement in one or more cities on their territory is like declaring that their country is in a state of non-international armed conflict, accepting also implicitly that international actors negotiate directly with sub-national local actors in order to provide basic humanitarian, security and development assistance (Milliken 2013, p. 9).

This struggle for and about external engagement for providing humanitarian assistance and making peace in the city also becomes visible when discussing other concepts usually applied to the state. For instance since the so-called "gang truce" of March 2012 in El Salvador, formats of peace mediation and negotiation processes with formalised inclusive agreements between conflict parties as the goal have been debated as possible instruments for the transition from on-going intra-city violent conflicts to building and keeping peace in the city. The El Salvador "gang truce" in fact took the form of a ceasefire arrangement for violent territorial conflicts between gangs in cities. Especially older members of the gang leaderships were involved in the process of reaching the ceasefire agreement (OAS 2015, p. 6). The "gang truce" lowered the number of murders committed, even if only temporarily. Despite being considered as having failed by now – with attempts of a renewal in 2016 – El Salvador's "gang truce" is still discussed as one possible model for building and keeping peace in twenty-first century cities through negotiated formalised settlements mimicking the practices of peace negotiations and agreements to settle inter- but also intra-state conflict (Macaluso and Briscoe 2015, p. 8).[17] Yet, instruments of preventive diplomacy and international mediation, most prominently of the UN, seem to have limited applicability to conflict constellations in cities in which armed groups show little interest in entering into such negotiations and the violent intra-state conflict becomes increasingly protracted (Sampaio 2016, p. 79).

Hence, this section's need to broaden the focus to the variety of intra-city violent conflicts for developing a better understanding of global comparative challenges of peace making in cites. The emerging political settlements approach, which has its roots in development practice, could serve for approaching such negotiation and dialogue processes in conflicted cities. Political settlements can be defined as "… the forging of a common understanding usually between political elites that their best interests or beliefs are served through acquiescence to a framework for administering political power." (Bell 2015, p. 12). Political settlements are the expression of a common understanding about how power is organised and exercised; they can include formal institutions for managing political and economic relations, such as electoral processes, peace agreements, parliaments, constitutions and market regulations. But they also include informal, often unarticulated agreements that underpin a political system, such as deals between elites on the division of spoils (see also Ingram 2014, p. 1 *et seq*). It would also mean turning the focus to continuous inclusive elite negotiations in cities for building and keeping peace. Thus, formal and informal political settlements in cities could create the foundations for inclusive sustainable peace in cities offering new forms of political and legal self-constitution and alternative modes of governance for twenty-first century cities that float on the continuum between on-going violent conflict and sustainable peace process. Yet, the potential of adapting the political settlements' approach to cities also comes with the risk that arrangements of bringing everyone to the table, including criminal actors and those behind them, could lead to the manifestation of formalised political *un*settlements in citys' formal and informal institutions.[18]

From today's perspective, building and keeping peace in cities ruptured by violent intra-city conflicts also needs active national and international mediation that facilitates an inclusive dialogue as well as informal and formal political settlements, one could even say peace agreements for cities (see eg OAS 2015, p. 16). These challenges raise the need for framework and comprehensive approaches avoiding ad hoc only responses to violence in the city but enabling case-by-case responses (see eg OAS 2015, p. 16 *et seq*). A core challenge is to develop a deeper understanding of local issues, actors, and power arrangements and to develop mechanisms for supporting local leadership for preventing and responding to violence that allows (post-conflict) cities to change relationships within the city, between community members, and between the city and the state. Thus, the focus turns to rebuilding cities that experienced intra-city violent conflict. Also, here we can witness a growing network of networks to address these challenges. For instance, the ICRC has been working with global initiatives like the New Urban Agenda and Habitat III, to create policy guidance on urban humanitarian action for national governments and city authorities for the future. According to Maurer:

> This guidance will be important in situations where municipal authorities need to partner with the ICRC and other humanitarian organizations to protect and assist their city's population and build essential urban services that are resilient in bad times as well as good times. There is probably no other context through which warfare and violence in urban areas are so clearly visible as in some of the cities in Yemen. While war and violations of IHL have taken their toll, at the same time violence and conflict have slowly killed economic activities, which are so essential to the survival of populations. With both trends combined, we end up with what we have: massive disruption of the economic, political and societal fabric, and the virtual impossibility of humanitarian actors functioning as a substitute for non-existent economic activities and social services for a whole population.
> (Maurer 2016, p. 646)

Moreover, the idea of "human security" has gained prominence in recent years. It complements "state security" by placing a greater emphasis on the security of people. Different authors point to the potential of "human security" in a broad sense for addressing cities' vulnerability to disasters as well as to low and high intensity violent conflict (Duijsens 2010, p. 363; Sampaio 2016, p. 74). "Human security" puts the focus on individual security, protecting individuals from physical violence by a state, another state, groups, or other individuals. In its interpretation and application "human security" can also focus on "community security" and "political security" offering protection for communities from ethnic violence and from human rights violations (Duijsens 2010, p. 363). In sum, it seems safe to claim that "human security" relates to global human rights protection and also makes relevant connections to international humanitarian law. "Human security" adds elements of human development to the concept; this includes economic security to sustain life and food security, as well as environmental security (Duijsens 2010, p. 363). The idea of relating "human security" to cities' vulnerability to disasters as well as to low and high intensity violent conflict can be read in conjunction with SDG 11 and the goal to promote safe, resilient and inclusive cities. In the end, responding to intra-city violent conflict and building sustainable peace in twenty-first century cities means more than guaranteeing the absence of violence, and authors consider "human security" as a useful concept for assessing violence and crisis situations in urban contexts; it also raises new challenges regarding to urban planning and proactive approaches to intra-city violence (Duijsens 2010, p. 363).[19]

Concluding Remarks and Outlook

This chapter explored the growing relevance of dealing with challenges of various forms and patterns of intra-city violent conflicts that will shape current and future processes of global urbanisation. It argued that responding to conflict potentials in and about twenty-first century cities needs adapted and new approaches to the regulation of violent conflict and building peace in the city. Jütersonke and Krause remind us that "... city 'disorder' need not imply that urban spaces are unable to cope with such challenges and ultimately transform. To the contrary, the 'resilience' of cities is a crucial feature that is often overlooked, and one that need to be explored further from the peacebuilding perspective." (Jütersonke and Krause 2013, p. 4). Thus, coming back to peace and security as basic conditions for reaching SDG 11, it remains to be explored whether and which opportunities cities offer to adapt and enhance concepts and practices of regulating (intra-city) violent conflicts and making peace as well as which role networks like the Global Alliance for Urban Crisis and their vision relating to SDG 11 will play in this regard in the future.[20]

This chapter's aim was to give an overview about the most recent emerging debates and eventually to invite and encourage further explorations of comparative and interdisciplinary urban conflict, peace building and political settlement research relating to the "glocal" visions and goals expressed in SDG 11. It remains for further future analysis to debate where to localise the state and other actors in the complex picture of contemporary intra-city violent conflicts and peacemaking processes. Thus, the chapter also encourages pushing further towards thinking about concepts of low and high intensity intra-city violent conflict, peacebuilding, political settlements, humanitarian aid and development and human security both beyond and below the state level and therewith expanding the perspectives on SDG 11's goal to make cities and urban communities inclusive, safe, resilient and sustainable spaces.

Notes

1 See Soja 2010; Blank and Rosen-Zvi 2010; Harvey 2001; Sassen 1991.
2 Also Peter Maurer draws an alarming picture by stating that: "The rapid urbanisation we are seeing is creating fragile cities – places like Bamako and Caracas – where violence is accelerating, fuelled by the drug trade, mass unemployment and civil unrest. It is not outright war but plain violence that kills in those cities, which enter the vicious circle of fragility, violence and, possibly, conflict. In some of the most violent cities in Latin America, as many people die by firearm violence as in Syria – a country at war. Many large cities of South Asia, Africa and Latin America are already suffering the consequences of rapid and unregulated expansion – most visibly in neglected and violence-affected slums and shanty towns." (Maurer 2016, p. 644).
3 Most people killed in urban conflict are civilians (Maurer 2016, p. 640).
4 A/RES/70/1, Transforming our world: The 2030 Agenda for Sustainable Development, 21 October 2015.

5 Alleged crimes committed in the context of the Maidan protests since 21 November 2013 and other events in Ukraine since 20 February 2014 are currently under preliminary examination by the International Criminal Court (ICC) in The Hague; although with a low probability to lead to a trial.

6 Evans comes to the preliminary conclusion that "... there is nothing that is certain or inevitable about armed violence in cities. From a security perspective, military researchers must learn to distinguish between the global city of influence, the megacity of sprawl and the emerging middleweight city, and between smaller peri-urban, semi-urban and inner-urban forms of human habitation. All are different. Indeed, when it comes to assessing the frequency and character of insecurity in a diverse range of cities, generalizations are misleading and good research will seek to adopt a strictly evidence-based approach." (Evans 2016, p. 47).

7 Aust focuses on cities and climate change, and other activities of cities and municipalities to get involved in areas that were traditionally perceived to belong to the sphere of a state's foreign policy, see Aust 2013, pp. 674–675; see also Frug and Barron 1999, pp. 27–29; Nijman 2011, pp. 228–229.

8 UN-Habitat – United Nations Human Settlements Programme.

9 For more on 'gang governance', see Macaluso and Briscoe 2015, pp. 7 *et seq;* for more on organised crime and gang violence in national and international law, see Hauck and Peterke 2010, pp. 407 *et seq.*

10 Bernard again underlines the complexities of contemporary conflict constellations by stressing that "... cities are again becoming the focal point of battles, partly because of a series of factors specific to modern conflicts. The vast majority of these conflicts involve armed groups fighting each other or government forces. Armed groups are sometimes born in cities, or they may hide in cities to benefit from the terrain: drawing the enemy into terrain […] fighting in a city allows armed groups to make up for their relative weakness in these 'asymmetric warfare' situations. In a sense, the city levels the playing field. The technological superiority of governments equipped with modern military hardware means that armed groups have no chance of success if a battle takes place in open country, so they hide in the urban fabric, blending in with the city's population" (Bernard 2016, p. 4).

11 See also Evans, who takes a strong security and military studies focus (Evans 2016, p. 37).

12 Available at: http://urbancrises.org/about-us (Accessed: 4 February 2018).

13 Available at: http://urbancrises.org/about-us (Accessed: 4 February 2018).

14 Available at: https://unhabitat.org/wp-content/uploads/2016/05/Global-Alliance-for-Urban-Crises-Overview-25-March-2016.pdf (Accessed: 4 February 2018).

15 Available at: https://unhabitat.org/wp-content/uploads/2016/05/Global-Alliance-for-Urban-Crises-Overview-25-March-2016.pdf (Accessed: 4 February 2018).

16 "The Alliance promotes a vision of inclusive, safe, resilient, and sustainable cities and towns (as laid out in the 2030 Agenda for Sustainable Development) in which urban communities, their leaders and members have the power, capacities and resources to address the risks and reality of humanitarian crises, to mitigate crisis impacts on the most vulnerable, including the displaced, and to enable affected people to determine, with dignity, the course of their lives and their futures." [online]. Available at: https://unhabitat.org/wp-content/uploads/2016/05/Global-Alliance-for-Urban-Crises-Overview-25-March-2016.pdf (Accessed: 24 February 2018).

17 El Salvador's gang truce: a lost opportunity? [online]. Available at: https://www.opendemocracy.net/opensecurity/mabel-gonzález-bustelo/el-salvador's-gang-truce-lost-opportunity (Accessed: 4 February 2018).

18 Regarding the conceptualization of formalized political *un*settlements, see Bell and Pospisil 2017.
19 Sampaio argues for pushing towards an 'urban strategic environment' (Sampaio 2016, p. 91).
20 Geneva Peacebuilding Platfrom 2015, p. 11.

Bibliography

Literature

Aust, Helmut Philipp. 2013. Auf dem Weg zum Recht der globalen Stadt? 'C 40' und der 'Konvent der Bürgermeister' im globalen Klimaschutzregime. *Zeitschrift für ausländisches öffentliches Recht und Völkerrecht*, 73, 673–704.

Bell, Christine and Pospisil, Jan. 2017. Navigating inclusion in transition from conflict: The formalised political unsettlement. *Journal of International Development*, 29, pp. 576–593.

Bell, Christine. 2015. What we talk about when we talk about political settlements, Towards inclusive and open political settlements in an era of disillusionment. *PSRP Working Paper (1)*. 1 September 2015. Edinburgh, UK: Global Justice Academy University of Edinburgh.

Bernard, Vincent. 2016. Editorial: War in Cities: the Spectre of Total War. *Review of the Red Cross*, pp. 98, 1–11.

Blank, Yishai and Rosen-Zvi, Issi. 2010. Introduction: The spatial turn in social theory *HAGAR: Studies in Culture, Polity & Identities*, 10, 1–6.

Blank, Yishai. 2006. The city and the world. *Columbia Journal of Transnational Law*, 44, 868–931.

Daase, Cindy. 2014. The global city in the 21st century: written and unwritten rules within and beyond the state. *ASIEN – The German Journal on Contemporary Asia*, 132, pp. 98–113.

Davies, Lance. 2016. Russia's 'governance' approach: intervention and the conflict in the Donbas. *Europe Asia Studies*, 68, 726–749.

Diuk, Nadia. 2014. Euromaidan, Ukraine's self-organizing revolution. *World Affairs*, 176, 9–16.

Duijsens, Raimond. 2010. Humanitarian challenges of urbanization. *International Review of the Red Cross*, 92, 351–361.

Evans, Michael. 2016. Future war in cities: Urbanization's challenge to strategic studies in the 21st century. *International Review of the Red Cross*, 98, 37–51.

Frug, Gerald E. 1999. *City Making: Building Communities without Building Walls.* Princeton, NJ: Princeton University Press.

Frug, Gerald E. and Barron, David J. 2006. International local government law. *The Urban Lawyer*, 38, 1–62.

Graham, Stephen. 2010. *Cities under Siege: The New Military Urbanism*. New York: Verso.

Guilfoyle, Douglas. 2016. Reading the city and the city as an international lawyer: reflections on territoriality, jurisdiction and transnationality. *London Review of International Law*, 4, 195–207.

Harvey, David. 2001. *Spaces of Capital: Towards A Critical Geography.* Edinburgh, UK: Edinburgh University Press.

Hauck, Pierre and Peterke, Sven. 2010. Organized crime and gang violence in national and international law. *International Review of the Red Cross*, 92, 407–436.

Ingram, Sue. 2014. Political Settlements: the History of an Idea in Policy and Theory. SSGM Discussion Paper 2014/5.

Jütersonke, Oliver and Krause, Keith. 2013. Peacebuilding and the City: Setting the Scene. Brief No. 9. Geneva Peacebuilding Platform.

Macaluso, Agnese and Briscoe, Ivan. 2015. *Trapped in the city: communities, insecurity and urban life in fragile states. Policy Brief.* The Hague, NL: Knowledge Platform Security & Rule of Law.

Maurer, Peter. 2016. War in cities: What is at stake, speech given by the ICRC President Peter Maurer, as part of the ICRC's Research and Debate Cycle on War in Cities, at the Graduate Institute, Geneva, on 4 April 2017. *International Review of the Red Cross*, 98, 639–646.

Neuman, Michael and Hull, Angela. 2009. The future of the city region. *Regional Studies*, 43, 777–787.

Nijman, Janne. 2009. The rising influence of urban actors. *The Broker - Special Report on 'Cities of the World Unite'*, 17, 14–17.

Nijman, Janne. 2011. The Future of the City and the International Law of the Future. In: Sam Muller et al (eds). *The Law of the Future and the Future of Law.* The Hague, NL: Torkel Opsahl Academic EPublisher. pp. 213–229.

Peterke, Sven. 2007. Brasiliens Herausforderung durch den Terror der Organisierten Kriminalität: Nach der Anschlagsserie von Rio: Kampf dem (Narco-) Terrorismus? *VRÜ – Law and Politics in Africa, Asian and Latin America*, 40, pp. 230–248.

Pieterse, Edgar. 2008. *City Futures: Confronting the Crisis of Urban Development.* London: Zed Books.

Sampaio, Antônio. 2016. Before and after urban warfare: Conflict preventions and transitions in cities. *International Review of the Red Cross*, 98, pp. 71–95.

Sassen, Saskia. 1991. *The Global City: New York, London, Tokyo.* Princeton, NJ: Princeton University Press.

Schroeder, Heike and Bulkeley, Harriet. 2009. Global Cities and the Governance of Climate Change: What is the Role of Law in Cities? *Fordham Urban Law Journal*, 36, 313–359.

Shveda, Yuriy and Park, JoungHo. 2016. Ukraine's revolution of dignity: The dynamics of Euromaidan. *Journal of Eurasian Studie*s, 7, 85–91.

Soja, Edward W. 2010. *Seeking Spatial Justice.* Minneapolis, MN.: University of Minnesota Press.

Wilson, Andrew. 2016. The Donbas in 2014: explaining civil conflict perhaps, but not civil war. *Europe Asia Studies*, 68, 631–652.

Documents

Geneva Peacebuilding Platform. 2015. White Paper on Peacebuilding. Geneva, Switzerland.

Milliken, Jennifer. 2013. Building Peace in Urban Settings, Lessons from the Ground and Recommendations for Collaboration. Paper No. 11. Geneva Peacebuilding Platform.

Organisation of American States (OAS). 2015. Searching for Common Approaches to Deal with Unconventional Conflicts and Violence in the Americas. Washington, DC: OAS.

United Nations Human Settlements Programme, UN-Habitat, The Global Campaign on Urban Governance. 2002. Concept Paper 2nd Edition: March 2002.

United Nations, Department of Economic and Social Affairs. 2014. World Urbanization Prospects The 2014 Revision, Highlights, ST/ESA/SER.A/352.

7 Ensuring Access to Public Space as a Dimension of "Safe Cities"

The Role of UN Entities in Shaping the Global Urban Governance Agenda

Hannah Birkenkötter

Introduction

"We envisage a world … where human habitats are safe" – this is one of the many visions proclaimed by the heads of state and government gathered at the 2015 United Nations Sustainable Development Summit (UN General Assembly 2015a, para 7). What does it mean for a human habitat, a city, to be safe? The 2030 Agenda and the New Urban Agenda promote an understanding of safety as access to public space that is free of violence, to be implemented by a variety of actors through multi-stakeholder partnerships. This chapter argues that this focus on the planning and design of public space is the result of slow normative change that has in part been shaped by the operational activities of UN entities.

The chapter proceeds in three steps. I first outline the substantive content of Sustainable Development Goal (SDG) 11.7 and the New Urban Agenda as they relate to public space management and safety. In this part, I further situate these two documents in the larger evolution of the UN's human settlements agenda. In a second step, I then take a closer look at operational activities relating to safer cities undertaken by the United Nations Human Settlements Programme (UN-Habitat), but also at a programme by an entity that is not directly charged with implementing the UN's human settlements agenda: the UN Entity on Gender Equality (UN Women). While UN entities' operational activities respond to their mandates, there is a large margin of interpretation as to how to discharge a given mandate, and entities will engage with one another as well as with several partners in devising measures to implement their mandates. The design of operational activities might be supervised, but is not primarily guided, by the state-composed governing structures. Instead, the governing bodies acknowledge these activities *ex post facto* and typically without restricting them. They do, however, appear to play no small role in legitimizing such activities and in scaling them up. The result is an interplay between interpretation and standard-setting, and between executive agencies and their principals. In a third and final step, I outline some implications for international institutional law resulting from a scrutiny of the operational activities of UN entities.

Access to Safe Public Space in Sustainable Development Goal 11 and the New Urban Agenda

It is beyond question that the 2030 Agenda with its 17 goals and no less than 139 targets will serve as one of the most salient normative yardsticks in the work of the UN for years to come, even if formally speaking the 2030 Agenda is a recommendation of the General Assembly, and as such does not create direct legal obligations for UN member states (Art. 10 UN Charter; but see White 2017). Secretary-General Antonio Guterres has announced significant institutional reforms in the organisation of the UN development cooperation system in view of the 2030 Agenda, which will affect the way in which UN entities cooperate both amongst one another as well as with partners at the regional, national and local levels (UN Secretary-General 2017). SDG 11 is specifically dedicated to cities and human settlements and aims to "make cities and human settlements inclusive, safe, resilient and sustainable." It needs to be read in the context of the broader human settlements agenda at the UN, which has evolved over some 40 years.

Providing Access to Safe Public Spaces as a Focus of the UN Human Settlements Agenda

Access to safe public spaces is one of several targets contained in SDG 11. Target 7 of SDG 11 aims to "[b]y 2030, provide universal access to safe, inclusive and accessible, green and public spaces, in particular for women and children, older persons and persons with disabilities." While SDG 11.7 does not necessarily imply that safety ought to be valued more than any of the other attributes of public spaces, the indicators for target 11.7 send out a clear signal. The first indicator measures the average share of built-up area of cities that is open space for public use for all, whereas the second indicator measures the proportion of persons who are victims of physical or sexual harassment (UN General Assembly 2017, Annex I, 11.7.1, 11.7.2). As the monitoring of the SDGs occurs primarily through data collection (Riegner 2016) – part of a larger trend of ever-growing sets of indicators in global governance, not free of critique (Merry et al. 2015) – increasing the amount of public space free of physical violence thus amounts to the main substantive content of SDG 11.7.

SDG 11 needs to be read jointly with the other SDGs, given that all goals are "integrated and indivisible" (UN General Assembly 2015a, preamble, paras 5, 18, 55). The second indicator for SDG 11.7 points to two goals that are immediately relevant to safety in cities: SDG 5 on gender equality and SDG 16 on peaceful societies. In addition, and regarding all SDGs, goal 17 on the means of implementation and the "Global Partnership for Sustainable Development" guides entities within the UN system and beyond in implementing the 2030 Agenda. That these goals need to be considered together was also the shared understanding of a Cross-Cutting Expert Group Meeting on “Safer Cities in the New Urban Agenda” held in 2016 prior to the Conference on Housing and Sustainable Development (Habitat III), which brought together representatives of UN-Habitat, the Global Network on Safer Cities, the European Forum on Urban Security and the International Centre for Crime Prevention, and was intended to ensure complementarity between the New Urban Agenda and the SDGs (UN-Habitat 2016, p. 3).

SDG 11 also needs to be read in conjunction with the New Urban Agenda, which was adopted at the Conference on Housing and Sustainable Urban Development (Habitat III) in 2016 (UN General Assembly 2016). The New Urban Agenda explicitly references the SDGs and stipulates that its implementation “contributes to the implementation and localisation of the 2030 Agenda … including Goal 11” (para 9). It consistently talks about “safe, inclusive, accessible, green, and quality public spaces” (paras 13, 37, 53, 67, 100, 109) in connection with a number of issues: persons with disabilities (para 36), social inclusivity (para 37), social and economic development (para 53), resilience (para 67), freedom from crime and violence, which specifically mentions sexual violence (para 100), and slum upgrading (para 109). The notion of public space also figures prominently in several paragraphs relating to housing (paras 97, 99).

The Substantive Evolution of the UN Human Settlements Agenda

Safety and public space as specifically urban concerns are a relatively recent addition to the global urban agenda. The first Habitat Conference in Vancouver in 1976 was largely dominated by environmental concerns. This is not surprising: the decision to hold a conference on human settlements was taken at the first UN Conference on the Human Environment in 1972 and the preparatory process was supervised by the newly established UN Environment Programme’s Governing Council (UN General Assembly 1972; UN General Assembly 1976, pp. 118–121). Next to environmental concerns, the first Habitat Conference emphasised the link between human settlements and economic development and placed this debate in the context of discussions on a New Economic Order (UN General Assembly 1976, 2 and Section II para 3, Section III para 2; recommendations A.1 (a), A.2 (c) (i) and F.2 (a)). Both the declaration as well as the national recommendations for action focus on this nexus and call for the establishment of national settlement policies. Safety is mentioned only once in the entire text, in the context of planning: “local planning must be concerned with social and economic factors … This means in particular: … the provision of infrastructure networks and systems required to link activities on the basis of economy, safety, convenience and environmental impact” (UN General Assembly 1976, recommendation B.7). Crime prevention and physical violence are not mentioned at all in the Vancouver declaration nor in its recommendations for national action and international cooperation.

This changed with the Istanbul Declaration and the Habitat Agenda adopted at the second Habitat Conference in Istanbul in 1996. Whereas the 1976 Vancouver Declaration aspired to create "more livable, attractive and efficient settlements" (UN General Assembly 1976, para 1b), the Heads of State or Government in the Istanbul declaration framed their goal as "making human settlements safer, healthier and more livable, equitable, sustainable and productive" and considered the Conference as marking "a new era of cooperation … of building together a world where everyone can live in a safe home with the promise of a decent life of dignity, good health, safety, happiness and hope" (UN General Assembly 1996, Annex I paras 1, 15). In the 1996 Habitat Agenda, safety advances to a widely used term, albeit characterised by a high degree of vagueness and openness. It is most often employed as a desideratum or goal to be achieved through various measures (UN General Assembly 1996, Annex II, eg in paras 2, 21, 32, 42, 85, 136, 142, 194), alongside the goals of health, welfare and environmental protection. The environment, in turn, is often joined with the attribute "safe" – measures ought to be implemented to achieve a "safe environment" (UN General Assembly 1996, Annex II, paras 9, 21). Safety is seen both as a goal and as a means to improve crime prevention efforts (UN General Assembly 1996, Annex II, eg in paras 25, 30, 84, 123). The back and forth from safety as an end to safety as a means is perhaps most visible in the section on shelters and the provision of basic infrastructure. One recommendation for action reads: "To safeguard the … safety … of all people … Governments … should promote … a high level of safety and public security." While analytically true, there is very little concrete guidance for action to be taken from this particular recommendation.

While safety is not exclusively connected to crime prevention and security, urban crime and other forms of violence were a major concern of the 1996 Habitat Agenda, building *inter alia* on the 1995 Economic and Social Council (ECOSOC) Guidelines for Cooperation and Technical Assistance in the field of Urban Crime Prevention, which had already stressed the importance of a local approach to urban crime prevention (UN Office on Drugs and Crime (UNODC) n/d). Crime is mentioned no less than 12 times in the Agenda (paras 8, 25, 123, 160), compared to only twice in the 2016 New Urban Agenda (UN General Assembly 2016, paras 100, 103). In turn, the New Urban Agenda's focus on the public dimension of urban space is a first: the sequence "safe, inclusive, accessible, green, and quality public spaces" occurs six times, "public spaces" a total of 11 times. While spatial planning was an issue on the settlement agendas before, the explicit nexus between public spaces and safety is a new addition to the human settlements agenda. But it did not come about overnight. Instead, it is the result of subtle substantive shifts between the different Habitat Agendas.

From Government Responsibility to Stakeholder Networks

In addition to shifts in the substantive content of the Habitat agendas, we can also witness an increasingly abstract language, both on the substance as well as concerning the addressees of its goals. Compare the following two paragraphs from the Istanbul Global Plan of Action (Habitat II) and the New Urban Agenda (Habitat III) concerning urban crime:

> To prevent, reduce and eliminate violence and crime, Governments at the appropriate levels, including local authorities, in partnership with all interested parties, should: (a) Design, create and maintain liveable human settlements that encourage the use of public spaces as centres of community life so that they do not become places for criminal activity . . .
>
> (Istanbul Global Plan of Action)

and

> We will support the provision of well-designed networks of safe, accessible, green and quality streets and other public spaces that are accessible to all and free from crime and violence, including sexual harassment and gender-based violence …
>
> (New Urban Agenda)

In a recent study of World Bank Reports, Franco Moretti and Dominique Pestre analyse how several changes in language lead to less concrete and discernible actions and instead promote abstract yet universal principles, making it hard to contest them (Moretti and Pestre 2015). While displaying different linguistic properties, a similar development towards more abstraction can be observed when comparing the different Habitat agendas. In the New Urban Agenda, it is not quite clear anymore which actor is responsible for ensuring access to public space. Taken at face value, the commitment from the New Urban Agenda, in conjunction with SDG 11 and its targets, stipulates that states as the drafters of the New Urban Agenda will "support" the provision of public spaces that are free from crime and violence. Contrast this with one of the Guidelines for Action from the 1976 Vancouver Declaration: "It is the responsibility of Governments to prepare spatial strategy plans and adopt human settlement policies to guide the socio-economic development efforts." Such a clear assignment of responsibility to the state is entirely absent from the language of the New Urban Agenda.

Rather, the New Urban Agenda understands itself as an Agenda that is neither exclusively authored by nor addressed to states. The introductory clause states that, "We, Heads of State and Government, Ministers and High Representatives, have gathered … with the participation of subnational and local governments, parliamentarians, civil society, indigenous peoples and local communities, the private sector, professionals and practitioners, the scientific and academic community, and other relevant stakeholders, to adopt a New Urban Agenda" (UN General Assembly 2016). While formal authorship rests with state governments, it is no longer "We, Heads of State and Government" exclusively, or, as the resolution establishing the former Centre for Human Settlements once stated, "primarily the responsibility of Governments" to improve the quality of life in human settlements (UN General Assembly 1977, preamble). Similarly, the 2030 Agenda states that implementation rests with "Governments as well as parliaments, the United Nations system and other international institutions, local authorities, indigenous peoples, civil society, business and the private sector, the scientific and academic community – and all people." (UN General Assembly 2015a, para 52). Ultimately, conferring normative value upon a set of substantive recommendations resides with state-composed organs. But the broader language – public spaces, prevention, coupled with a number of attributes of which safety is one – as well as the explicit targeting of actors besides states opens the door to a wide range of possible interpretations as to who should implement the New Urban Agenda, and how.

Discharging Mandates or Shaping Global Agendas? United Nations Operational Activities Revisited

Within the UN system, the entity primarily charged with issues of urban settlements is the UN Human Settlements Programme (UN-Habitat). Established in 2001 to replace the Commission on Human Settlements and its secretariat, it is a full UN programme governed by a Governing Council that reports directly to the General Assembly (UN General Assembly 2001). However, other UN entities and agencies have also worked on urban safety. In recent years UN Women has been one of the most prominent UN entities to work on safety in urban settlements. UNICEF has been another key entity with its "Child Friendly Initiative", launched as a follow-up to the Istanbul Declaration and the Habitat Agenda in 1996 (UNICEF n/d; cf also Riggio 2002 and Bishop and Corkery 2017). The UN Development Programme (UNDP) has also worked on safer cities (UNDP 2014 and UNDP 2016).

As with almost all international development cooperation agencies, there is a distinction to be made between the normative, policy level and the operational level (Riegner 2017, para 3 I 1 b)). But this distinction is not absolute: of course, the operational level is informed by the normative level. In addition, the argument presented here is that the operational level also has an impact on the normative level. The following sections will provide chronological overviews of the evolution of the UN-Habitat's Safer Cities Programme and the UN Women's Safe Cities and Safe Public Spaces flagship programme in order to illustrate the normative impact operational activities can have both at the local as well as at the global levels.

UN-Habitat's Safer Cities Programme

Established by a strategic policy decision of the Centre for Human Settlements (Habitat), the Safer Cities Programme was launched in 1996 at the request of African Mayors (cf UN-Habitat Governing Council 2011b, preamble). The programme was understood to fall squarely under the above-cited paragraph 123 of the 1996 Habitat Agenda, which aimed at the prevention and reduction of crime (UN-Habitat 2006, p. 24). In the first decade of its existence, the Safer Cities Programme was organised into a global project called "Safer Cities for Better Governance" and several local projects in cooperation with city governments (UN-Habitat 2006, p. 1). This separation into several projects can in part be explained through UN-Habitat's funding structure: The "Safer Cities for Better Governance" global project was funded by the Netherlands, whereas other sources of funding were procured through city-level projects (UN-Habitat 2006, p. 33). It goes beyond the scope of this contribution to elaborate on the funding structures of UN development cooperation in general and/or human settlement activities in particular, but it is important to acknowledge that the separation into various projects or project lines responds in part to funding necessities. Only about 5 percent of UN-Habitat's budget comes from the regular UN budget (cf UN Handbook 2016–17 (Ministry of Foreign Affairs and Trade of New Zealand 2017), p. 243 and Wortmann 2007, para 10). Important partners for the global project were the European Forum on Urban Safety, the International Centre for the Prevention of Crime and the Institute for Security Studies – two networks of local and regional authorities, where city governments cooperate directly with one another (cf Aust 2017, p. 344), and an independent research entity. The Safer Cities approach was ultimately the result of a collaboration of staff that were mandated by a wide variety of actors – states (UN-Habitat), cities (European Forum on Urban Safety, International Centre for the Prevention of Crime) and experts (International Centre for the Prevention of Crime and the Institute for Security Studies).

It appears that in this initial phase the focus of the Safer Cities programme was local, largely responsive and restricted to specific constituencies. A strategic review conducted in 2006 mentions Safer Cities approaches to youth at risk in Africa (with the prospect of developing similar context-specific approaches for other regions) and Safer Cities approaches to gender-based violence (UN-Habitat 2006, pp. 20 *et seq*). These approaches were streamlined and unified as the programme expanded: following the 2006 strategic review, the Safer Cities programme was further institutionalised through the Strategic Plan for Safer Cities 2008–2013 (UN-Habitat 2007a). The Strategic Plan emphasises the importance of the planning and design of public spaces in preventing crime (UN-Habitat 2007a, p. 6), thus shifting to an understanding of safety through urban planning. In addition, UN-Habitat's flagship publication, the annual Global Report on Human Settlements, also addressed safety and security in cities in 2007. The report proffers a broad conception of safety and security that is not only focused on crime prevention, but also considers insecurity of tenure and forced evictions as well as natural and man-made disasters as threats to security and safety in cities, although the Safer Cities programme is exclusively mentioned in conjunction with urban crime and violence (UN-Habitat 2007b, pp. 86–88, 258–259). In the Global Report, the Safer Cities programme is presented as an "international cooperation mechanism … an international initiative that is locally applied" (UN-Habitat 2007b, pp. 86 *et seq*). The report concludes with a call for the reinvigoration of the programme, "highlighting its strategic role as a normative and evaluation facility" (id. 259). With regard to crime prevention, it advocates "non-traditional approaches" to security (id. 260). On the substantive level, this entails a shift from responsive policies to approaches that enhance urban security and safety through effective urban planning and design and a furthering of the social crime prevention component.

Institutionally, both the 2007 Global Report as well as the Strategic Plan call for enhanced "partnership mechanisms", i.e. the identification of local partners – not only local public authorities, but also private actors such as businesses, community groups etc. – who are seen to be the "key players involved in delivery" (UN-Habitat 2007b, p. 260). There are at least two outcomes of the 2007 evaluation of the Safer Cities programme through the Global Report on Human Settlements and the Strategic Plan for Safer Cities. First, the substantive focus expands to consider dimensions of urban planning as safety concerns and specifically addresses public spaces. Second, the Safer Cities programme becomes firmly anchored in UN-Habitat's programme work: the Strategic Plan for Safer Cities calls for upscaling and resource mobilisation, as does the Human Settlements report. UN-Habitat now offers "Safer Cities Services" to cities that request them. The UN-Habitat staff supports local authorities in carrying out assessments of the safety situation in cities and will assist in the development of a local safety strategy and action plan to be implemented through a network of relevant stakeholders (UN-Habitat n/d, p. 3). The local safety strategy will routinely include a review and reform of existing laws. Law reform is thus an integral part of the operative activities of UN-Habitat, albeit not as the result of the direct implementation of a previously adopted normative standard, but rather as the result of multi-stakeholder partnerships.

Interestingly, the highest governance body of UN-Habitat, its Governing Council, did not explicitly address the Safer Cities programme until several years after its institutionalisation in 2007. While two resolutions from 2003 and 2005 on youth engagement in UN-Habitat activities take note of the Safer Cities programme's youth work (UN-Habitat Governing Council 2003 and UN-Habitat Governing Council 2005), none of the resolutions adopted by the Governing Council in 2007 or 2009 mention the Safer Cities programme, or explicitly mandate UN-Habitat's secretariat to further expand the programme. This does not mean that the Governing Council was not informed about the Safer Cities programme. UN-Habitat's secretariat lists its work on safer cities in the 2008–2009 and 2010–2011 proposed work programme and budget (UN-Habitat Executive Director 2007; UN-Habitat Executive Director 2009), both of which were subsequently adopted by the Governing Council. Nonetheless, it was only in 2011 that the Governing Council expressly addressed the nexus between urban development, safer cities and urban crime prevention as a matter of policy and encouraged member states to adopt local and national urban crime prevention policies (UN-Habitat Governing Council 2011b). Also in 2011, the Governing Council adopted a resolution on sustainable urban development through access to quality urban public space, which it explicitly placed in the context of its previous resolutions on youth and gender and safer cities (UN-Habitat Governing Council 2011a). Based on this resolution, UN-Habitat has since launched a Global Public Space Programme which has thus far resulted, *inter alia*, in the development of a Global Public Space Toolkit (UN-Habitat 2015). The vocabulary employed by the Governing Council is not new. Rather, it draws on language already in existence in the UN-Habitat's Safer Cities programme and confirms the existing normative agenda related to safer cities, coupled with a request to continue this work. Ultimately, then, the formal, state-composed decision-making governing body within UN-Habitat was not the primary driver in shaping the global agenda on safety in cities, but rather an observer that acknowledged and confirmed prior work that had been carried out for over a decade.

The same can be said for the institutional impact of the Safer Cities programme. One of its major results was the establishment of the Global Network on Safer Cities. Described by a UN-Habitat civil service officer as the "network hub" of the Safer Cities programme, the Global Network on Safer Cities was launched during the World Urban Forum in Naples, Italy, in September 2012 as an international forum for cities and urban stakeholders (Andersson 2014, p. 89). The World Urban Forum in turn is a multi-stakeholder conference launched under the auspices of UN-Habitat in 2001 (UN Commission on Human Settlements 2001, para 10). First affirmed by the General Assembly as a "non-legislative technical forum in which experts can exchange views in the years when the Governing Council does not meet" (UN General Assembly 2001, Section B para 3), it has since become a massive conference on urban issues, bringing together over 20,000 participants - national and local policymakers, non-governmental organisations, individuals, the private sector and practitioners in urban matters (UN-Habitat Executive Director 2015a) and is viewed today as "the foremost global arena for interaction" (UN General Assembly 2015b).

The Global Network on Safer Cities is intended to enable "local authorities and urban stakeholders to deliver urban safety" (Andersson 2014, p. 89). It is part of a wider trend of decentralisation that establishes local entities as sites of authority, and consequently challenges the century-old paradigm that views states as being exclusively responsible for the delivery of safety and security (Aust 2017, pp. 333–334). Like the C40 network in the realm of global environmental policy (Aust 2013; Bouteligier 2013), the Global Network on Safer Cities has the potential of becoming a central forum in shaping the substantive content of global normative standards in the area of safety. The actors connected within the Global Network on Safer Cities are UN-Habitat's primary cooperation partners for the Safer Cities programme. UN-Habitat connects directly with local actors, which are sometimes local public authorities, but often come from other constituencies – community groups, non-governmental organisations – as well. States have a role to play in ensuring safety and security within cities, but it is no longer an exclusive role, also regarding the cooperation with international institutions such as UN-Habitat.

Both the Safer Cities Programme and the Global Network on Safer Cities are now a recurring subject in the UN-Habitat's Governing Council (UN-Habitat Governing Council 2013; UN-Habitat Governing Council 2015, para 3; 2017). The UN-Habitat's international civil service officers in turn refer to these resolutions in order to lend additional support to their activities. For example, the 2015 report by the UN-Habitat's Executive Director to the Governing Council explicitly states that "[i]n *response to resolution 24/6*, the Global Network on Safer Cities continued to support the establishment of relevant policies and programmes in various countries", and that "[t]he Safer Cities Programme is now entering a period of transition, during which it is expected that this programme *will be scaled up* in the light of the lessons learned" (UN-Habitat Executive Director 2015b, paras 53, 55; emphasis added). Thus, the explicit consideration by the Governing Council appears to have contributed to an expansion and up-scaling of the programme.

UN Women's "Safe Cities and Safe Public Spaces"

While UN-Habitat has had a clear and explicit mandate to carry out projects related to urban safety since the 1996 Habitat Agenda, it is not the only entity within the UN system working on this issue. In recent years, UN Women has implemented programmes with a number of cities, under its Flagship Programme Initiative on "Safe Cities and Safe Public Spaces" (UN Women 2015). The Flagship Programme Initiative on Safe Cities and Safe Public Spaces builds on previous work done at the intersection of women's rights, violence against women and safety in cities, both by UN Women as well as other UN entities, and as of 2016 comprised the cities of Quito, Cairo, New Delhi, Port Moresby, Kigali, Cape Town, Mexico City, Rabat, Dublin, Winnipeg, Reykjavik, Sakai, and New York (UN Women 2016).

"Safe Cities and Safe Public Spaces" is one of 12 current Global Flagship Programme Initiatives. The Flagship Programme Initiatives were launched in 2015 by UN Women to better respond to UN Women's three-year strategic plan (UN Women Executive Board 2015, para 9) and have since been reaffirmed in the current Strategic Plan (UN Women 2017, paras 116–120). The Strategic Plan is routinely approved by UN Women's Executive Board, which, composed of 41 countries in regional distribution, provides operational policy guidance under the ultimate supervision of the Economic and Social Council and the General Assembly. UN Women's normative policy guidance is given by a separate, multi-tiered governance structure composed of the Commission on the Status of Women, the Economic and Social Council and the General Assembly (UN General Assembly 2010, para 57). The Commission on the Status of Women, in turn, is charged with monitoring and reviewing the implementation of both the Beijing Platform for Action adopted at the Fourth World Conference for Women in 1995 as well as SDG 5 on achieving gender equality (UN Economic and Social Council 1996; UN Economic and Social Council 2015). UN Women emphasises that its programmatic work through the Flagship Programme Initiatives responds to the Beijing Platform for Action as well as the 2030 Agenda, and thus implements a set normative frame (UN Women 2015, p. 1). The Safe Cities and Safe Public Spaces Programme Initiative responds to the strategic priority of eliminating violence against women, which is one target of SDG 5. SDG 5.2 calls for the elimination of "all forms of violence against all women and girls in the public and private spheres"; its indicator requests data disaggregated according to age and the place of occurrence (UN General Assembly 2017, Annex I Indicator 5.2.2).

The elimination of violence against women has been consolidated over the past three decades to become one of the most important norms on the women's rights agenda, as the result of a steady evolution. While it appears that violence against women was discussed during the first World Conference on Women in 1975, the outcome document mentions it only in passing (UN Economic and Social Council 1976, pp. 78, 93, 124, 133), and the 1979 Convention on the Elimination of Discrimination Against Women does not contain any explicit obligation to combat violence against women. In 1985, however, the third World Conference on Women in Nairobi explicitly acknowledged that "violence against women exists in various forms in everyday life in all societies [and] [...] is a major obstacle to the achievement of peace" and called for the establishment of legal measures to prevent violence against women and provide assistance to victims (UN General Assembly 1985, para 258; cf also paras 271, 297). In the wake of the 1985 Nairobi Conference, violence against women was a recurring item on the agenda of the Commission on the Status of Women, which resulted in several resolutions of the Economic and Social Council. In 1992, the treaty-monitoring body for the UN Convention on the Elimination of Discrimination against Women, the Committee on the Elimination of Discrimination against Women (UNCEDAW), issued a general recommendation on gender-based violence (UNCEDAW 1992). The Committee understood the broader term of "discrimination" to include violence against women and recommended *inter alia* that state parties to CEDAW report "on all forms of gender-based violence, and that such reports should include all available data on the incidence of each form of violence" (UNCEDAW 1992, para 24 (u)). One year later the General Assembly adopted the UN Declaration on the Elimination of Violence Against Women, which has been widely regarded as a binding guideline within the UN system (UN General Assembly 1993; on the normative force of declarations cf White 2017, p. 568). In 1994 the former Commission on Human Rights first appointed a Special Rapporteur on Violence against Women (UN Commission on Human Rights 1994, para 6). Finally, at the Fourth World Conference on Women, in 1995, violence against women was considered to be one of the critical areas of concern (UN General Assembly 1995, paras 112–130).

This is the normative background against which the Safe Cities and Safe Public Spaces Flagship Programming Initiative was developed. Note that none of the above documents identify public space as a particular concern. Thus, it is not clear that the normative request to eliminate violence against women was the exclusive reason why the UN Women's predecessor institutions chose to specifically address safety in public spaces. There appears to have been a cross-entity influence. As already said, UN-Habitat's Safer Cities programme had considered gender-based violence since the inception of its Safer Cities programme and had co-authored a study on women's safety with a number of international women's NGOs (UN-Habitat 2009). Prior to the creation of UN Women in 2010, one of its component entities, the UN Development Fund for Women (UNIFEM) had carried out smaller scale Safer Cities programmes in a number of Latin American countries (UN Development Fund for Women 2008, para 31). This reflects a growing tendency of much programmatic work within the UN system to explore overlaps and streamline efforts. Presumably, UN-Habitat's efforts to address violence against women in the context of its Safer Cities Programme since the early 2000s were guided in part by the normative instruments on violence against women, as much as UNIFEM's programme work on safer cities can be read in the context of UN-Habitat's work. But each entity responds to, and uses as an argument to justify its activities, a specific set of norms as its primary guidance.

Four outcomes are envisioned by the Safe Cities and Safe Public Spaces programme, namely: (1) gender-responsive pertinent and locally owned interventions that are identified through a scoping study; (2) comprehensive laws and policies that are developed to prevent and respond to sexual violence in public spaces; (3) a gender perspective that is included in the planning of public infrastructure and economic development; and (4) educational activities that result in a social and cultural transformation (UN Women 2015, p. 19). Law reform is thus an explicit aim of the operational activities carried out under the Safe Cities and Safe Public Spaces programme, and is embedded in a larger context of social reform.

UN Women self-identifies as a "strong technical partner" whose part in the cooperation consists of providing tools and packages adaptable to local contexts (UN Women 2016). This crucially includes concluding "Safe City Partnerships" with a range of local stakeholders – representatives from national and local government, grassroots women's organisations, community groups, international organisations, non-governmental organisations, researchers, the media and the private sector – and ensuring that these partnerships are inclusive of women in decision-making positions (UN Women 2015, p. 20). These partnerships are typically fixed through programme documents, complemented by monitoring and evaluation frameworks or mechanisms (UN Women 2015, p. 20), which is the usual procedure for results-based management in development cooperation (UN Development Group 2011).

The results of the "Safe Cities and Safe Public Spaces" programme advertised by UN Women include the amendment of a local ordinance in Quito, Ecuador, to strengthen action against sexual harassment in public, the establishment of vendors' associations for markets that include 50 percent women in executive positions in Port Moresby, Papua New Guinea (UN Women 2016), and the creation of a Safe Cities Committee within the Municipality of Marrakech, Morocco (UNICEF n/d). Quezon City, a satellite town of Manila, Philippines, enacted an ordinance against cat-calling as an explicit outcome of the Safe Cities programme (Quezon City 2016). These are a few examples of the potential impact on local legal regimes that programmes carried out under the "Safe Cities and Safe Public Spaces" Flagship Programme Initiative have had, an impact through partnership which distinctively differs from the direct implementation of international legal standards through entities other than states, perhaps most prominently exemplified by the implementation of CEDAW through a San Francisco ordinance (cf Resnik 2012, pp. 540–41).

In addition, the programme work on safe cities carried out by UN Women in response to its mandate to combat sexual and gender-based violence informed the work of the Commission on the Status of Women, which is tasked with providing normative guidance to UN Women's activities. As already said, none of the documents outlining action on violence against women address violence against women in public spaces and/or in urban areas as a distinct issue. This was taken up only in 2013, when the Commission on the Status of Women expressed "deep concern about violence against women and girls in public spaces, including sexual harassment" in its Agreed Conclusions (UN Commission on the Status of Women 2013, para 23), and most recently in 2017, when the Committee on the Elimination of Discrimination Against Women updated its General Recommendation on gender-based violence against women and specifically recommended that States parties "develop and implement effective measures to make public spaces safe for and accessible to all women and girls … measures should include ensuring adequate physical infrastructure, including lighting" (UNCEDAW 2017, para 30 (c)). It is probably not a coincidence that the issue of violence against women and girls in public spaces was explicitly addressed by the Commission on the Status of Women only *after* UN Women had started its work on Safer Cities: the operative part of the Agreed Conclusions on violence against women specifically calls to "[i]ncrease measures to protect women and girls from violence and harassment […] in both public and private spaces, to address security and safety, through […] programmes such as the UN Safe Cities initiative, improved urban planning, infrastructures, public transport and street lighting, […]" (UN Commission on the Status of Women 2013, section B para (zz)). Ultimately then, operational activities not only act as the implementation measures of a given mandate but also have an effect on the evolution of the very standards they are implementing.

Between Implied Powers and Organisational Independence? The Uncertain Status of UN Programmes and Funds

The preceding part presented illustrations of the operational activities of UN entities that have impacted on their governing bodies' normative agendas. We can observe some similarities between the UN-Habitat's Safer Cities programme and the UN Women's Safe Cities and Safe Public Spaces Flagship: both programmes were launched by civil servants of the entities in question (in the case of the Safer Cities programme responding to a request from mayors), not explicitly proposed and designed by their governing bodies. Both programmes do however contribute to discharging broad and comprehensive mandates stemming from World Conference outcomes and thus have a basis in multilateral negotiations. Through both programmes UN entities interact with a multitude of stakeholders, including governments at different levels, non-governmental organisations, expert networks and others. It is not uncommon for UN entities to interact with these partners in their own name, and on a par with them. For example, UN Women has concluded a Memorandum of Understanding with the City of New York (UN Women and City of New York 2016). UN-Habitat is a member organisation of the International Centre for the Prevention of Crime but also cooperates with it, a phenomenon that has elsewhere been called "networks of networks" (Slaughter 2004, Ch 4).

While the operational activities of the United Nations constitute an important bulk of its work, they have seldom been the main focus of international institutional law scholarship. Schermers and Blokker have pointed out that an estimated 60 percent of the UN budget is spent on operational activities regarding development (Schermers and Blokker 2011, para 946). Yet UN entities are not standardly considered when examples of subsidiary organs are given (eg Klabbers 2009 pp. 160–164). Even in comprehensive textbooks, programmes and funds are presented only by way of example and only in a scattered manner, typically in one to five paragraphs (Schermers and Blokker 2011). This is surprising, given the importance operational activities have within the UN system. The remainder of this chapter outlines some questions for international institutional law that arise from focusing on the operational activities of UN entities.

The status of entities such as the ones described in this chapter under international law is uncertain. Some of this uncertainty might be credited to the fact that the somewhat complex structure of programmes and funds in the UN system and the subsidiary bodies of the main organs in general has grown organically and not according to a consistent pattern (Rudolf 2006, para 29). In a way, this uncertainty reflects the limits of a functionalist account of international organisations (on these limits, Klabbers 2015). Legally speaking, the UN Women's Executive Board and the Commission on the Status of Women as well as UN-Habitat's Governing Council – the governing structures of each entity – are subsidiary organs that report to the Economic and Social Council and the General Assembly, in accordance with Arts. 7(2), 22 and 68 of the UN Charter. These provisions explicitly allow the establishment of such subsidiary organs as are deemed necessary for the performance of the UN's and the General Assembly's functions. As the General Assembly has the power to address any subject matter within the scope of the UN Charter – i.e. any subject matter of the global agenda – this provision confers a large margin of appreciation (Blokker 2009).

Of course, then, the work of entities such as UN-Habitat and UN Women can be understood as the work of subsidiary organs, deemed necessary for the UN to discharge its function of "achiev[ing] international co-operation in solving international problems" (Art. 1 (3) UN Charter). But it is obvious that not much can be said about the legal rights and constraints of these specific entities if we invoke only the broadest possible goal of the UN Charter to account for their existence. It is also obvious that there is a difference between entities such as UN-Habitat and UN Women on the one hand and for instance a Main Committee of the General Assembly, a subsidiary organ which is in charge of preparing draft resolutions for adoption by the Plenary (Rudolf 2006, paras 12–13). Simply focusing on the subsidiary organ status (see Wortmann 2007, for example) does not account for the institutional reality that these entities possess a certain level of autonomy, maintain administrative structures in the form of secretariats that are independent of the main Secretariat of the UN, and have their own governance structures. Both UN-Habitat and UN Women are good examples of entities that cannot unequivocally be categorised as either international organisations or subsidiary organs. The lines are blurred, and they are often characterised by the use of the more generic term of "international institution" (Klabbers 2009, pp. 9), and sometimes as "semi-autonomous" (Rudolf 2006, para 18; for UNDP also Riegner 2017, para 3 II a)) or, as in this chapter, "entity". In part because of the uncertain legal status of these entities, the partnerships that they conclude also escape clear-cut legal forms (Abbott 2010, para 7; Riegner 2019, in this volume).

There is thus a double uncertainty: It is uncertain whether these entities are endowed with distinct legal personality and it is uncertain whether the partnerships they conclude can be considered treaties under international law or what their legal nature is. While these questions are distinct on their surface, they are related in the following way: for an agreement to be considered a treaty under international law, it is necessary that it be concluded between two subjects of international law. (This is not sufficient, however. There are many agreements concluded between subjects of international law that are not treaties under international law, eg property purchases between states, cf Fitzmaurice 2010, p. 19). International legal personality in turn depends on whether an entity or an individual bears rights or obligations under international law. One way of incurring rights or obligations is through international treaties. One might think that this reasoning is circular (Riegner 2019, in this volume; Aust 2017, p. 145). But this is true only as long as we cannot determine either whether the parties to a given agreement are endowed with international legal personality independently of the contentious agreement, or whether an agreement ought to be considered as a treaty under international law for reasons other than that it was concluded between two or more subjects of international law. In other words, there might be considerations external to the specific situation we are examining when raising these questions. This appears to be the reasoning behind Michael Riegner's argument, in this volume, that loan and project agreements concluded between cities and the World Bank ought to be considered as treaties under international law: this is not so because cities are indisputably subjects of international law, but because such agreements are intended precisely to confer rights upon cities as distinct entities (Riegner 2019, in this volume).

But in the case of loan agreements between cities and the World Bank, the uncertainty regarding international legal personality extends to only one side of the agreement, namely the city as a sub-entity of the state. In the case of the project documents concluded under the auspices of the UN Women's Global Flagship Programme, for instance, the matter is much less clear. The parties to a given project are not only sub-state level governance actors (and often the national governments are part of the project alongside local governments) but also sub-international organisation-level entities, in addition to international and local non-governmental organisations and other non-state institutions. The form is distinctly *not* one that resembles international treaties. The Memorandum of Understanding concluded between UN Women and New York City explicitly states that it is "non-binding", but simultaneously speaks of an "agreement" (UN Women and City of New York 2016). In view of the double uncertainty, it appears as if the actors in question intentionally chose fluid notions, giving way to a "managerial mindset" that is informed by the optimisation of substantive outcomes rather than by the application of formal rules (Koskenniemi 2007).

However, emphasising substantive outcomes is neither free of normative constraints nor free of formality. Instead, the managerial mindset is one that is chiefly concerned with the effective implementation of existing normative standards or, put differently, with discharging mandates. Of course, discharging a mandate first requires the interpretation thereof, especially when the mandate is as broad as "the provision of [...] public spaces that are accessible to all and free from crime and violence." It ought therefore not to be surprising that operational activities undertaken in order to implement a specific normative agenda occur as part of a norm-cycle (Finnemore and Sikkink 1998) and will have an impact on the normative standards set by the principal. How to effectively ensure normative alignment and adequate control of the agent through the principal is a problem long known from the domestic context (cf eg McCubbins et al. 1987).

Within the UN context, this requires that we more closely examine and understand the existing legal constraints – mandates and procedural rules – that frame the activities undertaken by the composite parts of the UN system. The secondary law establishing subsidiary organs of various forms often refers to substantive standards that have hitherto been characterised as "soft law". For the entities in question, far from being soft, these standards constitute the frame within which their activities are designed. Even if recommendations are formally addressed to states, it is also the UN system and its composite entities who internalise the norms in question and advocate their implementation and their further advancement through direct interaction with relevant sub-state level or non-state actors. We have not only a disaggregated state (Slaughter 2004) but also disaggregated international organisations whose composite entities are instrumental both in shaping the substantive content of the norms that guide them as well as in forging networks immediately with sub-national authorities within the disaggregated state. One problem that arises from the disaggregation on both sides and from the existence of cross-cutting, abstract global norms such as "eliminating violence against women" or "creating safe public spaces" is that there is no longer one single entity that might be thought to be in charge of implementing a specific mandate. While many entities within the UN system were first set up to respond to concerns in a specific issue area, this vertical alignment has increasingly been complemented by horizontal, cross-cutting coordination entities (for the environment cf Chambers 2008, Part II). Within the UN system, Secretary-General Guterres has framed this as an accountability issue. He has asserted that there is "an evident accountability gap in the UN development system's interface with Member States on issues that do not belong to any individual governing body" (UN Secretary-General 2017, para 106).

Conclusion

To be clear, none of the above is to say that the entities within the UN system, alongside local, municipal actors, have replaced states as the main drivers of normative change. Rather, these entities are additional actors who have an impact on the formation of the substantive content of normative standards through a mode of norm-making that infers from the particular to the general. This chapter has sought to show that operational activities have played no small part in shaping the normative agendas of both UN-Habitat and UN Women in the realm of "safe cities", which in turn have contributed to the outline of SDG 11 and the New Urban Agenda. That safe cities are understood as cities that have large shares of public space accessible to all without the threat of physical violence is also the result of decades-long programme work by different UN entities. The state-composed entities reacted to already existing initiatives and confirmed concepts rather than proactively and intentionally setting norms. At the same time, operational activities are not designed in a vacuum either. They do respond to existing normative frames and, increasingly, to cross-entity impulses. UN-Habitat's work on safety in cities responded to a concern with urban crime voiced at the 1996 Habitat II conference. It is to be expected that the focus on public space management and planning rooted in SDG 11 and so clearly present in the New Urban Agenda will probably increase and will be informed by the other SDGs, other normative standards, and the many actors involved in their implementation.

While this makes future substantive shifts in the normative agenda hard to predict, this development is not necessarily negative. Rather, it allows for constituency groups that are otherwise excluded from formal procedures to be heard and to give input, providing a certain permeability of the international system. On the downside, however, this system (if ever there was only one) is evolving into an increasingly complex and convoluted web of different actors, entities, organs, constituencies and relations between them that partly overlap, contradict one another, or are ignorant of one another – an almost impenetrable thicket of standards, outcomes, best practices, projects and so forth. To identify, analyse, assess and evaluate elements of formality and legality in this thicket is, at least in this author's view, one of the most pressing challenges of international institutional law scholarship today.

Bibliography

Literature

Abbott, Kenneth. 2010. Public-Private Partnership. *Max-Planck Encyclopedia of Public International Law* [online]. Available at: http://opil.ouplaw.com/view/10.1093/law:epil/9780199231690/law-9780199231690-e1084?rskey=NpgYfa&result=1&prd=EPIL (Accessed: 7 May 2018).

Andersson, Cecilia. 2014. UN-Habitat's Safer Cities Programme In: Coester, Mark and Marks, Erich (eds). *International Perspectives of Crime Prevention 6*. Mönchengladbach, Germany: Forum Verlag. pp. 89–93.

Aust, Helmut Philipp. 2017. *Das Recht der globalen Stadt. Grenzüberschreitende Dimensionen kommunaler Selbstverwaltung*. Tübingen: Mohr Siebeck.

Aust, Helmut Philipp. 2013. Auf dem Weg zu einem Recht der globalen Stadt? „C40“ und der „Konvent der Bürgermeister“ im globalen Klimaschutzregime. *Zeitschrift für ausländisches öffentliches Recht und Völkerrecht*, 73, 673–704.

Bishop, Kate and Corkery, Linda (eds). 2017. *Designing Cities with Children and Young People*. New York: Routledge.

Blokker, Niels M. 2009. International Organisations or Institutions, Implied Powers. *Max Planck Encyclopedia of Public International Law* [online]. Available at: http://opil.ouplaw.com/view/10.1093/law:epil/9780199231690/law-9780199231690-e467?rskey=kjjoZW&result=1&prd=EPIL (Accessed: 7 May 2018).

Bouteligier, Sofie. 2013. *Cities, Networks, and Global Environmental Governance: Spaces of Innovation, Places of Leadership*. New York: Routledge.

Chambers, W. Bradnee. 2008. *Interlinkages and the Effectiveness of Multilateral Environmental Agreements*. New York:. United Nations University Press.

Finnemore, Martha and Sikkink, Kathryn. 1998. International norm dynamics and political change. *International Organization*, 4(52), 887–917.

Fitzmaurice, Malgosia. 2010. Treaties. *Max-Planck Encyclopedia of Public International Law* [online]. Available at: http://opil.ouplaw.com/view/10.1093/law:epil/9780199231690/law-9780199231690-e1481?rskey=yMNCcq&result=1&prd=EPIL (Accessed: 7 May 2018).

Klabbers, Jan. 2009. *An Introduction to International Institutional Law*. 2nd edn. Cambridge, UK: Cambridge University Press.

Klabbers, Jan. 2015. The EJIL Foreword: The Transformation of International Organizations Law. *European Journal of International Law*, 26(1), 9–82.

Koskenniemi, Martti. 2007. Constitutionalism as Mindset: Reflections on Kantian Themes About International Law and Globalisation. *Theoretical Inquiries in Law*, 8(1), 9–36.

McCubbins, Mathew D. and Noll, Roger D. and Weingast, Barry R. 1987. Administrative Procedures as Instruments of Political Control. *Journal of Law, Economics, & Organization*, 3(2), 243–277.

Merry, Sally Engle and Davis, Kevin E. and Kingsbury, Benedict (eds). 2015. *The Quiet Power of Indicators: Measuring governance, Corruption, and Rule of Law*. New York: Cambridge University Press.

Ministry of Foreign Affairs and Trade of New Zealand. 2017. *United Nations Handbook 2017–18*. 55th edn. Wellington, NZ: Crown Copyright.

Moretti, Franco and Pestre, Dominique. 2015. *Bankspeak: The Language of World Bank Reports, 1946–2012*. Stanford, CA: Stanford Literary Lab.

Quezon City. 2016. QC Law Penalizing Harassment of Women Signed [online]. Available at: http://quezoncity.gov.ph/index.php/recent-news/2029-qc-law-penalizing-harassment-of-women-signed (Accessed: 7 May 2018).

Resnik, Judith. 2012. Comparative (In)equalities: CEDAW, The Jurisdiction of Gender, and the Heterogeneity of Transnational Law Production. *International Journal of Constitutional Law*, 10(2), 531–550.

Riegner, Michael. 2016. Implementing the "Data Revolution" for the Post-2015 Sustainable Development Goals. Toward a Global Administrative Law of Information. *The World Bank Legal Review*, 7, pp. 17–39.

Riegner, Michael. 2017. *Informationsverwaltungsrecht internationaler Institutionen*. Tübingen, Germany: Mohr Siebeck.

Riegner, Michael. 2019. International Institutions and the City: Towards a Comparative Law of Local Governance. In: Aust, Helmut Philipp and du Plessis, Anél (eds) *The Globalisation of Urban Governance*, 38–64.

Riggio, Eliana. 2002. Child Friendly Cities: Good Governance in the Best Interests of the Child. *Environment & Urbanisation*, 14(2), 45–58.

Rudolf, Beate. 2006. United Nations Committees and Subsidiary Bodies, System of. *Max Planck Encyclopedia of Public International Law* [online]. Available at: http://opil.ouplaw.com/view/10.1093/law:epil/9780199231690/law-9780199231690-e547?rskey=wYx8OQ&result=9&prd=EPIL&print# (Accessed: 7 May 2018).

Schermers, Henry G. and Blokker, Niels M. 2011. *International Institutional Law*. 5th edn. Leiden, NL:Martinus Nijhoff Publishers.

Slaughter, Anne-Marie. 2004. *A New World Order*. Princeton, NJ: Princeton University Press.

White, Nigel D. 2017. Lawmaking In: Katz Cogan, Jacob, Hurd, Ian and Johnstone, Ian (eds). *The Oxford Handbook of International Organizations*. Oxford: Oxford University Press. pp. 559–580.

Wortmann, Martin. 2007. United Nations Human Settlements Programme (UN-Habitat). *Max Planck Encyclopedia of Public International Law* [online]. Available at: http://opil.ouplaw.com/view/10.1093/law:epil/9780199231690/law-9780199231690-e1715?rskey=owPyF8&result=1&prd=EPIL (Accessed: 7 May 2018)

Documents

Note: All UN documents with a document number should be accessible online through this link: http://undocs.org/DOCUMENTNUMBER, so eg http://undocs.org/E/CN.4/1994/132 or http://undocs.org/A/56/8(Supp)

UN Commission on Human Rights. 1994. Question of integrating the rights of women into the human rights mechanisms of the United Nations and the elimination of violence against women, Resolution 1994/45, contained in UN Doc. E/CN.4/1994/132, pp. 140–145.

UN Commission on Human Settlements. 2001. International cooperation and the review of mechanisms for monitoring the implementation of the Habitat

Agenda, resolution 18/5 adopted on 16 February 2001, contained in UN Doc. A/56/8 (Supp).

UN Commission on the Status of Women. 2013. Agreed Conclusions of the 57th session, contained in UN Doc. E/2013/27.

UN Committee on the Elimination of Discrimination Against Women. 1992. General Recommendation No. 19: Violence against women.

UN Committee on the Elimination of Discrimination Against Women. 2017. General Recommendation No. 35 on gender-based violence against women, updating general recommendation No. 19.

UN Development Fund for Women. 2008. Activities of the United Nations Development Fund for Women. UN Doc. A/63/205 (2008).

UN Development Group. 2011. Results-based Management Handbook. Harmonizing RBM concepts and approaches for improved development results at country level [online]. Available at: https://undg.org/wp-content/uploads/2016/10/UNDG-RBM-Handbook-2012.pdf (Accessed: 7 May 2018).

UN Development Programme. 2014. Citizen Security with a Human Face: Evidence and Proposals from Latin America. Regional Human Development Report 2013–14. [online]. Available at: http://hdr.undp.org/sites/default/files/citizen_security_with_a_human_face_-executivesummary.pdf (Accessed: 7 May 2018).

UN Development Programme. 2016. Safer City Pilot Initiative [online]. Available at: http://www.bz.undp.org/content/belize/en/home/presscenter/pressreleases/2016/08/01/safer-city-pilot-initiative.html. (Accessed: 7 May 2018).

UN Economic and Social Council. 1976. Report of the World Conference of the International Women's Year. UN Doc. E/CONF.66/34.

UN Economic and Social Council. 1996. Follow-up to the 4th World Conference on Women, resolution E/Res/1996/6, contained in UN Doc. E/1996/96, pp. 20–22.

UN Economic and Social Council. 2015. Future organization and methods of work of the Commission on the Status of Women. Resolution 2015/6, UN Doc. E/Res/2015/6.

UN General Assembly. 1972. United Nations Conference-Exposition on Human Settlements. UN Doc. A/Res/3001 (XXVII) Resolution adopted on 15 December 1972.

UN General Assembly. 1976. Report of Habitat: United Nations Conference on Human Settlements, Vancouver 31 May-11 June 1976. UN Doc. A/CONF.70/15.

UN General Assembly. 1977. Institutional arrangements for international co-operation in the field of human settlements. UN Doc. A/Res/32/162 resolution adopted on 19 December 1977.

UN General Assembly. 1985. Report of the World Conference to Review and Appraise the Achievements of the United Nations Decade for Women: Equality, Development and Peace. UN Doc. A/CONF.116/28/Rev.1 (1985).

UN General Assembly. 1993. Declaration on the Elimination of Violence Against Women. UN Doc. A/Res/48/104 (1993).

UN General Assembly. 1995. Report of the Fourth World Conference on Women, Beijing 4–15 September 1995. UN Doc. A/CONF.177/20/Rev.1.

UN General Assembly. 1996. Report of the United Nations Conference on Human Settlements (Habitat II), Istanbul 3–14 June 1996. UN Doc. A/CONF.165/14.

UN General Assembly. 2001. Strengthening the Mandate and Status of the Commission on Human Settlements and the Status, Role and Functions of the

United Nations. Centre for Human Settlements (Habitat). UN Doc. A/Res/56/206 Resolution adopted on 21 December 2001.

UN General Assembly. 2010. System-wide coherence. UN Doc. A/Res/64/289 Resolution adopted on 2 July 2010.

UN General Assembly. 2015a. Transforming our world: the 2030 Agenda for Sustainable Development. UN Doc. A/Res/70/1 (Resolution adopted on 25 September 2015).

UN General Assembly. 2015b. Implementation of the outcome of the United Nations Conference on Human Settlements (Habitat II) and strengthening of the United Nations Human Settlements Programme (UN-Habitat). UN Doc. A/Res/70/210 (Resolution adopted on 25 September 2015).

UN General Assembly. 2016. New Urban Agenda. UN Doc. A/Res/71/256 (Resolution adopted on 23 December 2016).

UN General Assembly. 2017. Work of the Statistical Commission pertaining to the 2030 Agenda for Sustainable Development. UN Doc. A/Res/71/313 (Resolution adopted on 10 July 2017).

UN-Habitat. 2006. Review: Safer Cities for Better Governance Final Report (May 2006).

UN-Habitat. 2007a. Strategic Plan for Safer Cities (2007).

UN-Habitat. 2007b. *Enhancing Urban Safety and Security. Global Report on Human Settlements.* London: Earthscan.

UN-Habitat. 2009. The Global Assessment on Women's Safety [online]. Available at: http://www.preventionweb.net/files/13380_7380832AssesmentFinal1.pdf (Accessed: 7 May 2018).

UN-Habitat. (n.d) Safer Cities – A Safer and Just City for All [online]. Available at: https://unhabitat.org/safer-cities-a-safer-and-just-city-for-all/ (Accessed: 7 May 2018).

UN-Habitat. 2015. Global Public Space Toolkit [online]. Available at: https://unhabitat.org/books/global-public-space-toolkit-from-global-principles-to-local-policies-and-practice/. (Accessed: 7 May 2018).

UN-Habitat. 2016. Habitat III Cross-Cutting Expert Group Meeting "Safer Cities in the New Urban Agenda: Reviewing the State of Safety in World Cities" [online]. Available at: https://resaud.net/docs/Docs/2016_07_Rapport_Geneve_En.pdf (Accessed: 7 May 2018)

UN-Habitat. 2017. World Urban Forum, [online]. Available at: https://UN-Habitat.org/wuf-past-sessions/ (Accessed: 7 May 2018).

UN-Habitat Executive Director. 2007. Draft Work Programme and Budget for 2008–2009. Report of the Executive Director. UN Doc. HSP/GC/21/4.

UN-Habitat Executive Director. 2009. Proposed Work Programme and Budget for the Biennium 2010–2011. Report of the Executive Director. UN Doc. HSP/GC/22/5.

UN-Habitat Executive Director. 2015a. Activities of the United Nations Human Settlements Programme: Seventh Session of the World Urban Forum. Report of the Executive Director. UN Doc. HSP/GC/25/2.

UN-Habitat Executive Director. 2015b. Activities of the United Nations Human Settlements Programme. Report of the Executive Director. UN Doc. HSP/GC/25/2/Add.2.

UN-Habitat Governing Council. 2003. Enhancing the Engagement of Youth in the Work of United Nations Human Settlements Programme, resolution 19/13 adopted on 9 May 2003, contained in Report of the Governing Council of the United Nations Human Settlements Programme Nineteenth Session. UN Doc. A/58/8(Supp), pp. 50–51.

UN-Habitat Governing Council. 2005. Youth and and Human Settlements, Resolution 20/1 adopted on 8 April 2005, contained in Report of the Governing Council of the United Nations Human Settlements Programme Twentieth session. UN Doc. A/60/8(Supp), pp. 14–17.

UN-Habitat Governing Council. 2011a. Sustainable Urban Development through Access to Quality Urban Public Spaces, Resolution 23/4 adopted on 15 April 2011, contained in Report of the Governing Council of the United Nations Human Settlements Programme Twenty-third session. UN Doc. A/66/8, pp. 13–14.

UN-Habitat Governing Council. 2011b. Sustainable Urban Development through Polices for Safer Cities and Urban Crime Prevention, Resolution 23/14 adopted on 15 April 2011, contained in Report of the Governing Council of the United Nations Human Settlements Programme Twenty-third session. UN Doc. A/66/8, pp. 31–34 (2011b).

UN-Habitat Governing Council. 2013. Supporting Action for the Creation of Safer Cities, Resolution 24/6 adopted on 19 April 2013, contained in Report of the Governing Council of the United Nations Human Settlements Programme Twenty-fourth session. UN Doc. A/68/8, pp. 17–18.

UN-Habitat Governing Council. 2015. Implementation of the Strategic Plan for 2014–2019, Resolution 25/4 adopted on 23 April 2015, contained in Report of the Governing Council of the United Nations Human Settlements Programme Twenty-fifth session. UN Doc. A/70/8, pp. 27–33.

UN-Habitat Governing Council. 2017. Promoting Safety in Cities and Human Settlements, Resolution 26/4 adopted on 12 May 2017, contained in Report of the Governing Council of the United Nations Human Settlements Programme Twenty-sixth session, UN Doc. A/72/8, pp. 20–21.

UNICEF (n.d) Safe Cities [online]. Available at: https://www.unicef.org/socialpolicy/files/Safe-Cities-Flyer-2.pdf (Accessed: 7 May 2018).

UN Office on Drugs and Crime (UNODC) (n/d). United Nations Standards and Norms in Crime Prevention at Your Finger Tips [online]. Available at: https://www.unodc.org/pdf/criminal_justice/UN_standards_and_norms_in_crime_prevention_at_your_fingertips.pdf (Accessed: 7 May 2018).

UN Office on Drugs and Crime (UNODC). 2016. Governing Safer Cities: Strategies for a Globalised World [online]. Available at: https://www.unodc.org/documents/justice-and-prison-reform/SaferCities.pdf (Accessed: 7 May 2018).

UN Secretary-General. 2017. Repositioning the United Nations Development System to Deliver on the 2030 Agenda: Ensuring a Better Future for All ("QCPR-Report"). UN Doc. A/72/124-E/2018/3.

UN Women. 2012. Safe Cities Free From Violence Against Women and Girls. Baseline Findings from the "Safe City Delhi Programme".

UN Women. 2013. Joining Forces with UN-Habitat to Promote Women's Voice, Acess and Safety in Sustainable Urban Development [online]. Available at: http://www.unwomen.org/en/news/stories/2013/6/joining-forces-with-un-habitat (Accessed: 7 May 2018).

UN Women. 2015. Flagship Programming Initiatives [online]. Available at: www.unwomen.org/-/media/headquarters/attachments/sections/library/publications/

2015/un-women-flagship-programmes-booklet-en.pdf?la=en&vs=357. (Accessed: 7 May 2018).

UN Women. 2016. Safe Cities and Safe Public Spaces [online]. Available at: www.unwomen.org/

UN Women. 2017. Strategic Plan 2018–2021. UN Doc. http://www.unwomen.org/-/media/headquarters/attachments/sections/library/publications/2015/un%20women-safecities-brief_us-web%20(1).pdf?vs=328 (Accessed: 7 May 2018).

UN Women and City of New York. 2016. Memorandum of Understanding [online]. Available at: http://www1.nyc.gov/assets/genderequity/downloads/pdf/mou-with-un-women-and-city-of-new-york.pdf (Accessed: 7 May 2018).

UN Women Executive Board. 2015. Report on the second regular session of 2015. UN Doc. UNW/2015/12.

8 The Challenges of Cultural Diversity for Safe and Sustainable Cities

Francois Venter

Introduction

The potential for development-inhibiting tension and conflict caused by improperly governed multi-cultural cohabitation in the urban environment is self-evident. It is in the city where people come in closest contact with their neighbours and where public spaces are shared for commercial, social and security purposes, even where communities are involuntarily or by choice segregated along cultural lines. Somewhat surprisingly, however, only oblique mention is made of this reality in the 2030 Agenda for Sustainable Development and its seventeen Sustainable Development Goals (SDGs) in the form of general reaffirmations of human rights, including religious freedom, cultural diversity and equality.

When the 2030 Agenda for Sustainable Development was adopted in September 2015, the Heads of State and Government and High Representatives at the United Nations (UN) confirmed their joint moral commitment to all human rights, including those related to culture as part of their vision, *inter alia* in paragraph 8 of the introductory declaration:

> We envisage a world of universal respect for human rights and human dignity, the rule of law, justice, equality and non-discrimination; of respect for race, ethnicity and *cultural diversity* [italics added]; and of equal opportunity permitting the full realization of human potential and contributing to shared prosperity. A world which invests in its children and in which every child grows up free from violence and exploitation. A world in which every woman and girl enjoys full gender equality and all legal, social and economic barriers to their empowerment have been removed. A just, equitable, tolerant, open and socially inclusive world in which the needs of the most vulnerable are met.

These sentiments were reiterated in paragraph 19 of the same Declaration[1] with reference to the Universal Declaration of Human Rights. In paragraph 54 of the 2015 Declaration, it is furthermore stated that "[t]he

Sustainable Development Goals and targets are integrated and indivisible, global in nature and universally applicable … ”

Against this background it may be assumed that all 17 SDGs and their associated targets are intended to be pursued with all the elements of the common vision in mind. Although the need for addressing cultural diversity is not specifically mentioned in SDG 11 or its concomitant targets, there should be no doubt that SDG 11 must be understood to acknowledge that the inclusiveness, safety, resilience and sustainability of cities will not be attainable if balanced governance by urban authorities of cultural diversity is not appropriately accounted for. This is also very strongly implied in the employment of the notions of "inclusiveness" and "resilience".

On the assumption that the various SDGs are to be read as mutually supportive and internally consistent, at least the following goals are also germane to the present discussion (italics added):

> Goal 10.2: By 2030, empower and promote the social, economic and political *inclusion of all*, irrespective of age, sex, disability, race, ethnicity, origin, *religion* or economic or other status.
> Goal 11.4: Strengthen efforts to protect and safeguard the world's *cultural* and natural *heritage.*
> Goal 16.10: Ensure public access to information and protect *fundamental freedoms*, in accordance with national legislation and international agreements.
> Goal 16.b: Promote and enforce *non-discriminatory laws* and policies for sustainable development.

Over the course of the history of the world, cultural diversity has often generated creativity, innovation and progress, but its impact as a cause of social tension has increased in recent times due to the migratory patterns of the world's population (see the next section on cultural diversity). The nature of these challenges quite often emerges in contested litigation and judgments of courts around the world (a selective survey of which is made in the section on local government and constitutionalism below). There is a strong tendency in law to seek solutions to intractable problems attending cultural tensions in the notion of imposing secular neutrality on organs of the state, which raises its own problems (which are discussed in the section on judicial processes below). This calls for an attempt to develop a principled solution for the mitigation of the tensions arising from the increasing cultural diversity of the cities of a globalised world, in order to promote cultural inclusiveness and urban safety. It is suggested (in cultural diversity below) that a solution is possible if state (including urban) authorities concede to the impossibility of dealing neutrally with cultural diversity.

Cultural Diversity as a Challenge to Urban Safety and Sustainable Development

A large proportion of the world's population is constantly on the move, not only because it has become possible to travel far and wide with increased speed and ease, be it for business, pleasure or for other reasons (Public Broadcasting Services 2017),[2] but also because there are always populations under existential stress due to economic, security and natural considerations. The world's population is close to 7.5 billion people, of whom approximately 3.3 percent are migrants, i.e. people not living in the countries where they were born, and the trend on both counts is rising. Add to this the trend of urbanisation, which indicates that 66 percent of the world's population will be urbanised by 2050 (UN Department of Economic and Social Affairs 2014).[3] Translated in terms of urban demographics, in many places a growing portion of city populations adhere to cultural mores different from those of the founding citizenry, and often also different from other migrant groups. Paragraph 29 of the Declaration acknowledges the implications of the current migratory patterns.[4] A closer analysis of this part of the Declaration reveals that two observations are made regarding the significance of migration: the need for cooperation for various purposes is underlined, and migrants' right to return to their states of origin and the duty of those states to receive returnees are reiterated.

Paragraph 29 attributes the significance of migration to –

- the potential contribution that migrants may make to *inclusive* growth and development; and
- its relevance, from a developmental perspective, to the migrants' countries of origin, transit and destination.

Flowing from these observations, the Heads of State recognise the need for international cooperation if the rights and safety of all migrants, refugees and displaced persons are to be protected, which is to be focused on the resilience of the communities hosting the refugees. The focus is said to be primarily on developing countries, although it obviously applies to all communities where refugees are present. The last part of the paragraph has the appearance of a defensive statement by destination countries taking the form of an emphasis on the right to return and the duty to receive returning migrants.

The phenomenon of the growing fraction of the world's migrant population is a function, *inter alia*, of globalisation. Dealing with the history of globalisation in the nineteenth and early twentieth centuries and its impact on the governance of the nation state, Löhr and Wenzlhuemer define globalisation as "the process of the gradual detachment of patterns of socio-cultural interaction from geographical proximity", and they consider "global" in this context to refer "to the increasing number of personal or institutional connections that transcend local horizons and let actors across the entire globe interact with each other" (Löhr and Wenzlhuemer 2013, p. 3).

Living in the second decade of the twenty-first century and being subjected to Western media coverage, one instinctively tends to associate migration with the politics, tragedies and growing challenges of refugees from the Middle East and Africa to Europe. According to the statistics of the Migration Policy Institute, in 2015 Germany ranked second in the world as a destination of international migrants, with almost 15 percent of its population being migrants, and South Africa seventeenth, with an almost six percent migrant population (Migration Policy Institute 2015).[5] These developments, however, represent only a fraction of migratory trends around the globe. Six percent of displaced people were hosted in Europe in 2015, 39 percent in the Middle East and North Africa and 29 percent in the rest of Africa (UNHCR 2017).

Another characteristic of globalisation is the dilution of the distinction between international, national and local governance and legal regulation (Halberstam 2012, pp. 150–212; Krisch 2010). Of this trend the 2030 Agenda for Sustainable Development is living proof, being an internationally negotiated and agreed to agenda for implementation at the regional, national and local levels to which governments have committed themselves.

Globalisation should not and does not, however, eradicate cultural pluralism. In the vast migratory patterns across the globe, migrants do not readily discard their diverse cultures when they resettle. Nor can global governance regulation diminish or erase cultural diversity. The international demand for the management of cultural difference in urban societies is indeed intensified by the globally agreed goals of promoting inclusion, non-discrimination, the protection of cultural heritage and fundamental freedoms which may be understood to be elements of constitutionalism (cf the SDGs cited above).

Local Government and Constitutionalism

"Constitutionalism" is a complex notion, and the intensity of its employment in a range of contexts is escalating (Tully et al. 2016, p. 1).[6] Its core meaning understandably evolved from constitutional law, of which urban governance should be considered to be a subset, although much of its manifestation at local level will depend on the measure of conformity with its precepts at national and regional/provincial level.

Elements of constitutionalism (Venter 2015, pp. 69–83)[7] that may be expected to be present in a balanced system of urban government should include fixed procedures for regulation and administration, the ability to maintain public order in conformity with protected fundamental rights, the democratic election and public accountability of political authorities, non-arbitrary decision-making and the execution of policies, and legality.

The implementation of the SDGs is indeed assumed to occur in an atmosphere of democracy, good governance, the rule of law (eg para 9 of the Declaration under "Vision"), and transparent, effective and accountable institutions (eg para 35 of the Declaration under "The New Agenda"), all elements universally assumed to be characteristic of constitutionalism. Local (in the sense of "urban") government is undoubtedly included in the desired scheme of constitutionalism, perhaps under some circumstances more so than at other levels, because a range of responsibilities of a culturally sensitive nature are typically entrusted to local government institutions. In South Africa these include abattoirs, cemeteries, public nuisances, noise pollution, and the control of the sale of liquor and food to the public, the promotion of social development and a safe environment, for example (see Schedule 5 of the Constitution). In Germany Article 28(2) of the Basic Law guarantees the right of municipalities to manage matters of local concern autonomously (*das Recht der Selbstverwaltung*), but it varies according to the relevant state (*Länder*) legislation, and would typically include matters such as theatre, sporting facilities, cemeteries, building regulations, food hygiene, population registration (*Meldeverwaltung*) and public safety (*Gefahrenabwehr*). These matters are generally similar to the competences of South African municipalities.

Considering the nature of these responsibilities, it is clear that there is a global demand for local authorities to moderate the potential for development-inhibiting tension and conflict that may be caused by improperly governed multi-cultural cohabitation. The administration and adjudication of culturally sensitive matters are naturally not encountered only at the local level, but they often are. In the next section selected examples of how problems of this nature have been dealt with, especially in litigation, are described.

Meeting the Challenges: A Review of Judicial Approaches

Around the world many issues concerning culture-related conflict, both between members of society and between the institutions of government and citizens, have challenged governments at all levels, and the cases that have reached the courts were more often than not concerned with the complexities of urban cohabitation. "Culture" is a comprehensive phenomenon[8] typically encompassing cultural heritage, cultural goods, cultural practices, a way of life, etc. One element frequently present in cultural life which holds strong potential for intercultural tensions is religion, and the practices, rituals and attitudes associated with specific religions (including assumed areligious stances such as atheism and agnosticism).

The relevance of jurisprudence for the present discussion of the difficulties that cultural diversity engenders for urban authorities responsible for safe and sustainable cities can be seen clearly in the role that "cases" perform in society. This was aptly described recently by Susanne Baer in an article which illuminates the complexity and interrelatedness of law, society, politics, culture, religion and the need to approach social issues from a multi-disciplinary perspective:

> To better grasp the power of law in its different practices, we should understand "the case" as the dominant and problematic frame for a complicated plurality of stories. Then, a different set of questions comes to mind. What is it that happens out there, really? How does a conflict enter the various arenas of law? What is litigated and by whom and in what manner? And who decides in what kind of institutional context the case shall be adjudged?
>
> (Baer 2017, p. 274)

In the following discussion some cases drawn from various jurisdictions are used to highlight the difficulties involved in the resolution of cultural "cases" arising within the sphere of urban governance. The selected judgments demonstrate the frequent need for courts to intervene in the exercise of the culture-related competences of city authorities to protect and promote, in the language of SDG 11, the inclusiveness, safety, resilience and sustainability of cities. From this it also becomes clear that not only the executive and legislative branches of government bear responsibilities for the realisation of the SDG's regarding cities, but that the judiciary also has a key role to play in ensuring compliance.

Public Disturbance

The loud and deliberate projection of sounds for cultural and more specifically religious purposes is frequently a bone of contention in the multicultural urban setting. Typically the tolling of bells and calls to prayer arouse the dissatisfaction of nearby residents.

In a matter emerging from a township development scheme initiated by a private company, the question whether the owner of land in the township established in 1979, an Islamic society, had breached the terms of their contract of sale came before the Cape Provincial Division of the High Court of South Africa some twenty years later (Garden Cities Incorporated Association not for Gain v Northpine Islamic Society 1999 (2) SA 268 (C)). The Islamic Society had agreed in the contract that they would not conduct any activities on the land which would, in the opinion of the developer, be a source of nuisance or disturbance to other owners of land in the township and, in particular, no sound amplification equipment would be used on the buildings to be erected. Furthermore it had been agreed that no "call to prayer" would be made from the buildings, and that a light installed on the minaret would be used instead in such a way that it would not be a nuisance or disturbance to others.

The respondent society, however, proceeded to build a mosque on the land and to install a loudspeaker through which calls to prayer were broadcast, causing surrounding residents to complain. When confronted with the obvious breach of contract, the respondent made it clear that it had never intended to comply with the limitation because the call to prayer is a basic tenet of Islam, and no Muslim may therefore "waive" the duty to call fellow Muslims to prayer. Although the contract had been entered into before the adoption of the Bill of Rights in the Constitution of the Republic of South Africa, 1996 (the Constitution), the respondent argued that the provision prohibiting sound amplification infringed upon its, its members and other Muslims' right to freedom of religion.

The court considered this claim to be "too dramatically stated", finding that "[t]he prohibition does no more than consensually regulate a particular ritual practised at a particular place. It does that in the interests of other members of the community" (Garden Cities, p. 271). To the argument that the Constitution did not permit the waiver or abandonment of a fundamental precept of one's faith, the court responded with the view that contracting parties would not necessary know whether a clause in a contract amounts to such abandonment, but that it should in any event not matter, because "the essence of individual freedom of religion is the right to discard established dogma and believe in something new or different or nothing at all" (Garden Cities, p. 272).[9]

In the course of the proceedings, it emerged that electronic amplification of the call to prayer was not a precept of the Islamic religion, and that calls made by the unassisted human voice would be acceptable to the surrounding residents. The court found the contractual conditions to be binding and that the offending loudspeakers had to be removed, implying, however, that if the call to prayer were made without a loudspeaker, it would neither infringe on the rights of the surrounding residents nor on the freedom of religion of the members of the respondent society.

If one considers the circumstances and the progression of this case, it becomes clear that various culturally related issues were involved. Among these are the view or attitude that contractual obligations are neutralised by the demands of religious belief, an assumption of the urban society that it is entitled to relative silence in a residential area, reciprocal disregard or rejection of the other's assumptions and attitudes, and the need to find a balanced solution to the conflicting outlooks. It is submitted that the judgment is an exemplary engagement with the relevant legal norms, while the court contrived to find a viable solution to the dispute, which required both parties to make certain concessions.

In 2012 the European Court of Human Rights handed down a judgment concerning complaints over the loudness of a church bell in Tilburg, Netherlands, intended to call parishioners to the services of worship (Schilder v The Netherlands ECtHR 2158/12 (16 October 2012)). Neighbouring residents complained that the ringing of the bell at 7:15 am disturbed their night's rest, upon which the parish priest reduced the ringing to one minute. After weighing the right to freedom of religion against the interests of others in the community, the municipal authorities warned the parish board to reduce the volume of the ringing, which was found to amount to an "intolerable noise nuisance", failing which a substantial monetary penalty would ensue. The parish board successfully appealed this decision in the courts, which led to the adoption in 2008 by the municipality of rules prohibiting calls to worship between 11 pm and 7.30 am exceeding 10 dB, and to the re-imposition of the monetary penalties if the church did not comply. Arguing *inter alia* that the sound limitations did not serve the local community's interest but only the special interests of the complaining residents, the parish board again appealed, but without success.

The parish priest then complained before the EUCtHR that the limitations on ringing the bell violated the rights to freedom of religion under Article 9 of the Convention. Emphasizing its approach that "Article 9 protects the sphere of personal beliefs and religious creeds, this being the area which is sometimes called the *forum internum*" (Schilder v The Netherlands, para. 18), the Court considered that

> [i]n democratic societies, in which several religions and beliefs coexist within one and the same population, it may be necessary to place restrictions on the freedom to manifest one's religion or belief in order to reconcile the interests of the various groups and to ensure that everyone's beliefs are respected.
>
> (Schilder v The Netherlands, para. 21)

Emphasising that different countries should be allowed a certain margin of appreciation due to the existence of variations in "national traditions and the requirements imposed by the need to protect the rights and freedoms of others and to maintain public order" (Schilder v The Netherlands, para. 22), the Court found that a fair balance between the competing interests involved was struck in the noise regulations of Tilburg (Schilder v The Netherlands, para. 23).

The assumption among the urban residents living near the church that they were entitled to demand silence during the hours of nightly rest even in the face of the church's insistence on the exercise of its freedom of religion is of interest, as is the involvement of the municipal authorities and the judiciary in finding a balanced solution to the dispute. Each of the opposing groups was required to make concessions without completely abandoning its claims to accommodation.

In both the cases described above the contesting parties showed a measure of inflexibility, which left the authorities with the responsibility of devising legal interventions in the interest of public order. The authorities could not simply stand back and allow the cultural tensions to escalate. The manner in which the courts should deal with such matters is not essentially different from the manner in which (local) government administrations and legislatures should approach them: that is to say, they need to find just and legally sound solutions to urban situations of tension generated by competing cultural interests.

Slaughtering of Animals

The ritual slaughtering of animals is practised in various cultural and religious contexts. Consequently the municipal management of abattoirs, food hygiene and animal protection is directly involved.

In South Africa a Zulu cultural ritual known as *Umkhosi ukweshwama* (Rautenbach 2011, Ch 4; Peté and Crocker 2012; Mnyongani 2012) or the "First Fruits Festival" came under judicial scrutiny in 2009 when a public benefit organisation approached the High Court in Pietermaritzburg in a bid to prevent the ritual bull killing at the festival on the grounds that the process involved severe cruelty to animals (Smit NO v King Goodwill Zwelithini Kabhekuzulu 2009 JDR 1361 (KZP)). Various South African and foreign institutions had protested against the performance of the ritual, believing without credible substantiation that it involved the killing of a bull by a group of fourteen-year-old boys using only their hands to rip out its tongue and eyes, mutilating its genitals and suffocating it by shoving handfuls of dirt into its mouth. In an affidavit submitted to the court by an historian, the ritual was described as follows:

> I personally have witnessed the ritual killing of a bull during the Ukweshwama ceremony. The bull was put to death in the usual way by twisting and breaking its neck in the complete absence of the type of mutilation and acts of cruelty the Applicants allege … acts [of cruelty to animals] have no place in Zulu culture and would not be tolerated for an instant. (Para 18 of Professor Jabulani Maphalala's affidavit quoted on pages 13-14 of the judgment.)

The judge significantly stated that he was "only too deeply aware of the consequences of vilifying the cultural and religious beliefs of communities and the polarization it causes." Also, that applications of this nature "are symptomatic of an intolerance of religious and cultural diversity", are "often an attempt to force the particular secular views and opinion held by one faction on others", and that the application was "harmful to the development of a democracy based upon tolerance and promoting diversity."

Against this background the application for an interdict to prohibit the performance of the ritual failed, based on considerations of the "balance of convenience", with the court considering the potential prejudice to the Zulu nation to be far greater than to the applicants.

In the vicinity of Gießen, Germany, a Muslim butcher had struggled since 1994 to obtain exceptional permission from the responsible local authority to slaughter cattle and sheep without numbing (anaesthesia), according to the religious prescripts demanded by his Muslim clientele, following a judgment of the *Bundesverfassungsgericht* in 2002 (BVerfGE 104, 337 (2002)) in which it was found that the administrative authorities and courts erred by applying the relevant legislation in a manner that caused them to infringe disproportionately on the fundamental rights of Muslims. Following this judgment, and after much administrative and judicial prevarication in the lower courts, the butcher was given preliminary permission to proceed under a number of restrictions, including a limitation on the number of animals that he was allowed to slaughter, and the requirement that a state veterinarian (*Amtsveterinär*) had to be present during the slaughtering process. When he returned to the *Bundesvefassungsgericht* in 2009 with a *Verfassungsbeschwerde*, it was found that the butcher's constitutional right of recourse to the law had been violated (1 BvR 1702/09).

It is likely that the bureaucratic and judicial obstruction over 15 years evidenced in this case was motivated by a measure of humanification of animals in opposition to an approach to the preparation of meat for human consumption, not motivated by cruelty, but by a different cultural perspective. Perhaps ironically, the outcome amounted to a judicial pointing of fingers at established German society, which is normally considered to be a pillar of constitutionalism, and the protection of a culture sometimes understood not to be completely compatible with the precepts of constitutionalism.

One could conclude that in both the cases discussed above, justice triumphed above cultural prejudice. The courts did indeed interpret and apply the law by means of established legal reasoning. However, the outcomes can hardly be said to have resulted in any measure of mediation between the contesting components of society other than identifying winners and losers.

This perspective causes the question to arise whether an abstract employment of legal logic and reasoning alone in adjudication and governance can sufficiently deal with the tensions, differences and conflict in a multi-cultural community. If the process produces only winners and losers, can it promote safety and sustainability in plural communities? To this question we will return below.

Public Holidays

The celebration of particular days of the week and days on the annual calendar is a frequent issue in multi-cultural societies. In addition to religious custom, historical, political and ethnic considerations also come into play. Various implications ensue, not the least being labour relations, hours of business, the celebration of festivities, and days of rest. An interesting approach to the problem of accommodating diversity in this regard is to be found in the Israeli Hours of Work and Rest Law, 5711–1951, which provides for at least 36 consecutive hours of rest per week for workers, including in terms of section 78(b) –

1 For a Jew – the Sabbath;
2 For someone who is not a Jew – the Sabbath or Sunday or Friday, all of which in accordance with what is acceptable to him as his day of weekly rest.

According to Kalman the *Hours of Work and Rest Law* –

> … is a conduit through which Israel's public, legislature, and court system debate religion in the public sphere, and it serves as a symbol of how Israelis attempt to define their society, their culture, and their identity as both a democratic and Jewish nation. Its interpretations are an opportunity to carve out precisely which Jewish and democratic values take precedence and which will prevail if they conflict.
> (Kalman 2013, p. 147)

When the constitutionality of the Law was considered in 2005, the Israeli Supreme Court endorsed it (Design 22 Shark Deluxe Furniture Ltd v Rosenzweig 2005 (1) Isr. L. Reps. 340 [2005]). The Court interpreted the "Jewish and democratic" nature of the State of Israel as having three constitutionally supported elements, namely Zionist and traditional-religious, democratic, and striving "to achieve an accord and harmony between the values of the State of Israel as a Jewish state and its values as a democratic state." The statutory arrangements regarding days of rest were found to be consistent with the constitutional values of the state because they served an important social purpose ("the welfare of the employer and his family"), and accommodated various religious convictions without coercion (Design 22 paras 22 and 23 of President Barak's judgment – also see para 2 of Justice Procaccia's supporting judgment).

In 1997 the South African Constitutional Court dealt with the constitutionality of a statutory provision in terms of which grocers' wine licences prohibited the sale of wine on Sundays, Good Friday and Christmas Day on the grounds, among others, of an infringement of the religious freedom of non-Christians (S v Lawrence; S v Negal; S v Solberg 1997 (4) SA 1176 (CC)). In the majority judgment the President of the Court stated, with reference to Canadian jurisprudence:

> I would have no difficulty in holding that a law which compels sabbatical observance of the Christian sabbath offends against the

> religious freedom of those who do not hold such beliefs … . This does not mean that the selection of a Sunday for purposes which are not purely religious and which do not constrain the practice of other religions would be unlawful simply because Sunday is the Christian sabbath.
>
> (S v Lawrence per Chaskalson P (as he then was), para 89)

The justices considered Sundays to have acquired a secular as well as a religious character, however, and that "[p]atterns established over the years by legislation have resulted in Sundays being the most common day of the week on which people do not work" (S v Lawrence, para 95) and that "[t]he secular nature of Sundays is evidenced by the ways in which many people spend their Sundays, engaging in sport and recreation rather than in worship" (S v Lawrence, para 96). The connection between the Christian religion and the statutory restrictions on the selling of wine on Sundays was found to be "too tenuous for the restriction to be characterised as an infringement on religious freedom" (S v Lawrence, para 105).

The measure of controversy of cultural and religious connotations associated with public holidays was demonstrated in this case by the two minority judgments, with two justices considering the possibility that the legislation amounted to religious favouritism to be marginal, but not constitutionally fatal, and three justices holding it to be discriminatory against non-Christians.

In the context of the idea that the constitutional state is required to be secular, the notion of state neutrality came up in the minority judgments. Thus, for instance, with reference to the constitutional provision dealing with religious freedom, Justice Sachs' view was (S v Lawrence, para 160):

> The objective of section 14 is to keep the state away from favouring or disfavouring any particular world-view, so that even if politicians as politicians need not be neutral on these questions, legislators as legislative drafters must.

Justice O'Regan, however, held (S v Lawrence, para 122):

> Requiring that the government act even-handedly does not demand a commitment to a scrupulous secularism, or a commitment to complete neutrality.

The question whether secular neutrality of the state is a characteristic or a constitutional requirement in South Africa was not settled in this judgment, nor elsewhere, but the fact that it was mentioned in the minority judgments is an indication of its relevance in the context of cultural and religious pluralism.

This was also clear in a judgment of the *Bundesverfassungsgericht* handed down in 2016 (1 BvR 458/10), when the constitutionality of the prohibition of activities of an association of atheists on Good Friday was tested. In the Bavarian Act on the Protection of Sundays and Public Holidays (*Bayerisches Gesetz über den Schutz der Sonn- und Feiertage*), Good Friday is recognised as a public holiday on which public peace and quiet is to be observed, and it does not allow for exemptions. A society recognised in public law which represents a particular world view (*Weltanschauungsgemeinschaft*), which is intended to represent the interests of religion-free (*Konfessionslosen*) persons subscribing to the tenets of the Enlightenment and secular humanism, planned an "Atheist Film Night" followed by a party of "heathen fun" (*Heidenspaß*) on Good Friday in a theatre in Munich. The occasion was partially prohibited by the administrative authorities on the ground that it would not conform to the legal requirements of public peace and quiet. The court found the legislation to be constitutionally tenable, but the provisions allowing for absolute prohibition of activities to be disproportionate. The secular neutrality of the German state was mentioned a number of times, both in the arguments before the court and in its judgment.

With reference to the foundational duty of the state to maintain ideological-religious neutrality (*weltanschaulich-religiöser Neutralität*), which had been developed in a number of previous judgments of the court, it was found that the recognition of Good Friday as a public holiday was constitutionally permitted and could therefore not be considered to be a privilege granted against the demand for neutrality (1 BvR 458/10 para 65). The constitutional understanding of neutrality also did not prohibit the specified protection of public peace and quiet (*Ruheschutz*) in accordance with Christian tradition (1 BvR 458/10 para 70).

Article 139 of the Weimar Constitution of 1919, which is incorporated in the *Grundgesetz*, provides that Sundays and officially recognised holidays continue to be protected in law as days of rest from labour and spiritual enhancement (*seelische Erhebung*). The court found that this expression has an ideological (*weltanschauliche*) and ethical meaning in addition to a religious meaning, which allows legislatures to establish various forms of Sundays and holidays without offending the neutrality principle. However, the neutrality of the state does have a limiting effect on the manner in which substantive religious or other content may be given to such days, because the state is prohibited from influencing the content of the "spiritual enhancement" of the populace. The state may respond to social circumstances and needs, but may not attempt in a specific manner to structure the secularised community in a religious or ideological fashion. It is left to the individual, alone or in community with others, to provide substance to the protected days (1 BvR 458/10 para 71).

From these judgments it is clear that the notion of the secular neutrality of the state is readily employed when a difficult situation involving contesting ideological interests calls for resolution by means of the exercise of legal authority. Although secularism is usually associated and specifically contrasted with religiosity, it is equally relevant in the broader cultural context. It amounts to an assumption that the constitutional state is a construct which is required to be culturally neutral, particularly in the face of exponentially growing cultural pluralism in communities (and cities) worldwide. This raises the question if such neutrality can be an effective mechanism in the hands of any branch of government for the enhancement of inclusivity, safety and security in the urban environment.

Seeking a Solution to the Unavoidable but Intractable Difficulties of Cultural Diversity

The facts of the cases referred to above suggest that cultural diversity in the urban setting, as common as it has become, is a recipe for tension. Paragraph 34 of the Declaration reflects an understanding of this reality where the heads of state recognise the importance of sustainable urban management for the quality of life. They therefore pledge to "work with local authorities and communities to renew and plan our cities and human settlements so as to *foster community cohesion*" (italics added), while taking "account of population trends and projections." SDG 11 implies, and the examples show, that governments – especially local administrations – cannot allow tensions emanating from cultural diversity to escalate by not seeking resolution. Furthermore, a mechanical application of legal norms will usually produce winners and losers, and if the losers lose because of their cultural preferences or requirements, tension may escalate even to the level of violence, which is obviously anathema to safety and sustainability. The neutral employment of authority in the resolution of cultural contestation in an urban environment effectively implies that the city must be without culture, without involvement, stripped of engagement with its multi-cultural population. Urban authorities must strive for a balanced resolution of cultural conflict, which is not possible if prejudiced "neutrality" is used as a pretext. Such an approach is clearly not sustainable and of no use for the promotion of safety and security in and of the city.

The question is therefore if a principled solution can be found for the mitigation of tensions arising from the increasing cultural diversity in the cities of a globalising world in order to promote cultural inclusiveness and urban safety? What should the approach of city governments be in the exercise of their culturally sensitive functions in order to maintain good order within their communities? Cultural preferentialism is evidently divisive, and authorities cannot simply disengage themselves from the realities of often conflicting cultural demands.

Through globalisation, the language of liberal democracy has become the constitutional *lingua franca* of the twenty-first century (Venter 2017).

Historically the idea of secular state neutrality flourished on the foundations of Western liberalism, which was the context within which the modern state evolved over the five centuries following the Reformation. The "separation between church and state" brought the notion of "secularism" to the fore. Secular neutrality continues to be a prominent official stance in the constitutional orders of North America and Europe, and particularly in Germany.

The term "neutrality" is often used loosely, without clear definition. It is also sometimes confused with or used as a synonym for "objectivity". On closer investigation it becomes clear that "neutrality" means not being engaged either positively nor negatively, but being disinterested. Put differently, it means not taking sides in the conflict of others, the conflict not being your "business". Being neutral therefore implies being coldly distant, not interested in the outcome of other people's contests, having no direct interest in them.

In Western democracies governments and courts tend to avoid difficult cultural and especially religious questions by subscribing to the notion of secular neutrality. Secular neutrality, however, offers only temporary cover for authorities who would prefer not to be involved in making cultural decisions in circumstances of cultural diversity in the community for which they are responsible. Such an avoidance of responsibility may bring about temporary clarity, but can hardly be said to produce credible solutions to tense cultural confrontations. According to Ladeur and Augsberg the courts, being one of the organs of state responsible for dealing with the problems generated by cultural pluralism, but not the only one, use the neutrality principle

> as an exit-option in order to avoid addressing problems which appear to be too complex for the law, relegating religion to sociological study. In this context, state neutrality merely functions as a *chiffre* for indifference. But this strategy of avoidance, though understandable in the light of the complexity of religious pluralism, undermines the law's function of conflict resolution.
>
> (Ladeur and Augsberg 2007, p. 144)

This illusion of liberal neutrality suffers from an absence of consistent moral and ethical standards, because the only available source of ethics and morality for the liberal functionary is human reason. Consequently, secular neutrality is devoid of a stable point of reference against which the difference between good and bad may be determined. Secular neutrality leaves the government functionary, the legislator and the judge only with subjective reason as a moral standard. Even Jürgen Habermas admitted that "In all cultures, religious beliefs and practices have had a crucial influence on the way individuals have understood themselves in ethical terms" (Habermas 2003, p. 9).

The assumption that neutrality is free from ontological prejudice is false. The "neutral" urban functionary or decision-making body assumes that exclusive reliance on human reason elevates decision-making above the arena of contesting cultural prejudice, allowing unencumbered rational thinking to resolve problems brought about by conflicting cultural demands. This is an illusion, because it is an attitude in which individual human reason replaces the supposedly irrational assumptions of other ontological stances that are culturally determined: "other" is the operative word here, because liberal neutrality is in itself based on an irrational assumption, namely the belief that human reason is consistent, unencumbered by prejudice and a guarantor of fairness and justice. In short, for the simple reason that no one is without a cultural predisposition, it is humanly impossible for those bearing authority to be neutral when confronted with the necessity of dealing with conflicting cultural interests.

In the interests of the promotion of inclusivity, safety and sustainability in city governance, the illusion that neutrality is achievable should be debunked. Neutrality assumes disengagement, the negation, among other things, of personal preference or prejudice. Being so disengaged is humanly impossible. No urban functionary can plausibly pretend to have the ability to be neutrally disinterested when taking decisions or implementing developmental policies in matters involving cultural tension. Were true neutrality in such matters possible and desirable, no human intervention would have been called for, and decisions and their implementation could then have been left to computers or to a cold-blooded, unthinking and mechanical application of rigid rules.

If neutrality is an impossible approach, the question then arises what an appropriate approach would be? It would after all obviously be unacceptable for city authorities to promote one, preferred cultural predisposition when facilitating the resolution of conflict induced by cultural divergence. Clearly, only in a mono-cultural and undiversified primitive society, which can hardly survive in the globalised world, would it be possible to employ a single culture as the exclusive source of ethics and morals.

What is therefore called for is the discovery of an objective ethical standard commonly occurring in the widest possible range of cultural contexts.

It is suggested that in attempting to find such a standard it is important to distinguish between *neutrality* and *objectivity*. In the judicial context the self-evident expectation is that adjudication is done objectively, i.e. "impartially and without fear, favour or prejudice", as section 165(2) of the South African Constitution employs this standard phrase. In the constitutional state, this is also expected of executive and administrative decision-making.[10]

Being "impartial" means not taking sides in a dispute with which one is seized. Put differently, it means that the functionary is required on the one hand not to pre-judge a matter in terms of personal predilection, such as being motivated by secularism. Objectivity requires one to deal with a matter without prejudice, which however, requires one to have knowledge and to concede to one's own inherent predisposition: one cannot avoid pre-judging subjectively if one pretends not to have a subjective opinion and if one is unaware of one's own involuntary standards of judging matters. As concrete examples, a city's natural museum director who is a devout believer in new earth creationism would be at fault if he rules out the accommodation of an archaeological exhibition of prehistoric life forms in order not to expose the public to a different perspective, and a municipal licensing official who is a practising vegetarian would have to develop an acceptably unprejudiced approach to decide on the award or withholding of abattoir licences. Objectivity requires the acknowledgement of difference and variety.

What is therefore required is not disinterested neutrality but consciously developed *objectivity*. In contrast to neutrality, objectivity demands warm-blooded engagement, active participation, and the conscious accounting for one's personal predispositions, accompanied by one's best efforts to be consistent and fair to all, regardless of one's personal approval or disapproval of the cultural (or other) preferences of those to whom justice must be done.

Fortunately there is a universal standard that can serve as a point of reference for the measurement of objectivity, known as "the golden rule". This is not the place to develop this approach fully (Wattles 1996 and Neuser and Chilton 2009 explored the topic admirably), but it can briefly be outlined.

The "golden rule", also referred to as "reciprocity", is a universal principle predating the mainstream contemporary cultural and religious traditions, while at the same time being absorbed by them. It is concisely expressed in the widely recognised injunction to treat others as you want others to treat you. This principle seems to have the same quality of intuitive rectitude as the general acknowledgment that compassion is good and that dishonesty, theft and murder are wrong. Reciprocity is therefore a profound and universally accepted moral standard against which authoritative law-based conduct may be measured, particularly in a situation of cultural pluralism and contestation.

The golden rule cannot be applied neutrally, however, because, as opposed to neutrality, confessional objectivity is possible. If I openly acknowledge my predilections, I am capacitated to consciously focus on reciprocal objectivity, meaning that I become free to strive to deal with the other in a manner that I would want to be dealt with, even if I have to endure some cultural limitations in the interests of justice.

Cultural diversity in the urban setting is a clear challenge on the way to the achievement of the ideal of SDG 11 to ensure that cities are safe, resilient, inclusive and sustainable. The urban (and other) authorities responsible for the realisation of these ideals cannot be expected to make real progress if they insist on dealing with cultural pluralism in a "neutral" manner. They need actively to engage with the cultural diversity in their communities in order to find solutions in an objective manner, whereby all contesting cultural groups can believe that they are being treated according to the ethics of reciprocity. This would inevitably require taking into account the possibly restrictive circumstances of the urban setting where diverse groups need to cohabit in mutual security, and the cultivation of a common culture of mutual accommodation, and where necessary, the sacrifice of exclusive privilege.

Notes

1 UNGA: RES. 70/1 – "Transforming Our World: The 2030 Agenda for Sustainable Development": "19. We reaffirm the importance of the Universal Declaration of Human Rights, as well as other international instruments relating to human rights and international law. We emphasize the responsibilities of all States, in conformity with the Charter of the United Nations, to respect, protect and promote human rights and fundamental freedoms for all, without distinction of any kind as to race, colour, sex, language, *religion*, political or other opinion, national or social origin, property, birth, disability or *other status*" (italics added).

2 A popular BBC television series "City in the Sky" assumes, presumably on the basis of sound factual information, that "[a]t any one time, there are a million people airborne somewhere in the world."

3 According to the UN Department of Economic and Social Affairs 54 percent of the world's population lived in cities in 2014, as opposed to 30 percent in 1950.

4 "We recognize the positive contribution of migrants for inclusive growth and sustainable development. We also recognize that international migration is a multidimensional reality of major relevance for the development of countries of origin, transit and destination, which requires coherent and comprehensive responses. We will cooperate internationally to ensure safe, orderly and regular migration involving full respect for human rights and the humane treatment of migrants regardless of migration status, of refugees and of displaced persons. Such cooperation should also strengthen the resilience of communities hosting refugees, particularly in developing countries. We underline the right of migrants to return to their country of citizenship, and recall that States must ensure that their returning nationals are duly received."

5 The figure for South Africa can only be a generalised estimate, because reliable immigration figures do not exist, mostly due to the large scale of illegal migration across poorly regulated borders. It is highly likely that the actual figure is much higher. Interestingly by comparison, the migrant population of Saudi Arabia was given as 32.3 percent, and that of the United Arab Emirates as 88.4 percent.

6 The editors reiterated that "[a]lthough there is a long history of global interaction among peoples, empires and colonies, the field [of global law and governance] was re-articulated as global and globalising after World War II and, with even more and widespread insistence, after the end of the Cold War. The field includes the law and politics of states and state-centred international law, but it situates these in the dense, global legal and governmental relationships, institutions and processes within, around and beyond the state and state-centred systems (that is, globalisation from above, in between and below)."

7 This is also underscored by the relevant statutory and constitutional provisions in South Africa (eg Sec. 152 of the Constitution of the Republic of South Africa, 1996 ("the Constitution")) and in Germany (Art. 28 of the German Basic Law of 1949, "the *Grundgesetz*").

8 Dictionary meanings include both "The arts and other manifestations of human intellectual achievement regarded collectively" and "The ideas, customs, and social behaviour of a particular people or society."

9 To substantiate this view, the judge cited Article 9.1 of the Convention for the Protection of Human Rights and Fundamental Freedoms (European Convention on Human Rights) (ECHR).

10 See eg Sec. 195(1)(d) of the Constitution of the Republic of South Africa, 1996 which requires public administration to be governed, *inter alia*, by the principle that "[s]ervices must be provided impartially, fairly, equitably and without bias."

Bibliography

Literature

Baer, Susanne. 2017. Speaking law: towards a nuanced analysis of 'cases'. *German Law Journal*, 19(2), 271–291.

Habermas, Jürgen. 2003. Intolerance and discrimination. *International Journal of Constitutional Law*, 1(1), 2–12.

Halberstam, Daniel. 2012. Local, global and plural constitutionalism: Europe meets the world. In: De Búrca, Gráinne and Weiler, Joseph H.H. (eds). *The Worlds of European Constitutionalism*. Cambridge: Cambridge University Press. pp. 150–202.

Kalman, Yael. 2013. Thou shalt accommodate the secular: Sabbath laws' evolution from 'day of rest' to 'day of leisure'. *Temple International and Comparative Law Journal*, 27, 111–147.

Krisch, Nico. 2010. *Beyond Constitutionalism: The Pluralist Structure of Postnational Law*. Oxford: Oxford University Press.

Ladeur, Karl-Heinz and Augsberg, Ino. 2007. The myth of the neutral state: the relationship between state and religion in the face of new challenges. *German Law Journal*, 8(2), 143–152.

Löhr, Isabella and Wenzlhuemer, Roland (eds). 2013. *The Nation State and Beoyond Governing Globalisation Processes in the Nineteenth and Early Twentieth Centuries*. Berlin: Springer.

Migration Policy Institute. 2015. Top 24 destinations of international migrants. Available at: www.migrationpolicy.org/programs/data-hub/charts/top-25-destinations-international-migrants?width=1000&height=850&iframe=true (Accessed: 12 April 2017).

Mnyongani, Freddy. 2012. The status of animals in African cosmology: a non-legal perspective. *SA Public Law*, 27, 88–102.

Neusner, Jacob and Chilton, Bruce D. (eds). 2009. *The Golden Rule – The Ethics of Reciprocity in World Religions*. New York: Continuum International Publishing.

Peté, Stephen Allister and Crocker, Angela Diane. 2012. Ancient rituals and their place in the modern world: culture, masculinity and the killing of bulls. *Obiter*, 33(2), 278–296, 580–599.

Public Broadcasting Services. 2017. City in the sky. Available at: www.pbs.org/city-in-the-sky/about/ (Accessed: 20 November 2017).

Rautenbach, Christa. 2011. *Umkhosi ukweshwama*: revival of a Zulu festival in celebration of the universe's rites of passage. In: Bennett, T.W. (ed). *Traditional African religions in South African law.* Cape Town. Juta. Chapter 4.
Tully, James, Jeffrey L. Dunoff, Anthony F. Lang jr, MattiasKumm and Antje Wiener. 2016. Editorial: Introducing global integral constitutionalism. *Global Constitutionalism*, 5(1), 1–15.
UN Department of Economic and Social Affairs. 2014. World urbanisation prospects. Available at: https://esa.un.org/unpd/wup/publications/files/wup2014-highlights.Pdf (Accessed: 12 April 2017).
UNHCR. 2017. Figures at a glance. Available at: www.unhcr.org/figures-at-a-glance.html (Accessed: 12 April 2017).
Venter, Francois. 2015. *Constitutionalism and Religion*. Cheltenham: Edward Elgar.
Venter, Francois. 2017. Rethinking the language of constitutional comparison. *South African Journal on Human Rights*, 33(1), 72–96.
Wattles, Jeffrey. 1996. *The Golden Rule*. Oxford:Oxford University Press.

Case law

European Court of Human Rights

Schilder v The Netherlands ECtHR 2158/12 (16 October 2012)

Germany

1 BvR 1702/09 (Beschluss vom 28. September 2009)
BVerfG, Beschluss des Ersten Senats vom 27. Oktober 2016–1 BvR 458/10.
BVerfGE 104, 337 (2002)

Israel

Design 22 Shark Deluxe Furniture Ltd v Rosenzweig 2005(1) Isr. L. Reps. 340 [2005]

South Africa

Garden Cities Incorporated Association not for Gain v Northpine Islamic Society 1999(2) SA 268 (C)
S v Lawrence; S v Negal; S v Solberg 1997(4) SA 1176 (CC)
Smit NO v King Goodwill Zwelithini Kabhekuzulu 2009 JDR 1361 (KZP)

Legislation

Bayerisches Gesetz über den Schutz der Sonn- und Feiertage, 1980
Constitution of the Republic of South Africa, 1996
German Basic Law of 1949 (*Grundgesetz*)
Israeli Hours of Work and Rest Law, 5711–1951

Part 3

9 Global Goals and Urban Development

The Territorial Effects of Implementing the MDGs in Brazil

M. Cecilia Oliveira

Introduction

The inclusion of a self-standing goal on cities in the Sustainable Development Goals (SDGs) is often portrayed as progress over their predecessors, the Millennium Development Goals (MDGs). Observers had long been critical that "the city is missing from the MDGs" (Cohen 2014). Indeed, the text of the MDGs did not refer to cities at all, and urban issues more broadly were addressed only as environmental concerns in sub-target 7.11 on slums. However, this textual lacuna does not mean that local governments were irrelevant for the MDGs. On the contrary, this chapter will show that municipalities and cities played a key role in implementing the MDGs in the United Nations (UN) member states. It argues that by studying the local implementation of the MDGs, we can draw some conclusions about the role of cities under the SDGs – not only with respect to SDG 11 on cities, but with regard to the crosscutting role of cities and local governments in the entire Agenda 2030.

This chapter demonstrates this point through a case study of the efforts to implement the MDGs in Brazil, at the local level generally and in the city of Rio de Janeiro more specifically. Brazil is an illustrative case study because it embraced the MDGs early on and incorporated them into policy frameworks at the national, state and local levels. The city of Rio de Janeiro not only exemplifies this countrywide trend, but also offers additional features of a "global city" that has inserted itself into the global economy and international relations at least since the 1990s (Confedaração Nacional dos Municípios (CNM 2011). Rio thus represents a good case through which to examine how the MDGs were implemented in cities and to demonstrate how cities were already covered by the MDGs, despite the lack of a specific goal on cities. More broadly, Rio illustrates the overlap between international agendas and domestic policy. Rio has hosted important international events on development, the urban agenda, and the environment, and was one of the first cities to create a municipal department for international relations. At the same time, Rio has been at the forefront of combining social development policies with a massive public security programme, both influenced by international developments.

By identifying the legacy of the MDGs, it is shown how SDG 11 carries the heritage of these attempts and interventions forward. It is important to stress these continuities because the discourse about the "newness" of SDG 11 obscures past experience and hampers a critical understanding of, and learning from, the problems produced by the localisation of the MDGs in urban contexts. The confluence of global development goals and domestic security apparatus is unlikely to be ruptured under the SDGs. These claims are developed in the remainder of this chapter, which proceeds in three parts. The next section sets out the national context within which the MDGs were implemented at the local level in Brazil. The subsequent section focuses on the role of cities under Brazil's MDG policies. The last section turns to the city of Rio and its efforts to localise the MDGs through a combination of social and security policies especially targeted at low-income neighbourhoods, the favelas.

Social Policy in Brazil and the Role of Local Governments

When analysing the implementation of the MDGs in Brazil, it is important to understand the political and legal context within which the localisation of global goals took place. This context is marked in particular by two elements of the Brazilian political and constitutional order: its social nature and its federal nature. The Constitution of the Federative Republic of Brazil of 1988 (the Constitution) – enacted as part of the democratic transition that occurred after the end of the civil-military dictatorship – contained strong social commitments. It was influenced by a Portuguese legal school which in the 1970s, after the Cravo revolution, supported the social and economic role of the Constitution in transforming state and society. In this sense, the Constitution would not be an exclusive juridicial and directive instrument of the state but rather a key expression of the joint relationship between state legitimisation and society (Bercovici and Massonetto 2006).

A second element is that of federalism, whose antecedents go back long before the 1988 Constitution. The state is composed of the federal level, the Union, the states, and municipalities. Article 30 of the Constitution gives municipalities powers to legislate upon matters of local interest, and to deliver public services, primary education and health services, with the cooperation of the federal government and the state. Article 16 guarantees municipalities local autonomy from other levels of government, and Article 182 contains the constitutional requirements for urban development.

In practice, Brazilian social policy has tended to involve all three levels of government. The role of municipalities has been strengthened over time. Supported and conditioned by World Bank loans, the federal governments of the beginning of the 1990s (particularly during Fernando Henrique Cardoso's presidency) followed a neoliberal approach, which attempted to reduce the role of the central state and social expenditure. To achieve this end, municipalities were to play a key role. The federal government created a social programme called "Comunidade Solidaria", to be implemented by the poorest municipalities. Federal funds were channeled to the local level and used by local governments and civil society for social programmes (Lenardao 2008; Peliano, Resende and Beghin 1995, p. 20).

During the 1990s the concept of human development popularised by the United Nations Development Programme (UNDP) became the international guiding idea for social policy in Brazil. The idea of measuring human development through an index, as practised by the UNDP internationally, was internalised in Brazil. With the decentralisation of social programmes the possibility of measuring the human development index (HDI) of municipalities became a core element of the management of poverty. Brazil is one of the only countries which developed municipality and neighborhood human development indexes, with the focus on urban areas and big cities. The first Brazilian UNDP HDI Report, launched in 1996, focused on introducing the HDI concept and data production for Belo Horizonte and Rio de Janeiro (Institute for Applied Economic Research (IPEA/PNUD), 1996). In addition, a series of specific conditional cash transfer programmes were developed in different categories to include access to social goods: food, water, gas, education, etc. At that time the central government was recognised by the UNDP as an example of how to implement human development. It made cities the main unit of governance for mapping the HDI and allocating funds to social programmes (Souza 2006).

The Role of Cities in Implementing the MDGs in Brazil

If human development had been the international guiding idea of the Cardoso government, the presidency of Ignacio Lula da Silva (2003–2010) turned to the MDGs as the international framework for its social policy. Under the Lula administration cities became the unit of governance for national policies to implement the MDGs in Brazil. The implementation of the MDGs took place within the framework of a nationwide policy platform, the "Hunger Zero" programme. This programme applied the MDG rationality of governmental practices in terms of discourse, the production of reports, technologies, and governmental participation in UN follow-ups. In this context, the already established role of cities in the country's social policy was further expanded.

Hunger Zero was a federal food-security policy designed to reduce hunger and poverty. It was composed of a variety of policies including the well-known "Bolsa Família" conditional cash transfer programme and the lesser known user database system, "Cadastro Unico" (CadUnico).

The goals of Bolsa Família were aligned with the MDGs and targeted poverty based on the international discourse of capability deprivation (Sen 2000). Poverty, in the context of Bolsa Família, was understood as a state of life that produces a gap between the production of income and access to fundamental rights.

Bolsa Família represented a consolidated attempt at achieving the MDGs and attracted financial support from international donors. These funds are important, not necessarily for their amount or frequency but for the reason of international investments in national programmes aligned to the MDGs that have enabled donor institutions to expand and justify their own course. In 2004 the World Bank accorded a loan of USD 520.2 million to the Bolsa Família Programme on the basis that "(t)he proposed project is at the centre of one of the core pillars of the Bank's CAS (Country Assistance Strategy) – achieving a more equitable Brazil – and is closely aligned with corporate priorities of achieving the Millennium Development Goals" (World Bank 2004). This alignment of the CAS and Bolsa Família expresses the close connection between Brazil's domestic approach and that of the international donors. The World Bank project sheet for the loan goes further in its analysis of the close connection between Bolsa Família and the MDGs: "… reduction of poverty (MDG 1) and inequality in the short- and long-term. In coordination with other government programmes, many of which are Bank supported, it will also contribute to reducing malnutrition (MDG 1), achieving universal education (MDG 2), reducing child mortality (MDG 4), and improving maternal health (MDG5) through the demand-side incentives it provides for investments in education, nutrition and health (for pregnant women and young children)" (World Bank 2004).

Brazil was one of the UN member states that not only supported the MDGs at the international level but also made a considerable effort to implement the goals via its own national law and policy framework. One of the incoming Lula government's first political steps was to create the Special Technical Committee on the MDGs at the national level. The committee's role was to advise and coordinate the national activities concentrated on each of the eight MDGs. It was to produce national reports and to work with UN agencies such as UNDP. This role was laid down in a presidential decree of 31 October 2003 that instituted the said technical group. The Technical Committee was composed of members drawn from the Presidency, the Ministry of Planning, Finance and Management, the Institute of Applied Economic Research (IPEA), the Brazilian Institute of Geography and Statistics (IBGE), and the Ministry of Social Development and Fight Against Hunger (Art. 3 of the Decree).

In 2004 the MDG Committee published the first national MDG report. The report stressed the Brazilian government's efforts to reduce poverty and eradicate hunger by putting emphasis on two concepts: development and social inclusion (Presidency of Brazil, First National MDG

Monitoring Report, 2004). The most profound policy measure in the first MDG report was the Hunger Zero programme (Lula da Silva 2003; Takagi 2010; Graziano, Belik and Takagi 2006). Hence, the implementation of the MDGs in Brazil was framed early on as a measure to fight hunger through "food security". This specific framing of the MDG in the national context drew on earlier attempts by the Brazilian government to ensure food security (Oliveira 2016).

Significantly, another key task of the MDG Committee was to work closely with international organisations, especially the UNDP. The latter, in turn, cooperated closely with the national association of municipalities, the Confederacao Nacional dos Municipios. This cooperation became instrumental in involving municipalities in the implementation of the MDGs. It resulted, *inter alia*, in the publication of guidelines and best practice examples for municipalities on the implementation of the MDGs (CNM 2008). This MDG guidebook for municipalities promoted the use of the city as a strategic actor in the Brazilian context: "The MDG indicators ... enable a broad look on the city and represent ideal tools to define and introduce transformative municipal policies. ... Local governance can be rewarded through the realised goals and thus gain visibility at the global and national, regional and local level" (CNM 2008, p. 18).

The guide also promoted the idea that municipalities are the main sources of national data with which to assess the implementation of the MDGs in Brazil. This aligned with the structure of the Bolsa Família cash transfer programme, which relied on the decentralisation of resources for implementation: "The MDGs have demonstrated to the world the importance of engaging local governments in actions to expand a more equitable development. ... This debate raises fundamental questions, like how to intensify the decentralisation of resources. In the Brazilian context, the main portion of the MDG indicators lies within the responsibility of the municipalities, be it because of their constitutional competences or because they execute national programmes like Bolsa Família" (CNM 2008, p. 20).

To be part of the Bolsa Família programme, families had to register in the CadUnico, a single register system to identify all low-income families in the country. The register developed a specific data system to identify and map the poor population nationally. This system covers the entire country and its data is collected by municipalities, which need to organise the distribution of benefits and the basic infrastructure of social policies by schools and health centers.

The multilevel administration of Bolsa Família applied a specific process in order to reach municipalities. To verify the eligibility of states and municipalities for Bolsa Família, the Decentralised Management Index was created to measure what is defined in Article 8 of Law 10386 on Bolsa Família: "The execution and management of the Bolsa Família Programme are public and governmental. It will be decentralised through the combination of efforts among the federated entities, observing intersectorality, community participation and social control." Thus, the Index was implemented in 2005 as a tool to improve the management of Bolsa Família in municipalities, which are responsible for dealing directly with the process of registration and the monitoring of conditionalities, thereby updating the CadUnico. A large financial contribution from the federal government funds the payment of six reais (around two USD) per family registered in each municipality. This accelerated the national mobilisation to update the CadUnico. The Index continues to serve to compare how different municipalities are being managed and to channel benefits to those with better performance (Oliveira 2016).

Registration is mandatory and supports a vast database. The latter points to the areas considered vulnerable and shows the beneficiaries of Bolsa Família. The CadUnico creates cartographies of poverty in the national territory. These maps assist the government to implement public security mechanisms and to provide public services.

Since it became operational in 2004, the CadUnico created a range of categories stratifying the population considered poor. It has at least 15 classified categories such as "(i)ndigenous families, gypsy families, families of prison inmates, homeless families, extractive families, families who are beneficiaries of the National Land Credit Programme, encamped families, waste collector families, and families affected by infrastructure and construction projects such as the 2016 Olympic Games or the 2014 World Cup" (Ministério do Desenvolvimento Social (MDS) 2014). The centralisation of the data becomes an important control mechanism achieved with the participation of the same target populations. They need to keep their data updated and follow the health and education conditions and contexts contributing to the national data that produces the national poverty cartography. By 2013 the CadUnico had collected information from 23 million families that represent roughly 80 million people. The CadUnico was managed during Dilma Roussef's term (2011–2016) under the National Secretary of Income and Citizenship by a special department, and has now become a special branch of the Ministry of Social Development and Fight against Hunger alongside the National Secretary of Food Security and Nutrition. It retains the same operational structure that it had under the previous government. The CadUnico continues to provide data for many national social programs. Other Brazilian government ministries and cities have started to use the CadUnico to identify the poor population for specific programmes.

The Bolsa Família numbers from CadUnico also fed into the Brazilian MDG reports, which in turn showcased the achievements towards the first MDG on poverty alleviation. The Hunger Zero programme, based in the Bolsa Família and the CadUnico, became an international model of how to pursue the MDGs by way of consolidated efforts across national, regional and local authorities within a single state.

The City of Rio de Janeiro and the MDGs: Sustainable Urban Development, Security and the Improvement of Slums

The city of Rio de Janeiro has taken a series of administrative steps towards internationalisation since the 1990s and went truly global during the MDG implementation period. As early as 1993 the municipality created its International Relations Department after hosting the UN Rio Earth Summit in 1992. The department was led by a former diplomat who facilitated exchange with the federal Ministry for International Affairs (CNM 2011).

Since 1996 Rio has acted as the host for a UN-Habitat regional office. The office supported Rio in hosting the global celebration of World Habitat Day in 2003 and in organising the Fifth World Urban Forum in 2010, which had the theme "The right to the city: bridging the urban divide", to give two examples.

Rio also became one of the 20 members of the United Nations Advisory Committee of Local Authorities (UNACLA), an advisory body that would serve the purpose of strengthening the dialogue of the UN System with local authorities from all over the world (UNACLA 1999). The Committee soon established itself as a representative body in the main local government networks and contributed to the implementation of global agendas at the local level (UNACLA 1999).

During the MDG period, the city of Rio implemented a series of programmes with international support: it administered the national Bolsa Família programme locally, it created a local variant of Bolsa Família to extend coverage (the so-called "cartao carioca"), it embarked on an infrastructure programme in the favelas (slums) including housing, transport, social policies, energy, sanitation, education and health, and combined these programmes with an intensive public security agenda aiming at the "pacification of territories", namely the favelas, and their integration into the city (Neri 2010). Each of these programmes had institutional or financial support from international agencies, whether UNDP, UN-Habitat, or the World Bank (World Bank 2012; UN 2011).

One of the key policy issues in the local programmes and within the international framework was the improvement of low-income neighbourhoods, namely the favelas. The 2010 Forum mentioned above addressed the "improvement of slums" under MDG 7.11, which aspired "to improve the lives of at least 100 million slum dwellers by the year 2020." During the Forum the discourse centred on integrated initiatives to improve slums, which would include: education, health, the control of risks, and environmental protection. The coordinated implementation of these elements would compose "the urban fabric of the city" (UN-Habitat 2010, p. 83).

One of the forum panels, "Integrated Slum Upgrading in Brazil", presented the policies for slum upgrading in Rio as a successful model: "(a)nother finding was that Brazil had a successful experience and scale of intervention that gave it a position of leadership. It was acknowledged that it was very advanced in the sector, but that challenges still existed and should be addressed" (UN-Habitat 2010). In the UN-Habitat report on the World Urban Forum, the governor of the state of Rio de Janeiro, Sergio Cabral, highlighted how certain urban policies were improving the quality of life of favela dwellers in the city of Rio: "He noted the achievements of the Growth Acceleration Programme, which had provided housing, water, and sanitation, and the provision of a number of other services to thousands of favela dwellers in Rio de Janeiro. A major national programme on public safety had also significantly reduced security threats in underprivileged communities" (UN-Habitat 2010, p. 12).

The Forum thus highlighted a particular combination of social and security policies that Rio was pursuing in the context of implementing national programmes and global goals. This combination is embodied by two programmes: the PAC Favelas, which focused on the urbanisation of slums, and the "Pacifying Police Unit" (UPP), later complemented by the "UPP Social" (renamed Rio + Social after the Rio+20 conference).

The UPP is a public security programme launched in 2008 by the state of Rio de Janeiro and aligned with the National Programme for Public Security and Citizenship. Both programmes coordinate their activities with urban infrastructure development programmes, providing social control and constant surveillance by the police to facilitate state intervention and to produce what they call "pacified territories". In the city of Rio, favela urbanisation and public security policies entailing a massive police presence complemented each other, promising attractive opportunities for public- and private-sector investments in these communities once vulnerability and violent armed conflict were under control. The pacification of favelas in Rio de Janeiro is an example of how security and social policies become integrated into national and local efforts to implement international development goals.

The practical functioning (and dysfunctionality) of the UPP programme is illustrated by its application to the "Complexo do Alemao", one of Rio's largest favela areas. In April 2010 Brazilian armed forces and police conducted a military operation in Complexo do Alemao, an area of Rio de Janeiro formed by 15 favelas with more than 60,000 inhabitants. The objective of this operation (Operação Arcanjo) was the military occupation of territories in order to reclaim them from drug-related violence, as well as the future implementation of a UPP network and the national favela urbanisation programme. It was also part of Rio's city security plan for the 2014 FIFA World Cup and the 2016 Olympic Games. The occupation by armed forces was said to be temporary, but it lasted for 19 months. Since the end of the military-civil dictatorship and the introduction of the Brazilian Constitution of 1988, this was the first time that the armed forces had been used in a large-scale operation for the purposes of law and order.

The armed occupation was followed by investments in urban infrastructure in Complexo do Alemao. The most prominent intervention was the construction of a cable car, which symbolised the slum's upgrading and the bridging of the urban divide between low- and middle-income areas. The cable car was intended to enhance mobility and to integrate the favela population into the city, reducing travel time from 50 to 16 minutes (Growth Acceleration Program PAC 2010, p. 39). In addition, social services were enhanced through the UPP Social Programme, which was supported by the World Bank. In its report the Bank wrote: "the Bank has been helping Rio to reinforce an integrated, multi-sectoral approach to the sustainable growth of the territory … the Bank has been providing support to *Social UPP* since its design stage, in 2010, through technical assistance services to strengthen social governance and territorially-based monitoring and evaluation. These and other areas being supported by the Bank, such as education, financial literacy, gentrification, and lack of income generation opportunities, are related to the 'second generation' of problems that are still present and/or still to come after favelas are pacified" (World Bank 2012).

The second-generation problems created by the pacification are related to police violence and the difficulties that the "newly pacified citizens" had in paying for public services such as water and energy, which were now supplied legally, but at unaffordable prices. The UPP Social Programme was created with the goal of managing the negative results of the original UPP's implementation and was also supported by UN-Habitat. Yet today's results remain sobering. The fate of the cable car is, again, symbolic: after four years, in September 2016 Alemao's cable car was closed due to a lack of public funds to maintain and operate it. The new plan was to convert the cable car stations into old-UPP-type police stations. Veloso and Santiago comment on this issue: "The case of the closed cable car is, however, also representative of an even more serious issue than mobility in Rio. According to Raul Santiago, an activist with the Collective Papo Reto, there was a plan to convert the closed stations of the cable car into a strategic base for the Pacifying Police Unit (UPP) in their confrontations with drug trafficking in Morro do Alemao. On the cable car, abandoned and mothballed by the same state that had built it and presented it as a definitive improvement to the daily lives of the Morro do Alemao habitants, mobility and violence combine, resulting in a context in which the second overlaps with the former, making what was already difficult impossible. It has almost become the basis for the UPP (…). The cable car consolidates as a metonym for the current situation that faces the Morro do Alemao inhabitants: 'nobody enters, nobody leaves'" (Veloso and Santiago 2017, p. 13).

One lesson learned from the cases of Brazil and Rio is that the merging of security and development policies does not necessarily improve slum areas but can instead see an increase in violence, the criminalisation of the poor, land speculation, and gentrification. Today Rio faces debt, security and corruption crises. In this respect, the environment in which the new SDG 11 will be implemented in Rio may be even less enabling than the original was in 2000.

Conclusion

Despite claims to the contrary, the city was not missing from the MDGs. At least in the case of Brazil, municipalities played a key role in the implementation of the goals and in data production. Today SDG 11 carries forward the heritage of these attempts and interventions. The new goal on cities can and will build on structures that emerged in the course of implementing the MDGs.

In this sense it is problematic to claim that the SDG 11 is a new achievement of the urban policy agenda. This argument obscures past experience and efforts and hampers a critical understanding of and learning from the problems produced by the localisation of the MDGs in urban contexts.

The experience with the MDGs in Brazil suggests that the localisation of global goals, even widely shared ones, is not enough to overcome the entrenched, problematic discourses and practices of poverty reduction. The combination of social policy and security policy ultimately neither improves living conditions nor "upgrades" slums. Instead, it risks contributing to the further growth of punitive institutions and to normalising the use of force – not only by the police but also by the military. The unintended result is the normalisation of violence against poor populations. This lesson is not limited to the specific context of Rio de Janeiro: the problematic confluence of poverty and security can be observed in many developing countries. This does not necessarily imply that localisation will have the same outcomes in other places, but it suggests hypotheses that need to be investigated in future research on the implementation of the SDGs.

The SDGs are unlikely to resolve the problem of securitising the poor in developing countries. The language of "slums" is still prominent in SDG 11.1. No lesson has been learned in this respect. While the further targets of SDG 11 broaden the focus beyond the previous MDG 7.11, the attempt to locate the entire urban agenda in one goal also carries risks. The introduction of a self-standing SDG on cities with an extensive list of targets might detract from the cross-cutting role of cities in all SDGs and may unnecessarily narrow down and compartmentalise urban development discourse in the frame of Agenda 2030. Cities remain relevant to most other SDGs. The reverse is also true: with respect to the lessons learned from implementing MDG 7.11 in Brazil, a particularly relevant addition in the Agenda 2030 is SDG 16, which addresses issues of the rule of law and access to justice. The implementation of this goal in cities like Rio would have to overcome deeply entrenched ideas about securitising the poor. In fact, there is even a risk that SDG 16's insistence on "peaceful societies" may legitimise further "pacification" of the kind seen in the UPP programmes in Rio.

If any lesson can be learned from the MDGs for the SDGs, then it is the necessity to critically observe the unintended consequences of implementing the SDGs in different local contexts. By acknowledging the ambivalent effects of MDG localisation we can question how the so-called "New Urban Agenda" accommodates or updates pre-existing concepts such as sustainable development or urban security. This is relevant not only for developing countries. Since the SDGs are now a universal commitment and do not exclusively address the urban disparities of developing countries, how will the historical experience of upgrading slums influence developed countries? These countries will leave behind the specific role of simply financing urban development elsewhere and potentially direct internationally guided interventions towards their own low-income neighborhoods, poor populations, refugees, (il)legal immigrants, and all those considered vulnerable. And, in the final instance, the "poverty" of slums as an urban challenge now officially leaves the geographic boundaries of the Global South and becomes a trans-territorial theme with universal reach denoting shared responsibility.

Bibliography

Literature

Bercovici, Gilberto and Massonetto, Luís Fernando. 2006. A constituição dirigente invertida: a blindagem da Constituição Financeira e a agonia da Constituição Económica. In: *Boletim De Ciências Económicas, Volume XLIX*. Coimbra, Portugal: Impactum Coimbra University Press. pp. 57–77.

Confederação Nacional dos Municípios (CNM). 2008. Objetivos de Desenvolvimento do Milênio – ODM: Estratégias da Gestão Municipal para Redução da Pobreza no Planeta Até 2015. Available at: www.santos.sp.gov.br/static/files_www/conselhos/PRO-ODM/coletnia_gesto_pblica_municipal_odm_2009-2012.pdf (Accessed: 30 January 2018).

Confederação Nacional dos Municípios (CNM). 2011. *As Áreas Internacionais dos Municípios Brasileiros: Observatório da Cooperação Descentralizada – Etapa 1*. Available at: www.paradiplomacia.org/upload/downloads/d360e8ef1e44fc88c858da5a2bf1ca2bmunic-bras-ii.pdf (Accessed: 30 January 2018).

Cohen, Michael. 2014. The city is missing in the Millennium Development Goals. *Journal of Human Development and Capabilities*, 15(2–3), pp. 261–274.

Graziano, José, Belik, Walter and Takagi, Maya. 2006. Os desafios de uma política de segurança alimentar no Brasil. In: Cidamadore, Alberto (ed.). *A Pobreza no Estado: Reconsiderando o Papel do Estado na Luta Contra a Pobreza Global*. Buenos Aires, Argentina: CLACSO. pp. 151–170.

Growth Accelaration Program (PAC). 2010. Favelas urbanisation: the PAC experience. Brasilia, Brazil: Ministry of Cities, National Housing Secretary.

Institute for Applied Economic Research (IPEA), United Nations Program for Development (PNUD/BRASIL). 1996. Relatório sobre o Desenvolvimento Humano no Brasil. Brasilia, Brazil:IPEA/PNUD-Brasil.

Lenardao, Elsio. 2008. The relationship between neo-liberal "modernization" and "backward" political practices in Brazil of the 1990s. *Revista de Sociologia e Política*, 16(31), pp. 197–214.

Lula da Silva, Luís Inácio. 2003. Speech at the 58th UN General Assembly, September 23rd. Available at: http://www.un.org/ga/search/view_doc.asp?symbol=A/58/PV.7 (Accessed: 30 January 2018).

Ministério do Desenvolvimento Social (MDS). 2014. Diversidade no Cadastro Unico – Respeitar e Incluir. Available at: www.mds.gov.br/webarquivos/publicacao/bolsa_familia/Cadernos/Diversidade_CadUnico.pdf (Accessed: 30 January 2018).

Neri, Marcelo. 2010. Cartão Família Carioca, o Bolsa Família 2.0. *Conjuntura Social*, 64(11), 60–64.

Oliveira, Maria Cecilia. 2016. The Millennium Development Goals: the secure life and planetary governmentality. PhD thesis. Catholic University of Sao Paulo.

Peliano, Ana Maria T., Resende, Luís Fernando de Lara and Beghin, Nathalie. 1995. O comunidade solidária: uma estratégia de combate à fome e à pobreza. *Planejamento e Políticas Públicas*,12 (Jan/Jun), 20–39.

Presidency of Brazil. 2004. Grupo tecnico para acompanhamento das metas e objectivos do milenio da Casa Civil da Presidencia da Republica do Brasil / First National MDG Monitoring Report of Brazil.

Sen, Amartya. 2000. *Social Exclusion: Concept, Application and Scrutiny.* Manila, Phillippines: Asian Development Bank.

Souza, Celina. 2006. *Evaluation of the National Human Development Report System/Case Brazil.* New York: UNDP.

Takagi, Maya. 2010. A implementação do Programa Fome Zero em 2003. In: Graziano, Jose, Del Grossi, Mauro and Galvao de Franca, Caio (eds). *Fome Zero: A Experiência Brasileira*. Brasilia, Brazil: Ministério de Desenvolvimento Agrário. pp. 53–83.

Veloso, Sérgio and Santiago, Vinícius. 2017. *Ninguém Entra, Ninguém Sai. Mobilidade Urbana e Direito à Cidade no Complexo do Alemão.* Rio de Janeiro: Heinrich Böll Stiftung.

Documents

UN (United Nations). 2011. Acordo entre ONU-Habitat e Prefeitura do Rio de Janeiro permitirá ampliação da UPP Social. Available at: https://nacoesunidas.org/acordo-entre-onu-habitat-e-prefeitura-do-rio-de-janeiro-permitira-ampliacao-da-upp-social/ (Accessed: 30 January 2018).

United Nations Advisory Committee of Local Authorities (UNACLA). 1999. Governing Council Committee UN-Habitat. Resolution 17/18 of 1999. Available at: https://unhabitat.org/unacla (Accessed: 20 January 2018).

UN-Habitat. 2010. Report of the Fifth Session of the World Urban Forum: Rio De Janeiro, Brazil. The Right to the City: Bridging the Urban Divide. Available at: https://unhabitat.org/wp-content/uploads/2016/07/wuf-5.pdf (Accessed: 30 January 2018).

World Bank. 2004. Integrated Safeguard Data Sheet. Report AC503. Washington DC: World Bank.

World Bank. 2012. Bringing the state back into the favelas of Rio de Janeiro: Understanding changes in community life after the UPP pacification process. Available at: http://documents.worldbank.org/curated/en/255231468230108733/pdf/760110ESW0P12300Rio0de0Janeiro02013.pdf (Accessed: 30 January 2018).

Legislation

Brazil. 2003. Decree 31st Oct. 2003. Technical Committee on the MDGs. Available at: www.planalto.gov.br/ccivil_03/DNN/2003/Dnn10011.htm (Accessed: 15 January 2018).

Federative Republic of Brazil. 1967. Constitución Política de 1967. Available at: http://pdba.georgetown.edu/Constitutions/Brazil/brazil67.html#mozTocId911334 (Accessed: 30 January 2018).

10 City Regions in Pursuit of SDG 11

Institutionalising Multilevel Cooperation in Gauteng, South Africa

Jaap de Visser

Introduction

Metropolitan areas are becoming more and more important in shaping the future of the planet. In 2017 there were 34 megacities worldwide, i.e. cities with a population of over 10 million. It is expected that this number will grow to 41 by 2030 (United Cities and Local Governments (UCLG) 2017a, p. 44). There are many more smaller urban conglomerations that can be defined as metropolitan areas, using criteria such as continuous growth, levels of density and perhaps most importantly, functional interdependence (UCLG 2017a, p. 44).

Metropolitan areas are growing fast and face tremendous challenges. In both developed and developing countries, they experience sprawl, social fragmentation, economic challenges and environmental threats. In developing countries this is compounded by the reality that 880 million people worldwide live in slums, most of them within metropolitan areas (UCLG 2017a, p. 46). The growth of metropolitan areas presents tremendous opportunities for an increase of the wellbeing of the city dwellers within them, but the reality is that many of the challenges fly in the face of the aspirations of Goal 11 of the Sustainable Development Goals (SDGs).

The Fourth Global Report on Decentralization and Local Democracy attributes this in large part to the fact that public policy and reform has not kept up with the growing importance of metropolitan areas, resulting in "weak political cooperation, government fragmentation and inconsistent bureaucratic authority discourage[ing] joint efforts to tackle externalities" (UCLG 2017a, p. 46).

City regions fit a somewhat narrower definition than metropolitan areas in that they are usually associated with a regional tier or level of government that operates in addition to or instead of the city level (UCLG 2017a, p. 44). For example, the Gauteng City Region (GCR) is a conglomeration of cities and towns around the City of Johannesburg, South Africa. It is a major contributor to the economy of the country and indeed the continent. Like its counterparts the world over, the population of the GCR is growing fast and its economy is vibrant.

However, spatial and institutional fragmentation in the GCR is hampering development. Some of the blame can be placed on the inability of government institutions in the GCR to align their programmes and projects, particularly with respect to infrastructure development. The Constitution of the Republic of South Africa, 1996 (the Constitution), in distributing powers with respect to infrastructure development across three jurisdictions, all of which are responsible for a space that is to all intents and purposes integrated, poses challenges to the GCR.

So what are the constitutional and legal options for closer collaboration? And how do these options relate to SDG 11 with its insistence on access to housing, transport systems, sustainable human settlement planning, resilience to disaster, linkages between urban, peri-urban and rural areas etc.? This chapter discusses these options with a specific focus on the provincial and municipal organs of state in the Gauteng Province of South Africa. It examines the question as to what legal avenues are available for the provincial government and municipalities to collaborate more closely around infrastructure development in order to support the development of the GCR. The question is whether in South Africa too, public policy and law reform have not kept up with the growing importance of its main metropolis in the pursuit of the SDGs, in particular SDG 11. The chapter commences with locating this debate in the international normative framework for decentralisation and urban governance.

The International Normative Framework and the Nature of South Africa's Multilevel Government

The international normative framework for decentralisation contains important pointers for the debate about suitable instruments for collaboration in the city region. The topic of intergovernmental collaboration does not feature strongly in instruments such as the European Charter for Local Self-Government (1985) and the International Guidelines on Decentralisation and Access to Basic Services for all (UN-Habitat 2009). However, the African Charter on the Values and Principles of Decentralisation, Local Governance and Local Development (2014) (African Charter) places a high premium on collaboration across the levels of government.

The African Charter contains a number of provisions that encourage member states to facilitate collaboration between local governments and other actors in the development arena. For example, the Charter's rendition of the subsidiary principle in article 6(1) is immediately followed by article 6(2), which provides that "central governments shall create enabling conditions for cooperation and coordination between national and all subnational levels of government and shall empower local governments or local authorities to discharge their duties and responsibilities." Article 6(3) provides that "[l]ocal governments or local authorities shall cooperate with central governments and other local actors to achieve increased efficiency and effectiveness in public action for the delivery of public services." Other examples are article 7(3) on central-local collaboration with regard to development investments and article 11 on collaborative development planning across the levels of government. Lastly, article 17 encourages horizontal and international cooperation among local governments.

It is suggested that the difference in emphasis is a result of the African Charter's placing less emphasis on local autonomy than its European or global counterparts. Its language pertaining to local self-governance is significantly diluted in comparison with that of the European Charter and the UN-Habitat Guidelines. Clearly, it sees cooperation and integration as an integral part of decentralisation, perhaps even more so than an insistence on local autonomy.

As will be discussed in this chapter, South Africa's system of multilevel government combines the same insistence on collaboration, with a strong emphasis on local autonomy. This is a specific challenge for the GCR region. South Africa's system of multilevel government is sometimes described as an "hourglass" model (Steytler 2017, p. 328). The national government is strong, exercising key exclusive powers over the judiciary, land, policing and, importantly, in firm control of the most buoyant taxing powers. The nine provincial governments are relatively weak, with most of their powers held concurrently with the national government, and their finances almost entirely dependent on the national government. On the other hand, local government is strong, with municipalities exercising constitutionally protected powers including the power to generate revenue (De Visser 2017, p. 226; see also Fuo 2019, in this volume). This is particularly true for large cities and metropolitan municipalities, many of which are located in the Gauteng Province. Municipalities must raise the bulk of their own revenue and practice zero-based budgeting. This renders them more prone to exercising self-government than provinces that rely on central government funding and largely implement national legislation (see below). However, it is also true that municipalities and provinces operate in a system that expects high levels of integration across the levels of government. The constitutional principle of "cooperation" with its many detailed provisions in Chapter 3 of the Constitution is a clear manifestation of this. The practice of integration across the levels of government is complex, however, as the remainder of this chapter will point out. The implications of this complexity, in South Africa or elsewhere are relevant to the localisation of the SDGs, in particular SDG 11. First, an overview of the socio-economic context of the GCR and the case of collaboration will be given.

The Gauteng City Region

Introduction

The Gauteng City Region is defined here as the areas made up of the municipalities in the Gauteng Province, one of nine provinces in South Africa. This area has linkages and flows of goods, capital and people that extend beyond such boundaries into neighbouring provinces, further into Southern Africa, and even globally, so that the GCR displays all the hallmarks of a global city region. However, for the purposes of this chapter the discussion will focus on the provincial and municipal bodies in the Gauteng Province, and the question is asked how they can increase their collaboration in order to more effectively pursue SDG 11 between now and 2030. The background to this inquiry is the need for multilevel governance arrangements in city regions such as the GCR, to step up to the challenge of tackling the externalities occasioned by fragmented governance because, as will be highlighted below, these externalities are impeding South Africa's efforts to realise the objectives related to access to housing, efficient transport systems, sustainable human settlement planning, resilience to disaster, linkages between urban, peri-urban and rural areas and other subsets of SDG 11.

Population, Economy and Spatial Form

Gauteng is South Africa's smallest but most densely populated province. It comprises only 1.5 percent of the country's land area (18,178 km^2) but is home to almost 24 percent (23.9 percent) of South Africa's 54m population (Statistics South Africa 2014, p. 12). Over the past years, its population has grown faster than the national average of 1.44 percent per annum.

The province is predicted to have a population of between 14.7m – 18.7m by 2037 (Gauteng Department of Roads and Transport 2013, p. 11). A substantial portion of that growth is as a result of in-migration. For example, between 2011 and 2015, Gauteng's net in-migration was estimated to be 543,109 people, of whom 343,308 came from outside the country's borders (Gauteng Provincial Government 2016, p. 24).

The GCR's one trillion ZAR GDP comprises about 36 percent of the country's GDP. Relative to the continent of Africa, the GCR contributes 11 percent of the continent's GDP (OECD 2011, p. 25). Despite the GCR's significantly high levels of economic activity and a growing population, it also has high levels of poverty, social exclusion and spatial distortions, including inefficient human settlement patterns (Gauteng Provincial Government 2015, p. 29).

Apartheid planning, which included condemning the black majority to dormitory townships to serve the mines and establishing race-based local institutions, has left a stubborn, cynical imprint on the area. In this respect the GCR was dealt a particularly hard hand in terms of setting out to achieve SDG 11's object of achieving inclusive urbanisation. The modern government institutions in the GCR have still not been able to make the desired progress in reversing this reality. This is in part for institutional reasons that are at the heart of this chapter.

Gauteng's spatial form is one of urban sprawl and fragmentation, which make it difficult to achieve the sustainability and inclusion that characterise the objectives of SDG 11. Its cities are struggling to combat inner city decline. The urban poor are spatially marginalised and travel long distances to work and to amenities. As an indication of the scale of the problem, households spend an inordinate proportion of their monthly income, about 21 percent, on transport (Gauteng Provincial Government 2016, p. 70). This disproportionally impacts black residents of the GCR. A study by Culwick et al. concluded that "African respondents travel 56 min to work compared with 42 min for white respondents. Black respondents consequently also start their daily journey to work much earlier in the day – 25 percent before 6 a.m. compared with just 5 percent of white respondents" (Culwick et al. 2015, p. 310).

To a large extent, race and income determine where people live. Transportation is car-oriented. There is a well-developed system of highways, particularly in high-income areas. Recent infrastructure development has largely followed this car-oriented model, and public transport remains seriously underdeveloped, despite the introduction of promising new initiatives such as rapid bus systems and the Gautrain (Gauteng City Region Observatory 2015, p. 6). The goal of "accessible and sustainable transport systems for all" thus remains a distant dream for the majority of the residents of the GCR.

Municipalities in the GCR

The GCR comprises three metropolitan municipalities –the City of Johannesburg, the City of Tshwane, and Ekurhuleni – and two district municipalities – Sedibeng and West Rand.

The three metropolitan municipalities have exclusive authority in their area and are responsible for all the local government functions

Table 10.1 Population growth in the Gauteng Province

Year	*Population size*
1996	7.6
2001	9.2
2015	13.2

Source: Gauteng Provincial Government 2016, p. 24.

(Constitution of South Africa 1996 Sec. 155(1)(a)). These functions include the supply of essential services such as water, sanitation, electricity reticulation, municipal public transport, municipal roads, waste management and planning (Constitution Sec. 156(1) read with Schedules 4(B) and 5(B)). The remainder of the province comprises of two-tiered local government structures, namely the two abovementioned district municipalities comprising a number of local municipalities – Emfuleni, Lesedi and Midvaal (part of Sedibeng) and Merafong, Mogale City, Randfontein and Westonaria (part of West Rand). These district and local municipalities share the responsibility for local government functions according to an intricate scheme set out in legislation (Constitution Sec. 155(1)(b)-(c) read with the Local Government: Municipal Structures Act 117 of 1998 ch. 5). The general thrust of this scheme is that the district municipalities are responsible for district-wide services, certain localised services, the bulk provision of services, and the performance of a coordinating and supporting role for the local municipalities. The division of the responsibilities between the district and the local municipalities is contested almost everywhere both inside and outside the GCR, and it has been on the agenda for legislative change for many years, adding complexity, instability and fragmentation to an already difficult GCR context (Steytler 2003, p. 241).

Fragmented Decision-making

It has proved to be difficult to address the spatial fragmentation inherited by apartheid. An important contributor to this problem is the issue of fragmented decision making and grant flows with respect to public and private infrastructure (National Planning Commission (NPC) 2011, p. 244). A few examples may elucidate this statement.

The provision of public transport services in the GCR, which is so critical to connect people to opportunities and amenities and central to the GCR's efforts to meet the targets set out in SDG 11, is often not aligned across the vertical and horizontal axes. Transport subsidies are paid by the central government to provincial governments, which perform many public transport services even when those public transport services begin and end within a municipality. Increasingly these transport subsidies are channeled through to municipalities but with considerable bureaucracy and delay. Similarly, grants for the building of subsidised housing are channeled to the provincial government even though the establishment of housing schemes intersects with a range of local government functions such as water, sanitation, electricity and municipal roads (De Visser and Christmas 2007, pp. 9–14).

SDG 11 enjoins South Africa to enhance its capacity for integrated and sustainable human settlement planning and to strengthen its national and regional development planning. The domestic legal and institutional context is complex, however. Land-use planning and management (or town planning) responsibilities are scattered across provincial and municipal governments. The provincial government is responsible for regional planning while the municipalities are responsible for municipal planning (Berrisford 2011, p. 254). In fact, many sectoral departments responsible for functions such as environmental protection, agriculture and heritage protection also exercise control over land use (see below). Municipalities are central to the management of land use and take land use planning decisions. However, many of their decisions will impact on the surrounding municipal areas and indeed on the exercise by the province of its functions.

This institutional fragmentation is often blamed for the lack of alignment between provincial and municipal services. For example, when metropolitan public transport services are incompatible and commuters cannot seamlessly utilise public transport across (otherwise irrelevant) administrative boundaries, the fragmentation of the institutions responsible for public transport is a big part of the problem. When a subsidised housing scheme runs into endless bureaucratic delays or when houses are built without the necessary services, there is often a trail of intergovernmental disputes behind the situation.

The Case for Better Institutional Collaboration

In 2011 the Organisation for Economic Co-operation and Development (OECD) conducted a study of the GCR and observed that it lacks a clear and widely shared city-region vision, and that it needs a dynamic body capable of coordinating action in this field (OECD 2011, p. 234). Implicit in the second part of the observation is that the GCR is advised to revisit the institutional arrangements that seem to play a role in perpetuating the fragmentation of service delivery.

That does not mean that the problem had hitherto not been a priority. In 2003, already the Gauteng Intergovernmental Forum, an intergovernmental structure comprising provincial and municipal executives in the province (see below), had agreed on the need to develop a common Gauteng region that is competitive. It had also agreed on the need for improved mechanisms for integration and intergovernmental relations and for improved coordination and consultation at sectoral and provincial levels (Gauteng Provincial Government 2006, p. 20).

It is those institutional arrangements to which this chapter is dedicated. What options are there in law for the provincial government and the municipalities to collaborate more closely? Before attempting to answer this question in greater detail, two specific issues that shape this debate are discussed below.

The Challenge of Cooperation Across Jurisdictional and Political Lines

Introduction

The above discussion strongly suggests that collaboration across provincial and municipal jurisdictions is much needed in the GCR. However, realising the collaboration is a serious challenge. This section discusses two dimensions of this challenge, namely the constitutional and the political.

The Legal Dimension: An Emboldened Local Government Sphere

As indicated earlier, municipalities in South Africa enjoy strong constitutional protection of their powers. These powers have been confirmed and clarified in a series of six Constitutional Court judgments (City of Johannesburg Metropolitan Municipality v Gauteng Development Tribunal and others [2008] 2 All SA 298 (W); Lagoonbay Lifestyle Estate (Pty) Ltd v The Minister for Local Government, Environmental Affairs and Development Planning of the Western Cape & Others [2013] ZASCA 13 (15 March 2013); Habitat Council and Another v Provincial Minister of Local Government, Environmental Affairs and Development Planning, Western Cape and Others [2013] ZAWCHC 112 (14 August 2013); Tronox KZN Sands (Pty) Ltd v KwaZulu-Natal Planning and Development Appeal Tribunal and Others 2016 (3) SA 160 (CC); Pieterse NO v Lephalale Local Municipality 2017 (2) BCLR 233 (CC); Maccsand (Pty) Ltd v City of Cape Town and Others 2012 (4) SA 181 (CC)). In these judgments, which will be briefly introduced below, the Constitutional Court delineated national, provincial and municipal powers over land-use management. For three reasons these judgments form an important backdrop to any effort towards developing a GCR with a defined institutional character beyond a voluntary and informal approach. First, they go to the heart of municipal autonomy over a crucial aspect of infrastructure development, namely decision making with respect to what can be loosely defined as "town planning". Secondly, they have broader relevance because they define how the Constitution protects local government powers. These powers include matters such as "municipal public transport", "municipal roads", "water and sanitation services" and "electricity … reticulation", all of which are central to the GCR debate. Third, they also elucidate the framework conditions for realising SDG 11 in the GCR and in South Africa generally.

The narrative surrounding the protection of local government's infrastructure powers commenced in City of Johannesburg Metropolitan Municipality v Gauteng Development Tribunal. In this case the City of Johannesburg asked the Constitutional Court to declare parts of the Development Facilitation Act (DFA) unconstitutional. The DFA empowered provincial planning tribunals to take land-use decisions, something that the Constitution reserves for municipalities, so the City argued. The Constitutional Court agreed with the City and declared the DFA unconstitutional. The judgment underscored the central role that municipalities play in land-use management and significantly reduced the scope for provincial interference with municipal powers. It essentially located municipalities at the centre of the land-use management framework.

In subsequent years more litigation surrounding municipal planning powers reached the Constitutional Court. In fact, this innocuous and technical part of the Constitution became the subject of five further Constitutional Court judgments, following each other in rapid succession. Without fail, each judgment confirmed the approach taken in Gauteng Development Tribunal, namely that national and provincial governments may not usurp the powers of municipalities with respect to "municipal planning". The national government does not trump municipal land-use decisions by issuing mining licences (Maccsand). Provincial governments may not subject municipal land-use decisions to a veto, even if the development impacts on an entire region (Lagoonbay). Provincial governments may also not subject municipal land-use decisions to provincial appeals (Habitat Council, Pieterse and Tronox). The six judgments are summarised below, for ease of reference.

The jurisprudential trend surrounding municipal powers and particularly how they interface with provincial powers is very clear. It indicates

Table 10.2 Overview of South African Constitutional Court judgments on "municipal planning"

Gauteng Development Tribunal (2010)	*Maccsand (2012)*	*Lagoonbay (2013)*	*Habitat Council (2014)/ Pieterse (2016)*	*Tronox (2015)*
Can province take "town planning" decisions?	Does having a national mining licence make municipal land-use approval unnecessary?	Can province overrule a municipality when the impact of the development straddles the municipal boundary?	Can the province be the appeal body for municipal planning decisions?	What if the provincial appeal board is an independent expert body?
No, the municipality takes town-planning decisions (rezoning and township development)	No, the municipality must still take its own decisions.	No, the municipality must still take its own decisions.	No, an appeal from a municipality to a province is not constitutional	No, an appeal from a municipality to a province is not constitutional (confirming Habitat Council)

that there are hard limits to how far the provincial government may go in imposing collaborative structures and mechanisms to facilitate the GCR. The provincial government may not pass any laws or take any action that removes executive authority from municipalities with respect to their constitutional powers. In the same vein, the provincial government may not pass any laws or take any actions that somehow "second-guess" municipal decision-making with respect to any of its constitutional powers, be they in the form of vetoes, appeals, or other attempts to override a municipality's powers. Lastly, the provincial government may not unduly circumscribe or restrict the exercise by municipalities of their constitutional powers.

It goes without saying that these constitutional realities limit the extent to which the Gauteng provincial government may impose collaborative structures and mechanisms on the municipalities in the province. The next section will examine the current relevant political realities, particularly as they have changed in the years preceding the publication of this chapter.

The Arrival of Competitive Politics

Recent changes in the political landscape in Gauteng present new challenges to the system of intergovernmental collaboration in Gauteng, and therefore to the GCR.

The government of the Gauteng Province was under the control of the African National Congress (ANC) from the time of the establishment of this province in 1994 until recently. Most of the municipalities in Gauteng were also governed by outright ANC majorities. In fact, before August 2016 all municipalities except Midvaal Local Municipality were governed by the ANC. Therefore, most of the municipalities in Gauteng were governed by the same party as that which governed the province. Intergovernmental relations in the province were complicated but not as a result of the dynamics between political parties.

The August 2016 local government elections brought about a significant change that was felt countrywide. The ANC lost a considerable amount of support, as evidenced by its national support dropping below 55 percent. More significantly, the ANC suffered major defeats in the metropolitan areas, losing three metros to the opposition, namely the City of Johannesburg, the City of Tshwane and Nelson Mandela Bay Metropolitan Municipality in the Eastern Cape. For intergovernmental relations in Gauteng, this means that two out of the three metropolitan powerhouses in the province are no longer controlled by the party that controls the provincial government.

A look at the financial aspect of this situation may underscore the significance of this development. Before the August 2016 elections the ANC controlled 85 percent of the 228-billion ZAR combined budget of the eight metros countrywide. The opposition Democratic Alliance (DA) controlled only 15 percent, because the City of Cape Town was the only city it controlled. The combined budget of the now opposition-controlled metros is

130- billion ZAR. The ANC has lost control of approximately 80 percent of the budgets of metros nationwide (Suttner 2017). A look at local government operating budgets throughout the country indicates that the ANC control of local government operating budgets has dropped from 82 percent to 41 percent, primarily as a result of the changes in the metropolitan municipalities.

For the GCR, the outcome of the 2016 local government elections makes intergovernmental relations more challenging than they were before August 2016. It will no longer be possible for intergovernmental disputes to be ironed out in party headquarters or for intergovernmental strategies to be informally sanctioned before the formal discussion. More reliance will have to be placed on the formal, institutional instruments for integration to which this chapter turns next.

The Instruments for Integration

Introduction

This section of the chapter provides a short overview of some of the most prominent legal instruments that could be utilised to institutionalise the Gauteng City Region and achieve greater integration. They are structured as a continuum of legal mechanisms that range from the most intrusive, i.e. involving interference with municipal autonomy, to the least intrusive, i.e. relying on voluntary cooperation.

Changing Municipal Institutions

On the far end of the spectrum is the changing of municipal institutions, i.e. the redrawing of boundaries and/or the recategorisation of municipalities in order to create a new GCR institution or institutions at municipal level. As indicated above, the GCR comprises of seven local municipalities, two district municipalities and three metropolitan municipalities. Redrawing boundaries, i.e. amalgamating municipalities has been considered in order to achieve greater coherence at local level. However, the provincial government does not have powers of its own to implement this. Boundaries are drawn by an independent Municipal Demarcation Board (Constitution Sec. 155(3)(b)).

Similarly, the declaration of more metropolitan municipalities could remove one level of complexity from the GRC scenario. If the GCR were to comprise metropolitan municipalities only, as has been mooted in the past, local government would comprise one tier only. The additional complexity of the district-local relations mentioned above could at least be eliminated. However, the same constraint as that in regard to the boundaries applies: the power to declare metropolitan municipalities resides with the Municipal Demarcation Board (Structures Act Sec. 4). Whether or not an area qualifies as a metropolitan municipality depends on three issues, namely the economy, intensity and interdependence. First, the area must contain a centre of economic activity whose economy is complex and diverse. Secondly, the area must be characterised by high population density, the intense movement of people, goods and services, and extensive development. Thirdly, it must have multiple business districts and industrial areas and there must be strong interdependence between its constituent units. It must thus be an area that requires integrated development planning (Structures Act Sec. 2). If all of the above criteria are complied with, the independent Municipal Demarcation Board declares the area a self-standing metropolitan municipality (Steytler and De Visser 2016, pp. 2–20). Prior to the 2000 elections the Demarcation Board proclaimed six metropolitan municipalities in the country, namely Johannesburg, Ekurhuleni (East Rand), Tshwane (Pretoria), City of Cape Town, eThekwini (Durban) and Nelson Mandela Bay (Port Elizabeth); with the 2006 elections, two more were added, namely Mangaung (Bloemfontein) and Buffalo City (East London).

Multi-jurisdictional Institutions

It seems then that changing municipal institutions is not within easy reach. The power to take the relevant decisions lies elsewhere, namely with the national Demarcation Board. In any event, the amalgamation and reclassification of municipalities is often a heavy-handed and controversial instrument.

A less intrusive mechanism to pursue the GCR objective may be the creation of multi-jurisdictional institutions. This mechanism still involves amending public institutions. In other words, it goes further than the intergovernmental dialogue and consultation discussed below. It involves creating institutions that exist in addition to the municipal and provincial organs of state in the province. These would be public entities and would therefore have to be established in terms of specific statutory provisions. They would bring together two or more organs of state into one legal entity with a particular mandate, drawn from the participating organs of state. Such entities could be particularly useful in consolidating those aspects of a specific public service, such as public transport, that are delivered at different government levels, thereby dealing with the externalities caused by different government levels. Being juristic persons in their own right with their own internal decision-making structures, they would be decidedly different from the intergovernmental structures provided under the Intergovernmental Relations Framework Act 13 of 2005 (IGRFA, see below), which are not juristic persons and depend on further decision making within the participating organs of state. In summary, the objective would be to create institutions that are (1) public in nature, (2) tasked with a joint mandate drawn from municipal and provincial spheres of responsibility and (3) managed jointly by the participating organs of state.

The question now is: what does the legal framework offer in this respect and how does it relate to the implementation of the global vision of good urban governance described in SDG 11? The reality is that the national legislative framework offers only a few options for the establishment of public entities that straddle jurisdictions. Key to the inquiry is the Public Finance Management Act 1 of 1999 (PFMA). For an institution to function as a public entity, exercising public functions, it must be recognised in terms of the PFMA, otherwise it may not handle public funds. The PFMA recognises national and provincial public entities, i.e. those that are accountable to Parliament or to a provincial legislature (PFMA Sec. 1). Furthermore, it recognises national and provincial business enterprises owned by national or provincial governments. However, when it comes to entities that straddle provincial and municipal jurisdictions, the PFMA offers little assistance. There is nothing in the PFMA on the basis of which a board, commission, company, corporation, fund, business enterprise or other entity that combines provincial and municipal governments can be duly recognised as a public entity. In other words, it does not recognise public entities that straddle national and provincial governments, or public entities that straddle two provincial governments. So it goes without saying that it does not recognise public entities that combine provincial governments and municipalities.

There are sector-specific laws that move closer to enabling a solution. The most prominent example is the establishment of an entity for the joint exercise of transport functions in terms of section 12 of the National Land Transport Act 5 of 2009. Section 12 provides for the combination of municipal and provincial functions into one arrangement which can be given effect by establishing a provincial entity. The provincial government may enter into an agreement with municipalities to provide for the joint exercise of functions. It goes a step further and provides that the province "may establish a provincial entity in this regard." However, the "provincial entity" referred to there is the same "provincial entity" defined in the PFMA as belonging to the province, not to the province and the participating municipalities. In other words, the joint entity becomes a provincial entity, making it unattractive for municipalities to take part in.

The local government legislation offers mechanisms for arrangements within the local government sphere. Section 87 of the Local Government: Municipal Systems Act 32 of 2000 (Municipal Systems Act) sets out a framework for multi-jurisdictional service utilities. A multi-jurisdictional service utility is a utility in which two or more municipalities combine their jurisdictions and collaborate in the performance of a municipal function in a designated area. It is a juristic person set up by agreement that is governed by a board of directors but reports regularly to the parent municipalities. So, for example, the three metropolitan municipalities could establish a joint utility responsible for the management of municipal roads within the combined area. As an instrument for use in achieving integration along the provincial-municipal axis, though, this mechanism is limited. It does not include the provincial government as a partner, and provincial functions may thus not be housed there. So, in our example the provincial road management functions could not be made a part of it. At best, the provincial government could be represented on the board of such a multi-jurisdictional service utility.

Furthermore, the legislation makes no mention of provincial involvement in the actual process of establishing the entity. (While the legislation acknowledges that senior levels of government may "trigger" such a collaborative arrangement, it somehow envisages this to be only the national government – Local Government: Municipal Systems Act Sec. 88.) The provincial oversight and coordination role also receives little attention in the law. While the national Minister is specifically mentioned as a possible "initiator" of a multi-jurisdictional service utility, the provincial government is not. This does not prevent the provincial government from actively engaging municipalities and facilitating the establishment of a multi-jurisdictional service utility, though. However, at the end of the day, it remains a "horizontal" arrangement.

In summary, the legal framework is not kind to the establishment of a provincial-local entity that (1) has separate legal personality and (2) is a public entity. It is suggested that the complaint registered in the Fourth Global Report on Decentralization and Local Democracy (United Cities and Local Governments 2017) resonates in this area of law in South Africa, namely that the growing importance of metropolitan areas in the pursuit of SDG 11 and the rest of the global urban development agenda is not matched by domestic law reform. It seems counterintuitive that a domestic legal framework is so parsimonious in offering safe statutory options for the members of the GCR to establish joint entities.

Other opportunities may need to be pursued if the establishment of a provincial-local entity is clearly on the cards. One example is establishing a private company under the Companies Act 71 of 2008, underwritten by an intergovernmental agreement. The legislation permits municipalities to establish or hold interests in private companies. Its interest does not have to be full ownership but may be a lesser interest as long as the other partners are provincial organs of state or municipalities (Local Government: Municipal Systems Act Sec. 86C). It becomes a PFMA-recognised entity if the ownership control is held by a national or provincial organ of state.

Provincial Regulatory Authority

A further option is for the provincial government to use its regulatory authority to achieve greater alignment in the GCR. This option does not involve the creation of any institution or agency but relates to the use of provincial regulatory power. It is suggested here against the backdrop of the complaint about the lack of alignment among municipalities in the GCR and between municipalities and provincial governments. The lack of alignment, particularly around key minimum standards for the delivery of infrastructure is often cited as a key concern, with incompatible public transport infrastructure as a prominent example. For example, why can the rapid bus transport in the three metropolitan municipalities not operate according to the same basic infrastructural standards, such as bus height, bus lane sizes and ticketing systems?

This is where the provincial regulatory authority could be utilised more effectively. With respect to the municipal functions listed in the Constitution (such as municipal public transport), each municipality in Gauteng enjoys constitutional protection. The provincial government may not remove a municipality's executive authority or compromise its decision making, as was clearly determined by the Constitutional Court (see above). This does not mean, however, that the provincial government does not have regulatory authority over local government functions. The local government matters are listed as provincial powers in Schedules 4B and 5B of the Constitution. Municipal autonomy is protected because the Constitution limits provincial power to "regulating" the exercise of these powers "to see to the effective performance" (Constitution Sections 155(6) and (7) read with Schedules 4(B) and 5(B)).

In order to pursue the GCR objectives, the provincial government is constitutionally permitted to establish minimum standards for municipal functions. There is no reason why these minimum standards could not be aimed at achieving basic harmonisation of municipal functions in the GCR. To take the public transport example, the Constitution empowers the Gauteng Province to prescribe minimum standards for the installation of rapid bus infrastructure so as to make the various systems more compatible.

The reality is that provincial governments have been very reluctant to exercise their legislative authority in areas where they share power with national government. This applies to both the provincial functions as well as to the regulation of local government functions. The "hourglass" model of South Africa's multilevel government referred to earlier is an important determinant of this. South Africa's provinces are reluctant to push the envelope of their constitutional powers to regulate local government (De Visser 2017, p. 229).

An example of one of the major provincial functions, namely "housing", may explain this. The example is apposite as the function permeates many of the targets set under SDG 11, most notably those related to access to adequate, safe and affordable housing, slum upgrading and human settlement planning. "Housing" is an area over which both national and provincial governments have concurrent competence. In other words, both national and provincial governments have the same legislative and executive authority. In the event of a dispute, the matter is ultimately resolved by the Constitutional Court on the basis of a constitutional system of overrides.

Throughout the country the nine provincial departments responsible for housing delivery, command impressive budgets to deliver subsidised housing. The provincial spend is very significant. No less than 72 percent of the ZAR 29.1 billion human settlements budget of 2014/15 was spent by provinces (National Treasury 2015). However, the practice of determining standards for housing delivery does not reflect this. The national government determines the legislative framework and disburses the funds while provinces identify projects and act as implementing agents of the national government. The legislative framework, including matters such as standards for housing subsidies and mechanisms to devolve housing functions to municipalities, is determined nationally. The National Housing Act 107 of 1997 and the National Housing Development Agency Act 23 of 2008 are as yet unmatched by rival provincial legislation (De Visser 2017, p. 231). The few provincial legislative initiatives in the housing arena were unfortunate attempts to facilitate eviction, as is discussed elsewhere in this volume (see Riegner 2019, in this volume). The absence of provincial legislation is symptomatic for most of the areas where provincial governments share authority with the national government.

It also applies to those areas where the provincial governments share authority with the national government to regulate local government matters. The regulation of municipal public transport is such an area: both the national and provincial governments may regulate municipal public transport, but only national government has done so.

The Gauteng Provincial Government is no exception. It has shown very little appetite to exercise its legislative powers to adopt frameworks for local government that are specific to Gauteng. In its recently adopted Integrated Urban Development Framework (IUDF), the Department of Cooperative Governance remarks that "the dynamics in the Gauteng Province are unique and require a distinct dispensation for coordination" (Gauteng Provincial Government 2016, p. 53). In the context of its desire to facilitate the GCR, which is very much a Gauteng-specific issue, there may be good reason for Gauteng to explore this competence.

Combined Decision-making

An important aspect of the concern underlying the GCR relates to the possibility that fragmented decision making may impede the roll-out of public and private infrastructure of the kind necessary for the pursuit of the SDG 11 targets in the years to come. A single development such as the establishment of a low-cost housing scheme, a rapid bus lane or a mall may attract the attention of many organs of state in different spheres of government, all of which exercise some form of regulatory authority over the required changes in land use. For example, a housing project may require a rezoning decision from the municipality, an environmental impact assessment from the provincial government, an agricultural approval from the department of agriculture and a water-use licence from the national government. It is not hard to imagine that these multiple approvals often result in delays in realising infrastructural development.

As this chapter moves from the most intrusive instruments (such as changing institutions or establishing new ones) to the less intrusive instruments (i.e. those that are more collaborative in nature), the statutory mechanisms to align decision making on land use come to mind. There are a number of provisions in legislation pertaining to land-use management that offer mechanisms to alleviate the burden of "red tape" caused by the many approvals required from different organs of state.

Section 30 of the Spatial Planning and Land Use Management Act 16 of 2013 (SPLUMA) empowers organs of state across spheres of government to jointly exercise their powers with respect to land use authorisation. In other words, when an infrastructure project in the GCR requires authorisation from more than one organ of state (as all big infrastructure projects do), they may exercise their powers jointly. They may do so in one of two ways. First, while issuing separate authorisations they may align the procedures to get there. For example, the provincial government and the city may combine their respective public participation procedures into one, but still take their own separate decisions. This already reduces the quantity of the red tape considerably. The second option goes further: the two may collapse their many separate authorisations into one single authorisation.

It is suggested that these mechanisms, if used effectively, could assist in mobilising organs of state in different spheres of government to collaborate around specific infrastructure projects.

Intergovernmental Relations

At the end of the spectrum of options to collaborate, on the cooperative side, exists a wide range of intergovernmental mechanisms. Most of them are regulated in local government laws or the IGRFA.

There is the Premier's Coordinating Forum (IGRFA Sections 16–20), a consultative structure where the Premier, selected members of the provincial cabinet (MECs) and the mayors meet. Another structure is the District Coordinating Forum (IGFRA Sections 24–27), of which the GCR region has two, one in each of the two districts. These are also consultative structures where the district mayor meets with his or her counterparts from the local municipalities. There are two more intergovernmental structures that do not have a basis in the IGRFA. The first is the Extended Executive Council, comprising of the entire provincial cabinet and the mayors of municipalities in the province. The second is the MEC-MMC forums (MEC stands for "Member of the Executive Council" (members of the provincial executive); MMC stands for "Member of the Mayoral Committee" (members of the city executive)), and "bilateral" forums where the

MEC responsible for a specific portfolio meets with his/her counterpart at the municipal level. The scope of work of these forums is limited to the functional area for which the MEC and the MMCs are responsible. All of the above forums are supported by technical structures where the relevant bureaucrats meet.

The IUDF points out that these forums have not been used optimally (Department of Cooperative Governance 2016, p. 45). From an institutional perspective there are two characteristics that crucially define all of these forums and set them apart from the more "coercive" or "institutional" options discussed above. First, they operate according to a consensus model: decision-making requires the agreement of all participating organs of state. Second, implementation depends on further decision making or adherence on the part of the participating organs of state. None of these forums are separate legal entities, and they are thus not capable to take executive decisions. From within the GCR, the question has arisen whether the regular intergovernmental structures are equipped to achieve greater alignment in the GCR region. IGR structures, where provincial and municipal executives come together, may take decisions, but these are not binding on the participating institutions. When one of them fails to follow through on a resolution taken by the IGR structure, there is little that can be done. They thus depend on voluntary participation and follow-through by the participating organs of state. In reality these forums have not been able to generate sufficient traction to facilitate the GCR.

A further intergovernmental relations mechanism to facilitate aligned infrastructure development is integrated development planning (IDP). Every municipality adopts a comprehensive five-year strategic plan called the IDP at the beginning of its term and reviews this annually (Local Government: Municipal Systems Act 2000 Ch. 5). This IDP is expected to be based on the aspirations expressed by communities, and triangulated with the resource capabilities of the municipality and the intergovernmental expectations of other spheres of government (also see van der Berg 2019, in this volume). It comprises and coordinates a range of municipal sectoral plans (on transport, water, economic development, electricity etc.) and, importantly, includes the municipality's spatial vision in the form of a spatial development framework (Local Government: Municipal Systems Act 2000 Sec. 26(3); SPLUMA 2013 Sections 20–21). All of this must be supported by a three-year financial plan (Municipal Systems Act 2003 Sec. 26(h); Local Government: Municipal Finance Management Act 56 of 2003 (MFMA) Sections 17(3)(b), (d) and 53(1)(b)), rendering the IDP the most critical vehicle for community-based and intergovernmental infrastructure planning. The IDP is regulated in the Local Government: Municipal Systems Act, the MFMA and SPLUMA. All three of these laws emphasise and structure intergovernmental alignment, both horizontal (neighbouring municipalities) and vertical (national-provincial).

However, over the past 15 years it has proven to be very difficult to take IDP alignment from high level political commitments into project-based alignment. With community participation often politicised, the process highly cyclical and overregulated, and linkages between strategy and funding often lacking (see Fuo 2019, in this volume), the IDP framework has not become what government intended it to be, namely government's primary vehicle for coordinated development (Pieterse 2007, pp. 20–24). Pieterse attributes this to a number of factors including the "the pressures that emanated from national and provincial governments, which were driving forward demanding sectoral programmes [and] created a cacophony of contradictory pressures that led to municipalities remaining in a reactive, fire-fighting mode" (Pieterse 2007, p. 21). It is very unlikely that the IDP framework alone, in its current form, will be capable of efficiently facilitating the realisation of the GCR.

A more targeted instrument exists in the form of the implementation protocol (IP), which is also regulated in the IGRFA (Sec. 35). The IP is a written agreement among the organs of state involved in the delivery of a particular function or the implementation of a particular project or programme, in which they coordinate their actions. The IP deals specifically with issues such as the roles and responsibilities of each participating organ of state, the contributions to be made by each organ of state, dispute settlement, timelines etc. It could be the umbrella for specific collaborative strategies such as the alignment of land-use procedures or the collapsing of land-use authorisations (see above). It is submitted that, given the limited potential of the IGR forums and IDPs to drive the realisation of greater integration in the GCR, the use of implementation protocols, to support specific large-scale infrastructure projects could be considered.

Conclusion

In a report consolidating the views of 400,000 local and subnational governments on the localisation of the SDGs, UCLG remarked that "[s]tronger institutional frameworks and new channels of dialogue and coordination may be an opportunity for sub-national governments to raise their stance in the process of implementation of the [sustainable development] goals. Many countries refer to these arrangements as a 'multilevel approach' to coordination and cross-level coherence" (UCLG 2017b, p. 11). This rings true for every country's efforts to implement the SDGs. It also plays out differently in every country, given the vast differences in state structures, in the role and status of subnational governments and cities, in histories, in capabilities in the public sector, and in appetites for reform.

In this chapter it is argued that for South Africa it ought to trigger a consideration of the legal framework for the GCR. Given its strategic importance for South Africa and Africa and given its challenges in ensuring alignment across the many organs of state active in the infrastructure sector, the GCR requires a robust institutional framework that can help unlock the potential of the GCR. The GCR must function as a coordinated platform to connect communities to opportunities right across its space, straddling the administrative boundaries of metropolitan, district and local municipalities as well as the provincial boundaries.

The constitutional and legal framework places a high premium on the protection of municipal and provincial autonomy. As has been pointed out in this chapter, the law, with its insistence on clear jurisdictional boundaries, is not always friendly towards collaboration. Aspects of it, such as the absence of a safe legal framework for multi-jurisidictional entities combining national, provincial and local authorities, may need to be reviewed.

While the Gauteng Provincial Government may wish to encourage and promote a more robust GCR framework, municipalities operate in a different incentive structure. They raise the bulk of their revenue and are held directly accountable for the implementation of their own budget. This does not incentivise them to surrender authority to opaque collaborative structures. In addition, competitive politics have arrived in Gauteng. At the time of writing, two of the three metropolitan municipalities are governed by a political party different from that governing the province. This has negated the use of party structures as viable mechanisms to seek policy and programmatic alignment around infrastructure projects and made intergovernmental relations in Gauteng more acrimonious. Reliance must be placed on the formal, legal structures to achieve alignment. Fortunately, there is no shortage of legal instruments and mechanisms, designed to facilitate collaboration across jurisdictional boundaries. Some of the possibilities arising from the existence of these those mechanisms have been discussed in this chapter. They range from the most intrusive actions, such as changing municipal boundaries and establishing institutions "co-owned" by provincial and municipal governments, to the least intrusive actions, such as utilising intergovernmental forums and concluding intergovernmental agreements. It has been argued that some of these mechanisms are under-utilised. Examples are the provincial power to regulate minimum standards for the delivery of infrastructure services and the conclusion of intergovernmental agreements.

Bibliography

Literature

Berrisford, Stephen. 2011. Unravelling Apartheid spatial planning legislation in South Africa. *Urban Forum*, 22, 247–263.

Culwick, Christina, Gotz, Graeme, Katumba, Samy, Trangoš, Guy and Wray, Chris. 2015. Mobility patterns in the Gauteng City-Region, South Africa. *Regional Studies, Regional Science* 2(1), 308–310.

Department of Cooperative Government and Traditional Affairs. 2016. Integrated Urban Development Framework. Pretoria, South Africa: Department of Cooperative Government and Traditional Affairs.

De Visser, Jaap. 2017. Concurrency in South Africa. In: Steytler, Nico (ed). *Concurrent Powers in Federal Systems: Meaning, Making, Managing*. The Hague: Brill/Nijhoff. pp. 222–240.

De Visser, Jaap and Christmas, Annette. 2007. *Developmental Local Government: Determining Appropriate Functions and Powers.* Bellville, South Africa: Community Law Centre.

Fuo, Oliver. 2019. Funding and Good Financial Governance as Imperatives for Cities' Pursuit of SDG 11. In: Aust, Helmut Philipp and du Plessis, Anél (eds). *The Globalisation of Urban Governance - Legal Perspectives on Sustainable Development Goal 11*. New York: Routledge. pp. 87–107.

Gauteng City Region Observatory. 2015. *Quality of Life Survey IV.* Johannesburg, South Africa: Gauteng City Region Observatory.

Gauteng Department of Roads and Transport. 2013. *25-Year Integrated Transport Master Plan*. Johannesburg, South Africa. Gauteng Provincial Government.

Gauteng Provincial Government. 2006. *Building Gauteng and a Globally Competitive City Region*. Johannesburg, South Africa. Gauteng Provincial Government.

Gauteng Provincial Government. 2015. *Concept Paper: Gauteng Spatial Perspective.* Johannesburg, South Africa: Gauteng Provincial Government, Planning Division.

Gauteng Provincial Government. 2016. Gauteng Spatial Development Framework 2030 - Draft for Public Comment. Johannesburg, South Africa. Gauteng Provincial Government.

National Treasury. 2015. *Database and Estimates of National Expenditure.* Pretoria, South Africa: National Treasury.

NPC (National Planning Commission). 2011. *National Development Plan.* Pretoria, South Africa: Presidency.

OECD (Organisation for Economic Co-operation and Development). 2011. *OECD Territorial Review: The Gauteng City Region, South Africa.* Paris: OECD.

Pieterse, Edgar. 2007. Tracing the "integration" thread in the South African urban development policy tapestry. *Urban Forum*, 18(1), pp. 1–30.

Riegner, Michael. 2019. International Institutions and the City. In: Aust, Helmut Philipp and du Plessis, Anél (eds). *The Globalisation of Urban Governance - Legal Perspectives on Sustainable Development Goal 11*. New York: Routledge. pp. 38–64.

Statistics South Africa. 2014. *Mid-year Population Estimates 2014*. Pretoria, South Africa: Statistics South Africa.

Steytler, Nico. 2003. District municipalities: giving effect to shared authority in local government. *Law, Democracy and Development*, 7(2), 227–242.

Steytler, Nico, 2017. The Constitutional Court in South Africa: reinforcing an hourglass system of multilevel government. In: Aroney, Nicholas and Kincaid, John (eds). *Courts in Federal Countries: Federalists or Unitarists?* Toronto, CA: University of Toronto Press. pp. 328–366.

Steytler, Nico and De Visser, Jaap. 2016. *Local government law of South Africa.* Durban, South Africa: LexisNexis.

Suttner, Raymond. 2017. The ANC in crisis – will it survive? *Daily Maverick*, 21 April [online]. Available at: www.dailymaverick.co.za/article/2017-04-21-op-ed-the-anc-in-crisis-will-it-survive/#.Wq5px-huaUk (Accessed: 18 April 2018).

UN-Habitat. 2009. *International Guidelines on Decentralisation and Access to Basic Services for All.* Nairobi, Kenya: UN-Habitat.

United Cities and Local Governments (UCLG). 2017a. GOLD IV 2016 - Fourth Global Report on Decentralization and Local Democracy – Co-Creating the Urban Future. The Agenda of Metropolises, Cities and Territories. Barcelona, Spain: UCLG.

United Cities and Local Governments (UCLG). 2017b. National and sub-national governments on the way towards the localization of the SDGs. Barcelona, Spain: UCLG.

Van der Berg, Angela. 2019. Through the Lens of Integrated Development Planning. In: Aust, Helmut Philipp and du Plessis, Anél (eds). *The Globalisation of Urban Governance - Legal Perspectives on Sustainable Development Goal 11.* New York: Routledge. pp. 208–226.

Case Law

City of Johannesburg Metropolitan Municipality v Gauteng Development Tribunal and others [2008] 2 All SA 298 (W).

Habitat Council and Another v Provincial Minister of Local Government, Environmental Affairs and Development Planning, Western Cape and Others [2013] ZAWCHC 112. (14 August 2013).

Lagoonbay Lifestyle Estate (Pty) Ltd v The Minister for Local Government, Environmental Affairs and Development Planning of the Western Cape & Others [2013] ZASCA 13. (15 March 2013)

Maccsand (Pty) Ltd v City of Cape Town and Others 2012(4) SA 181 (CC).

Pieterse NO v Lephalale Local Municipality 2017(2) BCLR 233 (CC).

Tronox KZN Sands (Pty) Ltd v KwaZulu-Natal Planning and Development Appeal Tribunal and Others 2016(3) SA 160 (CC).

Legislation

Constitution of the Republic of South Africa, 1996.

Intergovernmental Relations Framework Act 13 of 2005.

Local Government: Municipal Finance Management Act 56 of 2003.

Local Government: Municipal Structures Act 117 of 1998.

Local Government: Municipal Systems Act 32 of 2000.

National Housing Act 107 of 1997.

National Housing Development Agency Act 23 of 2008.

National Land Transport Act 5 of 2009.

Public Finance Management Act 1 of 1999.

Spatial Planning and Land Use Management Act 16 of 2013.

Documents

African Charter on the Values and Principles of Decentralisation, Local Governance and Local Development (2014).

European Charter of Local Self-Government (1985).

11 The Pursuit of SDG 11 Through the Lens of Integrated Development Planning

Angela van der Berg

Introduction

The United Nations (UN) predicts that the second and third decades of the twenty-first century will see irreversible and unprecedented urban growth. More than half of the world's population currently lives in cities, and it is anticipated that this number will increase to 60 percent by 2030 and 70 percent by 2050 (UN 2015, pp. 1–2). Much of the urbanisation is taking place in developing countries that generally have insufficient resources and capacity to be able to adequately provide the infrastructure necessary for managing growing cities and the needs of their inhabitants (UN 2014, pp. 7–10).

While urbanisation in itself is not necessarily problematic, rapid and unplanned urbanisation exacerbates the challenges that cities face in terms of sustainability specifically. Over the last two decades cities have emerged as a positive and potent force in driving the global sustainability agenda (UN-Habitat 2016c). Cities connect a wide range of actors, networks, infrastructures, resource flows, cultures, political and social processes, and have become valuable platforms for innovation and creativity, especially in terms of sustainable development (Sustainable Development Solutions Network (SDSN) 2013, pp. 9–12).

In 2015 the United Nations (UN) adopted the 2030 Agenda for Sustainable Development, which includes 17 sustainable development goals (abbreviated as the SDGs) aimed at fostering global social, environmental and economic sustainability. Of particular significance to cities is SDG 11, which seeks to ensure that cities and human settlements become inclusive, safe, resilient and sustainable. SDG 11 is to date the strongest international and political recognition of the key role of cities as drivers of the global sustainable development agenda (Kanuri et al. 2016, p. 1). As explained in the introduction to this volume, the goal provides a broad framework for what the notion of sustainable cities entails and lists specific targets to be met by 2030 to ensure urban sustainability around the globe.

While there are many legal and governance approaches to promoting sustainability within cities, it is increasingly accepted that "urban" or "municipal" planning[1] has a specific role to play (United Nations Environment Programme (UNEP), International Council for Local Environmental Initiatives (ICLEI) 2007, pp. 1–46). The law underpinning the planning function often hosts a number of governance instruments (such as spatial development frameworks, land-use schemes, zoning schemes, and strategic environmental assessments, for example) that shape the spatial form of cities. The instruments are aimed at reconciling and integrating social, economic, cultural and environmental concerns and challenges in the planning and design of cities (De Visser 2016, p. 84). Sustainable urban development is multi-dimensional and complex and necessitates a strategic and integrated approach to planning (International Council for Local Environmental Initiatives 1996, p. 14). Integrated development planning is increasingly distinguished as a valuable legal and strategic planning approach that assists city governments in the pursuit of urban sustainability (United Nations Development Programme (UNDP) 2016, p. 8). Several city governments across the globe employ forms of integrated planning to foster sustainable urban development in their areas of jurisdiction (UN-Habitat 2010, pp. 1–50).

The UN 2030 Agenda for sustainable development frames the context within which global sustainability must be pursued. SDG 11 requires specific action from cities to ensure sustainability in the urban context. This chapter questions how the notion of integrated development planning can serve as a vehicle for the pursuit of SDG 11. The application of integrated development planning in the South African context is employed as an example to illuminate the nexus between integrated development planning and the pursuit of SDG 11. Emphasis is placed on the Integrated Development Plan (IDP) of the City of Johannesburg Metropolitan Municipality. Johannesburg is situated in Gauteng – South Africa's smallest and most rapidly urbanising province (Gauteng Provincial Government 2016, pp. 3–5). The city is well-known for actively developing and driving innovative urban sustainability initiatives.

The second part of this chapter commences with a brief discussion of the origins, development and function of integrated development planning. The third part discusses what is generally expected of cities in the pursuit and maintenance of urban sustainability in the light of SDG 11. The chapter then moves on to an assessment of the application of integrated development planning in the South African context and critically examines the IDP of the City of Johannesburg in the context of SDG 11. Finally, the chapter offers a reflection on some of the inferences that have been drawn on the basis of the City of Johannesburg's IDP. This section also concludes with findings and lessons learnt on how the notion of integrated development planning can serve as a vehicle for the pursuit of sustainable cities.

Origins and Nature of Integrated Development Planning

Various approaches to urban planning exist, such as master planning, community planning, land-use planning, etc. (UN-Habitat 2015b, p. 3). The spectrum of planning methods is broad and reflects an evolving continuum within which planners and government authorities have attempted to influence and control urban forms and functions in different ways (UN-Habitat 2010 p. 5). Despite the existence of this multitude of planning approaches, integrated development planning, as opposed to modernist (master) planning[2] or traditional land-use planning,[3] is thought to be a valuable legal and strategic planning approach (United Nations Development Programme 2016, p. 7). Integrated development planning identifies and combines multiple strategies to address the challenges that cities face, in a manner that promotes holistic sustainable urban development (United Nations Development Programme 2016, p. 8).

Integrated development planning is said to be rooted in "strategic planning" practices originally employed in the private sector (Bryson 2012, p. 51). The private sector generally utilises strategic planning to identify strategies for corporate profit and to systematically plan for future development (Gordon 2005, p. 1). Strategic planning enables industry to incorporate many different stakeholders into the planning process, to conduct a detailed internal and external assessment of the organisation, to identify major challenges, and to establish viable strategies to address the challenges (Bryson 2012, p. 51). Strategic planning also entails budgeting, performance management, and evaluation, and enables an on-going learning process (Bryson 2010, p. 257).

Strategic planning emerged during the 1950s in the United States (Albrechts 2006b, p. 1151), and during the 1980s and 1990s in Western Europe, partly in response to an earlier disillusionment with master planning, but also in response to rapid and uncontrolled urban growth and pollution (Amirah et al. 2009, p. 60). Influenced by the successes of strategic planning in the private sector, government authorities started applying strategic planning practices to their public planning functions (Albrechts 2006b, pp. 1150–1151). In the city context specifically, authorities used strategic planning principles to enable them to predict and understand the present and future challenges that the community/municipal area might face and to develop consensus on a desired vision for the municipal area (Todes 2012, pp. 161–162). Adopting this approach also enabled the city authorities to describe the actions necessary to achieve the vision for the city and to design strategies to address the challenges foreseen; all within the context of the projected financial and human resources (Gordon 2005, p. 1).

Notably, the 1990s signified a turning point for municipal strategic planning. At this time municipal planning practice was influenced by a hegemony of ideas surrounding sustainable urban development (Pieterse

2004, p. 5). Questions relating to different scales of planning in the city, public participation in urban governance decisions, and the environmental imperatives of efficiency and ecological conservation dominated debates pertaining to the need for a paradigm shift in municipal planning practice (Pieterse 2004, p. 4). Proponents of the paradigm shift argued that planners should employ a more systematic and integrated approach to planning (Borja and Castells 1997, p. 153). It was also maintained that planning should cater for all aspects of urban living whilst being flexible enough to accommodate changes or forecast variables[4] that might hamper sustainable urban development (Yigitcanlar and Teriman 2015, p. 342). Similar ideas pertaining to planning and sustainable urban development were supported in the international policy discourses of the World Bank, the UN, and other bilateral agencies (Barraclough 2001, pp. 2–4). Accordingly, municipal planning became more integrated in nature (Barraclough 2001, p. 8). It also became more concerned with the interrelationship between human development and natural resource use (Lyle 1994, pp. 37–50).

One particular international policy development in 1992 is especially meaningful for municipal strategic planning practice (Miraftab, Silver and Beard 2008, p. 4). In June 1992 the UN Conference on Environment and Development (Earth Summit) in Rio de Janeiro, Brazil, adopted Agenda 21, which became widely recognised as the international guideline and plan of action for sustainable development. Chapter 28 established an agenda for local authorities (LA 21), which served to encourage local authorities in both developed and developing countries to improve the social, economic and environmental quality of human settlements. LA 21 noted the inadequacy of sector (silo)-based strategies and called for a holistic and integrated approach to sustainable development and planning (International Council for Local Environmental Initiatives I 1996, p. 80). By 1996 more than 1500 city governments from 149 countries worldwide had adopted integrated planning approaches to promoting sustainable development in their urban areas (UN 2002). This number had increased to nearly 6,500 local governments in over 100 countries by the end of 2001.

LA 21 requires local authorities to fundamentally change the way cities are planned. It necessitates a more responsive and flexible approach to planning. LA 21 includes several planning mandates, which range from cities undertaking community-based analysis to identify development challenges; to setting specific developmental goals and targets; to developing implementation plans to achieve the targets; and to monitoring and reporting on the achievement of their targets. Integrated development planning in terms of LA 21 is specifically guided by principles of integration, vision, linking local issues to global impacts, partnering with civil society, intergenerational equity, and ecological integrity (Venter 2011, pp. 100–102). The adoption of Agenda 21 and the subsequent LA 21 strategies significantly influenced planning in the municipal context to combine the principles and methods of corporate, community-based, and environmental planning with the purpose of creating a public-sector, strategic and integrated planning approach that reflects the imperatives of sustainable development (International Council for Local Environmental Initiatives 1996, p. 14). Integrated development planning requires planners to consider a city as a complex and interrelated system and enables more balanced development of the social, cultural, economic, and environmental domains of the city and its surrounding area (Yigitcanlar and Teriman 2015, pp. 350–352).

Envisioning Sustainable Cities in Terms of SDG 11

A key innovation within the SDGs is the introduction of a sub-national goal for the first time, focusing on urban areas (Arfvidsson et al. 2017, p. 100). SDG 11 has been heralded as "path-breaking, both within the UN system for acknowledging the development role of sub-national governments, and paradigmatically for global urban policy as it concedes that, in an urbanising world, cities can be pathways to sustainable development" (Parnell 2016, pp. 529). For example, the International Council for Local Environmental Initiatives (ICLEI) notes that SDG 11 is truly transformative in nature as it is the only goal that is location-specific and that can be pursued on a manageable scale (ICLEI 2015). The SDG further emphasises that responding to local contexts and stakeholder needs through engagement with a diverse range of local partners, and has become standard rhetoric in fostering urban transition (Patel et al. 2017, p. 786).

In essence, the goal seeks to ensure that cities and human settlements become inclusive, safe, resilient and sustainable. In terms of inclusivity, the goal envisions cities that are people-centred, ethical and just, without any form of the segregation, discrimination and exclusion from opportunities associated with urban living (UN-Habitat 2016a, pp. 4–5). Safety, in turn, is argued to include individual and community safety from violence and crime (UN-Habitat 2015a, pp. 1–10), but can also include the protection of all aspects of human security. Safety in terms of the latter entails meeting basic human needs and safeguarding political and social freedoms – both in terms of freedom from fear and freedom from want (Fukuda-Parr and Messineo 2012, pp. 2–3). As far as it pertains to resilience, the goal may be argued to envision cities with adequate physical structures, natural systems and human communities that function in a manner that enables people living and working in them (especially the poor and vulnerable) to survive and thrive, no matter what shocks (unexpected events) and stresses they encounter (Rockefeller Foundation and ARUP 2014, p. 3).

Sustainability itself, in terms of the SDG, is considered to be a broad notion. The goal envisions and depicts city sustainability by means of specific targets[5] that cities around the globe should collectively aspire to meet. The first seven targets are framed as outcomes (UN-Habitat 2016b, pp. 14–49) and range from requiring cities (by 2030) to ensure access to adequate, safe and affordable housing and basic services; provide safe and accessible transport systems; enhance inclusive, participatory and integrated human settlement planning; safeguard cultural and natural heritage; improve vulnerability to disasters; reduce environmental impacts and improve waste management; and provide access to safe public spaces. The remaining targets are framed in terms of procedure (UN-Habitat 2016b, pp. 50–55) and require cities to strengthen developmental links between urban, peri-urban, and rural areas; adopt and implement disaster risk reduction strategies in line with the Sendai Framework for Disaster Risk Reduction 2015–2030; and to support least developed countries through financial and technical assistance in building sustainable and resilient buildings, utilising local materials.

Integrated Development Planning and the Pursuit of Urban Sustainability: Learning from the South African experience

SDG 11 and its targets undoubtedly have implications for planning in one way or another. It is argued that in order to achieve the sustainable city as envisioned by SDG 11, city authorities will have to transform the way they plan, develop, govern and manage, and will have to deploy "sustainable, people-centred and integrated" approaches to urbanisation (Watson 2016, pp. 439). Some authors indicate that SDG 11 and its targets draw urban planning and design into the heart of the development debate in an unprecedented way (Klopp and Petretta 2017, p. 94). These authors also question how the aims of SDG 11 will integrate with and improve existing urban planning policies and approaches (Klopp and Petretta 2017, p. 94).

While it is entirely possible for many other questions pertaining to urban planning and SDG 11 to arise, this chapter questions how the notion of integrated development planning can serve as a vehicle for the pursuit of SDG 11. The following sections attempt to provide some answers in this regard. The arguments are based on a brief overview of integrated development planning in South Africa and on a critical evaluation of the IDP of the City of Johannesburg Metropolitan Municipality.

Integrated Development Planning in South Africa

The shift towards a more integrated planning approach in the South African context followed a somewhat similar trajectory to that in the international context (see the discussion in the section above). Early forms of integrated development planning were introduced in the 1990s in order to address South Africa's apartheid planning system, which had rendered the country's towns and cities socially imbalanced, racially segregated, and resource-intensive (Gueli, Liebenberg and Van Huyssteen 2007, pp. 100–101). During the late 1980s and early 1990s planning practice was, *inter alia*, rooted in new public management (NPM) theory (Todes 2012, pp.

161–162). NPM is underpinned by corporate values concerned with economic efficiency and identifying challenges and strategies tailored to a specific organisation (Harrison 2006, p. 188). The characteristics of NPM in the context of planning include, for example, the adoption of strategic planning techniques to develop rational frameworks to inform budgeting, resource allocation, the definition of targets and the division of labour between managers and agencies; various forms of sanctions and incentives to improve performance; and procedural steps to solve specific problems (Pieterse 2007, p. 8). NPM thinking also encourages the formation of partnerships with different sectors as part of the planning practice (Harrison 2001, pp. 178–180).

During the early 1990s planning activities were mostly implemented at regional or provincial levels of the South African government[6] (Pycroft 1998, p. 155). It was only after the demise of Apartheid in 1994 that attention started to shift to the role of local government in planning (Harrison 2006, p. 194). The newly elected African National Congress (ANC) implemented a number of policies aimed at redressing the country's apartheid planning legacy and at ensuring an improved and integrated approach to planning (see, for example, the Reconstruction and Development Programme 1994). It was only with the enactment of the Constitution of the Republic of South Africa, 1996 (Constitution) and the publication of the White Paper on Local Government of 1998 (White Paper) that local government became responsible for integrated development planning in the country. The Constitution (Schedule 4(B) and Sec. 153) and the White Paper (Section B) entrust the local government with a developmental mandate. This mandate requires municipalities to work with citizens and groups in the community to find sustainable ways to meet their social, economic and material needs and improve the quality of their lives (Section B of the White Paper). Municipalities are also expected to incorporate the strategic planning principles of performance management, community participation, and partnerships for service delivery into their planning practices (Retief and Cilliers 2016, pp. 174–176). Despite the clarity provided by the White Paper and the Constitution regarding the role of local government in the pursuit of sustainable development and planning, there was still a great need to provide a more adequate legislative basis for integrated development planning and to provide clarity regarding the content and scope of IDPs (Harrison 2006, p. 197). Accordingly, the government developed and approved the Local Government: Municipal Systems Act 32 of 2000 (hereafter Systems Act) in November 2000. The Systems Act *inter alia* provides the required legislative basis for IDPs and, amongst other provisions, details their content.

The IDP required in terms of the Systems Act is South Africa's direct response to the implementation of LA 21 (Todes 2004, p. 851). The IDP has become the principal strategic planning instrument of the municipality, and is expected to guide and inform all planning, and development, and all decisions with regard to planning, management, and development in the municipal area (Bekink 2006, pp. 498–499). It is also the primary tool by which to ensure the integration of local government activities and strategies with development planning policy at national, provincial and international levels (Visser 2001, p. 1680). Every IDP has the force of law as it is legally binding on municipalities in the exercise of their executive authority, and it binds all other persons and entities within their jurisdictions (Sec. 35(1)(b) of the Systems Act). IDPs are specifically designed to assist municipalities to fulfil their developmental mandate (Retief and Cilliers 2016, pp. 167–170) and must be informed by the constitutional rights in the Bill of Rights (eg procedural rights and the rights of access to housing and sufficient water, the right to dignity and equality, as well as the environmental right (Ch. 2 of the Constitution). IDPs must also be informed by the constitutional provisions that place a service delivery mandate on local government *inter alia* to ensure the provision of services to communities in a sustainable manner; and to promote social and economic development (Sec. 152 of the Constitution). The aim of the IDP is to integrate economic, sectoral, spatial, social, institutional, environmental, and fiscal strategies in order to support the optimal allocation of resources between sectors and geographical areas and across the jurisdiction of the municipality in a manner that promotes sustainable growth, equity and the empowerment of the poor and marginalised (Retief and Cilliers 2016, pp. 169–170). Municipalities are further legally required to consult the local community in the drafting and adoption of an IDP (Sec. 29 (1)(i) of the Systems Act). Communities are generally consulted by means of public participation procedures which facilitate the consultation of all urban stakeholders in the development of localised strategies that support local citizens' understandings of how the city ought to develop. The IDP therefore facilitates the assessment of the varied needs of the community and different interest groups, and prioritises these needs in order of urgency, importance and constitutional and legislative imperatives (Visser 2001, p. 1678).

Every IDP must include a vision for the long-term development of the municipality (Sec. 26(a) of the Systems Act). IDPs also contain legal instruments that shape the spatial form of cities and facilitate future growth and development (such as spatial development frameworks and land-use schemes). They also include the operational strategies and implementation plans of the municipal council and its line departments (Sec. 26(f) of the Systems Act). All strategies are tied to key performance indicators and targets (Sec. 41(1)(a) of the Systems Act). Each strategy must further be aligned with the municipality's annual budget (Sec. 26(h) of the Systems Act). IDPs are flexible instruments, however. Their contents, goals, and time-frames may be adjusted to new challenges or the changing needs of the municipality and community (Du Plessis 2008, pp. 464–465).

Integrated Development Planning in the City of Johannesburg

The City of Johannesburg is the largest and most populous city in the Gauteng Province (Gauteng Provincial Government 2016, pp. 3–5). It is classified as one of ten cities situated in developing countries that are projected to become megacities (cities with ten million inhabitants or more) between 2016 and 2030 (UN 2016, p. 6). Despite its significant transformation since 1994, substantial challenges remain if it is to move beyond the entrenched spatial and racial divisions and inequalities of South Africa's apartheid past, build democratic values and forge new, more sustainable development paths.

Recently the City reviewed and developed its 2016–2021 IDP. The IDP sets the strategic priorities for the next five years and is based on the City's long-term development strategy, namely, the City of Johannesburg Growth and Development Strategy Vision 2040. It is also aligned with South Africa's national strategic policies such as the country's National Development Plan Vision 2030 (National Development Planning Commission 2011); including regional strategic policies such as the African Union Agenda 2063: The Africa We Want (African Union 2016), and international policy instruments such as Agenda 2030 and SDG 11.

The main vision of the City as it is expressed in its IDP is to ensure that Johannesburg becomes a "world class African city". This entails that the city environment should by 2040 be "resilient, sustainable and liveable." It includes the aim that the City should secure an improved quality of life for all, foster human and infrastructural resilience, promote an inclusive and competitive local economy, and advance the administrative and governance performance of the City administration (IDP 2016–2021, p. 2 (City of Johannesburg 2016)). The City also describes a "world class African city" as one "that protects its resources for future generations, which is built to last and offers a healthy, clean and safe environment" (IDP 2016–2021, p. 2 (City of Johannesburg 2016)).

The IDP is divided into four main parts. The first part contains a broad overview of the City as pertains to the general developmental aims. It also contains information regarding the demographics and age distribution of the population of the city; the number of households and dwelling units in the city; economic and employment figures; and the current level of inequality and service delivery in the city. The first part also includes a brief description of the city's developmental and political history, lists key areas of strategic success in the city, and highlights key challenges the City intends to address by means of prioritised strategies. The second part of the IDP lists and describes the strategies in place to address the challenges the city faces, while part three contains priority implementation plans, and part four contains provisions regarding performance management.

The IDP includes 11 priority implementation plans (PIPs) that collectively aspire to ensure that Johannesburg reaches its goal of becoming a world class African city. Of specific significance to SDG 11 is the city's PIP aimed at "Transforming Sustainable Human Settlements" (PIP 4 in the IDP). In this regard the City emphasises the provision of basic services and infrastructure to all settlements, regardless of the level of formality of the settlement. The City also aims to improve the living conditions of people in Johannesburg by increasing access to water[7] and access to sanitation[8] (PIP 4 in the IDP). Additional objectives include improving people's quality of life by increasing access to electricity in informal settlements,[9] and by increasing the number of social housing units developed for disadvantaged beneficiaries.[10] The role of transport and mobility is also recognised for transforming the city's human settlements. The City intends to use transport systems to foster social inclusion and cohesion, stimulate economic development, and transition to a low carbon economy. Subsequently, the City aims to improve road infrastructure,[11] increase access to public transport systems,[12] and reduce congestion.[13]

In addition to the above, the City actively strives to protect the environment and to mitigate against the effects of climate change. Its "Environmental Sustainability and Climate Change" implementation plan is geared towards reducing the consumption of natural resources, and carbon emissions, to minimise environmental pollution (air, water and waste-to-land), and to protect the City's ecosystem goods and services. Specific activities in this regard include the installation of solar water heaters in social housing projects, ensuring that rapid bus transit systems use cleaner fuel technologies, employing integrated waste management practices (such as separation at source, biogas and recycling projects) and reducing natural resource consumption (specifically water and energy). The City also includes a separate implementation plan that intends to reduce the city's carbon emissions by implementing a green mobility programme which includes, *inter alia*, the use of "green buses" (PIP 3 in the IDP).

The City places the voice of the public in high regard in its decision-making processes. It's "Community Building and Engage Citizenry" goal (PIP 9 in the IDP), aims to promote participatory citizenship and to ensure that the needs and concerns of persons from all races, cultures, and economic backgrounds are reflected in the City's planning processes. For this purpose the City intends to improve its community-based planning framework by increasing access to public participation channels with the use of technology (i.e. SMS networks), especially with respect to service delivery programmes and spatial planning instruments.

The City also prioritises individual and community safety. Its "Building Safer Communities" implementation plan specifically emphasises the need to ensure that public open spaces are free from violence and crime (PIP 8 of the IDP). Activities for this purpose include promoting public safety through urban design and collaborating with the South African Police Service in the policing of public spaces. The City also intends to reduce the mortality rate of victims of violent crimes, and also of persons who are victims to other emergency situations, such as the occurrence of natural disasters.

The implementation plans discussed thus far may be argued to directly promote urban sustainability as envisioned by SDG 11. Through these plans the City aspires to ensure increased and equitable access to adequate housing, basic services and public transport. The city also prioritises the reduction of its environmental impact, especially as pertains to waste management and carbon emissions. It also aims to strengthen public participation in governance matters and the decisions of the City. Safety from violence and crime and other broader aspects of human security relating to the occurrence of disasters also enjoy priority in the IDP (see the discussion pertaining to SDG 11 above).

Notably, the City also goes beyond what is expected by SDG 11 in terms of urban sustainability. The IDP includes several implementation plans that are not necessarily related to SDG 11 but are also generally aimed at promoting urban sustainability in a broader sense. These "additional" implementation plans are focused on addressing specific challenges that are unique to the City of Johannesburg. The City's "Economic Growth, Job Creation, Investment Attraction and Poverty Reduction" implementation plan (PIP 1 in the IDP), in combination with the "Informal Economy, Small Micro and Medium Enterprise (SMME) Support" implementation plan (PIP 2 in the IDP), is specifically aimed at addressing high levels of poverty and unemployment. Through these plans the City aims to create new job opportunities, increase support for SMMEs, and improve employability. Activities in this regard include establishing food gardens, supporting local farmers, providing early childhood development training, and establishing feeding schemes for underweight persons. In addition, the City's "Smart City and Innovation" implementation plan (PIP 5 in the IDP) envisages the City integrating smart technologies with service provision. For this purpose the City intends to provide free WiFi in public spaces, develop a "City App", and establish e-learning programmes for children. Moreover, with its "Financial Sustainability" implementation plan (PIP 6 in the IDP) the City intends to ensure sustainable financial management. For this purpose the City intends to update the revenue management system to include customer incentives, for example. Finally, the City also recognises the role of good governance. With its "Good Governance" implementation plan the City intends to improve its governance practices in a democratic, participatory, transparent and accountable manner (PIP 11 in the IDP).

Integrated Development Planning and the Pursuit of Urban Sustainability: Mismatch or Success?

An IDP is, in essence, a roadmap and a decision-making tool that must guide and inform all decisions taken by city councillors and management (Retief and Cilliers 2016, p. 167). It enables city authorities to strategically determine their challenges and apply an integrated and multi-sectoral approach when seeking solutions, with the cooperation of all line functions and departments in the municipal administration. IDPs also allow city authorities to incorporate strategies that may assist in incremental ways in the pursuit of sustainability on a global scale.[14] IDPs help ensure that cities are accountable and that their decisions are transparent. The IDP development and review process encourages public participation and requires city authorities to give feedback regarding the adjustment of goals and the implementation of programmes (Africa, Magwaza, and Patel 2014, pp. 36–44). Moreover, every implementation plan included in an IDP must be aligned with the city's budget (Sec. 21(1)(a) of the Local Government: Municipal Finance Management Act 56 of 2003). The latter is intended to prevent the mismanagement of funding and to ensure that all implementation plans are carried out with the necessary financial resources. Integrated development planning moves beyond the passive, top-down planning approaches that are synonymous with older-order planning regimes (see the discussion pertaining to the South African experience of integrated development planning). Integrated development planning is people-centred and is responsive to the changing conditions of urban environments (McEwan 2003, p. 472).

It is important to note that integrated development planning also faces significant challenges. Research has indicated that, whilst on paper integrated development planning promotes a balanced approach to urban development, practice has shown that economic considerations can take precedence over addressing issues of socio-spatial exclusion, or environmental degradation and pollution, for example (Amirah et al. 2009, p. 63). In addition, many smaller municipalities lack the human and financial capacity to adequately design and implement an IDP (Municipal Institute of Learning and South African Loca Government Association 2016, p. 58). The latter directly effects the quality of their IDPs, which leads to fragmented urban development and dissatisfied local communities (Gibbens 2008, pp. 10–13). It is also argued that line-function departments in municipalities often operate in isolation from one another in developing the IDP (Amirah et al. 2009, p. 63). Not all IDPs in South Africa take note of or are integrated with national and provincial development goals, priorities and challenges (Municipal Institute of Learning and South African Local Government Association 2016, p. 59). True integration (which is the purpose of integrated development planning) is, in many instances, not institutionally embedded.

South Africa's local government political climate may also pose challenges for successful integrated development planning. Sustainable urban development is a long-term process, whereas a municipality's IDP reflects a specific municipal council and political party's five-year development objectives for the municipal area. New municipal councils and political parties are elected every five years. Long-term success in terms of sustainable urban development may be hampered with each new election, as different political parties may favour different aspects of urban sustainability (South African Local Government Association 2015).

Despite the challenges mentioned above, it may be argued that integrated development planning has assisted the City of Johannesburg to attain some of the sustainability aspirations underpinned in SDG 11. In terms of what is required by SDG 11, the City's IDP emphasises basic service provision and access to social housing; increased access to public transportation and mobility; engaging in and increasing participatory citizenship; the reduction of vulnerability to climate change, the protection of natural resources and minimising environmental impact; and fostering public safety. The IDP is noticeably silent, however, on the SDG 11 targets pertaining to efforts aimed at protecting and safeguarding the world's cultural and natural heritage; supporting positive economic, social and environmental links between urban and rural areas; aligning disaster management plans with the Sendai Framework for Disaster Risk Reduction 2015–2030; and providing financial and technical support to least developed countries. The City focusses instead on addressing specific challenges that are barriers to achieving a "world class African City" with an environment that is "resilient, sustainable and liveable", as envisioned in the IDP. For this purpose, the City includes implementation plans that are aimed at increasing employment opportunities (also in the informal economy); alleviating the effects of poverty; promoting economic development, increasing the use of smart technologies (specifically for infrastructure and service delivery); and encouraging good governance and sound financial management. Through its IDP the Johannesburg Metropolitan Municipality has identified the challenges to its sustainable urban development, determined which SDG 11 targets are most suited to promoting urban sustainability in the city's specific context, and developed key goals with implementation plans. It has also established goals and implementation plans to promote its sustainability in a broader sense, not necessarily related to SDG 11, but relevant to addressing specific challenges that hinder sustainable development in the city. Notably, the performance monitoring mechanisms in the IDP enable the municipality to monitor and report on progress.

Johannesburg's IDP is merely one example, however. The details of the goals and implementation plans included in IDPs will surely differ from one city to the next. Several factors will influence the design features of a specific city's IDP.[15]

Conclusion

The purpose of this chapter was to question how the notion of integrated development planning can serve as a conduit for the pursuit of SDG 11. The chapter has considered the application of integrated development planning in the South African context and evaluated the IDP and the practice of integrated development planning in the City of Johannesburg

Metropolitan Municipality. It has considered the origins and function of integrated development planning, and found that integrated development planning was originally rooted in corporate strategic planning practices, and is, in the urban or municipal government context, significantly influenced by the principles of sustainability emphasised in international policy documents of the 1990s. Considering that many city authorities over the globe have since 1992 shifted to adopting the integrated planning approach to promoting sustainable urban development, this chapter has critically examined the case of Johannesburg in the context of the new SDG 11 imperatives.

It has been found that the IDP of the City of Johannesburg is a partial translation of SDG 11 into a specific local context. While the IDP promotes urban sustainability in accordance with what is required by SDG 11, it seems to prioritise certain targets over others. This may be because the IDP is specifically tailored to the City's own developmental, social, and economic challenges, and because the IDP is significantly informed by the voices and needs of local community members. The City may also have considered city politics, its administrative resources, and its financial capacity in selecting certain development goals over others. Overall, it is submitted that integrated development planning is a valuable legal and governance instrument that allows city authorities to pursue urban sustainability in a flexible, holistic, informed, and integrated manner. All action taken towards the pursuit of urban sustainability is tailored to local circumstances and planned in combination with citizen engagement and partnerships with civil society. The development of an IDP enables municipalities to conduct extensive assessments of the social, environmental, and economic reality in the municipal area, to audit available resources, skills and capacities, and to prioritise needs in order of urgency and long-term importance (De Visser 2005, pp. 103–105).

The case of Johannesburg seems to indicate a general success in the use of integrated development planning in the pursuit of urban sustainability. It is important, however, to note that integrated development planning practice is also susceptible to multi-dimensional challenges. It is also necessary to be mindful of the fact that Johannesburg is a metropolitan city with considerably more human and financial resources and expertise than other smaller (and more rural) municipalities in South Africa. The success of integrated development planning depends on the existence of political drive, on the existence of support for the normative values underpinning sustainable urban development, and on being able to make a concerted effort to move beyond a silo-based approach to planning. Nevertheless, it is concluded that integrated development planning is a key, globally acknowledged public management tool that may serve the purpose and intent of SDG 11. The way in which this will happen is context, resource and time dependent, however, and will vary from city to city and from one continent to the next.

Notes

1 Various descriptions of the terms "urban planning" or "municipal planning" exist. It is generally agreed, however, that urban or municipal planning pertains to the "authority of the most decentralised level of government to guide and shape development in a spatially demarcated area" (Berrisford 2011, p. 254). It entails, for example, the regulation and governing of land-use rights, changes in existing land-use rights, and the facilitation of a specific spatial area's social, environmental, and economic development trajectory (Blowers and Evans 2003, p. 10). For the purpose of this chapter, the terms urban planning and municipal planning are used interchangeably.

2 Modernist planning emerged in Western Europe and other advanced capitalist countries during the latter part of the nineteenth century in an effort to manage the negative externalities of industrialisation and urbanisation. Modernist planning is technocratic in nature and generally involves a process of producing master plans which are "top down" and expert led, and regarded as solely a function of government. Modernist planning also perpetuates a particular urban form characterised by low densities, private vehicle use, high-rise buildings and set quantities of green open space (Arimah et al. 2009, p. 47). Modernist planning is widely criticised for failing to integrate the interests of the urban poor, women, youth and indigenous people in the physical and socio-economic spaces of the city. It also neglects to consider the effects of urban development on the environment (UN-Habitat 2016b, p. 125).

3 Traditional land-use planning entails a passive planning approach aimed at identifying land use and determining where and how land use occurs. (Albrechts 2006a, p. 1489). Different land uses are generally separated and controlled by zoning schemes and regulations. Traditional land-use planning is generally criticised for following economic considerations over social, cultural and environmental considerations, and for implementing a silo-based approach to planning (Berke 2002, pp. 21–22).

4 Such as population fluctuations, economic instabilities, changing natural resource conditions and housing needs, for instance.

5 The targets are accompanied by a set of indicators with metadata that provide statistics/benchmarks for the targets. The metadata are aimed at providing a means to measure progress on the fulfilment of the SDG 11 targets (Riegner 2016, p. 16). For a more detailed discussion in this regard, see Riegner 2019, in this volume.

6 Local government at the time was responsible for only a narrow range of traditional local government functions such as local roads and sewerage (Van Wyk and Oranje 2014, pp. 353–355).

7 The city intends to increase the number of households with access to water from 94 percent to 100 percent by 2021.

8 The city intends to increase the number of households with access to sanitation from 45.65 percent to 52.53 percent by 2021.

9 The city intends to ensure that 12 000 new houses have access to electricity by 2021.

10 The city intends to develop 6,852 social housing units for disadvantaged beneficiaries by 2021.

11 The city intends to improve road infrastructure by resurfacing 1,334 km of roads and upgrading 1,547 km of gravel roads by 2021.

12 The city intends to provide access to 60,000 additional Bus Rapid Transit users per day, and 51,000 additional Metro Bus users per day by 2021.

13 The city intends to increase the number of walkways and cycle lanes from 77 km in 2016 to 200 km by 2021.

14 IDPs are generally attuned to policy developments and imperatives in the context (Africa, Magwaza and Patel 2014, p. 5).

15 International requirements, city politics, national and regional developmental imperatives, inputs from community members through public participation procedures, and available human and financial resources significantly influence the interpretation and understanding of urban sustainability, for instance.

Bibliography

Literature

Africa, E., Magwaza, Esme, and Patel, Yusuf. 2014. IDP Guide Pack: General Overview. Pretoria: Department of Provincial and Local Government.

Albrechts, Louis. 2006a. Bridge the gap: from spatial planning to strategic projects. European Planning Studies, 14(10), 1487–1500.

Albrechts, Louis. 2006b. Shifts in strategic spatial planning? Some evidence from Europe and Australia. *Environment and Planning*, 38(6), pp. 1149–1170.

Arfvidsson, Helen, Simon, David, Michael, Oloko, and Moodley, Nishendra 2017. Engaging with and measuring informality in the proposed urban sustainable development goal. *African Geographical Review*, 36(1), 100–114.

Arimah, Ben C., Jensen, Inge, Mutizwa-Mangiza, Naison D., and Yemeru, Edlam Abera. 2009. *Global Report on Human Settlements 2009: Planning Sustainable Cities.* Nairobi: UN-Habitat.

African Union. 2016. *Agenda 2063: The Africa We Want*. Addis Ababa: African Union.

Barraclough, Solon Lovett. 2001. *Toward Integrated and Sustainable Development? UNRISD Overarching Concerns.* Geneva: UNRISD.

Bekink, Bernard. 2006. *Principles of South African Local Government Law.* Durban, South Africa: LexisNexis Butterworths.

Berke, Philip R. 2002. Does sustainable development offer a new direction for planning? Challenges for the twenty-first century. *Journal of Planning Literature*, 17(1), 21–36.

Berrisford, Stephen. 2011. Unravelling Apartheid spatial planning legislation in South Africa. *Urban Forum*, 22(3), 247–263.

Blowers, Andy and Evans, Bob (eds). 2003. *Town Planning into the 21st Century.* New York: Routledge.

Borja, Jordi and Castells, Manuel (eds). 1997. *Local and Global: The Management of Cities in the Information Age.* London: Earthscan.

Bryson, John M. 2010. The future of public and non-profit strategic planning in the United States. *Public Administration Review*, 70, 225–267.

Bryson, John M. 2012. *Strategic Planning and Management*. London: SAGE.

Chaitanya, Kanuri, Revi, Aromar, Espey, Jessica, and Khule, Holger. 2016. *Getting Started with the SDGs in Cities. A Guide for Stakeholders.* New York: Sustainable Development Solutions Network.

De Visser, Jaap. 2005. *Developmental Local Government: A Case Study of South Africa.* Antwerp, NL: Intersentia.

De Visser, Jaap. 2016. Devolution by court injuction: the case of land use planning and management in South Africa. *The Ugandan Journal of Managment and Public Policy Studies*, 10(1), 84–99.

Du Plessis, Anél A. 2008. *Fulfilment of South Africa's Constitutional Environmental Right in the Local Government Sphere*. LLD thesis, North-West University, Potchefstroom.

Fukuda-Parr, Sakiko and Messineo, Carol. 2012. *Human Security*[illegible] *Review of the Literature*. Leuven, NL: Centre for Research on [illegible]ical Development.

Gauteng Provincial Government. 2016. *Gauteng Spatial Development Framework 2030*. Pretoria, South Africa: Gauteng Provincial Government.

Gibbens, Menini. 2008. *The Invisible Director: An Exploration of the Role of Power in Intergovernmental Communication on Meaningful Municipal Integrated Development Planning*. MT&RP thesis, University of Pretoria.

Gordon, Gerald L. 2005. *Strategic Planning for Local Government*. Washington, DC: International City/Country Management Association.

Gueli, Richard, Liebenberg, Sybert and Van Huyssteen, Elsona. 2007. Integrated development planning in South Africa: lessons for international peacebuilding? *African Journal on Conflict Resolution*, 7(1), 89–112.

Harrison, Philip. 2001. The genealogy of South Africa's integrated development plan. *Third World Planning Review*, 23(2), 175–193.

Harrison, Philip. 2006. *Integrated Development Plans and Third Way Politics*. Cape Town, South Africa: HSRC Press.

International Council for Local Environmental Initiatives. 1996. *The Local Agenda 21 Planning Guide: An Introduction to Sustainable Development Planning*. Bonn: International Council for Local Environmental Initiatives.

International Council for Local Environmental Initiatives. 2015. Cities and the Sustainable Development Goals. Available at: www.redesparaodesenvolvimento.org/ficheiros/file/iclei-briefing-sheets-02-cities-and-the-sustainable-development-goals.pdf (Accessed: 19 March 2018).

City of Johannesburg. 2011. *Johannesburg Growth and Development Strategy Vision 2040*. Johannesburg, South Africa.

City of Johannesburg. 2016. Integrated Development Plan 2016 – 2021. Johannesburg, South Africa

Klopp, Jacqueline M. and Petretta, Danielle L. 2017. The urban sustainable development goal indicators: complexity and the politics of measuring cities. Cities, 63, 92–97.

Lyle, John Tillman. 1994. *Regenerative Design for Sustainable Development*. London: Wiley.

McEwan, Cheryl. 2003. Bringing government to people: women, local governance and public participation in South Africa. *Geoforum*, 34(4), 469–481.

Municipal Institute of Learning and South African Local Government Association. 2016. Strategic planning and IDP. Available at: www.mile.org.za/QuickLinks/News/Urban%20Strategic%20Planning%20Master%20Class%202016/Day%201.2-Puven%20Akkiah-Case%20Study-IDP%20experiences%20of%20eThekwini.pdf (Accessed: 19 March 2018).

Miraftab, Faranak, Silver, Christopher and Beard, Victoria A. 2008. Introduction: Situating contested notions of decentralized planning in the global South. In: Beard, Victoria A., Miraftab, Faranak and Silver, Christopher (eds). *Planning and Decentralization: Contested Spaces for Public Action in the Global South*. New York: Routledge. pp. 1–18.

National Planning Commission. 2011. *National Development Plan Vision 2030*. Pretoria, South Africa: National Planning Commission.

Parnell, Susan. 2016. Defining a global urban development agenda. *World Development*, 78, 529–540.

Patel, Zarina, Greyling, Saskia, Simon, David, Arfvidsson, Helen, Moodley, Nishendra, Primo, Natasha, Wright, Caro. 2017. Local responses to global sustainability agendas: learning from experimenting with the urban sustainable development goal in Cape Town. *Sustainability Science*, 12(5), 785–797.

Pieterse, Edgar. 2004. Untangling integration in urban development policy debates. Urban Forum, 15(1), pp. 1–35.

Pieterse, Edgar. 2007. Participatory local governance in the making: opportunities, constraints and prospects. In: Parnell, Susan (ed). *Democratising Local Government: the South African Experiment*. Cape Town, South Africa: UCT Press. pp. 1–18.

Pycroft, Christopher. 1998. Integrated development planning or strategic paralysis? Municipal development during the local government transition and beyond. *Development Southern Africa*, 15(1), 151–163.

Retief, F. and Cilliers, D. 2016. Municipal integrated development planning. In: Du Plessis, Anél A. (ed). *Environmental Law and Local Government in South Africa*. Claremont, South Africa: Juta. pp. 167–191.

Riegner, Michael. 2016. Implementing the "data revolution" for the post-2015 sustainable development goals toward a global administrative law of information. *The World Bank Legal Review*, 7, 15–39.

Rockefeller Foundation and Arup Consulting Engineers 2014. *City Resilience Framework*. London: ARUP.

South African Local Government Association. 2015. *15 Years of Developmental and Democratic Local Government: 2000 – 2015*. Pretoria: South African Local Government Association.

Sustainable Development Solutions Network. 2013. *The Urban Opportunity: Enabling Transformative and Sustainable Development*. New York: Sustainable Development Solutions Network.

Todes, Alison. 2004. Regional planning and sustainability: limits and potential of South Africa's integrated development plans. *Journal of Environmental Planning and Management*, 47(6), 843–861.

Todes, Alison. 2012. Urban growth and strategic spatial planning in Johannesburg, South Africa. *Cities*, 29(3), 158–165.

UN. 2002. Second Local Agenda 21 Survey. Available at: www.un.org/documents/ecosoc/cn17/1997/background/ecn171997-1.rpt1.htm (Accessed: 19 March 2018).

UN. 2014. World urbanisation prospects: the 2014 revision. New York: UN.

UN. 2015. Population consumption and the environment. New York: UN.

UN. 2016. The world's cities in 2016: data booklet. New York: UN.

UN-Habitat. 2010. Planning sustainable cities: practices and perspectives. Nairobi, Kenya: UN-Habitat.

UN-Habitat. 2015a. Habitat III issue paper 3: safer cities. Quito, Ecuador: UN-Habitat.

UN-Habitat. 2015b. International guidelines on urban territorial planning. Nairobi, Kenya: UN-Habitat.

UN-Habitat. 2016a. The city we need 2.0: towards a new urban paradigm. Nairobi, Kenya: UN-Habitat.

UN-Habitat. 2016b. SDG Goal 11 monotoring framework: a guide to assist national and local governments to monitor and report on SDG Goal 11 indicators. Nairobi, Kenya: UN-Habitat.

UN-Habitat. 2016c. World cities report: urbanisation and development emerging futures. Nairobi, Kenya: UN-Habitat.

United Nations Development Programme. 2016. Integrated planning and sustainable development: challenges and opportunities. New York: United Nations Development Programme.

United Nations Environment Programme, International Council for Local Environmental Initiatives and Alliance C. 2007. *Liveable cities: the benefits of urban environmental planning*. Washington, DC: The Cities Alliance.

Van Wyk, Jeannie and Oranje, Mark. 2014. The post-1994 South African spatial planning system and Bill of Rights: a meaningful and mutually beneficial fit? *Planning Theory*, 13(4), 349–369.

Venter, Annelise. 2011. Integrated development planning as an approach to sustainable development. In: Van der Waldt, Gerrit (ed). *Municipal Management: Serving the People.* Cape Town, South AfricaJuta. pp. 93–108.

Visser, Gustav. 2001. Social justice integrated development planning and post-apartheid urban reconstruction. *Urban Studies*, 38(10), 1673–1699.

Watson, Vanessa. 2016. Locating planning in the new urban agenda of the urban sustainable development goal. *Planning Theory*, 15(4), 435–448.

Yigitcanlar, Tan and Teriman, Suharto. 2015. Rethinking sustainable urban development: towards an integrated planning and development process. *International Journal of Environmental Science and Technology*, 12(1), 341–352.

Documents

Agenda 21, UN Doc A/Conf.151/26 (1992)

Reconstruction and Development Programme (1994)

White Paper on Local Government (1998)

Legislation

Constitution of the Republic of South Africa, 1996

Local Government: Municipal Finance Management Act 56 of 2003

Local Government: Municipal Systems Act 32 of 2000

12 Governance in the Smart City

Sketches of a Research Programme in Legal Theory

Peter Gailhofer

Introduction

The legal implications of the globalisation of urban governance are being addressed from a variety of perspectives in this volume. This contribution adds another dimension to this variety, which can without doubt be considered no less dramatic than the diagnosis of the "urban century" and is equally omnipresent in public and scientific discourse. Smart cities are a ubiquitous topic in current explorations surrounding the economic, ecologic and societal transformation of the world`s urban settlements. Smart city concepts are diverse. In a nutshell, they promote information technologies which are supposed to achieve participatory, efficient and sustainable cities (Gabrys 2014), and the deployment of sensor-based ubiquitous computing across urban infrastructures and mobile devices. Thereby they conceive urban territory as informational territory that is hybrid, i.e. physical and virtual/digital at the same time (Milakovic and Novocovic 2017, p. 87). The subject of the smart city therefore can be seen to enrich (and further complicate) the jurisprudential inquiry of the urban by matching it to the "mega-trend" of digitisation. Although discourses about smart cities sometimes seem to be focused on detailed, technical questions like "smart" street lighting, waste management or digitally interconnected parking lots, they capture political, societal and economic transformations or disruptions which are very much relevant for the subject of this volume.

First and most obviously, the role of smart city-solutions is prominent in the pursuit of the objectives of SDG 11. Many of the instruments promoted by champions of the smart city – like technical solutions for sustainable transport, energy efficiency, or digitally enabled "decentralised urban planning" are considered to be adequate transformative tools for the implementation of the SDGs (cf Marsal et al. 2017, p. 14). More generally speaking, "city smartness" relates to most of the aspects that appear to be desirable or solution-driven in the – at times quite dystopian – context of urbanisation and sustainable development. It promises technical solutions to achieve ecological sustainability, social and institutional inclusiveness, communal self-sufficiency, quality of life for all inhabitants and the decentralisation of governance, "true" participation and all-embracing democratisation. This utopian dimension of a so-far predominantly technical concept is startling. Paradoxically and contrary to their supposed "emancipatory potential" (Sadowski and Pasquale 2015), notions of digitised urban spaces, even in seemingly profane applications, at the same time inspire a range of dystopian perspectives. Critical scholars denounce the installation of a "seamless web of surveillance and power" (Sadowski and Pasquale 2015), the takeover of formerly public spheres of governance by private actors, and even the end of urban politics (cf Mozorov 2017).

Second, smart cities may be seen to be ideal-typical "glocal" spaces. The intersection of dimensions of the global, regional, national and local dimensions of urban governance as accentuated in the introduction to this volume can be explored with respect to the digitisation of urban spaces in a probably quite radical way. In the realm of public international law, urban governance is increasingly relevant: Cities are becoming important actors in international politics and governance and are more and more frequently being acknowledged as such (Aust 2017). The concept of the smart city integrates a domestic, specifically spatial perspective on these phenomena, which nevertheless is embedded in a global context. It is an interesting question, if this new configuration of "glocal" governance can be reconstructed in a plausible way by drawing on given theoretical concepts of "networked" law and decentralised governance.

Third, a theoretically informed reconstruction of the ambivalent dimensions of "smart" urban/digital decentralisation and its disruptive potentials, risks and pathologies may be helpful to establish a theoretical place for global yardsticks like SDG 11 in the analysis of "smart" urban governance. A socio-scientific research programme for the reconstruction of the normative substance, the potentialities and the intended and unintended effects of digitised urban spaces has already been proposed (Rabari and Storper 2015, p. 28). I argue in this chapter that it is equally important for jurisprudence and legal theory to deal with the fundamental implications of the digitisation of cities and the related concept of digitised governance for the law. I will therefore, necessarily in a sketchy, preliminary manner, outline some suggestions for further research. While sociological reconstructions predominantly deal with a critical theoretical foundation needed to articulate the smart city's emancipatory potential (Sadowski and Pasquale 2015), legal theory may offer the tools for a reconstructive account. It shows the conceptual and practical relation of decentralised or "polycentric" urban digital governance to overarching or "meta" rules, principles and objectives like those in SDG 11. Such reconstruction has certain methodological implications and points to an "epistemological primacy of (legal) practice" (Weinberger 1991, p. 4). The substantive question of how the normative premises of decentralisation and urban democratisation could be processed by legal theory in a plausible way may point to a specifically spatial dimension of civil or fundamental rights.

Promises and Pitfalls of the Digitisation of Urban Governance

What are Smart Cities?

The concept of the smart city is as diverse as it is ubiquitous.[1] In a very general way, it can be conceived as denoting "informational territory", understood as a "framework of real time monitoring of movement and flow of both people and information" (Milakovic and Novakovic 2017, p. 87). By integrating sensors "into nearly all parts of the physical urban fabric", a "digital skin" is created, which is "composed of connected, digitally enabled objects, network nodes, communication devices and posts for monitoring and analysing data fed into servers" (Rabari and Storper 2015 p. 27). Smart cities thus implicate spatial hybridity, i.e. an interconnection between "real" and "virtual" urban spaces and a sort of interexchange between them (Mela 2014).

Besides this hybrid nature of smart cities, "smart solutions" can be, in an instrumental way, regarded as innovative tools to solve the social, political, economic and environmental problems faced by city-regions. Its proponents emphasise the transformative role of these technologies. In the near future they expect to see smart cities with buildings that are net producers of renewable energy, connected and optimised transport systems, electric cars that drive a zero emission economy and a range of e-services such as e-health, e-education, e-commerce, e-governance and teleworking resulting in major changes across society (UN-Habitat and Ericsson 2014, p. 6). The "smart" aspect is thereby "progressively connected not only to the presence and use of digital infrastructure, but also to human, social and relational capital" (Zucchardi-Merli and Bonollo 2014, p. 141). Smart cities thus can be defined as spaces "where information technology is combined with infrastructure, architecture, everyday objects and even our bodies to address social, economic, and environmental problems" (Townsend 2013, p. 15).

Much of the new, technical instruments of smart cities can be conceived as managerial applications of "big data", which is gained by sensors and IT devices and used to improve the effectiveness and efficiency of a city's traffic, waste or water systems. Cities are supposed to be able to respond to changes quickly and accurately and to get better results by predicting and optimising future events (see Cronin, 2010, p. 5), to be sustainable, and to be "well-performing in a forward-looking way" (Giffinger et al. 2007, p. 11).[2] Smart city concepts thus focus on technological solutions that are also at the heart of discourses about the effective implementation of the SDGs by using innovative data collection techniques and technologies (cf UN Sustainable Development Solutions Network (UN SDSN)

2015). However, it would be mistaken to reduce smart cities to this "managerial dimension". The idea of governance such concepts promote also has a utopian dimension which may be insightful for theoretical reflections about the function and the importance of global normative yardsticks for urban governance like SDG 11.

Smart Governance and its Utopian Dimensions: Decentralisation, Emergence, Cosmopolitism

Besides technical possibilities to realise well informed "top-down" "policies and programmes, eg for targeting sustainable development ..." (Albino et al. 2015, p. 5), the idea of using data, sensors and networks to "manage" urban life also draws on a specific approach to "smart" urban governance. This approach can be conceived as a specific reformulation of the concept of governance, which, in the introduction to this volume, is associated with the supplementation of rather formal, hierarchical state power by more diffuse, decentral modes of the exercise of power (Aust and du Plessis 2019, in this volume). In the international realm, scholars have long observed ongoing processes of de-formalisation: from formal intergovernmental organisations through informal intergovernmental networks and public-private partnerships to private standard-setting practices (Benvenisti 2014, p. 25). Smart city concepts equally can be seen to promote a philosophy of governance that counts on the informal networks and actions of non-state parties (Bria and Morozov 2017, p. 44). This philosophy implies notions of political decentralisation, emergence and cosmopolitism that have strong normative implications, and may therefore quite adequately be called a "new utopia" (Townsend 2013). At the same time it has to be understood in a specifically glocal context.

"Smart" ideas of urban governance implicate, first of all, radical notions of decentralisation, in the sense of civic participation and a shift away from hierarchical modes of governance. A "bottom-up approach" to smart cities considers the empowerment and participation of citizens and other stakeholders to be "an essential requirement" (Zucchardi-Merli and Bonollo 2014, p. 141). Platforms for participation are supposed to lead to the construction of an open, transparent and collaborative city.[3] This may implicate feedback-tools, eg apps for people to report graffiti or faulty street lighting in their area,[4] concepts for improved participation by using "digital tools in participatory planning" (Wallin et al. 2010), instruments for citizens to invest in local real estate (Rabari and Storper 2015, p. 31), and apps through which people can transparently and selectively share personal data "to help companies or government groups [...] to improve the city" (Reynolds 2017) and use the decentralised block chain-technology to connect the idea of citizen participation with urban "data collection". Information technology in a more general manner is supposed "to strengthen democratic engagement by offering services enabling people to engage in politics

[…] to encompass true public participation and involve the urban poor and other marginalised groups in decision making forums" (UN Habitat and Ericsson 2014, p. 5).

Secondly, the idea of decentralised, interaction-based smart governance implicates not only "truly" participatory, more interactive governance and city management but quite often implies even "more revolutionary or utopian" premises (cf Rabari and Storper 2015, p. 37), which are reminiscent of the early hopes for the emancipatory potential of the internet. The confidence of the champions of cyberspace in the "emergence" of legitimate governance "from ethics, enlightened self-interest and the commonwealth" is well-known (see Rabari and Storper 2015, p. 36; Barlow 1996). "Smart" governance likewise postulates "superior" forms of crowd-based, decentralised interactions, and reflects and relies on a "new wisdom of crowds" (Rabari and Storper 2015, p. 37). The smart city is conceived as a self-organising, emergent system beyond all centres and peripheries, which is operated based on the aggregated outputs of the citizens` practices. The connection of stakeholders (like citizens, politicians, NGOs and businesses) via the web, according to Portmann and Finger, promises access to complexity. It allows addressing emergence, non-linearity and self-organisation, self-reference and self-regulation by enabling cooperation (Portmann and Finger 2015, p. 471). The city thus is supposed to manage itself in an automated, entirely decentralised way using network-based communications informed and enhanced by "ubiquitous computing". This eventually is supposed to lead to a kind of "collective intelligence achieved by symbiotic cooperation of man and computer" (Portmann and Finger 2015, p. 471). The normative quality of management and governance consequently seems to emerge out of a quasi-organic mechanism. The "digitally enhanced, postmodern city [is] a cybernetic mechanism that accommodates interaction and actuation in its capacity as a spatial system, capable of extracting contextual information, acknowledging the inhabitants' desires and needs, and adopting behaviour patterns based on what it learns" (Nabian and Ratti 2011, p. 13). It appears adequate to consider this kind of idea as "free-floating utopianism about governance as a machine" (Sadowski and Pasquale 2015).

Accounts of the smart city finally entail an understanding of citizenship which, in the "glocalised" context, may be considered to implicate certain cosmopolitan notions. Smart city practices such as "monitoring and managing data in order to feed-back information into urban systems" may become constitutive of citizenship, which is diagnosed to "transform into citizen sensing" (Gabrys 2014). With the internet as the "backbone" (Portmann and Finger 2015, p. 2) of urban digitisation, potentially global platforms, global codes and algorithms determine the structure of such actions, interactions or deliberations in smart cities. By attaching digitised technologies closer to communal policies and to physical urban space – for instance in the case of technologies concerning planning decisions with respect to physical infrastructure – the smart city may be seen to introduce its own configuration of the idea of "glocalised governance". Works about smart cities predominantly stress the economic implications of this spatial configuration of globally networked citizens (cf Wall et al. 2015, p. 106) However, as information technology is considered a tool for the globalisation of civil society and to constitute a kind of global democratic infrastructure (Peters 2009, p. 314), this concept potentially implies more substantive notions of cosmopolitanism. The fact that digitised deliberations in the virtual public spaces of the internet are embedded in global "spaces of flows" (Castells 2016, p. 229) and "cosmopolitan and glocal media platforms" leads sociologists to reflect on a concept of "hypercitizenship" based on a globalised "understanding of science and technology for governance" (Pitasi and Angrisani 2013, p. 318).

The observation about the utopian dimension of many of the discourses about smart cities is, of course, also true for the debates about global urbanisation in general. Quite often, implicitly or explicitly, such discourses have a progressive tone and a transformative orientation, especially with respect to ideas of more democratic, more equitable, "bottom up" governance. Cities could, it was said in a recent publication, "be the places of radical innovation in politics, spaces of actual reinvention of democracy" (Caccia 2017, p. 38), of "democratic regeneration", even with respect to the growing problems of the legitimacy of international or supranational institutions (De Magistris 2017, p. 45). Such hopes and expectations are, quite often, related to certain normative approaches to the spatial qualities of cities. Cities are "complex and incomplete systems" (Sassen 2013, p. 210), or "problems of organised complexity" (Jacobs 1992, p. 432), which by means of their spatial make-up (Sennett 2006, p. 4) or urban capability to enable dense "intersections of time/space/people/routinised practices" (Sassen 2013, p. 214) have a specifically spatial, organic, democratic quality. They are key spaces for "the material practices of freedom [...] where the powerless can make speech, presence, a politics" and "transform conflicts into a strengthened civicness" (Sassen 2013, p. 210). As big cities are also "arrival cities" for migrants and refugees, hubs for globalised enterprises, global value chains and transnational social networks, these potentially liberating intersections and encounters already take place on a transnational, or "translocal" scale, within a "network of networks, which is unfolding on different spatial scales" and by "global processes" which "are concentrated and localised" (Krätke et al. 2012, p. 3). Discourses about the democratic quality of cities therefore already suggest a certain notion of "glocalised" cosmopolitanism (cf Roudometof 2005, p. 122). The transnational situation of cities and the urban multiplicity of identities and interactions, according to Appadurai and Holston (1996), – although it also suggests the emergence of an almost medieval body of overlapping, heterogeneous, non-uniform and increasingly private memberships – is likely to produce new forms of overlapping citizenship, and multiple jurisdictions can spawn new and more democratic forms of citizenship. "It may even be, after all, that there is something irreducible and non-transferable, necessary but not quite sufficient, about the city's public street and square for the realization of a meaningfully democratic citizenship" (Appadurai and Holston 1996, pp. 198, 199, 202).

Pathologies of Digitised Urban Spaces

The exact form of the very young configuration of governance in the smart city and its potentially disruptive societal, political and legal implications are, without doubt, complex and can hardly be predicted. However, sociological findings about the properties and the functioning of a digitally induced "structural transformation of the public sphere" (cf Celikates 2016; Papacharrisi 2009) as well as critical theoretical approaches on smart cities suggest a wide range of concerns about the "potential unintended effects" of the digital urban transformation (Rabari and Storper 2015, p. 40; Kitchin 2014; Sadowski and Pascuale 2015). Such a critical sociological reconstruction of specific "pathologies of modernity" (cf Kneer 1990, p. 19), i.e. the pathological or paradoxical nature of societal progress follows a long tradition. Early sociologists like Weber and Horkheimer already described modern rationalisation as a process in which increasing knowledge, predictability and efficiency, which are meant to enhance individual freedom, may lead to a serious loss of individual agency and freedom, when rationalisation and efficiency become an end in themselves and an individual is reduced to being a "cog in a machine" (cf Kim 2012; Horkheimer 1991, p. 136). Critical scholars observe dynamics in smart cities that can be conceived in a comparable way. An "inherent tension [...] in the creation of systems that seek to enable more effective modes of governance which also threaten to stifle rights to privacy, confidentiality, and freedom of expression" is obvious for "smart" applications for big data, where datastreams are centralised and stored by data control centres (Kitchin 2014, p. 11). Decentralised governance relying on IT and a digitally enabled "wisdom of the crowds" may implicate pathological consequences in a more subtle manner. "Smart" ideas of a decentralised, self-organising, emergent city which might have the potential to contribute to emancipation and human well-being are at the same time prone to becoming pathological by creating new asymmetries by themselves.

The complex implications of digitisation on the public sphere cast doubt on the emancipative potential of "smart governance". Instead of amplifying the democratic potential of urban spaces, the smart city and its decentralised governance could endanger the democratic quality which Sassen, Jacobs or Appadurai ascribe to urban public spaces. The idea of dense, urban spaces or "open systems" allowing for heterogeneity, spontaneity and creativity or pluralistic "vibrant clashes of democratic political positions" (cf Mouffe 2016) depends on actual urban density, actual interactions and encounters. Recent findings, however, raise the question if the digitisation of the public sphere may seriously compromise this space for plurality, density and encounters with the other instead of strengthening it. Decentralising phenomena in online media seem to reproduce Weber's and Horkheimer's description of the ambivalence of processes of modernisation and rationalisation. Digital media convergence and "prosumerism" with respect to the decentral production of digital information are suspected to lead to a polarisation or fragmentation of the public sphere by extreme diversification and specialisation of public discourses (cf Weber and Druecke 2012). The disruptive, disintegrating nature of social platforms as "privately generated narratives published in [reflexive] commercially public spaces" (Papacharissi 2009, p. 244) has been an increasingly omnipresent topic in the last years. An interesting question about smart cities and their physical *and* digital nature consequently is: Could phenomena like "filter bubbles" caused by personalised, algorithm-based filters for information (Pariser 2011), or an emergent, self-energising, ideological or even "epistemological" segregation and polarisation of online communities (cf Roberts 2017; Seemann and Kreil 2017) thus lead to a "tendency towards fragmentation and local homogeneity" (Pariser 2011, p. 70) in the hybrid spaces of Smart Cities? Rabari and Storper's (2015) critical sociological analysis of the smart city seems to confirm this possibility:

> The language of feedback and control in the current discourse about the digital skin may appear to involve more room for spontaneity and decentralised interactions, but upon closer examination, at the core of this vision is [what according to Lantier (2010) can be called] "cybernetic totalism", where individuals are channelled and shaped to be "users" of a "cybernetic mechanism", with its inbuilt categories of interaction and algorithms that reinforce mass culture and median tastes and preferences. This is because a geo-tagged map or an algorithmically organised index may create "filter bubbles" and an unintended, but still very real, virtual segregation or, its extreme opposite, herd effects that end up limiting diversity.
>
> (Rabari and Storper 2015, p. 35; cf Gillespie 2014)

The decentralised, informal nature of digital networks and digital communication – the core and basis of the hopes of the advocates of digitisation and self-organising governance and their emancipative effects – could turn out to be self-defeating if they lead to an aggravation of already existing tendencies of segregation and fragmentation of urban societies.

In addition to risks of fragmentation, a smart city "heavily structured by the algorithms, presentation styles, search channels and economic incentives of private-sector actors" (Rabari and Storper 2015, p. 32) may imply problems which can be associated with de-formalisation. Naturally, the exercise of functions of coordination by autonomous networks does not at all guarantee the absence of new hierarchies or configurations of power. Algorithms or codes for smart city technologies are one example of potential new asymmetries caused, for example, by superior information or technological lock-in effects (cf Rabari and Storper 2015, p. 39; Kitchin 2014, p. 11). Data-driven methods and the privatisation of digital services could, according to critical scholars, also lead to a further shift from territorial to functional sovereignty and replace formal rules and procedures:

> Who needs city housing regulators when AirBnB can use data-driven methods to effectively regulate room-letting, then house-letting, and eventually urban planning generally? Why not let Amazon have its own jurisdiction or charter city, or establish special judicial procedures …? […] [O]nline rating systems could replace state occupational licensure so rather than having government boards credential workers, a platform like LinkedIn could collect star ratings on them.
>
> (Pasquale 2018)

A comparable ambivalence might be associated with new configurations of institutionalised governance. In political reform endeavours regarding communal (self-)administration, lawyers observe significant standardising and centralising tendencies towards a digital platform state (Rittgen 2017, p. 1012). Digitised structures of participation and governance, which are commonly conceived as instruments for a digital (or virtual) decentralisation of politics, could thereby challenge the constitutional configuration in federal states and lead to new, problematic centralising dynamics. Thus, digital decentralisation sometimes seems to turn against the physical and organisational decentralisation of federalism.

Finally, horizontal, interaction-based approaches to smart city-governance seem to exclude the necessity of policy choices and substantiated decision-making. The idea of replacing government with flexible networks of governance (cf Mozorov 2017; Pierre and Peters 2005, p. 2), digitised participation and feedback loops, ubiquitous computing and data analytics, not only risks losing sight of new, diffuse power structures. It also implies that a political output that replaces substantially oriented decision making or formalised procedures of collective choice could "emerge" out of processes or patterns of interaction which can be automatically yet reasonably processed. However "digital interaction does not solve problems of collective choice, or obviate the need for universal rules and government, and public goods" as there are "externalities, economies of scale, irreversibilities and sunk costs, positionalities, and many other features that require social choice and collective provision" (Rabari and Storper 2015, p. 36). This inability of smart governance to account for public interest and overarching objectives or values seems to run counter to the transformative potential of smart technologies.

Sketching a Legal Theoretical Research Agenda on Smart City Governance

Smart cities will bring about their own legal problems and transformations. It is foreseeable that ICT and Big Data will lead to new legal problems related eg to privacy laws, copyright and media law. The connection of the new technologies to physical space, such as the hybridity of the smart city, might also bring into being new, hybrid legal configurations. For example, planning law and media law may be considered to overlap when city planners have to take into account privacy laws or digital copyrights. However, more fundamental jurisprudential implications of smart city governance remain to be clarified. While the potentially pathological consequences of smart governance technologies are being critically reflected upon by scholars, legal theoretical reflections on the issue so far are not discernible. This is unfortunate, as legal theory could make its own, relevant contributions to the observation of the ambivalent topic of smart cities. A legal theoretical perspective asks if and how the findings, critiques and aspirations of sociological accounts of the smart city can be "translated" into the concepts of law and, based on this translation, may strive to reconstruct these issues in a normatively meaningful way.

As I have suggested, "bottom up" crowd- and interaction-based approaches to smart cities can be understood as specifically glocalised reformulations of ideas of informal, network-based governance on the global stage. A plausible starting point to tackle the conceptual and normative problems of the issue thus may consist of an examination of established ways to legally and theoretically understand the idea of the self-organisation of networks, the avoidance of hierarchies and the complementing or replacing of existing centralised structures (cf Boysen et al. 2007, p. 1081). Such a reconstruction would have to recognise important variances between global and glocal governance. With respect to relevant aspects, however, parallels might prevail. The properties of smart cities discussed above, the ambivalent implications of decentralised governance and the problems of fragmentation are leitmotifs of debates about transnational governance. The consequences of the structural conditions of networks and decentralised governance for the law are conceptualised by theories on legal "polycentricity" (Petersen and Zahle 1995), legal pluralism and normative fragmentation. These established theories, I propose, offer some appropriate instruments to capture the said properties within a legal theoretical framework and may point to an interesting possibility of integrating substantive reflections about SDG 11 into a legal theoretical framework – a closer look at such an integration, however, reveals the necessity to think about some conceptual supplements.

A Legal Pluralist Reconstruction of "Smart" Urban Governance

Legal pluralist theories provide some conceptual tools to depict the structural implications of decentralised governance for the law and thus to reconstruct the properties of smart urban governance within their theoretical framework.[5] Traditionally describing parallel legal practices of non-state communities, post-modern accounts of legal pluralism refer to the fragmentation of the legal system as the legal counterpart of governance practices following a "networked logic". In such accounts, "the separation between public and private, between universal and particular interest … and the hierarchically graded deciding organisation … can henceforth act to create order only to a limited extent." (Ladeur 2013, p. 629) As public sovereignty and private actions have become supposedly "undistinguishable" within the "heterarchical overlapping network" and the state cannot claim to regulate universal as opposed to particular interests, new forms of normative regulations arise (Ladeur 2013, p. 630). The legal dimension of the decentralised networks of governance therefore is represented by legal pluralism or legal polycentricity, and the assumed consequence is normative fragmentation. New private or public-private regimes are emerging out of the networked interactions of civil society and are diverging in their normative meaning, for example considered to be "functionally differentiated", that is, "structurally coupled" to particular systemic (economic, technical, political, for instance) rationalities (Fischer-Lescano and Teubner 2007, p. 833).

As in sociological descriptions of the pathologies of "smart" governance, scholars of global governance and legal pluralism diagnose the risk of new asymmetries and the "serious problem" that the seemingly "cosy and consensual nature" of informal governance arrangements may in fact be "a consensus dictated by the stronger players" (Pierre and Peters 2005, p. 93). Recent contributions discuss the fundamental divergences between private interests, which motivate interactions and communications that might lead to the emergence of the new transnational regimes, and public interest (Senn 2016, p. 40). A pluralism of "spheres of of authority" (Rosenau 1999, p. 295) and the absence of normative hierarchies lead lawyers to ask how "in the messy world of multilevel governance and global Legal Pluralism" it is possible to subject actors to a formal rule of law (Heupel and Reinold 2016, p. 2) or to safeguard individual and collective rights (Benvenisti 2014, p. 25).

Just as in the preliminary reconstructions of "smart" urban governance, the diagnosis of the absence of overarching normative orientation is a characteristic and specifically problematic feature of legal pluralist theories (to which I shall return in the next paragraph). There supposedly is no legal "meta-layer" in a decentralised, networked world which could help to address the collisions of different regimes and the contradictions between particular interests and general public goods and values (cf Fischer-

Lescano and Teubner 2006, p. 40). However, the reconstruction of "meta" norms, rules or principles is a recurring theme in legal theoretical or jurisprudential theories on legal pluralism (cf Berman 2005; Teubner and Korth 2009). Empirically grounded theories of legal pluralism describe how legal actors draw on substantive norms, rules or principles to justify decisions between conflicting orders (Allott 1960, p. 154). Legal theories on legal pluralism may also provide a starting point for an integration of such substantive reflection into a legal theoretical account of smart urban governance: Theories of radical fragmentation draw on specific ideas of inclusion to cope with the severe normative problems of legal pluralism, and thereby indicate potentially fructuous parallels to the concept of inclusiveness in the context of sustainable development. Inclusion in a legal pluralist sense, may, for example, mean to open up the concept of law by including normative practices of non-state communities (Davies 2005). In another respect, the inclusion of individuals into the formalised communications of legal systems is supposed to inhibit disenfranchisement within the plural legal structures of decentralised governance (Fischer-Lescano 2005, p. 141; Merry 2006, p. 43; Boysen et al. 2007, p. 1085). Inclusion, in other words, is considered a central precondition of the legitimacy of plural orders, as it prevents the "universalisation of partial logics" within fragmented regimes (Fischer-Lescano and Christensen 2005, p. 237).

Outlook: Aspects of a Legal Theory of Inclusive Urban Governance

Thinking about a concept of inclusiveness in the context of urban governance on the grounds of a theoretical legal pluralist framework could address the ambivalent nature of smart cities in a couple of constructive ways, which of course can be only roughly outlined here. First, legal pluralism helps to make sense of the normative conditions of decentralised governance characterised by informal structures and interactions or partly privatised regulatory mechanisms, and illustrates the normative conflicts, tensions and potential incoherencies under these conditions. Particularly, this normative complexity – which is highlighted by sociological descriptions of the utopian *and* potentially pathological nature of smart city governance – points to the necessity and some relevant properties of having overarching yardsticks to provide orientation for legal decisions on normative conflicts (cf Brousseau 2007) as well as for the adoption of appropriate governance instruments (cf Gupta et al. 2015, p. 549).

Second, an elaborated theory of the legal conditions of inclusiveness may be a promising candidate for such a substantial yardstick. A further examination of such a notion of inclusiveness would be able to draw on the growing literature on the SDGs and sustainable development as well as on jurisprudential reflections on urban governance. A complex concept of participation in the context of inclusive development for example may enrich legal pluralist concepts that rely on overly formalised ideas of legal inclusion as a source of the legitimacy of plural legal orders. Inclusiveness may for example presuppose multidimensional "processes of empowered participation", which point not only to procedural configurations but also to material conditions of meaningful participation, like the access to resources (Dugarova 2015, p. 9), civic amenities or public infrastructure (Gupta et al. 2015, p. 551). From a legal perspective, this implies that preventing unjust exclusions from plural orders presumes a reference to (multidimensional) human rights as preconditions of legal inclusion (cf Niederberger 2007, p. 156; Gailhofer 2016, pp. 317–325): If citizen feedback, crowd-based funding or participation in decentralised governance regimes replace formal procedures of representation and regulation "this brings into focus the inclusion of individuals and a 'novel' horizontal effect of fundamental rights in [networked] transnational regulatory structures" (cf Boysen et al. 2007, p. 1085). With respect to the interaction-based, networked governance of urban spaces, this notion of a rights-based inclusion would also have to take the hybrid nature of "smart" urban spaces into account. Physical urban space, with its normative implications for the "material practices of freedom" and democracy, is as much concerned as its virtual "second skin" (Rabari and Storper 2015). Normative reconstructions of a "right to public space" (Siehr 2016) or a "right to the city" (Khan 2016), or elaborations on the legal implications of "exclusion from public space" (Moeckli 2016) would have to consider this additional dimension.

Finally, a legal theoretical approach would have to be able to sensibly include such reflections and practices of normative justification into its theoretical framework. It should be able to integrate a conceptual space in legal theory for the methodological jurisprudential reconstruction of normative yardsticks for urban governance. This kind of normative reasoning about values, objectives or "codes", as I have argued elsewhere, (cf Gailhofer 2016, pp. 179–183, 195–198) takes place in legal pluralist theories but remains strangely alienated from the very concepts and theories that descriptively reproduce narratives of hopeless fragmentation. Just like apologists of decentralised "bottom up" governance, legal pluralists count on emergent phenomena like "spontaneous patterns of order" that emerge out of networked cooperation and coordination (Fischer-Lescano and Teubner 2007, p. 61) or even systemic, agent-less "auto-constitutionalisation" (Teubner 2003, p. 25). Even non-hierarchical variants of democracy are supposed to function without procedural safeguards and substantive rights, but "would focus …on producing a distributed self-observation and the observation of others made possible by a 'network of networks' and the associated productive association possibilities …" (Ladeur 2013, p. 632). The reason for this sometimes lies in a problematic theoretical foundation of theories, such as in positivist theory of law as a functionally differentiated system (cf Gailhofer 2016, pp. 179–183) or in essentialist concepts that romanticise quasi-organic notions of "bottom-up" plurality (cf Gailhofer 2016, pp. 128–129). One feature such theories share is their blindness to the legally productive and socially effective capacity of meaningfully oriented, creative actors who cope with complex normative situations and legal plurality. Such theories of legal pluralism, that exclusively focus on code or structure or conflate legal norms and practices with culturally or socially determined normative convictions, cannot conceive such subjective productivity due to their theoretical premises. Approaches that try to reconstruct individual behaviour under conditions of decentralised governance often draw a one-sided picture of legal agency. Citizens, state agencies and organisations use norms of governance as mere "vehicles, by which different parties attempt to gain and maintain control" (Nader 2002, p. 117), and are thus conceived of as strategic actors trying to maximise their particular interest (Benda-Beckmann and Benda-Beckmann 2006, p. 10).

Tendencies of fragmentation are crucial for an adequate understanding of "smart" decentralised governance and its legal consequences and so are the phenomena of the instrumentalisation of legal or quasi-legal instruments by powerful actors. A theory that exclusively focuses on social determinants or the aggregated effects of the actions of self-interested actors, however, will be able to explain neither the function nor the conditions for effectivity of universal rules, principles or overarching objectives. It therefore has little relevance for a practical reflection of the problem of approaches to decentralised governance identified above. It is also theoretically blind to important drivers of change in the structures of law and governance: The structure of law or any other social institution is constituted through active social practice (Hoekema 2008, p. 11). Normative deliberation, substantive reasoning and justification are vital elements of the social practices of law and governance (cf Dale and Samara 2008) and can be conceptualised in a plausible way as productive elements of social and legal dynamics (Wrase 2010; Bourdieu and Wacquant 2006; Weinberger 1991; cf Gailhofer 2016, pp. 256–262, 292–295). In situations of Legal Pluralism or polycentricity, as in methodological legal reasoning in general (cf Müller and Christensen 2009, pp. 321; 549), such reasoning and justification imply a reference to normative reasons, principles or values that claim overarching validity (Alexy 1991, pp. 264, 410). A theory of decentralised governance and legal polycentricity should therefore integrate practices of justification and decision making as effective elements of social reality in a more comprehensive framework of structural and individual drivers of legal dynamics. Such a comprehensive theoretical approach would integrate a perspective on the normative criteria legal actors refer to as justifying reasons for their legal practices in constellations of decentralised governance (cf Mahlmann 2011, p. 345; Weinberger 1991, p. 100; Aust 2016). In these searches for yardsticks, against which the alleged smartening of the city must be measured (cf Sadowski and Pasquale 2015), it can be assumed that SDG 11 will play an important role.

Notes

1 For an overview of definitions see Albino et al., 4; Zucchardi-Meli and Bonollo (2014)
2 It remains an open, empirical question, of course, if these managerial sustainability goals can really be realised by using digital instruments or if digitisation leads to unintended consequences with effects contrary to the goals of SDG 11 – eg to rebound effects.
3 www.decidim.barcelona/?locale=es
4 www.fixmystreet.com/
5 Legal pluralism has its historical roots not in a conceptualisation of global normative orders but in local fields of colonial states and the subversive "asphalt-law" in big cities (cf de Sousa Santos 1977) - the attempt to grasp the implications of "smart" urban governance by drawing on Legal Pluralist concepts is therefore less exotic than it may seem.

Bibliography

Literature

Albino, Vito, Berardi, Umberto, Dangelico, Rosa, Smart cities, definitions, dimensions, and performance, *Journal of Urban Technology*, 22, 3–21.

Alexy, Robert. 1991. *Theorie der juristischen Argumentation: Die Theorie des rationalen Diskurses als Theorie der juristischen Begründung*, 2nd edn. Frankfurt: Suhrkamp.

Allott, Antony N. 1960. *Essays in African Law: With Special Reference to the Law of Ghana*. London: Butterworth.

Appadurai, Arjun and Holston, James. 1996. Cities and Citizenship. *Public Culture*, 8187–204.

Aust, Helmut Philipp. 2016. The rules of interpretation as secondary rules. In: Heupel, Monika and Reinold, Theresa (eds). *The Rule of Law in Global Governance*. London: Palgrave. pp. 59–94.

Aust, Helmut Philipp. 2017. *Das Recht der globalen Stadt – Grenzüberschreitende Dimensionen kommunaler Selbstverwaltung*. Tübingen: Mohr Siebeck.

Aust, Helmut Philipp and du Plessis, Anél. 2019. Introduction: The Globalisation of Urban Governance – Legal Perspectives on Sustainable Development Goal 11. In: Aust, Helmut Philipp and du Plessis, Anél (eds). *The Globalisation of Urban Governance - Legal Perspectives on Sustainable Development Goal 11*. New York: Routledge. pp. 3–16.

Barlow, John Perry. 1996. A declaration of the independance of cyberspace. Available at: https://www.eff.org/de/cyberspace-independence.

von Benda-Beckmann, Franz and von Benda-Beckmann, Keebet. 2006. The dynamics of change and continuity in plural legal orders. *Journal of Legal Pluralism and Unofficial Law*, 38(53–54), 1–44.

Benvenisti, Eyal. 2014. *The Law of Global Governance*. The Hague: Brill.

Benkler, Yochai. 2006. *The Wealth of Networks: How Social Production Transforms Markets and Freedom*. New Haven, CT: Yale University Press.

Berman, Paul Schiff. 2005. Choice of law and jurisdiction on the internet. Towards a cosmopolitan vision of conflict of laws. *University of Pennsylvania Law Review*, 153, 1819–1882.

Börzel, Tanja A. and Panke, Diana. 2007. Network governance: Effective and legitimate? In: Sorensen, Eva and Torfin, Jacob. *Theories of Democratic Network Governance.* New York: Palgrave. pp. 153–168.

Bourdieu, Pierre and Wacquant, Loic J. D. 2006. *Reflexive Anthropologie*, 3rd edn. Frankfurt/Main: Suhrkamp.

Boysen, Sigrid, Bühring, Ferry, Franzius, Claudio, Herbst, Thomas, Kötter, Matthias Kreutz, Anita, Lewinski, Kai, Meinel, Florian, Nolte, Jakob, Schönrock, Sabrina. 2007. Networks in public law. *German Law Journal*, 8(11), pp. 1079–1089.

Bria, Francesca and Morozov, Evgeny. 2017. Die Smarte Stadt neu denken, Rosa Luxemburg Stiftung Germany [online]. Available at: www.rosalux.de/publikation/id/38134/die-smarte-stadt-neu-denken/. (Accessed: 15 November 2017).

Brousseau, Eric. 2007. Multilevel governance of the digital space: Does a "second rank" institutional framework exist? In: Brousseau, Eric and Curien, Nicolas (eds). *Internet and Digital Economics.* Cambridge: Cambridge University Press. pp. 617–648.

Caccia, Giuseppe. 2017. The magnet and the container: A transnational space of expression for "Cities of change" through Europe. In: Büllesbach, Daphne, Cillero, Marta, Stolz, Lukas (eds). *Shifting Baselines of Europe.* pp. 37–41. Bielefeld: Transcript.

Castells, Manuel. 2016. Space of flows, space of spaces: Materials for a theory of urbanism in the information age. In: LeGates, Richard T. and Stout, Frederic. *The City Reader*, 6th edn. New York: Routledge. pp. 229–240.

Celikates, Robin. 2016. Digitalization: Another structural transformation of the public sphere? In: Feger, Hans and Dikun, Xie and Ge, Wang. *Yearbook for Eastern and Western Philosophy.* 1. pp. 39–54.

Cronin, Mary J. 2010. *Smart products, smarter services: Strategies of embedded control.* Cambridge, MA: Harvard University Press.

Dale, John G. and Samara Tony Roshan. 2008. Legal pluralism within a transnational network of governance. *Law, Social Justice & Global Development* [online]. Available at: https://warwick.ac.uk/fac/soc/law/elj/lgd/2008_2/daleandsamara/daleandsamara.pdf (Accessed: 15 November 2017).

Davies, Margaret. 2005. The Ethos of Pluralism. Sydney Law Review 4, (2005) 27(1).

De Magistris, Luigi. 2017. Rebel cities are not utopia (Interview). In: Büllesbach, Daphne, Cillero, Marta, Stolz, Lukas (eds). *Shifting Baselines of Europe.* Bielefeld, Germany: Transcript. pp. 45–48.

De Sousa Santos, Boaventura. 1977. The law of the oppressed, the construction and reproduction of legality in Pasargada. *Law & Society Review*, 12(1), 5–126.

Dugarova, Esuna. 2015. Social Inclusion, Poverty Eradication and the 2030 Agenda for Sustainable Development. United Nations Research Institute for Social Developlment Working Paper 2015-14 [online]. Available at: www.unrisd.org/80256B3C005BCCF9/(httpAuxPages)/0E9547327B7941D6C1257EDF003E74EB/$file/Dugarova.pdf (Accessed: 30 September 2018).

Fischer-Lescano, Andreas. 2005. *Globalverfassung: Die Geltungsbegründung der Menschenrechte.* Weilerswist: Velbrück.

Fischer-Lescano, Andreas and Christensen, Ralph. 2005. Auctoritatis interpositio. Die Dekonstruktion des Dezisionismus durch die Systemtheorie (mit Ralph Christensen), in: Der Staat. Zeitschrift für Staatslehre und Verfassungsgeschichte, deutsches und europäisches öffentliches Recht. pp. 213–242 [online]. English translation available: http://journals.sagepub.com/doi/pdf/10.1177/0964663911423698. (Accessed 30 September 2018).

Fischer-Lescano, Andreas and Teubner, Gunther. 2006. *Regimekollisionen: Zur Fragmentierung des globalen Rechts.* Frankfurt: Suhrkamp.

Fischer-Lescano, Andreas and Teubner, Gunther. 2007. *Fragmentierung des Weltrechts.* In: Albert, Mathias and Stichweh, Rudolf (eds). *Weltstaat und Weltstaatlichkeit: Beobachtungen globaler politischer Strukturbildung.* Wiesbaden: Springer. pp. 37–62.

Gabrys, Jennifer. 2014. Programming environments: Environmentality and citizen sensing in the smart city. *Environment and Planning: Society and Space*, 32(1), 30–48.

Gailhofer, Peter. 2016. *Rechtspluralismus und Rechtsgeltung.* Baden-Baden, Germany: Nomos.

Giffinger, Rudolf, Fertner, Christian, Kramar, Hans, Meijers, Evert. 2007. *Smart Cities: Ranking of European Medium-Sized Cities.* Vienna, Austria: Vienna University of Technology.

Gillespie, Tarleton. 2014. The relevance of algorithms. In: Gillespie, Tarleton, Boczkowski, Pablo and Foot, Kristen. *Media Technologies.* Cambridge, MA: MIT Press. pp. 167–194.

Gupta, Joyeeta, Pouw, Nicky, Ros-Tonen, Mirjam 2015. Towards an elaborated theory of inclusive development. *European Journal of Development Research*, 27 (4). pp. 541–559.

Heupel, Monika and Reinold, Theresa. 2016. Introduction: The rule of law in an era of multilevel governance and global legal pluralism. In: Heupel, Monika and Reinold, Theresa (eds). *The Rule of Law in Global Governance.* London: Palgrave. pp. 1–25.

Hoekema, André. 2008. Multicultural judges and national judges: A general approach. *Law, Social Justice & Global Development Journal* [online]. Available at: https://warwick.ac.uk/fac/soc/law/elj/lgd/2008_2/hoekema/hoekema.pdf (Accessed: 12 January 2018).

Horkheimer, Max. 1991. *Zur Kritik der instrumentellen Vernunft. Gesammelte Schriften Bd. 6.* Frankfurt: Fischer.

Jacobs, Jane. 1992. *The Life and Death of Great American Cities.* New York: Vintage Books Edition.

Khan, Sabaa A. 2016. *Limits of Formalization and Horizons of Urban Citizenship.* Montreal, Canada: McGill University Libraries.

Kim, Sung Ho. 2012. Max Weber. *The Stanford Encyclopedia of Philosophy.* Fall 2012 Edition [online]. Available at: https://plato.stanford.edu/archives/fall2012/entries/weber/ (Accessed: 12 January 2018).

Kitchin, Rob. 2014. The real-time city? Big data and smart urbanism. *GeoJournal*, 79(1),1–14.

Kneer, George. 1990. *Die Pathologien der Moderne: Zur Zeitdiagnose in der ‚Theorie des kommunikativen Handelns' von Jürgen Habermas.* Düsseldorf, Germany: Westdeutscher Verlag.

Krätke, Stefan and Wildner, Kathrin and Lanz, Stephan (eds). 2012. *Transnationalism and Urbanism.* London: Routledge.

Ladeur, Karl-Heinz. 2013. Globalisation and the conversion of democracy to polycentric networks. In: Vesting, Thomas and Augsberg, Ino and Ladeur, Karl-

Heinz (eds). *Das Recht der Netzwerkgesellschaft*. Tübingen, Germany: Mohr Siebeck. pp. 609–638.

Mahlmann, Matthias. 2011. Neue Perspektiven einer Soziologie der Menschenrechte. In: Mahlmann, Matthias (ed), *Gesellschaft und Gerechtigkeit: Festschrift für Hubert Rottleuthner*. Baden-Baden: Nomos. pp. 331–346.

Marsal, Lluisa, Llorente, Tomas, Braga, Graciela, Curtis, Stan, Garcia, Jordi, Garcia, Javier, et al. 2017. Implementing SDG 11 by connecting sustainability policies and urban planning practices through ICTs. Geneva: United 4 Smart Sustainable Cities[online]. Available at: www.unece.org/fileadmin/DAM/hlm/documents/Publications/U4SSC_Brochure_Implementing_sustainable_development_goal_11.pdf (Accessed: 12 February 2018).

Mela, Alfredo. 2014. Urban public space between fragmentation, control and conflict. In: City, Territory and Architecture [online]. Available at: https://cityterritoryarchitecture.springeropen.com/articles/10.1186/s40410-014-0015-0 (Accessed: 2 November 2017).

Merry, Sally Engle. 2006. Transnational human rights and local activism: mapping the middle. *American Anthropologist*, 108(1), 38–51.

Milacovic, Anita and Novocovic, Nevena. 2017. Integral approach to urban design in a data-rich city-context. In: Certoma, Chiara, Dyer, Mark, Pocatilu, Lorena, Rizzi, Francesco, *Citizen Empowerment in the data rich city*. Heidelberg, Germany:Springer. pp. 79–90.

Moeckli, Daniel. 2016. *Exclusion from Public Space. A Comparative Constitutional Analysis*. Cambridge: Cambridge University Press.

Morozov, Evgeny. 2017. "Smarte Müllabfuhr? Von wegen!". Süddeutsche Zeitung [online]. Available at: www.sueddeutsche.de/kultur/digitaler-wandel-smarte-muellabfuhr-1.3721915 (Accessed: 5 November 2017).

Mouffe, Chantal. 2016. Democratic politics and conflict: An agonistic approach. *Politica Comun* [online]. Available at: http://dx.doi.org/10.3998/pc.12322227.0009.011 (Accessed: 5 November 2017).

Müller, Friedrich and Christensen, Ralph. 2009. *Juristische Methodik, Band I: Grundlagen Öffentliches Recht*. Berlin: Duncker & Humblodt.

Nabian, Nashid and Ratti, Carlo. 2011. The senseable city and mechanisms of actuation: networks and neo-cyborgs. In: Nabian, Nashid and Robinson, Prudence (eds). *Senseable City Guide*. Cambridge, MA: SENSEable City Laboratory Massachusetts Institute of Technology. pp. 18–27.

Nader, Laura. 2002. *The Life of Law. Anthropological Projects*. Berkeley, CA: University of California Press.

Niederberger, Andreas. 2007. Politisierung des Rechts oder Verrechtlichung und Demokratisierung der Politik? In: Niederberger, Andreas and Wolf, Markus (eds). *Politische Philosophie und Dekonstruktion*. Bielefeld: Transcript. pp. 143–164.

Papacharrisi, Zizi. 2009. The virtual sphere 2.0, the internet, the public sphere and beyond. In: Chadwick, Andrew and Howard, Philip N. (eds). *Routledge Handbook of Internet Politics*. London: Routledge.

Pasquale, Frank. 2018. From territorial to functional sovereignty [online]. Available at: www.opendemocracy.net/digitaliberties/frank-pasquale/from-territorial-to-functional-sovereignty-case-of-amazon (Accessed: 29 January 2018).

Pariser, Eli. 2011. *The Filter Bubble. What the Internet is Hiding from You*. New York, London: Penguin.

Peters, Anne. 2009. *Dual Democracy*. In: Klabbers, Jan and Peters, Anne and Ulfstein, Geir (eds). *The Constitutionalization of International Law*. Oxford: Oxford University Press.

Petersen, Hanne and Zahle, Henrik. 1995. Legal Polycentricity: Consequences of Legal Pluralism in Law. London: Dartmouth.

Pierre, Jon and Peters, Guy. 2005. Governing Complex Societies: Trajectories and Scenarios. New York: Palgrave Macmillan.

Pitasi, Andrea and Angrisani, Mariarosalba. 2013. Hyper citizenship and the evolution of a new global identity. *Journal of Sociological Research*, 4(2), pp. 138–335

Portmann, Edi and Finger, Daniel. 2015. Smart Cities. Ein Überblick. *HMD Praxis der Wirtschaftsinformatik*, 52(4), 470–481.

Rabari, Chirag and Storper, Michael. 2015. The digital skin of cities: urban theory and research in the age of the sensored and metered city, ubiquitous computing and big data. *Cambridge Journal of Regions, Economy and Society*, 8(1), 27–42.

Reynolds, Matt. 2017. Citizens give up data in blockchain project to improve cities [online]. Available at: www.newscientist.com/article/2131950-citizens-give-up-data-in-blockchain-project-to-improve-cities/ (Accessed 30 September 2018).

Rittgen, Klaus. 2017. Rechtliche und tatsächliche Herausforderungen bei der Entwicklung ländlicher Räume. *Deutsches Verwaltungsblatt*, 16, 1007–1015.

Roberts, David. 2017. Donald Trump and the rise of tribal epistemology [online]. Available at: www.vox.com/policy-and-politics/2017/3/22/14762030/donald-trump-tribal-epistemology (Accessed: 15 November 2017).

Roudometof, Victor. 2005. Transnationalism, cosmopolitanism and glocalization. *Current Sociology*, 53(1), 113–135.

Rosenau, James N. 1999. Toward an ontology of global governance. In: Hewson, Martin, Sinclair, Timothy J. (eds). *Approaches to Global Governance Theory*. Albany, NY: New York State University Press, pp. 287–302.

Sadowski, Jathan and Pasquale, Frank. 2015. The spectrum of control: A social theory of the smart city. *First Monday*, 20 (No. 7). Available at: http://firstmonday.org/article/view/5903/4660 (Accessed: 30 September 2018).

Sassen, Saskia. 2013. Does the city have speech? *Public Culture*, 25(2), 209–221.

Seemann, Michael and Kreil, Michael. 2017. Digitaler tribalismus and fake news [online]. Available at: www.ctrl-verlust.net/digitaler-tribalismus-und-fake-news/#fn-2153-2 (Accessed: 05 November 2017).

Senn, Myriam. 2016. Towards reinforcing or contesting the vision of the rule of law? In: Pazartzis, Photini and Gavouneli, Maria (eds). *Reconceptualizing the Rule of Law*. London: Hart Publishing. pp. 31–41.

Sennett, Richard. 2006. The open city [online]. Available at: http://downloads.lsecities.net/0_downloads/Berlin_Richard_Sennett_2006-The_Open_City.pdf (Accessed: 15 November 2017).

Siehr, Angelika. 2016. *Das Recht am Öffentlichen Raum, Theorie des Öffentlichen Raumes und die räumliche Dimension der Freiheit*. Tübingen: Mohr Siebeck.

Teubner, Gunther. 2003. Globale Zivilverfassungen, Alternativen zur staatszentrierten Verfassungstheorie. *Zeitschrift für ausländisches öffentliches Recht und Völkerrecht*, 63, 1–28.

Teubner, Gunther and Korth, Peter. 2009. Zwei Arten des Rechtspluralismus: Normkollisionen in der doppelten Fragmentierung der Weltgesellschaft. In:

Kötter, Matthias and Folke Schuppert, Gunnar. *Normative Pluralität ordnen: Rechtsbegriffe, Normenkollisionen und Rule of Law in Kontexten dies- und jenseits des Staates.* Baden-Baden, Germany: Nomos. pp. 137–168.

Townsend, Anthony. 2013. *Smart Cities: Big Data, Civic Hackers, and the Quest for a New Utopia.* New York: W.W. Norton & Company.

Thorn, Claire and Griffiths, Catherine. 2014. Smart, smarter, smartest: Redefining our cities. In: Rosenthal-Sabroux, Camille and Dameri, Renata Paola. *Smart City. How to Create Public and Economic Value with High Technology in Urban space.* New York: Springer. pp. 89–99.

Wall, Robert, Stravropoulos, Spyrion, Edelnbos, Jurian, Pajevic, Filipa. 2015. Evaluating the smart city in the global economic network. In: Rodríguez-Bolívar, Pedro. *Transforming City Governments for Successful Smart Cities.* New York: Springer. pp. 87–113.

Wallin, Sirkku, Horelli, Lisa and Saad-Sulonen, Joanna. 2010. Digital tools in participatory planning, Centre for Urban and Regional Studies Publications, Aalto University [online]. Available at https://aaltodoc.aalto.fi/bitstream/handle/123456789/4832/isbn9789526032603.pdf?sequence=1 (Accessed: 30 September 2018).

Weber, Karsten and Drüeke, Ricarda. 2012. *Konvergente Medien, Fragmentierung der Öffentlichkeit und medienethische Anmerkungen* [online]. Available at: www.researchgate.net/publication/256474315_Konvergente_Medien_Fragmentierung_der_Offentlichkeit_und_medienethische_Anmerkungen (Accessed: 4 November 2017).

Weinberger, Ota. 1991. *Law Institution and Legal Politics: Fundamental Problems of Legal Theory and Social Philosophy.* London: Kluwer Academic Publisher.

Wrase, Michael. 2010. Recht und soziale Praxis – Überlegungen für eine soziologische Rechtstheorie. In: Cottier, Michele and Estermann, Josef and Wrase, Michael (eds). *Wie Wirkt Recht?* Baden-Baden, Germany: Nomos. pp. 113–146.

Zuccardi Merli, Mara and Bonollo, Elisa. 2014. Performance-measurement in smart cities. In: Rosenthal-Sabroux, Camille and Dameri, RenataPaola. *Smart City. How to Create Public and Economic Value with High Technology in Urban Space.* New York: Springer. pp. 139–155.

Documents

UN-Habitat and Ericson. 2014. The role of IDCT in the proposed Urban Sustainable Development Goal and the New Urban Agenda [online]. Available at: https://unhabitat.org/the-role-of-ict-in-the-proposed-urban-sustainable-development-goal-and-the-new-urban-agenda/ (Accessed: 15 November 2017).

UN Sustainable Development Solutions Network (UN SDSN). 2015. Tools for designing SDG strategies and roadmaps [online]. Available at: https://sdg.guide/chapter-3-tools-for-designing-sdg-strategies-and-roadmaps-a8172680d5ef (Accessed: 20 January 2018).

13 The Tensions Between Local Resilience-Building and Transnational Action

US-Mexican Cooperation in Crime Affected Communities in Northern Mexico, and What this Tells Us about Global Urban Governance

Alejandro Rodiles

Introduction

In 2006 Mexico's then President Felipe Calderón (National Action Party – PAN, 2006–2012) mobilised federal forces and started a frontal combat against organised crime, targeting the illicit narcotics business. This anti-crime strategy which, despite some minor rhetorical adjustments, remained in place under the administration of Enrique Peña (Institutional Revolutionary Party – PRI, 2012–2018) became known as "Mexico's war on drugs" or "Mexico's narco war", since it involves the military in assistance of civil authorities who, in several municipalities and some entire states, lack the capacity to control very rich and well-armed criminal syndicates (Rodiles 2018a). Specialists and public intellectuals in Mexico agree almost unanimously that the "war" has failed (Aguilar and Castañeda 2009; Astorga 2012; Dresser 2012; Guerrero 2012) because it has led to a spiralling of violence, especially in those parts of the country where local authorities are most fragile (i.e. the least professional and the most corrupt).

Calderón's government pushed for the recognition on behalf of the US administration of a "shared responsibility" in this situation, due to the high demand for drugs north of the Rio Grande and the heavy flow of arms and dollars from north to south. George W. Bush's government reacted positively. In 2007 the two governments entered into a far-reaching bilateral partnership called the Mérida Initiative. To this day the main purpose of this informal arrangement is to strengthen cooperation between the two countries in the fight against organised crime through information-sharing, financial assistance, weaponry donation, capacity-building, and joint security operations, although the latter are not officially recognised.

By 2009 the situation of extreme violence had become critical in northern Mexico, especially in those cities along the most frequently crossed international border which, also because of this geography, are amongst the most affected by the failed war on drugs. Ciudad Juárez (or "Juárez"), on the border to El Paso, Texas, and Tijuana, which together with San Diego and other counties and municipalities along Baja California Norte and California forms a transnational metropolitan conurbation, figured among the cities with the highest murder rates in Mexico during that period. Juárez actually acquired the tragic reputation of being the most violent city in the world outside actual war zones. Monterrey, which is not on the border but is a major communication, commercial and industrial hub in northern Mexico and thus also an important point in one of the most profitable drug smuggling routes in the world, was affected by this situation as well.

Around that time, Barack Obama designated Carlos Pascual as Ambassador to Mexico. Together with other US diplomats and foreign policy thinkers like Stephen Krasner and Condoleezza Rice, this specialist in state-failure promoted a less state-centered approach to state-building (Krasner and Pascual 2005; Rice 2006; Jones, Pascual and Stedman 2009). From 2009 on, *Mérida* began to evolve into what some have called "Beyond Mérida" (see Olson and Wilson 2010). More attention was accordingly paid to crime prevention through non-aggressive means focused on directly strengthening the affected communities. This strategy complements the initiative as its "Pillar IV", officially called *Build Strong and Resilient Communities* (US Embassy to Mexico 2010). Juárez, Monterrey, and Tijuana were chosen as pilot cities for this endeavour, and in all three cases encouraging developments have taken place.

However, "building strong and resilient communities" is still attached to the broader bilateral security partnership, which has helped to maintain the aggressive anti-crime strategy of Calderón beyond his administration, both in terms of the financial assistance needed to carry it out, as well as in relation to its embeddedness in a transnational narrative of a "global war against drugs and crime" (Rodiles 2018a). This very same narrative has been a major obstacle to the adoption of alternative approaches such as treating the drug problem as a public health matter and the legalisation of certain illegal drugs, as well as a more attuned strategy of preventing, persecuting, and prosecuting those crimes which most affect the inhabitants of these cities and communities in their day-to-day lives (kidnapping, extortion, violent robbery etc.), and which, as some have noted, are not part of the illegal narcotics business as such (Aguilar and Castañeda 2009). What is more worrisome is that in December 2017 a new *Law on Interior Security* (Diario Oficial de la Federación (DOF) 2017) was adopted by the Mexican Congress, which intensifies the war approach, prolonging a quasi-state of exception.

In this chapter, I inquire into the emancipatory force of Mérida's Pillar IV, and of community resilience-building programmes in particular. After the framing of resilience within this initiative has been analysed, as well as some instances of its instrumentality, it will become clear that even in this case there are different and often differing conceptions of resilience at play. Being part of a broader, transnational security plan, community resilience is also constantly at risk of being captured, and of reducing itself to a legitimacy-conferring device in service of actually contrary policies of security. At the same time, in this vulnerability rests its very potential and strength, since resilience can be constantly re-appropriated and re-configured: "If resilience represents anything, it represents the possibility of change" (Rogers 2017, p. 14). Indeed, it is the resilience of resilience that makes it a risky and a promising adventure at the same time, also in the context of community-building measures.

Both as a discourse and a strategy, resilience is full of contradictions, and this is not exclusive to the Mérida Initiative. It is likely to be present in other anti-crime programmes and counter-terrorism strategies, whenever the involvement of communities in urban as well as rural areas become part and parcel of the former. But what about the place of resilience within the kind of urban governance that concerns this volume? Mérida's Pillar IV has no direct relationship with the 2030 Agenda of the United Nations (UN). However, a closer look at the tactics that have been developed for achieving the goals of Pillar IV reveals the understanding that safety should be intrinsically tied to the positive reconfiguration of the social web through inclusiveness, the promotion of individual capabilities, and the recovery of public space. This resonates all too well with Sustainable Development Goal 11 (SDG 11). A way of analysing this relationship is to trace the genealogy of resilience in urban governance, and to make the correlations between UN-led, US-led, and other discourses on the subject-matter. This chapter has no such ambition. Instead, I limit myself to arguing that resilience is a governance technique that has penetrated the urban on a global scale, as it has done in the security, environmental, and development realms. Indeed, in parallel to the notion of resilience as a strategy for making communities and cities safe, both within Mérida's Pillar IV as well as within SDG 11, resilience appears as an end in itself. This is baffling – even paradoxical –inasmuch as the management of risk entails the peril of perpetuating the vulnerability of those who are to cope with crime and insecurity (Evans and Reid 2014), closing up spaces for political action aimed at the transformation of the public good (Aradau 2017, pp. 85–88, based on Arendt 1958). It is in this sense that the tensions that this chapter identifies between local resilience-building and transnational action in the framework of the Mérida Initiative should not fall on deaf ears to those concerned with global urban governance more broadly.

The Mérida Initiative and Its Fourth Pillar

The Mérida Initiative is best described as an informal bilateral security arrangement between Mexico and the US to combat organised crime, mostly in Mexico. It involves, on the one hand, a US multi-year funding programme approved by Congress, and on the other an unprecedented partnership between both countries on matters of security cooperation. It is contained in a joint political declaration of Presidents George W. Bush and Felipe Calderón, made in Mérida, Yucatán, on 14 March 2007 (Cámara de Diputados LX Legislatura 2008). Adopted under the understanding of a "shared responsibility" in regard to the increasing problem of organised crime in Mexico, the US provides funds, equipment, and training to Mexican law-enforcement authorities and the military, and it establishes mechanisms for enhancing cooperation among the authorities of the two countries, mainly through information-sharing.

Read in isolation the initiative does not say much. It is, indeed a "little paper", as former Foreign Secretary and Senator, Rosario Green (PRI), put it, in clear disapproval of its informal nature, lack of transparency, and the bypassing of parliamentary participation along the process (Ascención 2012). But the informality of transnational initiatives should not be confused with purely political intentions (Rodiles 2018b). The Mérida Initiative has evolved over the years through bilateral consultation mechanisms, like the High Level Consultative Group on Bilateral Cooperation against Transnational Organised Crime and the Policy Coordination and the Bilateral Coordination Groups. These working groups function like those bi-national commissions established in bilateral treaties for the purposes of developing their rather general provisions over time. According to treaty law, the agreements reached in these commissions may constitute subsequent agreements in terms of article 31 (3) (a) of the Vienna Convention on the Law of Treaties (VCLT), which amount to authentic interpretations of the treaty text (see Nolte 2013; International Law Commission (ILC) 2018). Subsequent practice and agreements have the potential of transforming rigid treaties into quite flexible treaty-governance regimes. In a similar fashion, subsequent joint political declarations and action plans have turned the Mérida Initiative into a very broad framework arrangement that now goes well beyond bilateral cooperation in the field of enhanced law-enforcement.

In September 2009 the High Level Consultative Group, chaired by former foreign ministers Patricia Espinosa and Hillary R. Clinton, established four strategic pillars to guide the work between the two governments (US Embassy to Mexico 2010); these are:

- Pillar I - Disrupt the Capacity of Organised Crime to Operate
- Pillar II - Institutionalise the Capacity to Sustain the Rule of Law
- Pillar III - Create a Twenty-First Century Border Structure; and
- Pillar IV - Build Strong and Resilient Communities

The first pillar did not introduce anything new. It is basically about enhanced law-enforcement cooperation in order to "systematically capture and incarcerate" the leaders of Mexican drug cartels. It is the war approach to public security that has led to a spiral of violence in the country. Pillar II was also well under way before 2009. It deals with institutional capacity-building of the police, the judiciary and customs, reminding the reader of the kind of security sector reform (SSR) promoted by the UN, mostly in post-conflict scenarios. It must be mentioned that Pillar II was instrumental in Mexico's penal law reform of 2008, which has transformed an inquisitorial criminal justice system into an adversarial one, as well as for its implementation afterwards and until today. In contrast, Pillars III and IV do represent innovations vis-à-vis the original plan envisaged by Presidents Calderón and Bush in 2007. Pillar III is basically concerned with not impeding commercial flows along the border, which thanks to the North American Free Trade Agreement (NAFTA) amount to almost one and a half billion dollars a day, while curtailing the illicit trafficking of people, weapons, cash and drugs. For this goal, big infrastructural projects with the participation of private investment are planned. Moreover, the "twenty-first century border" establishes a bi-national capacity-building working group for customs officers and foresees the identification of best practices to be followed by them, as well as the pre-screening, pre-clearance, and pre-inspection of people and goods on both sides of the border.

Finally, Pillar IV is said to "strengthen communities by creating a culture of lawfulness and undercutting the lure and power of drug trafficking organizations" (US Embassy to Mexico 2010). This includes the promotion of transnational social networks through *inter alia* students' exchange programmes, especially among law schools. Most importantly, Mérida's fourth pillar envisages financial assistance and overall support to local communities, mainly via the US Agency for International Development (USAID), in the design and implementation of social, educational, cultural, sports, and job-creating programmes, as well as those concerned with sustainable urban development. In helping to fortify or restructure the social web of the locales affected, Mérida's Pillar IV is supposed to curb the vulnerability of communities affected by crime. Transnational cooperation is thus channeled through multiple actors, including civil society and academia on both sides of the border. The idea is that these communities will acquire the ability to resist and counter the threats and temptations posed by heavily armed, highly organised, and very rich criminal syndicates, in a self-sufficient and evolving way: citizen security guaranteed by the citizens themselves.

Hence, Mérida's Pillar IV can be described as a transnational (binational) programme that engages the private sector and the affected communities in the design and execution of measures aimed at improving daily local life. Thus, it fits into the broader scheme of urban (security) governance spurred by programmes and initiatives that transcend not only the local but also the purely public aspect of so-called public policies (Aust and du Plessis 2019, in this volume). In doing this, at least in theory it defies traditional conceptions of international cooperation. Local resilience-building promoted transnationally (or internationally, for that matter) also shifts the discourse from interventionist state-building policies imposed by a donor on a recipient country to a post-sovereignty legitimacy anchored in the needs, realities and practices of affected locales. However, given its place within the broader Mérida Initiative, this particular resilience discourse also denotes inner tensions, legitimacy problems, and even questions about its longer-term effectiveness.

Again, due to its informal nature, the few available documents of the Mérida Initiative (joint statements and declarations, as well as fact sheets and reports to Congress, mainly in the US) do not reveal much about how resilience is concretely understood in this context, beyond the notion of generating the capacity of crime-affected communities to withstand the effects of crime. So how can we get a grasp on what specific sort of resilience is invoked within Mérida's framework and how its instrumentation is supposed to function? In order to come a bit closer to this it is necessary to analyse how resilience is understood by USAID, the main US governmental agency through which Pillar IV is channeled (see Seelke and Finklea 2017). This will also allow us to compare the resilience-framings involved in Mérida and SDG 11, which in turn would lead to a better comprehension of the global promotion of the role of resilience in urban governance.

The Mérida Initiative's Resilience Framing

The USAID Mexico Country Development Cooperation Strategy for the fiscal years 2014–2018 (USAID 2014) is the main document in regard to the resilience-building strategies sponsored by the US in Mexico. Development Objective 1 (DO1) is concerned with facilitating mechanisms for the instrumentality of Mérida's Pillar IV, for which three pilot cities were chosen: Juárez, Monterrey, and Tijuana. This is due to the extreme violence that these cities experienced during Calderón's administration, but also because they – especially Monterrey – already had better capacities in place to build resilience, and in some instances community-resilience-like initiatives were already under way so that USAID could build on them. A prime example of this is Nacidos para Triunfar (NPT), which brings together members of rival gangs in sports and cultural activities, like soccer games and graffiti competitions, seeking to bridge among them, with the aim of negotiating and adopting "peace treaties". It has already led to the conclusion of seven intergang truces in Monterrey's metropolitan area. Also in Monterrey, public-private partnerships (PPPs) involving the city's powerful business and industry sector have successfully pushed for police reform, taking active part, for example, in the creation of its "civil force" (The Economist 2013).

USAID channels its work on local resilience-building in crime affected communities in northern Mexico according to three major approaches: 1) assisting in constructing or fortifying ties between the Mexican federal, state, and municipal governments, and affected citizens; 2) promoting and channeling the involvement of the private sector also in order to improve the socio-economic environment of marginalised locales; and 3) providing financial assistance and technical guidance in the articulation and instrumentality of educational, cultural, sports, work-insertion, and other initiatives aimed at improving the capacity of at-risk youth "to play a productive role in their communities" (USAID 2014, pp. 17–26). Thus, USAID sponsors and enables the creation of cooperation schemes that involve different levels of government on both sides of the border, the private sector, and the affected individuals themselves. The aim of this is to build strong communities in violence-driven places, so that the members of these communities can resist crime and extreme violence.

This basic notion of resilience-building is compatible with the traditional concept of resilience as it emerged in mechanical engineering and in thermodynamics more concretely, and which refers to the ability of materials to resist external exposure and to bounce back (Rogers 2017, p. 14). It corresponds to the first paradigm of resilience as a matter of preservation rather than transformation, also called the "homeostatic approach" (Chandler and Coaffee 2017, p. 5). Importantly, the homeostatic approach to resilience also emphasises dynamic self-organisation in the process of maintaining stability while adapting to threat. Here, the fluidity of the resilience metaphor comes to the forefront as it is already closely connected to biology and ecological systems, which in turn are related to organic understandings of societal self-regulation. I dwell on this because, as Rogers makes clear, the genealogy of the resilience concept, eg how it has travelled over time relying on diverse concepts drawn from analogies of different sciences (engineering, mathematics, physics, biology, ecology, neurosciences, and psychology) is crucial for understanding the different purposes that are attached to this broad concept, also according to those using it (Rogers 2017, pp. 13–14).

DO1 further states that it focuses "on developing and testing crime and violence prevention models that can ultimately be replicated by local stakeholders" (USAID 2014, p. 17). The role of prevention within the resilience discourse has several possible and interrelated connotations. Depending on these differences, the meaning of "strong communities" varies, and with it also the means to be deployed for such purposes.

First, the prevention facet of resilience is linked to the risk-based approach (RBA). Accordingly, vulnerable or "at-risk" communities should develop mitigation and adaptation skills that help them to cope with extreme violence. This understanding of local resilience-building hardly leads, in and of itself, to the making of stronger communities – at least not in the sense of "weaving and bolstering webs of positive human relationships" (Slaughter 2017, p. 109) inside particular community groups and across the whole community, i.e. in the sense of "bonding" and "bridging" social capital (Putnam 2000). As explained by Koonings and Kruijt (2015, p. 19), who analyse different models of resilience used in various Latin American cities, urban resilience to violence and insecurity manifests itself on different levels according to the particular models employed. The "coping with" model is the most rudimentary one, which hardly translates into a fortified social web. The level of local resilience which it produces is rather limited to vigilantism, criminal governance, and the privatisation of security.

Strictly tied to this model is the idea of developing the ability to anticipate risks as far as possible. Hence, a proactive approach to security threats is promoted, and with it the temptation of engaging in strategies like profiling and, as far as the participation of community members is concerned, of turning fellow citizens into police informants. This may render effective results in some instances. However, and as has been noted in relation to terrorism prevention activities in Muslim communities in Western cities, it also raises serious concerns from the perspective of community-building through bonding and bridging, since it may alienate members of these communities, provoking divisions that, in the long run, may complicate peaceful coexistence (Walklate and Mythen 2015, pp. 93–115). Moreover, the management of danger may also lead to an acceptance of the perpetuation of the vulnerability of certain parts of the population (Evans and Reid 2014), and this may contribute to the mushrooming of gated communities and the correlated ghettoisation of neighborhoods and even entire city areas.

But there is also a more positive aspect of resilience as a crime prevention strategy. In this case prevention works through the improvement of living conditions, like the recovery of public spaces and the enhancement of public services, as well as through the creation of capabilities. Here, development work in the sense of the "human development approach" (Nussbaum 2011) starts making sense in urban security matters, and resilience appears as the *conduit* that connects the creation of individual and collective capabilities with crime prevention – the latter becoming almost a corollary of the former. An example of this is Jóvenes con Rumbo, which explicitly forms part of Mérida's fourth pillar. This bilateral PPP is facilitated by USAID and involves the Mexican and US private sectors (Nacional Monte de Piedad and Prudential Foundation), civil organisations south and north of the Rio Grande (YouthBuild, Servicios a la Juventud, Jóvenes Constructores de la Comunidad), as well as the municipalities of Tijuana, Monterrey, and Guadalupe. It seeks to offer young people in these cities (Guadalupe is part of the metropolitan area of Monterrey) prospects for their future insertion (or re-insertion) into social life and the labour market. In the end, it remains a fact that young people with better chances for realising their free personal development do not fall so easily into the cartels' payroll. It should be stressed, at the same time, that Jóvenes con Rumbo seeks to go beyond the mere professional perspective. It emphasises the need to develop "human leadership", which is about the role of these young women and men in regenerating the social web, from family life and neighbourhood (physical and social) reconstruction (bonding) to the wider social context in which they interact (bridging), for example through cultural activities. Tijuana has one of Mexico's most vivid cultural scenes today. For this, it has created "youth centres" where young people are individually oriented and trained in different crafts according to their personal histories and life experiences, individual capabilities and interests. Accordingly, Jóvenes con Rumbo seems to reject the "Choose Life. Choose a job. Choose a career. Choose a family" morality that is so fervently denounced at the ending of the Trainspotting movie, denying, at least in discourse, one-size-fits-all solutions. Inspired by the critical pedagogy of the Brazilian Paulo Freire (Freire 1969), as mentioned in its mission statement, it looks more into the different capabilities of individuals and their transformative potentials as active members of their communities and the broader society. This resonates with the root-causes discourse, as it does with the intuitive idea that people and their interactions make strong or weak communities in the first place. Here, resilience is about fortifying local agency, which in turn enables change. Thus, it is a bouncing-forward conception that does not solely seek mitigation and adaptation, but ultimately seeks transformation. Indeed, here resilience serves as a *conduit for change* instead as an end that pushes for change for its own sake.

According to USAID, those resilience strategies which prove to be successful should be replicated (USAID 2014, p. 17). This has several implications as well. First, there is the trans-border dimension of Mérida's Pillar IV, as evidenced through the import into Monterrey's suburbs of models which have been successful in crime-affected communities in US cities, such as initiatives to mitigate gang violence in East Los Angeles (such as GRYD – Gang Reduction and Youth Development).[1] The promotion of mimesis processes does not only have the US as a frame of reference. For instance, USAID has financed travels from Juárez to Medellín, Colombia, so that people involved in resilience-building in the former can learn first-hand how urban planning has been successful in the latter, including in reducing violence (see Carpenter 2013).

Second, the replication of successful models is not meant only to export/import programmes and initiatives to those places lacking them, but it resonates too with the role of redundancy in the building of resilience networks: the idea that overlapping instances and tasks do not pose so much of a problem, but they rather strengthen the complex, thus making it possible to rely on more than one single form of organisation (or community programme) in situations of severe stress (Slaughter 2017, p. 81).

Third, the role of mimesis is also related to the notion of building resilient communities through an on-going process of trial and error. Here, an analogy can be drawn to a governance technique, namely experimentalist governance (Sabel and Zeitlin 2012). Local resilience building may not be *prima facie* about regulation, but seen from this angle, it is about the idea that instead of finding fixed solutions provided in more or less detailed laws and regulations, a pro-active and continuously evolving approach based on mutual learning is more appropriate for managing problems which are themselves dynamic.

Local Resilience Building in Northern Mexico: Beyond Mérida?

USAID and other US governmental agencies involved in Mérida IV, most clearly the US Embassy in Mexico City and the General Consulates in Juárez, Monterrey, and Tijuana, are not mere supportive bystanders but additional layers in a multilevel game of cross-scale interaction (Aust and du Plessis 2019, in this volume) that involves the international and transnational, the national, the regional and the local levels, the private and the public sectors, as well as community members. This network-logic of organisation is, in principle, non-hierarchical, and each layer interacts with others as the issues at hand demand. Moreover, while the federal, state, and municipal authorities are important players, they are not so in their own right, so to speak, but in the relational aptitudes among them, with international and most importantly with the affected locales – the communities and their individual members. It is within this network-complexity, or in this regime complex of resilience-building that the relationship with the global level and with SDG 11 in particular has to be sought.

In the present context, local resilience-building in crime-affected communities is tied to a concept of urban governance. Given its place within Mérida, one would be inclined to think of it as an instance of bilateral urban governance, i.e. the design of local policies within an informal but inter-governmental setting. But then again, the very purpose of Mérida IV is to depart from a state-centric approach so that the "transnational" is to be understood as "trans-border", but not as mainly "bi-national" or "inter-national". The agency-conferring element of the fourth pillar, on its part, emphasises the role of the local, but this through a globally embedded discourse and foreign assistance. So, might it be accurate to speak in this context of "glocal governance"? Might it be the case that urban governance cannot but be glocal, i.e. globally informed local interpretations of communications, housing, environmental, and safety policies? Be that as it may, this shows that whenever the concept of governance is in place, it becomes extremely difficult to keep local, national, international and transnational levels, public and private realms apart. It is the "global" with all its ambiguities and uncertainties that insinuates itself (Walker 2015). And this is why Mérida's Pillar IV is a case in point for the *globalisation of urban governance*, or *global urban governance*, which is pretty much the same thing.

Neither in USAID documents nor in other documents from the US Embassy, nor in reports to the Mexican and US congresses on the implementation of Mérida's Pillar IV could I find a single reference to SDG 11. Moreover, UN work on urban resilience is rarely acknowledged in Mérida's framework. However, the Mexican federal government and several state governments have committed to the implementation of the 2030 Agenda, and USAID recognises that since Mexico is an upper-middle income country, it does not fit into its typical development work. Accordingly, it emphasises that its programmes are in close relationship with existing ones of the Mexican government. Most relevant in this context is the National Programme for the Social Prevention of Violence and Crime (DOF 2014), a document which contains a series of public policies in the field of crime prevention, premised on the recognition that law enforcement alone is not sufficient for ameliorating Mexico's violence. Adopted as a federal administrative act, it establishes the legal basis for the cooperation among the three levels of government, which is then further implemented through administrative agreements between specific federal, state, or municipal agencies. It is clearly in line with Mérida's fourth pillar, but also with UN programmes, in particular with UNDP policy papers and recommendations on urban governance and citizen security tailored for Latin America (UN Development Programme (UNDP) 2013).

The National Programme (DOF 2014) is prior to the SDGs and the UN Habitat's New Urban Agenda (A/RES/71/256 2017). However, its articulation of the "right to the city" matches with elements contained in the latter, especially those that relate city safety to good urban planning and the promotion of social integration (A/RES/71/256 2017 paras 13 (b), 99, 103).

Another indirect connection between the contents of Pillar IV and those of SDG 11 can be found in the Toolkit for Urban Resilience in Situations of Chronic Violence (USAID/MIT 2012), elaborated by the MIT Centre for International Studies in 2012, and sponsored by USAID. This report, which contains concrete recommendations for the work of USAID, was elaborated under the leadership of Professor Diane E. Davis, Chair of the Department on Urban Planning and Design at Harvard University, and a longtime specialist on city violence in Latin America, particularly in Brazilian and Mexican urban areas (Davis 2009; Davis 2016).

The Toolkit's recommendations on urban planning and the transformation of violent spaces are so very consistent with the section of the New Urban Agenda on "planning and managing urban spatial development" (A/RES/71/256 2017, paras 93–125) that one may even think of it as a forerunner. A guiding premise for Davis and her colleagues is that instead of concentrating on the perpetrators of violence (the law enforcement work), it is more useful to focus on the spaces where violence thrives (USAID/MIT 2012, p. 8). Therefore, spatial re-orientation is conceived as a powerful means of reducing armed non-state actors' capacities, especially since territorial control is quintessential to them. Moreover, it is acknowledged that aggressive tactics to combat civilian armed actors (through the military, enhanced law-enforcement, or the militarisation of the police through the increased use of SWAT teams and the like (Lieblich and Shinar 2017) "alienates affected communities and fuels broad political dissatisfaction" (MIT/USAID 2012, p. 4). This alienation can in turn lead to what these authors call "negative resilience", i.e. the coerced alignment of communities with criminal organisations that gain effective control over certain areas, neighborhoods, or even entire cities. In order to avoid this, or to decolonise spaces of violence and relocate the transaction centers of illicit lucrative business away from neighborhoods, social networks of resilience are the most promising means of establishing "relatively autonomous control over the activities, spaces, and social or economic forces and conditions that comprise their daily lives" (MIT/USAID 2012, p. 5). Resilience-building becomes thus a matter of "ensuring access to public spaces", and this in turn is understood as "a dimension of 'safe cities'" (Birkenkötter 2019, in this volume). It is about bridging social fragments through the recovery of *la plaza pública*. Literally translated as the "public square", the use of this phrase invokes public life in the sense of *res publica. La plaza pública* can be described as a positive web of human relations literally bridged through infrastructure. This is why functional public services like transport and street-lighting, as well as the rehabilitation of lost spaces, or "placemaking" (PPS/UN-Habitat 2012), are essential in this kind of resilience work, as positive experiences from Mexico City, Medellín, and other cities in Latin America show. Precisely drawing on these experiences, the Toolkit identifies best practices on projects of urban renovation, including public transportation, participatory budgeting, community-led reconstruction, sanitation projects, and so on. It also emphasises the need to tackle the problems generated by urban informality (informal settlements) in order to recover (and in some cases, create) public spaces. This is so because, according to Davis and her colleagues, informal urban settlements further complicate the relationship of the affected communities with municipal authorities, making the former more vulnerable to negative resilience.

The MIT/USAID Resilience Toolkit highlights three broad approaches to urban chronic violence: 1) "bridging" connections among members of the communities, i.e. building upon and strengthening social capital (Putnam 2000; for a critique: DeFilippis 2010); 2) fostering cooperative autonomy, in particular by engaging private business in the economic boosting of communities, which in turn contributes to lively neighborhoods where people go out on the streets, but also where they find jobs, all-in-all, it is about developing a sense of normalcy and spatial allegiance; and 3) reimagining state-community relations through the participation of citizens in the design and implementation of public policies, something which not only benefits from the street-knowledge[2] of those directly affected by making these policies more attuned, but also enhances the transparency and accountability of public servants.

As can be observed, these three approaches are consistent with the three dimensions of local resilience-building activities that USAID envisages for Mexico in its country strategy 2014–2018, described above. As already said, this is the juxtaposition of bouncing back and forward, of the "homeostatic approach" and ecology-inspired societal dynamic self-regulation. It remains to be seen, however, whether this theoretical juxtaposition has been successful in overcoming the tensions between a transnational action plan that has helped maintain a situation of extreme violence that resilience is supposed to ameliorate and change in the first place. In the next and final section, I will argue that, despite some successful instances of local resilience-building in the framework of Pillar IV, this has not been the case. Beyond the case of Mérida's Pillar IV, this failure is tied to a predominant concept and instrumentality of resilience as a governance technique of risk management. But I will also argue that this is not the only meaning of resilience. Hence, its transformative potential is not foreclosed.

Concluding Remarks: Local Resilience as a Technique of Global (Urban) Governance

Ciudad Juárez is the major success story of Mérida's fourth pillar. In February 2010 the administration of Calderón installed the Mesas de Seguridad y Justicia ("roundtables for peace and justice"), a platform for cooperation between the federal, state, and local authorities, as well as civil society represented by a variety of actors from the private sector to academia to neighbourhood leaders. Significant efforts and money were put into local crime prevention instead of kingpin-chasing. Although not framed in postmodern vernacular, the Mesas initiative, which quickly became known as Todos Somos Juárez ("We're all Juárez") can be described as a resilience network (Slaughter 2017, pp. 80–110) that incorporates a variety of actors from several levels of government and the society in a heterarchical decision-making process with a view to restructuring and fortifying the social web. Note that integrating authorities into this network does not just break the dependence on state-centered, hierarchical settings, giving place to alternative solutions. It also has the potential of ameliorating state dysfunctionality by two means: first, as part of the *mesas*, authorities must submit their decisions and actions to ongoing scrutiny through dialogue, which enhances accountability; second, these decisions are not self-contained orders to be implemented, but become part of a trial-and-error procedure that facilitates the correction of otherwise rigid prescriptions covered by the mantle of public authority.

The murder rate of Juárez has dropped constantly since 2013, showing a 92 percent decline by 2015, and it has become a growing economy and an attractive city for young people around the country. As seen in the previous sections, the programmes and initiatives carried out under the framework of Pillar IV in Monterrey and Tijuana, be it through active engagement of USAID, financial support, or just as favoured by this transnational discourse on city and citizen security, have successfully promoted local agency. Jóvenes con Rumbo and NPT have been emancipatory for young people living under the siege of crime, inefficient and corrupt authorities, and complicit police forces.

Thus, there are good reasons for describing this integral part of the Mérida Initiative as a promising case of the improvement of the quality of local life through transnational action. It is important to note that in this context the "improvement of local life" is not to be understood only as the result of *living* in more secure communities but also as a crucial means of *making* communities secure. It is therefore a holistic concept of local security which resembles the integral approach to cities' safety of the SDG 11, which is intrinsically tied to sustainability and inclusion, and the human development approach focused on building capabilities (Nussbaum 2011). Moreover, community resilience building with its focus on local agency represents a change from traditional interventionist state-building enterprises. This has been celebrated as "the end of intervention" (Finkenbusch 2016; Finkenbusch 2017).

However, this narrative is incomplete. Violence is on the rise again in Juárez and Tijuana, especially since the extradition to the US of Joaquín Guzmán Loera ("El Chapo"), the leader of the Sinaloa Cartel. The National Programme for the Social Prevention of Violence and Crime of Peña's government, which tried to expand nationwide the "integral" approach to insecurity undertaken during Calderón's term in office in Juárez, received ample public support and was praised by NGOs, the media, and scholars as a measure that began shifting paradigms in the fight against crime, but it practically ceased to exist in late 2016, when federal funding was suspended (in the framework of major cuts to public spending). During Peña's administration the war-approach to public security has not ceased, and murder rates have even surpassed those from 2006 to 2012. Actually, in December 2017 the failed war on drugs was sadly reinvigorated through the adoption by Congress of the Law on Interior Security, which has been rightly criticised for further militarising the country and prolonging a quasi-state of exception – bypassing the constitutional provisions on the law of exception (Art. 29 of the Mexican Constitution), which are actually tailored in a way that efficiently contains executive abuse (Rodiles 2018a). Not surprisingly, the constitutionality of this law has already been challenged before Mexico's Supreme Court by several political groups, subnational governments, the National Human Rights Commission and the Human Rights Commission of Mexico City.

Looking at these developments it must be said that, despite some instances of success, Pillar IV has not lived up to the expectations of it as an emancipatory force. It is being used instead as a means of legitimising the war approach favoured and facilitated by the rest of the Mérida Initiative, in particular by Pillar I. In the end, the resilience narrative underlying Pillar IV is "fully embedded as a policy metaphor for envisioning future local place-making and community building activities alongside broader-scale national [and transnational, AR] security concerns", which tend to lead to "contradictory practices" (Coaffee and Fussey 2017, p. 304). This also suggests that little has changed. The traditional interventionist policies of the US in Latin America, including but not limited to the "war on drugs", have usually been accompanied by development work, which has often been strategically employed as a legitimacy-conferring device (Humphreys 2010, pp. 149–155). Although it must be acknowledged that the Mérida Initiative is a bilateral arrangement for which the government of Calderón actively lobbied, it still follows the overall logic of an ineffective and counterproductive "global war on drugs and crime" promoted in Washington DC all over Latin America, and beyond. Pillar IV and its resilience narrative does not break this paradigm, and hence comes closer to a spin on intervention than to its end. Intervention is re-framed in more amicable terms that fit our postmodern mindset of the inevitability of complexity, the power of networks, and the strength of persuasion. David Chandler has critically observed that the empowerment of communities is the result of the disillusionment with fixing state-failure through international liberalism, i.e. the sober conclusion that imposing good governance practices on the level of political elites and promoting legal reform just does not work, or at least not alone, and that therefore informal change in society has to be facilitated and inculcated (Chandler 2013, p. 277). Inherent in this novel developmental rhetoric is the conviction that local resilience-building cannot succeed without external (foreign, international) assistance, since the barriers to progress also lie within the society itself (Fukuyama 1995). This has implications beyond Mérida, because it suggests that resilience as part of a new development agenda has not fully disassociated itself from the old epistemic assumption of the civilising mission (N'Zatioula Grovogui 1996; Anghie 2007).

Both in Mérida's Pillar IV as well as in SDG 11, resilience stands as an end in itself. This is perplexing. Why should change be pursued for its own sake? It would seem far more appropriate and useful to conceive of it as a conduit to safety, or sustainability for that matter, where the bouncing-forward elements of societal reorganisation are properly accentuated. This would also better unleash the potential of resilience as a powerful discourse for re-conceptualising – and not merely reframing in terms of spin – development towards the creation (or liberation) of human capabilities that are needed in different contexts and places, beyond unidirectional prescriptions informed by international elites (Nussbaum 2011). Framing resilience as an objective in and of itself is tied to the risk-based approach mentioned above (RBA). "Coping and adapting to crime" (USAID/MIT 2012) means that becoming a resilient community is to remain an *at-risk* community that constantly finds new ways of *living with* the risk. This represents a shift away from a politics of promise to one that embraces contingency, as it happens where it happens. This may lead to the evasion of responsibilities in the longer term, diminishing the conditions for collective political action aimed at the transformation and reconfiguration of the public good (see Aradau 2017, pp. 85–88, based on Arendt 1958). It also entails the danger of perpetuating and normalising the vulnerability of certain sections of society (Evans and Reid 2014).

RBA resilience poses a paradox: By embracing change as its *telos*, it actually rejects change. Indeed, building resilient communities (and cities) reduces itself to the global promotion of an experimentalist mode of local governance that is dynamic and even proactive, but inasmuch as it serves the management of risk, i.e the management of insecurity, inequality, and growth. Management sounds innovative, but it is more conservative than orthodox ruling. The concept and instrumentality of resilience as risk management turns it into a powerful medium of governmentality (Foucault 2004), i.e. of "conducting conduct" (Foucault 1994, p. 237) through non-sovereigntist and non-traditional legal means that serve to reject political transformation: an anti-law law that is also an anti-politics politics (Rodiles 2018b, p. 257).

But, as stated in the introduction, the meaning of resilience is not fixed and RBA-resilience is not its only possible manifestation. The meanings of this polysemous buzzword are construed and re-construed over time through the interactions of the different paradigms advanced by different epistemic communities, from foreign policy elites to bureaucracies, from development agencies to affected locales. Thus, resilience can be viewed as an open-ended struggle for appropriation and re-appropriation. I have described some instances of this local re-appropriation in the framework of Mérida's Pillar IV, which have not overcome the overall understanding and instrumentality of resilience as the management of insecurity in a transnational setting, but are nonetheless encouraging beyond Mérida. However ambiguous and inconclusive they are, it is my belief that these lessons from transnationally informed local resilience-building in northern Mexico can help us sharpen the awareness of SDG 11, and the enterprise of global urban governance.

Notes

1 It should be noted that Latino gangs that emerged in major US cities and prisons (Mara Salvatrucha, Barrio 18, Barrio Azteca) have also settled in Mexican and Central American cities. Far from solving gang-related violence in the US, deportation has often the ironic effect of gang-transnationalisation (Zilberg

2011). Transnational gangs are, then again, best-suited for moving drugs and weapons inside cities and towns here and there, thus becoming valuable partners to major transnational criminal organisations.

2 "Street-knowledge" is an often-used catchphrase by rappers in US cities and suburbs who contrast this concept, eg their knowledge of how the "hood" works and how to survive in it, to police intervention. This is the case, for instance, with Niggers with Attitude (N.W.A.), its Best of album being precisely called The Strength of Street Knowledge. Street-knowledge is, of course, an old-school way of referring to resilience (positive and negative) in Compton, LA, Independencia, Monterrey, or Altavista, Juárez.

Bibliography

Literature

Aguilar, Rubén V. and Castañeda, Jorge G. 2009. *El Narco: La Guerra Fallida.* Mexico City: Punto De Lectura.

Anghie, Antony. 2007. *Imperialism, Sovereignty and the Making of International Law.* Cambridge: Cambridge University Press.

Aradau, Claudia. 2017. *The promise of security: resilience, surprise and epistemic politics.* In: Chandler, David and Coaffee, Jon (eds). *The Routledge Handbook of International Resilience.* New York: Routledge. pp. 79–91.

Arendt, Hannah. 1958. *The Human Condition.* Chicago: University of Chicago Press.

Ascención, Arturo. 2012. La 'Iniciativa Mérida' es un papelito insuficiente: Rosario Green. [online]. Available at: http://mexico.cnn.com/mundo/2012/09/10/la-iniciativa-merida-es-un-papelito-insuficiente-rosario-green (Accessed: 31 January 2018).

Astorga, Luis. 2012. Estado, Drogas Ilegales y Poder Criminal: Retos Transexenales. *Letras Libres*, 167, 26–31.

Aust, Helmut Philipp and du Plessis, Anél. 2019. Introduction: The globalisation of urban governance – legal perspectives on Sustainable Development Goal 11. In: Aust, Helmut Philipp and du Plessis, Anél (eds). *The Globalisation of Urban Governance - Legal Perspectives on Sustainable Development Goal 11.* New York: Routledge. pp. 3–16.

Birkenkötter, Hannah. 2019. Ensuring access to public space as a dimension of "safe cities": The role of the UN entities in shaping the global urban governance agenda. In: Aust, Helmut Philipp and du Plessis, Anél (eds). *The Globalisation of Urban Governance - Legal Perspectives on Sustainable Development Goal 11.* New York: Routledge. pp. 127–150.

Carpenter, Ami C. 2013. Changing lenses: Conflict analysis and Mexico's "drug war". *Latin American Politics and Society*, 55(3), 139–160.

Chandler, David. 2013. International statebuilding and the ideology of resilience. *Politics* 33(4), 276–286.

Chandler, David. 2014. Beyond neoliberalism: Resilience, the new art of governing complexity. *Resilience: International Policies, Practices and Discourses*, 2(1), 47–63.

Chandler, David and Coaffee, Jon. 2017. Introduction: contested paradigms of international resilience. In: Chandler, David and Coaffee, Jon (eds). *The*

Routledge Handbook of International Resilience. New York: Routledge. pp. 3–10.

Coaffee, Jon and Fussey, Pete. 2017. The politics of security-driven resilience. In: Chandler, David and Coaffee, Jon (eds). *The Routledge Handbook of International Resilience.* New York: Routledge. pp. 293–306.

Davis, Diane E. 2009. Non-state armed actors, new imagined communities, and shifting patterns of sovereignty and insecurity in the modern world. *Contemporary Security Policy*, 30(2), 221–245.

Davis, Diane E. 2016. The production of space and violence in cities of the global south: Evidence from Latin America. *Nóesis, Revista de Ciencias Sociales y Humanidades*, (January-June 2016), 1–15.

DeFilippis, James. 2010. The myth of social capital in community development. *Housing Policy Debate*, 12(4), 781–806.

Dresser, Denise. 2012. Repensar la Guerra, *Reforma.* p. 15.

Evans, Brad and Reid, Julian. 2014. *Resilient Life: The Art of Living Dangerously.* Cambridge: Polity Press Ltd.

Finkenbusch, Peter. 2016. Expansive intervention as neo-institutional learning: Root causes in the Merida Initiative. *Journal of Intervention and Statebuilding*, 10(2), 162–180.

Finkenbusch, Peter. 2017. The demise of the intervention paradigm – resilience thinking in the Merida Initiative. *Conflict, Security & Development*, 17(4), 313–332.

Foucault, Michel. 1994. *Dits et Écrits (1954–1988) tome IV 1980–1988*. Paris: Gallimard.

Foucault, Michel. 2004. *Sécurité, Territoire et Population.* Paris: Gallimard. Édition du Seuil.

Freire, Paulo. 1996. *La educación como práctica de la libertad.* Mexico City, Mexico: Siglo Veintiuno Editores.

Fukuyama, Francis. 1995. *Trust: The Social Virtues and the Creation of Prosperity.* New York: Free Press.

Guerrero, Eduardo. 2012. La Estrategia Fallida. Nexos Hoy [online]. Available at: www.nexos.com.mx/?p=15083 (Accessed: 31 January 2018).

Humphreys, Stephen. 2012. *Theatre of the Rule of Law – Transnational Legal Intervention in Theory and Practice.* Cambridge: Cambridge University Press.

Jones, Bruce and Pascual, Carlos and Stedman, John. 2009. *Power & Responsibility - Building International Order in an Era of Transnational Threats.* Washington DC: Brookings Institution Press.

Krasner, Stephen D. and Pascual, Carlos. 2005. Adressing state failure. *Foreign Affairs*, 84(4), 153–163.

Koonings, Kees and Kruijt, Dirk. 2015. Urban fragility and resilience in Latin America: conceptual approaches and contemporary patterns. In: Koonings, Kees and Kruijt, Dirk (eds.). *Violence and Resilience in Latin American Cities.* London: Zed Books. pp. 1–29.

Líderes Unidos por la Paz A.C. 2011. Nacidos Para Triunfar [online]. Available at: http://www.npt.org.mx/home.html (Accessed: 31 January 2018).

Lieblich, Eliav and Shinar, Adam. 2017. The case against police militarization. *Michigan Journal of Race & Law*, 23(1) [online]. Available at: https://papers.ssrn.com/sol3/papers.cfm?abstract_id=2840715 (Accessed: 31 January 2018).

N'Zatioula Grovogui, Siba. 1996. *Sovereigns, Quasi Sovereigns and Africans.* Minneapolis, MN: The University of Minnesota Press.

Nolte, Georg (ed). 2013. *Treaties and Subsequent Practice.* Oxford: Oxford University Press.

Nussbaum, Martha C. 2011. *Creating Capabilities – The Human Development Approach.* Cambridge, MA: Harvard University Press.

Olson, Eric L. and Wilson, Christopher. 2010. Beyond Merida: The Evolving Approach to Security Cooperation. Woodrow Wilson International Center for Scholars, Mexico Institute [online]. Available at: www.wilsoncenter.org/sites/default/files/beyond_merida.pdf (Accessed: 31 January 2018).

Putnam, Robert D. 2000. *Bowling Alone. The Collapse and Revival of American Community.* New York: Simon & Schuster.

Rice, Condoleezza. 2006. *Transformational Diplomacy.* US Department of State Archive [online]. Available at: https://2001-2009.state.gov/secretary/rm/2006/59306.htm (Accessed: 31 January 2018).

Rodiles, Alejandro. 2018a. Law and violence in the global south: The legal of framing of Mexico's "Narco War". *Journal of Conflict & Security Law,* 23(2), 269–281.

Rodiles, Alejandro. 2018b. *Coalitions of the Willing and International Law – The Interplay Between Formality and Informality.* Cambridge: Cambridge University Press.

Rogers, Peter. 2017. The etymology and genealogy of a contested concept. In: Chandler, David and Coaffee, Jon (eds). *The Routledge Handbook of International Resilience.* New York: Routledge. pp. 13–25.

Sabel, Charles F. and Zeitlin, Jonathan. 2012. Experimentalist governance. In: Levi-Faur, David (ed). *The Oxford Handbook of Governance.* Oxford: Oxford University Press. pp. 169–184.

Seelke, Clare R. and Finklea, Kristin. 2017. U.S.-Mexican Security Cooperation: The Mérida Initiative and Beyond. Congressional Research Service [online]. Available at: https://fas.org/sgp/crs/row/R41349.pdf (Accessed: 31 January 2018).

Slaughter, Anne-Marie. 2017. *The Chessboard and the Web: Strategies of Connection in a Networked World.* New Haven, CT: Yale University Press.

The Economist. 2013. The new face of Mexican Policing. A public-private effort to reduce violence in Mexico's wealthiest city. *The Economist,* 15 June 2013 [online]. Available at: www.economist.com/news/americas/21579457-public-private-effort-reduce-violence-mexicos-wealthiest-city-new-face-mexican (Accessed: 24 April 2018).

Walker, Neil. 2015. *Intimations of Global Law.* Cambridge: Cambridge University Press.

Walklate, Sandra and Mythen, Gabe. 2015. *Contradictions of Terrorism – Security, Risk and Resilience.* New York: Routledge.

Zilberg, Elana. 2011. *Space of Detention: The Making of the Transnational Gang Crisis Between Los Angeles and San Salvador.* Durham, N.C.: Duke University Press.

Documents

Cámara de Diputados LX Legislatura. 2008. Iniciativa Mérida Compendio [online]. Available at: www.diputados.gob.mx/cedia/sia/spe/SPE-CI-A-02-08.pdf (Accessed: 31 January 2018).

Diario Oficial de la Federación (DOF). 2014. National Program for the Social Prevention of Violence and Crime 2014–2018. Mexico City, Mexico: Federal Office.

Diario Oficial de la Federación (DOF). 2017. Law on Interior Security. Mexico City, Mexico: Federal Office.

Estrategia Todos Somos Juárez [online]. 2010. Available at: www.conadic.salud.gob.mx/pdfs/todos_somos_juarez_28junio.pdf (Accessed: 31 January 2018).

International Law Commission (ILC). 2018. Report on the Work of the Seventieth (2018), Chapter IV. Subsequent agreements and subsequent practice in relation to the interpretation of treaties, UN Doc. A/73/10.

Líderes Unidos por la Paz A.C. 2011. Nacidos Para Triunfar [online]. Available at: www.npt.org.mx/home.html (Accessed: 31 January 2018).

Massachusetts Institute of Technology (MIT) and United States Agency for International Development (USAID). 2012. A Toolkit for Urban Resilience in Situations of Chronic Violence. MIT Center for International Studies [online]. Available at: http://graduateinstitute.ch/files/live/sites/iheid/files/sites/ccdp/shared/Docs/Projects/urban_resilience_toolkit-1.pdf (Accessed: 31 January 2018).

Programa Jóvenes con Rumbo [online]. 2013. Available at: http://jovenesconrumbo.org/ (Accessed: 31 January 2018).

Project for Public Spaces/UN Habitat. 2012. Placemaking and the Future of Cities. Available at: https://daks2k3a4ib2z.cloudfront.net/5810e16fbe876cec6bcbd86e/59f1fb530aad1d00010a6186_PPS-Placemaking-and-the-Future-of-Cities.pdf (Accessed: 31 January 2018)

UNDP. 2013. Regional Human Development Report 2013–2014. Citizen Security with Human Face: Evidence and Proposals for Latin America.

USAID. 2017. New Urban Agenda, A/RES/71/256 [online]. Available at: http://undocs.org/A/RES/71/256 (Accessed: 31 January 2018).

United States Agency for International Development (USAID). 2014. Mexico Country Development Cooperation Strategy (FY2014-FY2018) with addendum as of November 2015 [online]. Available at: https://www.usaid.gov/sites/default/files/documents/1869/Mexico%20CDCS%202014%202018.pdf (Accessed: 31 January 2018).

U.S. Embassy to Mexico. 2010. Facts Sheet: The Four Pillars of M *érida*. Ciudad de México: U.S. Embassy & Consulates in Mexico [online]. Available at: https://photos.state.gov/libraries/mexico/310329/7abril/The%20Four%20Pillars%20of%20Cooperation%20Final.pdf (Accessed: 31 January 2018).

14 Conclusion

Summary of Observations and Pointers for Future Research

Anél du Plessis and Helmut Philipp Aust

Scholarly Responses to the City-centric Shift in Global Policy

While the adoption of SDG 11 and the New Urban Agenda, as well as urbanisation itself are often celebrated for their potential to help make cities more prosperous, many cities of the world have been described as being "grossly" unprepared for the multidimensional challenges associated with urbanisation (UN-Habitat 2016, p. 2; Parnell 2016, p. 530). The demands made on so-called "good urban governance" are high, considering the complexity of the legal and many other systems, processes and governance actors involved (Sassen 2013, pp. 244–248). SDG 11 confirms a turn in the real and perceived global position of cities and their authorities worldwide. In UN circles, cities are now officially acknowledged as meaningful participatory actors globally, in the pursuit of inclusive, safe, resilient and sustainable urban spaces. It is mainly in international law and governance scholarship that the broader sustainable urbanism narrative has in recent years been accompanied by a growing number of analyses of the ecological challenges embedded in the Anthropocene (Biermann et al. 2016, p. 341).

Still, for some time now cities themselves have routinely faced complex immediate societal, economic and environmental challenges brought about by changing climates, resource depletion and unprecedented urbanisation. These challenges are not confined to specific countries, which explains why during the past decade what is happening in the urban space has also become more and more prominent in and relevant to the global governance discourse. It is as a direct result of this development that new concepts such as "localisation" came about in sociological studies (Robertson 1995, p. 25), and global governance circles agreed that urbanisation is "a socially and economically driven transformation process that hugely impacts most socio-ecological systems of the planet"(Biermann et al. 2016, p. 342; Parnell 2016, p. 533).

The SDGs focus on sustainable development, but Goal 11 specifically envisions cities that are not only sustainable but are also inclusive, safe and resilient. As alluded to in Chapter 1 of this book, the combination of separate inter-related SDG 11 aspirations may be criticised for the fact that it suggests that the characteristics of safety, resilience and inclusiveness may fall outside of the purview of urban sustainability in its totality. The items on the wish list of the urban Goal may not all be compatible with one another – more inclusive urban development may compromise (unintentionally so) issues of urban safety, for example. On the other hand, it is very meaningful that a global goal, as a single normative base for all nations, has been adopted which speaks to a more or less delineated geography – the city space. SDG 11 and the New Urban Agenda have resulted in what Parnell describes as 'a city-centric shift in global policy' (Parnell 2016). It is therefore safe to assume that "a fair amount of reframing and clarification [of SDG 11] will be necessary, especially as national, regional and city governments move towards implementation and indicators" (Revi et al. 2014, p. 8).

The scholarly and policy discourse on the subsidiary goals of inclusivity, sustainability, resilience and safety in SDG 11 is in the process of being developed. We trust that this book adds value to this unfolding discourse and emerging body of scholarship. The contributors did not, however, adopt any fixed meanings for any of the goals. As stated at the beginning, the meaning, level of relevance and parameters of any of the goals are largely dependent on national and local contexts and should be considered in relation to all the other SDGs. The authors accordingly acknowledged and worked with the fluidity of the meaning and impact of SDG 11. Its indefiniteness in fact made it possible for authors from different disciplines and countries to select a number of questions and consider them through a law and governance lens.

The themes in this book range from the conceptualisation and negotiation of SDG 11 to the nexus between multiple levels of state intervention and the global flows of commodities, capital and people, and their impact on urban sustainability. The phenomenon and effects of fast-changing urban conflict constellations were discussed, as well as the challenges in law posed by digitisation and urbanisation as twenty-first century megatrends. The book also looked at the transition from the MDGs to the SDGs and the relationship between cultural and religious diversity on the one hand and co-habitation in the urban space on the other. Some chapters addressed the compatibility of resilience-building in cities with transnational cooperation with reference to specific cases in and examples from South Africa, Mexico and Brazil.

In the collective, the preceding chapters in this book have succeeded in showing a) how urban governance is being globalised and what role SDG 11 plays in this regard; and b) how international, national and local law and governance systems are reacting or may have to react and adjust in future. The authors have presupposed that the globalisation of urban governance suggests some kind of standard for (local) governance practice and the quality of life of those inhabiting the urban space. They have accordingly used SDG 11 as a globally recognised yet non-legally binding reference point to assess how urban governance is globalising, and to establish what the concomitant implications and effects are. Each chapter has explored one or more key aspects of the globalisation of urban governance from a law and/or governance perspective.

As is often the case with an edited book that is the result of a collaborative, cross-border research project, all of the contributors have embraced a form of contextualising comparative analysis. We have deliberately refrained from a strict comparative investigation. Instead, where relevant, the authors have focused on relative similarities and comparable phenomena. Several of the authors have adopted a comparative outlook to determine and explain, for instance, how domestic and international legal systems respond to urban spatial disparities and fragmentation in today's globalised urban areas. Comparison also played a useful role when discussing why good financial governance is imperative at the local level. Similar considerations apply to the discussion of digital governance and how it plays out locally. The World Bank's direct entry into agreements with local governments has also been analysed with respect to different jurisdictions. It follows that the collective focus has been on SDG 11 in relation to a wide array of different law and governance systems and on the legally relevant developments and governance instruments at different levels and in various contexts. In our view, this makes for a novel contribution to the global governance literature, which is often more interested in informal processes, international relations and political workings than in concrete questions of the architecture of governance and the functioning of existing and future domestic and international law. It also informs the fields of urban studies, urban ecology and urban politics, which frequently explore very specific local contexts or locations.

The Globalisation of Good Urban Governance from a Legal Perspective: Some Observations

Realising SDG 11 requires novel legal interventions and the establishment of new or the strengthening of existing types of legal relationships within and across state borders. Understanding is needed of how different legal frameworks applicable to urban governance are being transformed (directly and indirectly) by informal practices, transnational lobbying and non-binding international commitments such as the SDGs. It is also necessary to be aware of the limitations created by existing domestic law and governance systems, where the SDG commitments and international peer pressure are expected to make a difference in the short to medium term. The contributors to this volume have attempted to make some inroads in this regard.

One can draw any number of matrix charts to join the dots between the inquiries in the different chapters of this book. This in itself is indicative of how rich the scholarly probing of the globalisation of good urban governance can be – whether from a law, governance or any other analytical perspective. In this conclusion we aim to highlight some of the main moments in the three overarching focus areas in this book.

Part One focused on the genesis and origins of SDG 11 in context and analysed what it means for the globalisation of urban governance. Chapters One to Four revealed that the relevance afforded to cities as actors in and as delivery sites for the global development agenda embodied in SDG 11 is tainted with global political and economic forces, and that not all state parties are equally optimistic about the prospects of states losing some of their "national ownership" over development policy. This suggests some degree of tension between the escalation of city authority and the hitherto and still predominant preponderance of national governments in the international arena. It also became evident that the curious phenomenon of international institutions allying themselves with individual cities to fulfil their global mandates extends the boundaries of the notion of sovereignty and may have implications (some of which may be unintended) for global delivery of the targets in the SDGs. This ties in with the observation in relation to the planetary infrastructure regime that there are path dependencies and uncontrollable relationships that characterise the politics of globalisation on different levels of government, so that various questions need to be asked: Who governs? Whom does urbanisation benefit and whom does it harm? How sustainable and democratic are processes of integration and convergence?

Part Two considered specific contexts of the globalisation of urban governance. This is a particularly vast area of inquiry which called for the selection of specific themes. Chapters Five to Eight singled out the matters of funding and financial governance; violent urban conflict and peace in cities; public space management and safety in cities; and cultural diversity and inclusiveness in the urban environment. The chapters collectively show how the globalisation of urban governance may intensify pre-existing problems and needs in cities and city governance. Yet they also demonstrate how this development demands the reconceptualisation of existing governance regimes and approaches. With reference to South Africa it is shown that due to poor financial management in local government, local fiscal autonomy may blow up in the face of the sub-targets set in SDG 11, even if national fiscal and financial policy and law are intact. The conclusion is that executives (or elected politicians) who fail local communities must be held accountable – whether by electorates or by other control mechanisms. Furthermore, it is essential for the pursuit of SDG 11 to craft an enabling governance environment with access to sufficient financial resources and good fiscal management. Examples of how violent conflicts have historically played out and/or continue to do so in various cities of the world were used to argue that responding to conflict potentials in and about twenty-first century cities needs the adoption of new approaches to the regulation of violent conflict and to building peace in the city. The point was made that peace and security are basic conditions for achieving SDG 11. Yet it remains to be explored how cities may adapt their ideas and practices in order to regulate (intra-city) violent conflicts and make peace, as well as what role networks like the Global Alliance for Urban Crisis and their visions relating to SDG 11 may have to play. It has also been further observed, with reference to international institutional law and the normative agendas of both UN-Habitat and UN Women in the realm of safe cities, that despite their complexity, entities in the UN system are governance forces to be reckoned with, and that they too will be critical to the eventual success of SDG 11. Finally, this part turned to the challenge of cultural diversity. Only rarely would cities be homogenous units of shared cultural, religious and social norms. Accordingly, it was argued that urban authorities should adopt a "balanced" governance approach to cultural diversity and matters of cultural and religious pluralism, including in the process of implementing SDG 11.

Part Three focused on the local dimensions of the phenomenon of the globalisation of urban governance with reference to specific local contexts. Chapters Nine to Thirteen took the reader from Rio de Janeiro in Brazil, to Johannesburg in South Africa, and onwards again to various areas in Mexico, while being mindful of the new digital realities in which good urban governance is to take place today. With reference to some historical and future developments in specific city contexts, it was explained how planning and programmatic developments by (and sometimes for) local government may have significant bearing on the outcomes of SDG 11 years from now. From the discussions in this part of the book, we glean that years of experience with the implementation of the MDGs may assist when countries and cities devise strategies aimed at the local implementation of SDG 11 and also that despite the universalist jargon in SDG 11, local strategies tailored for local circumstances will be critical. It was also observed that the notion of "city regions" is gaining traction in some parts of the world and that the establishment of and vision for these regions challenges the ways in which we understand the governance of metropolitan areas and their interconnectedness with smaller urban, semi-urban and rural areas. In this vein, the case of the Gauteng City Region in South Africa was used to highlight the role of competitive party politics, and the significance of legal systems and instruments for cooperation in government and between multi-jurisdictional institutions, as well as the alignment between typical critical services and infrastructure to forge governance connections and connectivity in the urban space.

Still focused on the South African context, it was explained that the country's existing domestic law and policy framework on municipal integrated planning is at this point one of the most useful governance instruments for cities' internalisation and city-level translation of the SDG 11 targets. In a more general sense, the complexity of the philosophy of governance that counts on the informal networks and actions of non-state parties as based on the notions of political decentralisation and cosmopolitism, was illustrated with reference to the notion of the smart city. The conclusion is that a theory of networked governance should more comprehensively integrate practices of justification and decision making as elements of socio-legal reality. In Chapter 13, the discussion of the *Mérida Initiative* offered a case study that tied in with the latter idea, as it showed the potential for there to be a positive reconfiguration of the social web and urban fabric through inclusiveness, the promotion of individual capabilities, and the recovery of public space. The *Mérida* case also confirmed how resilience (as undefined as it may be in SDG 11 and other paradigms) may be both a governance strategy and an end in itself, and how transnational responses to risk and insecurity can form part of a feedback loop with resilience-building in cities.

In summary, the chapters in this book have illuminated how legal, social, economic, political and technological forces have been at play in the build-up to the formulation and adoption of SDG 11 and how these very forces are likely to determine the future trajectory of the global urban goal. These forces operate in traditional and more novel relationships between governance actors (with different degrees of global and local governance autonomy, access to resources and technologies, and political backing) as well as between such actors and those people and institutions that are 'governed'. While it is clear that international, regional, national and local legal systems are at work it is hard to pinpoint the ways in which and the pace at which "the law" is adapting to and/or facilitating the globalisation of urban governance.

A Future Research Agenda

When reflecting on a future research agenda it is necessary to ask what we know and what we don't. It seems fair to say that through the lens of the law it is more or less understandable how and why SDG 11 came into being and what it seeks to achieve, globally. Not as clear, though, is how the law can and should be employed in countries and cities now moving forward to realise the urban Goal. The final destination is hard to imagine because of the difficulty in visualising a world where every city meets the expectations and targets set forth in SDG 11. It would indeed be a utopian world where people that live and work in cities are able to declare that their basic and other needs are met, that communities and infrastructure are resilient and safe, that natural resources are no longer threatened by unsustainable urban pressures and urbanisation, and that every single person feels welcome, included and valued, all of the time. In such an imaginary world we would be much better positioned to understand the real role of cities in sustainable development.

Bulkeley et al. recently argued that the city comprises a "multiplicity of connections and alignments" and that for this reason there is limited value in confining the role of cities in transition and striving for sustainable development to that of an *actor,* and of confining the city itself to being *a theatre (space) for action* (Bulkeley et al. 2015). The findings in this book support this view. The staggering dynamics of the global governance system and the manner in which it involves and affects every city as a microcosm (of the very same system) make it futile to try and conceptually confine the manner in which urban governance is globalising and its concomitant legally relevant implications and effects.

For this reason, as stated from the outset, various substantive issues could not be addressed in this book, a fact which highlights the need for further research on the globalisation of urban governance. Some of these issues include, for example, the development of international, domestic and local indicators for sustainable cities and the meaning of the so-called right to the city in the context of SDG 11 and in international, regional and domestic legal frameworks. Furthermore, the complexity of the rural-urban interface and the interdependence between places and people in rural and urban areas would merit more detailed attention. The prominent role of global and party politics and the economic forces in how city governments actually plan space and the use of land is another issue deserving of more attention, including from a legal perspective. In addition, the impact of international institutions and forces such as economic and geopolitical drivers, international migration patterns and international conflict on the contemporary trend of urbanisation await further analysis. Other questions remain, about the democratisation and decentralisation of city governance, the working of the principle of institutional subsidiarity, and the meaning of bottom-up community participation at the city level. There is an increasing need to critically assess the strengths and weaknesses of responsive and accountable democratic local government in an era of populism. Likewise, the role of courts in the design, interpretation and application of domestic laws and policies on the entitlements of city-dwellers in various SDG 11-related issues awaits more research.

In the limited scope of this book we could not fully do justice to the critical links between city governance, geographical frontiers and the ever-expanding spheres, scales and jurisdictional limitations of global governance. We acknowledge that within and outside of state boundaries it is necessary to investigate how city networks, metropolitan or so-called city regions and international local government projects, for example, may contribute to the pursuit of safe, sustainable, inclusive and resilient cities.

Another area in need of further research is the relationship among methodologies of different scholarly disciplines working on the globalisation of urban governance. It will be necessary to ask how different methodologies in the legal, social, socio-legal, political, urban governance and geographical fields support one another and what researchers in these fields should guard against when undertaking multi-disciplinary or interdisciplinary projects.

In the final instance, we deem it necessary for scholars to contemplate the recipients of the research that they produce. The scholarly discourse on the SDG 11 subsidiary goals of inclusivity, sustainability, resilience and safety is increasing in volume and sophistication, and ultimately it should have tangible impact. In a nutshell, there is a rich research agenda to be explored on the future of SDG 11. This volume understands itself as a starting point for a debate that will continue for years to come, if not for decades. It is our hope that future research on the globalisation of urban governance will inform those responsible for transformative approaches to urban governance and empower those living and working in cities. In order to make SDG 11 work, we need short-, medium- and long-term pathways and strategies leading to the realisation of the utopian city where law, justice and sustainable development thrive.

Bibliography

Literature

Biermann, Frank, Revi, Aromar, Simon, et al. 2016. Down to Earth: Contextualizing the Anthropocene. *Global Environmental Change*, 39, 341–350.

Bulkeley, Harriet, Castán Broto, Vanesa, and Edwards, Gareth A.S. 2015. *An Urban Politics of Climate Change: experimentation and the governing of socio-technical transitions.* New York: Routledge.

Parnell, Susan. 2016. Defining a Global Urban Development Agenda. *World Development*, 78, 529–540.

Revi, Aromar, Featherstone, Mike, Lash, Scott and Robertson, Roland et al.. 2014. Consultation on the UN Open Working Group on the SDG's Urban SDG Goal 11: Targets and indicators [online]. Available at: www.africancentreforcities.net/consultation-un-open-working-group-sdgs-urban-sdg-goal-11-targets-indicators-%E2%80%A8/ (Accessed: 5 June 2018).

Robertson, Roland. 1995. Globalisation: Time-space homogeneity-heterogeneity. In: Featherstone, Mike et al. (eds). *Global Modernities.* London: Sage.

Sassen, Saskia. 2013. A focus on cities takes us beyond existing governance frameworks. In: Stiglitz, Joseph and Kaldor, Mary (eds). *The Quest for Security: Protection without Protectionism and the Challenge of Global Governance.* New York: Columbia University Press.

Documents

UN-Habitat. 2016. New Urban Agenda.

UN-Habitat. 2016. World Cities Report. Available at: http://wcr.unhabitat.org/wp-content/uploads/sites/16/2016/05/Chapter-1-WCR-2016.pdf (Accessed: 5 June 2018).

Index

Adaptation 20, 23–24, 94, 253
African Charter on the Values and Principles of Decentralisation, Local Governance and Local Development 87, 187–188
African National Congress (ANC) 195, 214
African Union 89, 91, 216
2030 Agenda 10, 12, 14, 17–19, 25, 27–31, 92, 127–129, 132, 137, 151, 154, 173, 182, 208–209, 216, 249, 257
Anthropocene 267
Apartheid 56, 189, 191, 213–214, 216
Armed conflict –> see war

Bilateral agreements 41, 43, 46
Bilateral cooperation 47, 202, 211, 247–248, 250, 254, 256, 261
Bloomberg, Michael 46
Brazil 13, 21, 24, 38–39, 42, 53–54, 57, 173–183, 255, 268, 271
Brenner, Neil 71
Bretton Woods institutions 75–76
Budgeting 55, 70, 88, 90–93, 96–99, 188, 195–196, 201, 205, 210, 214–215, 219, 258
Bush, George W. 247, 250

Calderón, Felipe 247, 250, 252
C40 – Climate Leadership Group 5, 19, 21, 46, 136
CEDAW 138–140
City networks 5, 10, 20–21, 39–40, 43, 45, 56, 67–77, 80, 117–118, 120, 122, 131, 133, 140, 143, 179, 208, 230, 232, 271, 273
City rankings 43, 46, 65–66, 68
Climate change 3–5, 7, 21, 23–24, 39, 46, 58, 80, 94, 112, 114, 217, 220
Clinton, Hillary 250
Constitutionalism 13, 152–155, 160
Cohabitation 13, 151, 155
Courts 10, 13, 55–56, 98–99, 152–165, 273
Corruption 89–92, 96, 99–102, 182
Credit rating 94, 101
Crime 15, 19, 114, 116, 129, 133–140, 143–144, 212, 217–218, 247–262
Cultural diversity 7, 13, 151–168, 271

Decentralisation 14, 39, 54–55, 87, 92, 136, 175, 177, 187–188, 228, 230–233, 235, 272–273
Democracy 13, 18, 55, 68, 79–80, 155, 159, 164, 186, 199, 232, 239
Development 40–43, 45–47, 55–57, 89, 175–183, 208–222, 249, 251–255, 257, 260–262, 268, 270
Digitisation 14–15, 227–240, 268
Disaster 4, 18, 24, 29, 114, 121, 134, 187, 189, 213, 218, 220
Donbas 111, 116
Donetsk 111, 116,
Drugs 57, 180–181, 247–262

Earth Summit 1992 179, 211
Economy 14, 57, 65–80, 129, 173, 186–189, 197, 216–220, 229, 260
Emissions 21, 58, 217–218
Equality 21, 109–110, 151, 176, 215–216, 262, –> see also Gender equality
Espinosa, Patricia 250
European Charter of Local Self-Government 87, 187–188
Eviction 49–50, 56–57, 134, 201,

Favelas 14, 57, 174, 179–181, –> see also Informal settlements, Slum, Township
FIFA World Cup 56, 178, 180
Financial governance 7, 12, 87–103, 269
Fiscal power 12, 20, 75, 87–103, 215, 270
Fragmentation 14, 186–187, 190–192, 234–240, 269

Gangs 57, 110, 113–116, 119, 252
Gauteng City Region (GCR) 14, 56, 186–205, 209, 216, 271
Gender equality 4, 13, 26, 127–128, 131
Geography 71, 80, 248, 268
Germany 7, 9, 21–23, 25, 42, 53–55, 154–155, 160, 165
Glaeser, Edward 65
Global city 11, 39, 51, 53, 66–68, 75, 77, 173
Global city-region 67, 189
Global governance 4, 8–11, 21, 31, 39, 45, 128, 154, 237, 267, 269, 273
Globalisation 4–8, 10, 12–13, 51, 65–80, 153–154, 164, 227, 232, 257, 268–274
Global markets 58, 69, 77
Global Network on Safer Cities 129, 135–136
Global North 5, 11, 65, 113
Global South 5, 11, 40, 43, 48, 51–52, 66, 113, 183
Global urban governance 15, 127–145, 249, 257, 262
Glocal governance 11, 15, 38–58, 112, 228, 230–232, 236, 256, 258
Glocalisation –> see Glocal governance
Good governance 18, 21, 25, 91, 109, 155, 218, 220, 261
Governance –> see Global governance, Global urban governance, Glocal governance, Good governance and Local governance
Government intervention – see state intervention

Habitat III 20, 30, 41, 120, 129, 131, –> see also UN-Habitat; New Urban Agenda
Heritage 4, 24, 46, 54, 152, 154–155, 192, 213, 220
Hobbes, Thomas 69
Housing 4, 9, 18, 40, 42, 48–50, 56–57, 70, 78, 110, 179–180, 187, 189, 191–192, 200–201, 213, 215, 217–218, 220, 235, 256,
Human development 121, 175, 211, 254, 260
Human Development Index (HDI) 175
Humanitarian aid 110, 117–122
Humanitarian law 113–115, 117
Human rights 19, 21, 23, 40–42, 48–50, 54, 56–57, 121, 138, 151, 239
Human security 121–122, 212, 218
Human settlement 3, 11–12, 17–27, 31, 127–133, 164, 187, 189, 191, 200–201, 209, 211–213, 217

ICLEI 5, 87, 95, 212
Imperial infrastructure regime 68, 72–74, 77
Inclusiveness 3, 4, 8–10, 13, 15, 17–18, 22–26, 30–31, 56, 65–66, 68, 88, 98, 110, 113–115, 118–122, 152–153, 156, 164, 167, 190, 213, 216, 227, 238–239, 249, 268, 270, 272
India 24–25
Indicators 4, 10–11, 21–22, 26–31, 46–47, 49, 128, 137, 177, 215, 268, 273
Informal settlements 3, 40, 46–49, 51, 56, 217, 258, –> see also Favela, Slum, Township
Information technology 229–232
Infrastructure 3, 9, 38, 44, 49, 55–57, 67–80, 87, 89, 92–94, 101–102, 109, 129–130, 139–140, 177–181, 187, 190–193, 200–205, 208, 217, 220, 227, 229, 232, 238, 258, 270–272
Integrated Development Planning 14, 98, 197, 203, 208–221
International Committee of the Red Cross (ICRC) 109, 117, 120–121
International Guidelines on Decentralisation and Access to Basic Services to all 187
International institutional law 11, 13, 38–65, 127, 141, 145, 271
International law 4, 6, 9–10, 12, 38–39, 41–45, 48, 52–53, 112, 115, 141–142, 228, 267, 269
International Monetary Fund (IMF) 76
International Organisation for Standardisation (ISO) 5

Johannesburg 14, 40, 53–54, 56, 110, 114, 186–205, 209, 213, 216–221, 271

Keynesian-Fordist infrastructure regime 68, 72–76
Krasner, Stephen 248
Kyoto Protocol 94

Land tenure 48, 143
Land use 192–194, 201–204, 209–210, 215
Latin American countries 54, 138, 254, 257–258, 261
Legal pluralism 236–238, 240
Legitimacy 39, 47, 54, 58, 77, 232, 238–239, 249, 252, 261,
Local Agenda 21 (LA 21) 22, 211, 214
Local governance 5–6, 8, 10–11, 17, 21, 23, 25, 38, 47, 154, 177, 187, 262, 268, 272
Local government 4–8, 10–11, 13, 22–24, 27, 29, 38–41, 45–47, 51–58, 68, 74–75, 79, 87, 94–98, 100–103, 111–112, 132, 139, 143, 152, 154–155, 159, 173–175, 177, 179, 186–205, 211, 214–215, 219–220, 269–271, 273
Localisation 51–52, 129, 174, 182–183, 188, 204, 267
Locke, John 69
Luhansk 111, 116,

McKinsey 78
Mérida-Initiative 15, 247–262, 272
Metropolitan areas 14, 44, 55–56, 66–68, 77, 80, 101, 186–205, 209, 213, 220–221, 248, 252, 254, 271, 273
Mexico 9, 53, 137, 247–262, 268, 271
Migration 10, 25, 108, 153–154, 189, 273
Millennium Development Goals (MDGs) 13–14, 18, 23, 27, 29, 31, 42, 46–50, 56, 173–183, 268, 271
Mitigation 13, 23, 94
Municipal bylaws 54
Municipal government –> see local government
Multilevel governance 11, 14, 29, 39, 186–205, 237

Natural disasters 4, 24, 114, 218
New Deal 72, 74
New Urban Agenda 12, 30, 41, 120, 127–132, 144, 183, 257, 267–268
Non-governmental organizations (NGOs) 6–7, 50, 57, 88, 135–136, 138, 139–140, 143, 231, 260
Non-state actors 24, 116, 143, 258

Obama, Barack 248
Occupy Wall Street 80

Paes, Eduardo 46
Paris Agreement on Climate Change 94
Peace 12, 26, 108–122, 128, 137, 163, 183, 252, 254, 259, 270–271
Peacebuilding 21, 114–115, 118–122
Peña, Enrique 247, 260
Peri-urban areas 26, 48, 187, 189, 213,
Planetary infrastructure 65–80, 270
Planetary urbanisation 65–80
Planning 4, 6, 12, 14, 18, 21–26, 29–30, 49, 57–58, 75, 88–89, 92–93, 98, 121, 127, 129–130, 134, 139–140, 144, 176, 187–189, 191–194, 197, 200, 202–203, 208–221, 227, 230–231, 235–236, 255, 257, 271
Polycentricity 14, 236–237, 240
Poverty 4, 17, 19–20, 102, 108, 114, 175–176, 178, 182–183, 189, 218, 220
Private sector 6, 23, 44, 78, 94, 132, 135, 139, 180, 210, 235, 251, 253–254, 259
Procurement 88, 90–91, 97, 99–100
Public nuisance 155–158
Public participation 7, 10, 21, 29, 49, 90, 91, 96, 98, 109, 178, 202, 204, 211, 214–215, 217–219, 228, 230–231, 235, 239, 254, 258, 273
Public policy 186–187
Public-private-partnerships 6, 38, 44, 55–56, 70, 76, 94, 102, 230, 237
Public safety 155, 180, 217, 220
Public services 49, 56, 96, 117, 174, 178, 181, 188, 197, 254, 258
Public space 4, 12, 18, 25, 111, 114, 127–145, 151, 213, 217–218, 232–234, 239, 249, 254, 258, 270, 272
Public transport 96, 140, 190–193, 197, 200–201, 217–218, 220, 258

Refugees 153–154, 183, 232
Religion 152, 155–158, 161–163, 165

Resilience 3, 15, 18, 24, 101, 109, 111, 115, 122, 129, 152–153, 156, 187, 189, 212, 216, 247–262, 268, 272
Rice, Condoleezza 248
Right to the city 10, 40, 42, 57, 110, 179, 239, 257, 273
Rio de Janeiro 13, 38, 40, 45–46, 53, 56–57, 110, 114, 173–183, 211, 271
Rio+20 10, 17, 180
Rural areas 9–10, 21, 24–26, 31, 78, 102, 108–109, 187, 189, 213, 220–221, 249, 271, 273

Sanctuary cities 80
Safer Cities Programme 13, 127–145
Safety 3, 9, 10, 12–13, 47, 109, 127–145, 152–153, 155–156, 160, 164, 166, 180, 212, 217–218, 220, 249, 256–257, 260–261, 268, 270, 274
San Francisco 139
Sanitation 18, 20, 96, 179–180, 191, 193, 217, 258
Security 9, 11, 14, 25, 56, 69–70, 108–122, 130, 134, 136, 140, 151, 153, 164, 168, 174–183, 212, 218, 247–262, 271–272
Segregation 212, 234
Service delivery 3, 49, 55, 192, 214–217, 220
Slums 4, 18, 42, 46–49, 56, 114, 129, 173, 179–183, 186, 200, –> See also Favela, Informal Settlements, Township
Smart city 14–15, 65–66, 78–79, 218, 227–240, 272
Smart governance 230–237
Smith, Adam 69
South Africa 7, 9, 12, 14, 53–57, 89, 95–103, 154–157, 159, 161–162, 166, 186–205, 208–221, 268, 270–271
Southern African countries 25
Sovereignty 4, 40–41, 44, 114, 119, 235, 237, 252, 270
Spatial form 5, 189–190, 209, 215
Spatial planning 30, 130, 202, 217
Special Economic Zones 77,
State intervention 11, 66–67, 69–72, 76–77, 180, 268
Subsidiarity 113, 273
Sustainability 11–12, 14–15, 17, 24, 26, 42, 66–69, 79, 87–89, 91–92, 95, 97–98, 100, 113, 160, 164, 166, 190, 208–209, 212–221, 227, 260–261, 268, 274
Sustainable Development Goals (SDGs), generally 3–4, 8–9, 11, 13–14, 17–31, 38, 42, 47, 110, 128–129, 151–152, 154–155, 173, 182–183, 204, 208, 229, 238, 257, 268–269
SDG 1 4
SDG 5 4, 128, 137
SDG 10 152
SDG 11 3–5, 8–10, 12, 14–15, 17–31, 38, 42, 47–48, 66, 68, 87–90, 92–96, 100, 103, 110, 115, 117–118, 121–122, 127–129, 131, 144, 152, 156, 164, 167, 173–174, 182–183, 186–191, 193, 198–201, 208–209, 212–213, 216–218, 220–221, 227–230, 236, 240, 249, 252, 256–257, 260–262, 267–274
SDG 13 4
SDG 16 90, 128, 152
SDG 17 92, 128, 182

Taxation 23, 75–78, 89, 91–92, 102, 188
Technical assistance 43–44, 46, 181, 213
Terrorism 249, 254
Township 56, 156, 189, 194 –> see also Favela, informal settlement, slum
Transition management 88, 98
Transparency 46, 88, 90–91, 96–97, 113, 250, 259
Transportation 4, 9, 18, 65, 70, 73, 76–77, 96, 109, 140, 179, 187, 189–193, 197–198, 200–201, 203, 213, 217–218, 220, 227, 229, 258
Treaties 40–41, 43–47, 53, 70, 142–143, 250, 252

Ukraine 111, 115–116
UNESCO 41, 44, 46, 54
UN-Habitat 13, 19–20, 22–23, 26, 30, 40–42, 45–46, 48–49, 76, 113, 120, 127, 129–144, 179–181, 187–188, 193, 257, 271
United Nations 5, 38–43, 50, 57 66, 76, 109, 127–145, 173
United Nations Advisory Committee on Local Authorities (UNACLA) 179
United Nations Development Programme (UNDP) 41, 50, 132, 175–177, 179, 209, 257

United Nations Environmental Programme (UNEP) 19, 23, 209
United Nations Global Compact 20
United States 7, 9, 11, 65–80, 247–262
Universal Declaration of Human Rights 23, 151,
UN Women 13, 127, 132, 136–145, 271
Urban Age 3, 66, 77, 79, 108, 110
Urban development 11, 17, 19–21, 23, 30, 38, 40–44, 46–50, 56–57, 110, 117, 129, 135, 174, 179–183, 199, 201, 209–211, 219–221, 251, 268
Urban governance 4–15, 42, 48, 51, 68–69, 71–72, 110, 113, 154, 156, 187, 198, 211, 227–230, 237–239, 249, 252, 256–257, 259, 262, 267–274
Urban planning –> see Planning
Urban warfare 12, 111, 113, 115–116
USAID 251–260

Violence 12, 15, 57, 108–122, 127–145, 151, 164, 180–182, 212, 217–218, 247–262, 270–271

War –> See Urban warfare
War on drugs 247–262
Waste management 18, 191, 213, 217–218, 227
Women 26, 127–145, 176, 255, 271
World Bank 5, 8, 38–58, 76, 78, 131, 142, 174, 176, 179, 181, 211, 269
World Trade Organisation (WTO) 76

Zoellick, Robert 46

For Product Safety Concerns and Information please contact our EU
representative GPSR@taylorandfrancis.com
Taylor & Francis Verlag GmbH, Kaufingerstraße 24, 80331 München, Germany

www.ingramcontent.com/pod-product-compliance
Ingram Content Group UK Ltd.
Pitfield, Milton Keynes, MK11 3LW, UK
UKHW022117190926
475702UK00013B/1484

9780367663827